STRESS, APPRAISAL, AND COPING

Richard S. Lazarus, Ph.D.
Susan Folkman, Ph.D.

Springer Publishing Company
New York

Copyright © 1984 by Springer Publishing Company, Inc.
536 Broadway, New York, NY 10012

Springer Publishing Company, Inc.
536 Broadway, New York, NY 10012

Library of Congress Cataloging in Publication Data

Lazarus, Richard S.
     Stress, appraisal, and coping.
     Bibliography: p. Includes index.
     1. Stress (Psychology) I. Folkman, Susan. II. Title
BF575.S75L32 1984   155.9   84-5593
ISBN 0-8261-4191-9

Printed in the United States of America

Stress, Appraisal, and Coping

Richard S. Lazarus, Ph.D., has been Professor of Psychology at the University of California, Berkeley, since 1957. After obtaining his doctorate in 1948 from the University of Pittsburgh, he taught at Johns Hopkins University and at Clark University where he was Director of Clinical Training. He has published extensively on a variety of issues in personality and clinical psychology, and was the recipient of a Guggenheim Fellowship in 1969. He has been a pioneer in stress theory and research, exemplified by his 1966 book, *Psychological Stress and the Coping Process,* and by his influential psychophysiological research during the 1960s. Professor Lazarus maintains an active program of research as Principal Investigator of the Berkeley Stress and Coping Project, and continues to be a major figure in emotion theory, as well as personality and clinical psychology.

Susan Folkman, Ph.D., is Associate Research Psychologist at the University of California, Berkeley, and Co-Principal Investigator of the Berkeley Stress and Coping Project. After a career of full-time parenting, Dr. Folkman began her doctoral work in 1975 and received her Ph.D. from the University of California, Berkeley, in 1979. She has published numerous journal articles and book chapters based on her research, and has rapidly gained a reputation for her ability to expand appraisal and coping theory and to test it empirically.

To Bunny;
To David

Contents

Preface

The idea for this book originated about 10 years after the publication of *Psychological Stress and the Coping Process* by Lazarus in 1966, when it became evident that the field had not only grown and matured, but that it had also changed greatly in character. Cognitive approaches to stress had become widely accepted and, along with renewed interest in emotions and psychosomatic (or behavioral) medicine, the issues of stress and coping in adult life and aging, as well as stress management, were gaining attention. Most important, the concepts of cognitive appraisal and coping, not yet in the mainstream of thought in 1966, had become major themes of interdisciplinary theory and research, and our own approaches to these concepts had further developed and expanded. It was again time to pull together the field of stress, coping, and adaptation from the perspective of our current research and thought. This book, then, has a historical connection with its 1966 forebear; it shares its objectives and metatheoretical orientation, but its character and basic content are new.

We have three main objectives. First, we present in detail our theory of stress, focusing on cognitive appraisal and coping. Our approach is plainly partisan, and reflects a longstanding stake in certain theoretical and metatheoretical perspectives. Second, we examine major movements within the field from the perspective of our theory, including issues of behavioral medicine and concern with the life course, emotion, stress management, and treatment. Third, since stress, coping, and adaptation represent both an individual psychological and physiological human problem—and a collective problem because humans function in society—our concerns are multilevel and multidisciplinary. Therefore, our intended audience includes clinicians (psychiatrists, social workers, nurses, and clinical psychologists), sociologists, anthropologists, medical researchers, and physiologists. Although our own emphasis is clearly psychological and centered on individual coping and adaptation, our concerns touch on each of these disciplines.

A book such as this requires choices, sometimes painful ones, about how much to cover, in how much detail, with how much scholarship, and at what level of complexity. We have not tried to be encyclopedic or to cover every topic that could conceivably be included under the rubric of stress. The research literature is now voluminous; we have not here reviewed it for each of the topics covered, but emphasize the most important issues and research relevant to our conceptualization. We have had to be highly selective and have experienced ambivalence about whether or not to cite particular discourses or research studies. This is an idea book, not a review of research; where possible, we cite reviews the reader can turn to. We closed the book on new citations in the summer of 1983. We have tried to keep the text to a manageable size, which may disappoint those researchers whose work is not included.

We made the decision to forgo an examination of the physiology of stress, on which there are numerous treatments, whereas there are few scholarly books devoted to the psychological and social aspects of stress from the cognitive standpoint. A workable pyschophysiology of stress depends as much on a vigorous understanding of psychological and social processes as it does on a sound knowledge of physiology. We view our contribution as mainly in the former areas. We also chose not to examine developmental issues. Relevant research on developmental aspects of stress and coping is growing, but as of this moment it seems premature to examine the topic in this book.

This is not an undergraduate text or a self-help book; it is oriented toward professionals in many disciplines who might appreciate an integrative theoretical analysis of the subject matter. When one writes a book for biological and social scientists and practitioners, however, one must be wary of overestimating knowledge across disciplines. We have made every effort to be clear without assuming such prior knowledge. We hope sociologists will understand that we are not sociologists and that we are not writing exclusively for them; and similarly for physiologists, anthropologists, and so on. It is our hope not only that social and biological scientists and practitioners can read what we have written with understanding, but that graduate students, advanced undergraduates, and educated laypersons too would appreciate this book.

We acknowledge with gratitude the contributions of a number of persons who read specific chapters and gave us comments and advice. These include James Coyne, Anita DeLongis, Christine Dunkel-Schetter, Rand Gruen, Theodore Kemper, D. Paul Lumsden, and Leonard Pearlin. We have also benefited from our collaboration with graduate students, postdoctoral fellows, and visitors who have participated in the Berkeley Stress and Coping Project, including Carolyn Aldwin, Patricia Benner, Judith Cohen, Gayle Dakof, Gloria Golden, Darlene Goodhart, Kenneth Holroyd, Allen Kanner, Ethel Roskies, Catherine Schaefer, and Judith Wrubel. Carol Carr, of the Berkeley Stress and Coping Project, has carried heavy responsibility for the management of the manuscript and provided major editorial assistance. Ursula Springer, the publisher, has also given substantial editorial assistance and encouragement. Finally, a number of federal and private granting agencies have helped with our research, some of which is reported in the book: The National Institute on Aging, the MacArthur Foundation, and the National Institute on Drug Abuse. This ongoing research has encouraged us to keep our feet on the ground of observation and has prevented us from allowing our speculations to depart too far from reality.

1

The Stress Concept
in the Life Sciences

It is virtually impossible today to read extensively in any of the biological or social sciences without running into the term *stress*. The concept is even more extensively discussed in the health care fields, and it is found as well in economics, political science, business, and education. At the popular level, we are flooded with messages about how stress can be prevented, managed, and even eliminated.

No one can say for sure why interest in stress has gained such widespread public attention. It is fashionable to attribute this to rapid social change (e.g., Toffler, 1970), to growing anomie in an industrial society in which we have lost some of our sense of identity and our traditional anchors and meaning (Tuchman, 1978), or to growing affluence, which frees many people from concerns about survival and allows them to turn to a search for a higher quality of life.

The issues encompassed by the concept of stress are certainly not new. Cofer and Appley (1964) wisely pointed out some years ago that the term stress ". . . has all but preempted a field previously shared by a number of other concepts . . ." (p. 441), including anxiety, conflict, frustration, emotional disturbance, trauma, alienation, and anomie. Cofer and Appley went on to say, "It is as though, when the word stress came into vogue, each investigator, who had been working with a concept he felt was closely related, substituted the word stress . . . and continued in his same line of investigation" (p. 449).

A Bit of History

As with many words, the term *stress* antedates its systematic or scientific use. It was used as early as the 14th century to mean hardship, straits, adversity, or affliction (cf. Lumsden, 1981). In the late 17th century Hooke (cited in Hinkle, 1973, 1977) used stress in the context of the physical sciences, although this usage was not made systematic until the early 19th century. "Load" was defined as an external force; "stress" was the ratio of the internal force (created by load) to the area over which the force acted; and "strain" was the deformation or distortion of the object (Hinkle, 1977).

The concepts of stress and strain survived, and in 19th century medicine they were conceived as a basis of ill health. As an example, Hinkle (1977) cites Sir William Osler's comments on the Jewish businessman:

> Living an intense life, absorbed in his work, devoted to his pleasures, passionately devoted to his home, the nervous energy of the Jew is taxed to the uttermost, and his system is subjected to that stress and strain which seems to be a basic factor in so many cases of angina pectoris. (p. 30)

Here, in effect, is an old version of the current concept of the Type A personality—hardly limited, incidentally, to any ethnic group—with a special vulnerability to cardiovascular disease. Some years later, Walter Cannon (1932), who gave much research vitality to the physiology of emotion, considered stress a disturbance of homeostasis under conditions of cold, lack of oxygen, low blood sugar, and so on. Although he used the term somewhat casually, he spoke of his subjects as "under stress" and implied that the degree of stress could be measured.

By 1936, Hans Selye was using the term stress in a very special, technical sense to mean an orchestrated set of bodily defenses against any form of noxious stimulus (including psychological threats), a reaction that he called the General Adaptation Syndrome. Stress was, in effect, not an environmental demand (which Selye called a "stressor"), but a universal physiological set of reactions and processes created by such a demand. In the early 1950s Selye published an *Annual Report of Stress* (1950, 1951–1956) on his research. This work was pulled together in 1956 in a major book called *The Stress of Life*. By that time, the literature on the physiology of stress had already amounted to nearly six thousand publications a year (Appley & Trumbull, 1967). An invited address by Selye to the American Psychological Association in 1955 also helped spread interest in the concept from physiology to psychology and other behavioral sciences. Although the enormous volume of work on hormonal stress secretions that stemmed from Selye's work had obvious implications at the sociological and psychological levels of analysis, it did not actually clarify the latter processes. Nonetheless, Selye's work and its spinoffs have played a dominant role in the recent expansion of interest in stress.

Hinkle (1977) also accords an important role in the evolution of the stress concept in medicine to Harold G. Wolff, who wrote about life stress and disease in the 1940s and 1950s (e.g., Wolff, 1953). Like Selye and Cannon, who conceived of stress as a reaction of an organism besieged by environmental demands and noxious agents, Wolff appears to have regarded stress as a state of the body, although he never tried to define it systematically, as Selye did. He wrote (as cited in Hinkle, 1973, p. 31):

> I have used the word [stress] in biology to indicate that state within a living creature which results from the interaction of the organism with noxious stimuli or circumstances, i.e., it is a dynamic state within the organism; it is not a stimulus, assault, load, symbol, burden, or any aspect of environment, internal, external, social or otherwise.

This emphasis by Wolff on a "dynamic state" involving adaptation to demands, and by Selye on an orchestrated physiological response pattern, is important for several reasons. First, the term stress as used in the physical sciences refers to an inactive or passive body that is deformed (strained) by environmental loads. However, in the biological usage, stress is an active process of "fighting back"; the living body engages in adaptational efforts crucial to the maintenance or restoration of equilibrium, a concept derived from the French physiologist Claude Bernard (1815–1878) and based on his dicovery of the sugar-storing functions of the liver. Second, stress as a biological process of defense offers an interesting analogy to the psychological process we shall later call "coping," in which a person struggles to manage psychological stress. Third, the concept of a dynamic state points us toward important aspects of stress processes that might otherwise be missed, such as the resources available for coping, their costs, including disease and distress, and their benefits, including growth of competence and the joy of triumph against adversity. Finally, when one views stress as a dynamic state, attention is turned toward the ongoing relationship between the organism and the environment, and interplay and feedback. With a dynamic formulation we are less likely to settle for incomplete and inadequate definitions of stress that are based solely on what is happening within the organism.

We should also be aware of what was occurring during this period in relation to stress in sociology and psychology. Sociologists Marx, Weber, and Durkheim wrote extensively about "alienation." Durkheim (1893) viewed alienation as a condition of anomie that arises when people experience the lack or loss of acceptable norms to guide their efforts to achieve socially prescribed goals. To speak of powerlessness, meaninglessness, normlessness, isolation, and self-estrangement, which Seeman (1959, 1971) regards as the five variants of the concept of alienation (see also Kanungo, 1979; McClosky & Schaar, 1965), is clearly to place alienation under the general rubric of stress (see also Chapter 8).

More contemporary sociologists have tended to prefer the term strain rather than stress, using it to mean forms of social disruption or disorganization analogous to Wolff's view of stress in an individual as a disturbed state of the body. Riots, panics, and other social disturbances such as increased incidence of suicide, crime, and mental illness are consequences of stress (strain) at the social level; they refer to group phenomena rather than to phenomena at the individual psychological level. There is often an overlap, however, between stress in sociology and psychology that is well illustrated by Smelser's (1963) sociological analysis of collective behavior (panic, riot, etc.) and the research literature on natural disaster (Baker & Chapman, 1962; Grosser, Wechsler, & Greenblatt, 1964). Other examples include Lucas's (1969) study of a coal mine disaster, Mechanic's (1978) studies of students facing examination stress, Radloff and Helmreich's (1968) study of the group stress effects of working and living under water, and studies of organizational stress (Kahn, Wolfe, Quinn, Snoek, & Rosenthal, 1964). The borderline between sociological and psychological thought becomes exceedingly difficult to draw in these instances. In addition, the terminology used is chaotic, with stress (or strain) sometimes the agent and sometimes the response. Whatever language is employed, such research surely falls within the field of stress and is part of its recent history.

On the strictly individual psychological side, stress was, for a long time, implicit as an organizing framework for thinking about psychopathology, especially in the theorizing of Freud and later psychodynamically oriented writers. However, *anxiety* was used rather than stress. The word stress did not appear in the index of *Psychologi-*

cal Abstracts until 1944. Freud gave anxiety a central role in psychopathology. Blockage or delay of instinctual discharge of gratification resulted in symptoms; in later Freudian formulations, conflict-induced anxiety served as a cue or signal of danger and triggered defense mechanisms, unsatisfactory modes of coping that produced symptom patterns whose characteristics depended on the type of defense. A similar formulation, dominant in American psychology for many decades, was the reinforcement-learning theory of Hull (1943) and Spence (1956). Anxiety was viewed as a classically conditioned response that led to unserviceable (pathological) habits of anxiety-reduction (cf. Dollard & Miller, 1950). In most of the first half of the 20th century, this concept of anxiety was a major influence in psychological research and thought. The existential writings about anxiety by Kierkegaard and others were popularized in the United States by Rollo May (1950, 1958). If one recognizes that there is a heavy overlap between the concepts of anxiety and stress, and does not feel it necessary to quibble about which term is used, it could be said that the dominant view of psychopathology thus formulated was that it was a product of stress.

Empirical research on anxiety got a boost in the early 1950s with the publication of a scale for the measurement of anxiety as a trait (Taylor, 1953). The scale generated a huge amount of research on the role of anxiety in learning, memory, perception, and skilled performance, mostly from the standpoint of anxiety serving either as a drive (see Spence & Spence, 1966) or as a source of interference in cognitive activity. Much of this research was reviewed in a book edited by Spielberger (1966). Books continue to appear with the term anxiety rather than stress in the title, or using both terms, reflecting the fascination with anxiety and anxiety as stress (e.g., Sarason & Spielberger; and Spielberger & Sarason, 1975; Spielberger, 1966, 1972).

World War II had a mobilizing effect on stress theory and research. Indeed, one of the earliest psychological applications of the term stress is found in a landmark book about the war by Grinker and Spiegel (1945) entitled *Men Under Stress*. The military was concerned with the effect of stress on functioning during combat; it could increase soldiers' vulnerability to injury or death and weaken a combat group's potential for effective action. For instance, soldiers became immobilized or panicked during critical moments under fire or on bombing missions, and a tour of duty under these conditions often led to neurotic- or psychotic-like breakdowns (see Grinker & Spiegel).

With the advent of the Korean War, many new studies were directed at the effects of stress on adrenal-cortical hormones and on skilled performance. Some of the latter were done with a view to developing principles for selecting less vulnerable combat personnel, and others to developing interventions to produce more effective functioning under stress. The war in Vietnam also had its share of research on combat stress and its psychological and physiological consequences (cf. Bourne, 1969), much of it influenced by Selye. Also concerned with stresses of war were books on the impact of bombings on civilian morale and functioning (e.g., Freud & Burlingham, 1943; Janis, 1951), manipulation of military prisoners (e.g., Biderman & Zimmer, 1961), wartime survival (e.g., von Greyerz, 1962), and the concentration camp (e.g., Bettelheim, 1960; Cohen, 1953; Dimsdale, 1980).

A major landmark in the popularization of the term stress, and of theory and research on stress, was the publication by Janis (1958) of an intensive study of surgical threat in a patient under psychoanalytic treatment. This was followed by an increasing number of books also devoted to the systematization of stress theory and methodology, and an increase in concern with the social sources of stress in the environment. Examples are books by McGrath (1970) and Levine and Scotch (1970).

Since the 1960s there has been growing recognition that while stress is an inevitable aspect of the human condition, it is coping that makes the big difference in adaptational outcome. In *Psychological Stress and the Coping Process* (Lazarus, 1966) the emphasis began to shift somewhat from stress per se to coping. Aside from popular accounts, however, there are still relatively few treatises devoted extensively to coping, but more are beginning to appear. Examples include Coelho, Hamburg, and Adams (1974), Haan (1977), Horowitz (1976), Menninger (1963), Vaillant (1977), Levinson, Darrow, Klein, Levinson, and McKee (1978), Lazarus and Launier (1978), Murphy and Moriarty (1976), Pearlin and Schooler (1978), Folkman and Lazarus (1980), Lazarus and Folkman (1984), and some anthologies on coping with diverse forms of life stress (cf. Monat & Lazarus, 1977; Moos, 1977).

Modern Developments

Five relatively recent developments have also stimulated interest in stress and coping: the concern with individual differences, the resurgence of interest in psychosomatics, the development of behavior therapy aimed at the treatment and prevention of disease or life styles that increase the risk of illness, the rise of a life course developmental perspective, and a mounting concern with the role of the environment in human affairs. Let us examine each of these briefly.

Interest in *individual differences* grew out of the research on the effects of stress on performance that was stimulated by World War II and the Korean War. This problem, which was obviously relevant to people in nonmilitary settings as well, led to hundreds of laboratory and field experiments during the 1950s (see Lazarus, 1966, for a list of reviews). The dominant view had been quite simplistic: stress or anxiety resulted in the impairment of skilled performance either by excessively heightening drive tension or by creating interference or distraction. Psychologists who were involved in this research often cited a universal law propounded by Yerkes and Dodson (1908), the so-called inverted U-shaped curve in which increments of arousal or drive tension improved task performance up to a certain level, beyond which increasing disorganization and performance impairment resulted.

It became increasingly apparent, however, that there were important individual differences in response to stress; performance was not uniformly impaired or facilitated. Lazarus and Eriksen (1952), for example, found a marked increase in variance instead of an average increase or decrease in performance effectiveness under failure-induced stress. Performances were made more variable by stress, some experimental subjects doing much better and others doing much worse. This and other studies made it clear that one could not predict performance simply by reference to stressful stimuli, and that to predict performance outcomes required attention to the psychological processes that created individual differences in reaction. For example, people could differ in their optimal level of arousal, or in the ways they appraised the encounter or coped with its demands.

The growing realization of the importance of person factors such as motivation and coping (cf. Lazarus, Deese, & Osler, 1952) led to changes in the formulation of the problem of stress and skilled performance. For example, many researches (e.g., Sarason, 1960, 1972, 1975) began to look at the possible effects of mediating or moderator variables and their interactions. As the definition of the problem shifted toward person factors and the processes intervening between the stressful demands of the environment and the short-term emotional and performance outcomes, studies of skilled performance under stress were largely preempted by studies of stress-related processes (e.g., cognitive appraisal and coping) that could account for individual differences in reaction.

Yet the original problem, the effects of stress on performance, has not been totally abandoned. For example, in an analytic review of current research on stress and fatigue in human performance, Schönpflug (1983) and his colleagues bring us back to familiar concepts and variables such as time pressure and the effects of noise on fatigue and the efficiency of problem solving, but with a new twist: cognitive, motivational, and coping concepts have been grafted onto the earlier concern with performance effectiveness. This keeps alive the important issues of stress and performance, yet in a way that encourages the investigation of individual differences.

Psychosomatic medicine burgeoned about 50 years ago (Lipowski, 1977) but subsequently underwent a dramatic decline until quite recently. The reasons for the decline are complex but include a poor data base for the oversimple idea that various types of disorders such as ulcers and colitis could be explained on the basis of special kinds of psychodynamic processes. Unsuccessful attempts were made to use psychodynamic formulations to identify an "ulcer personality" (Alexander, 1950), a "colitis personality," a "migraine personality," and so on. Over the past 20 years, traditional psychoanalytic concepts have lost favor, and there has been more interest in environmental factors in illness. As a result, psychosomatic medicine, which had been heavily committed to an intrapsychic emphasis, suffered a crisis of confidence.

Revival of current interest has been prompted by a number of recent changes in outlook concerning stress and illness. A major contributor is Selye's work, which gives strong support to the general conviction that social and psychological factors are, indeed, important in health and illness. Psychophysiology and medicine, for instance, have moved away from the view that disease is strictly a product of environmental agents such as bacteria, viruses, and damaging accidents and toward acceptance of the idea that vulnerability to disease or "host resistance" is also important. Advanced research on stress and hormone effects on the tissues (Mason, 1971, 1974, 1975a, b, c; Mason et al., 1976) has made the concept of vulnerability acceptable to many of those suspicious of traditional psychodynamic formulations. Current psychosomatic thought is thus heavily embedded in stress theory and research and seems to have taken on a new vitality promoted, in part, by this broader, more interdisciplinary approach. A number of books on psychosomatic or behavioral medicine, including those by Weiner (1977), Weiss, Herd, and Fox

(1979), and Norton (1982), attest to this resurgence of interest, as do Ader's (1981) book on the comparatively new field of psychoimmunology, and Stone, Cohen, and Adler's (1979) volume on health psychology.

We might note in passing that interest in the immune response as a factor in all kinds of illness is by no means new, but it has gathered great momentum in recent years. Broadening the concept of psychosomatics from a specific set of ailments such as ulcers and hypertension to the general concept that all illness could have psychosocial etiology in a multicausal system (cf. Weiss, 1977) has stimulated the examination of the immune response as a possible factor even in cancer, a disorder far removed from the original meaning of psychosomatic. We should expect increased multidisciplinary research activity on the immune process, and the psychological and social factors affecting it, in coming years.

More evidence of the growing commitment to the consideration of psychological factors in health comes from the decision of the American Psychological Association to form the Division of Health Psychology (Division 38), and from the publication of journals including *Health Psychology, The Journal of Behavioral Medicine, Psychophysiology, The Journal of Human Stress, The British Journal of Medical Psychology, Psychological Medicine, The Journal of Psychosomatic Research,* and the *Journal of Health and Social Behavior,* in addition to the longstanding journal *Psychosomatic Medicine.* A number of more specialized journals (e.g., dealing with biofeedback or treatment) contain related research, and more broadly based journals (e.g., *The Journal of Personality and Social Psychology, The British Journal of Clinical Psychology*) have also begun to publish studies that center on psychosomatic or health-related topics.

Behavior therapy has also emerged in recent years as an alternative to traditional psychodynamic therapy. At first its outlook was preciously scientific, positivist, and narrow, focused around classical and operant conditioning, and militantly dissociated from psychoanalytic thought. Later it began developing greater flexibility and spawned within it the cognitive behavior therapy movement (e.g., Ellis, 1962; Ellis & Grieger, 1977), which takes into account, as central factors in psychopathology and successful coping, how a person construes adaptational encounters, and focuses on interventions to change thought as well as feeling and action. Growing numbers of cognitive behavior therapists see their work as the basis of rapprochement between behavioral and psychodynamic approaches (e.g., Goldfried, 1979; A. Lazarus, 1971; Lazarus, 1980; Mahoney, 1980; Wachtel,

1980). This has led them into the realm of stress and coping, as can be seen in Meichenbaum's (1977) cognitive coping interventions, Meichenbaum and Novaco's (1978) use of the concept of "stress inoculation," in which people are trained to cope with upcoming stressful situations, and Beck's (1976) treatment of depression.

A major realignment of interest in *developmental psychology* is a fourth factor facilitating interest in stress, coping, and adaptation. The psychology of development had traditionally been focused on infancy, childhood, and adolescence. In the 1960s, stimulated in part by the marked increased in the numbers of people reaching old age, there was a growing concern with adulthood and its problems. The writings of Erikson (1963) helped turn psychology from a Freudian focus on the early years of life and the resolution of the oedipal struggle in adolescence to the realization that major psychological transformations also took place in young adulthood and even later. Developmental psychology became a field devoted to change over the life course.

At the popular level, interest in adult transitions was given impetus by Gail Sheehy's (1976) book *Passages*, which borrowed from the more scholarly and systematic work by Levinson and his colleagues (e.g., Levinson et al., 1978) on midlife transitions and crises. Writings by Neugarten (1968 a, b), Lowenthal (1977; Lowenthal, Thurnher, & Chiriboga, 1975), and Vaillant (1977) also reflected and contributed to the growing interest in adult development. At the same time, the political and social repercussions of an aging population resulted in the establishment of the National Institute on Aging and a shift of research funds toward the study of the problems of aging.

One of the central themes expressed in this new literature concerns the stress of transitions and social change and how they are coped with. There is great interest, for example, in the empty nest, midlife crises, widowhood, and retirement. At the same time, there has never been more interest than at present in the emotional development of infants and children and the ways a child comes to understand the personal significance of social relationships and interactions. Whether the focus is on development in adults or in children, issues are frequently organized around stress, coping, and adaptation.

A final factor in the increased interest in stress and coping is the emergence of a strong *environmental or social ecological focus* in behavioral science research. Clinical psychology and psychiatry had already begun to move away from a strictly intrapsychic emphasis, in which the processes thought to underlie psychopathology resided primarily within the person, and toward an environmental focus. Psychological thought in general has shifted in the same direction, toward a greater interest in the environments within which humans live. Environmental psychology (or social ecology) itself has been facilitated by the rise of ethology as a naturalistic science. As they witnessed the impact of ethological studies, social scientists became aware of their lack of understanding of the natural habitats of humans. Stress depends, in part, on the social and physical demands of the environment (Altman & Wohlwill, 1977; Proshansky, Ittelson, & Rivlin, 1970; Stokols, 1977). Environmental constraints and environmental resources (Klausner, 1971) on which the possibilities for coping depend are also important factors. Therefore, the advent of a science of environment brought stress theory and research an extended perspective as well as new converts.

The Concept of Stress

Not everyone concerned with stress-related issues is sanguine about the value of the term stress. Members of an Institute of Medicine panel (Elliott & Eisdorfer, 1982), for example, state: ". . . after thirty-five years, no one has formulated a definition of stress that satisfies even a majority of stress researchers" (p. 11). Ader (1980), in a presidential address to the American Psychosomatic Society, is more pointed in his criticism:

> For our purposes . . . there is little heuristic value in the concept of "stress." "Stress" has come to be used (implicitly, at least) as an explanation of altered psychophysiological states. Since different experiential events have different behavioral and physiologic effects that depend upon the stimulation to which the individual is subsequently exposed and the responses the experimeter chooses to measure, the inclusive label, "stess," contributes little to an analysis of.the mechanisms that may underline or determine the organism's response. In fact, such labeling, which is descriptive rather than explanatory, may actually impede conceptual and empirical advances by its implicit assumption of an equivalence of stimuli, fostering the reductionistic search for simple one-cause explanations. (p. 312)

In 1966 Lazarus suggested that stress be treated as an organizing concept for understanding a wide range of phenomena of great importance in human and animal adaptation. Stress, then, is not a variable but a rubric consisting of many variables and processes. We still believe that this is the most useful approach to take. It is incumbent upon those who use this approach, however, to adopt a systematic theoretical framework for examining the concept at multiple levels of analysis and to specify antecedents, processes, and outcomes that are relevant to stress phenomena and the overarching concept of stress. This indeed is the main purpose of this book.

Some researchers and writers have been troubled about the tendency to expand the concept of stress to all the activities normally considered under the rubric of adaptation. Much that people do to adapt, however, goes on routinely and automatically through cognitive processes and specific actions and styles of living that do not necessarily involve stress. If we are to regard stress as a generic concept, we must therefore further delimit its sphere of meaning. Otherwise stress will come to represent anything and everything that is included by the concept of adaptation. We shall propose such a sphere of meaning below, after we consider three other classic definitional orientations: stimulus definitions, response definitions, and relational definitions.

Stimulus and Response Definitions

In keeping with psychological traditions of the recent past that portray humans and animals as reactive to stimulaton (S-R psychology), the most common definition of stress adopted by psychologists has been that it is a stimulus. Stress stimuli are most commonly thought of as events impinging on the person. Stimulus definitions also include conditions arising within the person, for example, drive stimuli such as hunger or sex, which are based in tissue conditions, and stimuli arising from neurological characteristics, as in White's (1959) "effectance drive."

What kinds of environmental events are typically cited as stress stimuli, or in Selye's terms, "stressors"? Lazarus and Cohen (1977) speak of three types: major changes, often cataclysmic and affecting large numbers of persons; major changes affecting one or a few persons; and daily hassles. As to the first, certain cataclysmic phenomena are usually treated as universally stressful and outside anyone's control. Included here are natural disasters, man-made castastrophes such as war, imprisonment, and uprooting and relocation. These may be prolonged events (e.g., imprisonment) or over quickly (earthquake, hurricane), although the physical and psychological aftermath of even a brief disaster can be extended over a long time.

Cataclysms and other disastrous events can also occur to only one person, or to relatively few, but the number of people affected does not crucially alter the power of such events to disturb. These events may be outside individual control, as in the death of a loved one (Bowlby, 1961; Lindemann, 1944; Parkes, 1972), a life-threatening or incapacitating illness (Hackett & Weisman, 1964), or being laid off from work (Kasl & Cobb, 1970); or the event may be heavily influenced by the person to whom it happens, as in divorce (Gove, 1973), giving birth (Austin, 1975), or taking an important examination (Mechanic, 1962). The above list consists largely of negative experiences that are harmful or threatening. Some writers (cf. Holmes & Masuda, 1974) maintain that any change, positive or negative, can have stressful impact. We shall examine this question in greater detail in Chapter 10.

To equate environmental stress stimuli with major catastrophe or change is, in our view, to accept a very limited definition of stress. Our daily lives are filled with far less dramatic stressful experiences that arise from our roles in living. In our research we have referred to these as "daily hassles," the little things that can irritate and distress people, such as one's dog getting sick on the living room rug, dealing with an inconsiderate smoker, having too many responsibilities, feeling lonely, having an argument with a spouse, and so on. Although daily hassles are far less dramatic than major changes in life such as divorce or bereavement, they may be even more important in adaptation and health (cf. DeLongis, Coyne, Dakof, Folkman, & Lazarus, 1982; Kanner, Coyne, Schaefer, & Lazarus, 1981).

It is also possible to identify a number of *formal* properties of situations that could affect their stressfulness, either quantitatively or qualitatively. For example, we could emphasize the difference between chronic and acute demands, as in Mahl's (1949, 1952, 1953) observation that gastric acid secretion occurs only with chronic stress. Other potentially fruitful distinctions include the magnitude of adjustive demands, the kinds of adjustment called for, the extent to which a person has control over the event or can predict it, the positive or negative valence of the event, and so on. Consider, for example, the possible differences between the unexpected loss of a loved one in an automobile accident and the slow and predictable loss that occurs in a lingering terminal illness. The degree and quality of stress reactions may differ markedly in these two situations even though the loss is the same.

Still another formal taxonomy of stressors has been proposed by the Panel on Psychosocial Assets and Modifiers of Stress in the Institute of Medicine report on *Stress and Human Health* (Elliott & Eisdorfer, 1982). It proposes four broad types of stressors that differ primarily in their duration, and overlap some of the distinctions made above. The four types of stressors are (Elliott & Eisdorfer, 1982):

> (1) *Acute, time-limited stressors,* such as going parachute jumping, await-ing surgery, or encountering a rattlesnake; (2) *Stressor sequences,* or series of events that occur over an extended period of time as the result of an initiating event such as job loss, divorce, or bereavement; (3) *Chronic intermittent stressors* such as conflict-filled visits to in-laws or sexual difficulties, which may occur once a day, once a week, once a month; and (4) *Chronic stressors* such as permanent disabilities, parental discord, or chronic job stress, which may or may not be initiated by a discrete event and which persist continuously for a long time. (pp. 150–151)

The above illustrates what is essentially a stimulus definition of stress in which certain situations are considered normatively stress-ful. Although it is sensible to search for a sound taxonomy of envi-ronmental stressors, whether defined in terms of content or of·for-mal characteristics, such as duration or chronicity, one must be wary, because there are individual differences in vulnerability to such stressors. External events are considered normatively stressful on the basis of the most common response, which is always far from universal. In other words, the creation of a taxonomy of stressful situations is dependent on an examination of patterns of stress re-sponse. Once patterns of response are taken into account, the pro-perties of persons that give stimulus situations potency and mean-ing must be considered, and the definition of stress is no longer stimulus-bound but becomes relational, an outlook we will examine shortly.

We noted earlier that in biology and medicine stress is most commonly defined in *response* terms, as in the work of Selye and Harold Wolff. When the response of the person or animal is empha-sized, we speak of a state of stress, an organism reacting with stress, being under stress, being disrupted, distressed, and so on. If we try to define stress by the response, we then have no systematic way of identifying prospectively what will be a stressor and what will not. We must await the reaction. Furthermore, many responses can be taken to indicate psychological stress when such is not the case.

Heart rate, for example, will rise sharply from jogging while the individual seems to feel psychologically relaxed and at peace. The response cannot reliably be judged as a psychological stress reaction without reference to the stimulus.

In short, all stimulus-response approaches are circular and beg the crucial questions of what it is about the stimulus that produces a particular stress response, and what it is about the response that indicates a particular stressor. It is the observed stimulus-response relationship, not stimulus *or* response, that defines stress. Consider, for example, Selye's definition of stress as "the non-specific response of the body to any demand." Aside from the fact that it is limited to the physiological level of analysis (e.g., Selye, 1980), this definition is essentially like earlier ones that treat stress as a disturbance of homeostasis produced by environmental change. There are many psychological parallels. For example, Miller (1953) defines stress as ". . . any vigorous, extreme, or unusual stimulation which being a threat, causes some significant change in behavior . . . ," and Basowitz, Persky, Korchin, and Grinker (1955) define it as "stimuli *more likely* to produce disturbances." A stimulus is a stressor when it produces a stressful behavioral or physiological response, and a response is stressful when it is produced by a demand, harm, threat, or load.

A further pitfall in the stimulus-response conceptualization lies in the definition of a stress response. It is all well and good to speak of a stress response as a disturbance of homeostasis, but since all aspects of living seem to either produce or reduce such disturbance, stress becomes difficult to distinguish from anything else in life except when the degree of disturbance is unusual. Moreover, it is difficult to define a steady-state or baseline on which to judge disturbance. Given this difficulty, rules are needed for determining when a condition will disturb homeostasis, create a stress response, or restore homeostasis.

The need for rules is made obvious by considering Selye's words "demand" or "stressor." For Selye, the property of a stimulus that makes it a stressor is that it is noxious to tissues. Mirsky (1964) has made the same observation:

If one examines the literature dealing with "stress," it becomes apparent that almost every energy transformation can be interpreted to be a stressful phenomenon. Phenomena that I used to regard as most pleasurable . . . are apparently stressful nowadays. I would suggest that we stop using the term "stress" in a loose sense and instead refer to what we are dealing with in more specific terms. Usually we are really talking about noxious stimuli. Let us use some description of the meaning of any event, noxious or otherwise, to the subject—be it a rat (only other rats can tell me what a rat feels) or be it a man. (p. 534)

Mirsky's comments might as readily have been cited in our earlier discussion of the overlap in meaning between stress and adaptation, and of Ader's and others' dissatisfaction with the loose meaning of the term stress. Mirsky's solution is equally useless, however, and like all stimulus definitions places the burden on a stimulus parameter without clarifying the rules for differentiating a stressor from a nonstressor. When one says that anything noxious to tissues is a stressor, confusion arises when we try to test what is meant by "noxious." For example, although it may be obvious, a bullet is not noxious or harmful unless it is fired from a fairly high-powered rifle at a vulnerable target. Even a bullet minimally capable of wounding or killing a person will not kill most game animals, surely not an elephant or rhinoceros, unless directed at a vulnerable soft spot. Similarly, bacteria do not create illness in species or individuals with high resistance to infection, and even severe pressures of living do not usually result in heart attacks in persons with well-functioning cardiovascular systems. In contrast, alcohol will have far more serious consequences for a person with existing liver damage than for a person whose liver is healthy; to a diabetic, sugar in the diet can mean disaster, whereas to a healthy person it is readily handled through the release of insulin; and to a person with a poor defense against the tubercle or smallpox bacillus, contact with those organisms is highly dangerous, whereas to one with high resistance, contact is of little consequence.

If the problem is difficult at the tissue level, consider the psychological level, where the properties of the person that create vulnerability are so difficult to assess. Miller's (1953) definition, cited above, is a case in point. In speaking of stress as "unusual stimulation which being a threat, causes some significant change in behavior . . .," Miller highlights the need for psychological principles about what makes stimulation unusual and threatening so as to produce a stress reaction. If, as Selye (1980) avers, ". . . emotional arousal is the most common cause of stress . . . ," it is all the more essential to understand the psychodynamics of that emotion. It is this latter task that we attempt to address in later chapters of this book.

Relational Definitions

We have noted the development of interdisciplinary scientific thought, and with it the gradual emphasis on relations among systems and the importance of the context in which phenomena occur. Most dramatic are shifts in the concept of disease in medicine. A major medical breakthrough was the 19th century discovery that microorganisms and other external environmental agents were causes of disease. Pasteur, Lister, Koch, and others showed that disease could be treated and even prevented by mounting assaults on these environmental agents or by keeping them at bay with vaccines, quarantine (which had been practiced much earlier without an understanding of how it worked), mosquito abatement, surgical asepsis, and so on.

A classic true story told to student epidemiologists illustrates an ideal of epidemiological research that derived from this 19th century emphasis on single environmental causes of disease, an ideal that still flourishes today. The story is about a pump handle and the research of John Snow on the cause of the cholera epidemic in London in 1855. It was believed at the time that the disease was caused by bad air. Snow, however, thought it had something to do with the presence of fecal matter in the Thames. Two companies, one located upstream, the other downstream, supplied this water to the residents of London. Snow accomplished the first epidemiological mapping of a cholera outbreak by conducting a census of households for both the presence of cholera and the water source. He found that water from only one source was implicated. Thus, all that was needed to control or even eliminate the disease would be to shut off the one pump handle that controlled the polluted water. For each student of epidemiology, then, the search for the right pump handle expresses the hope that he or she will discover the cause of a disease that can then be "shut off."

As we noted earlier, the concept of external causes of disease has given way in recent years to a newer concept of illness, namely, that a pathogen must be *united with* a susceptible organism. The characteristics or status of the system under attack (e.g., the organism, a person) are as important as the external noxious agent. A person does not become ill merely as a result of noxious agents in the environment—viruses and bacteria, for example, are always present—but as a result of being vulnerable to those agents. It is the person–environment *relationship*, one, incidentally, that is always changing, that determines the condition of disease.

Dubos (1959) described elegantly why it is that this 19th century search for a specific causal agent had to be abandoned for today's major health problems such as cardiovascular disease, cancer, and mental illness, which are multicausal. He writes:

> Koch and Pasteur wanted to show that microorganisms could cause certain manifestations of disease. Their genius was to devise experimental situations that lent themselves to an unequivocal illustration of their hypothesis-situations in which it was *sufficient* to bring the host and parasite together to reproduce the disease. By trial and error, they selected the species of animals, the dose of infectious agents, and the route of inoculation which permitted the infection to evolve without fail into progressive disease. Guinea pigs always develop tuberculosis if tubercle bacilli are injected into them under the proper conditions; introduction of sufficient rabies virus under the dura of dogs always gives rise to paralytic symptoms. Thus, by the skillful selection of experimental systems, Pasteur, Koch, and their followers succeeded in minimizing in their tests the influence of factors that might have obscured the activity of the infectious agents they wanted to study. This experimental approach has been extremely effective for the discovery of agents of disease and for the study of some of their properties. But it has led by necessity to the neglect, and indeed has often delayed the recognition, of the many other factors that play a part in the causation of disease under conditions prevailing in the natural world—for example, the physiological status of the infected individual and the impact of the environment in which he lives. (pp. 106–107)

The "pump handle" story has two important implications for our present discussion. First, stress and disease are prime examples of a multicausal system of the sort Dubos discusses. As is true of microbes, stress alone is not a sufficient cause of disease. To produce stress-linked disease other conditions must also be present such as vulnerable tissues or coping processes that inadequately manage the stress. The primary task of research is to study the contribution of these other variables and processes as mediators of the stress–illness relationship. Second, the self-same reasoning applies to our definition of stress as a particular kind of relationship between person and environment; here, too, researchers must identify the variables and processes that underlie that relationship. To the extent that epidemiologists and others concerned with behavioral or psychosomatic medicine and health psychology come to terms with this principle, it should require no further intellectual gymnastics to see the point with respect to the definition of stress itself and to recognize that many factors in the environment and the person must combine to generate stress and its outcomes.

It is true that *extreme* environmental conditions result in stress for nearly everyone, just as certain conditions are so noxious to most tissues or to the psyche that they are very likely to produce tissue damage or distress. However, the disturbances that occur in all or nearly all persons from extreme conditions such as military combat, natural disasters, imprisonment, torture, imminence of death, severe illness, and loss of loved ones must not be allowed to seduce us into settling for a simplistic concept of stress as environmentally produced. Such extreme conditions are not uncommon, but their use as a model produces inadequate theory and applications. The main difficulties arise when we overlook the great variations in human response to so-called universal stressors.

As one moves away from the most extreme life conditions to milder and more ambiguous ones, that is, to the more ordinary, garden-variety life stressors, the variability of response grows even greater. What now is stressful for some is not for others. No longer can we pretend that there is an objective way to define stress at the level of environmental conditions without reference to the characteristics of the person. It is here that the need for a relational perspective is most evident, and where it is particularly urgent to identify the nature of that relationship in order to understand the complex reaction pattern and its adaptational outcomes, as well as to draw upon this understanding clinically.

We are now ready to indicate the sphere of meaning in which stress belongs. *Psychological stress is a particular relationship between the person and the environment that is appraised by the person as taxing or exceeding his or her resources and endangering his or her well-being.*

Our immediate concern must be with what causes psychological stress in different persons (see Chapters 7 and 8 for discussions of stress at the social and physiological levels of analysis). We approach this question through the examination of two critical processes that mediate the person–environment relationship: cognitive appraisal and coping. Cognitive appraisal is an evaluative process that determines why and to what extent a particular transaction or series of transactions between the person and the environment is stressful. Coping is the process through which the individual manages the demands of the person–environment relationship that are appraised as stressful and the emotions they generate. In the chapters immediately following we shall elaborate these concepts, examine what is known and believed, raise important issues that have caused confusion in the field, and provide a theoretical and

methodological framework within which to think about the processes that mediate psychological stress and its relationship to
health and adaptation.

Chapters 2, 3, and 4 are concerned with the key concept of
cognitive appraisal. In Chapter 2 we discuss why this concept is
important and give a brief overview of related research. In Chapter 3
we focus on person factors that influence appraisal, and in Chapter
4 we look at the role of situation factors in the appraisal process.
Chapters 5 and 6 are about coping. In Chapter 5 we examine traditional formulations of coping, and their limitations. In Chapter 6 we
present our own process-oriented approach to coping. Chapter 7 is
concerned with the impact of appraisal and coping processes on
short- and long-term adaptational outcomes, including morale, social functioning, and somatic health. The subjects of coping effectiveness and learned helplessness are covered within this context.
Chapter 8 shifts from the psychological to the social levels of analysis. Here we look at society as a factor in adaptation and at its role in
individual stress and coping. Chapter 9 deals with cognitive theories
of emotion and the relationship between emotion and cognition. In
Chapter 10 we compare traditional approaches to theory and research with our process-oriented transactional formulation and address issues of research design and measurement. In Chapter 11 we
move to more applied questions and consider the implications of our
theory of stress and coping for management and intervention.

It is rare today to find stress, coping, and adaptation discussed
without reference to the topic of personal control. There is no single
concept of control; rather, it has many meanings and is used differently by different writers and even by the same writer at different
times. There is no one chapter on control in this book. Instead, the
theme of control weaves in and out, appearing, for example, in
Chapter 3 in our discussion of the ways control expectancies influence appraisal, in Chapter 6 in the context of coping, and in Chapter
7 in the section on effective coping in situations that are appraised as
uncontrollable and as an outcome of coping, as in learned helplessness. Control, in short, appears in at least three guises: as an antecedent situation or person variable; as a mediator, for example, a coping process; and as an outcome, as in loss of control or learned
helplessness. We hope that researchers who have a particular interest in this important topic will find that the system of thought and
approach to research that is presented in this book is clarifying and
that it encourages a systematic, multifaceted treatment of control
and of the many ways it operates in stress and coping processes.

Summary

The concept of stress has been around for centuries, but only recently has it been systematically conceptualized and a subject of research. World War II and the Korean War gave an impetus to stress research because of its significance for military combat. Later it was recognized that stress is an inevitable aspect of life and that what made the difference in human functioning was how people coped with it. Developments in psychosomatics, behavioral medicine, health psychology, and clinical intervention, growing interest in the stressful transitions of aging, and concern with the physical environment and how it affects us, all have had a stimulating effect on the study of stress and on individual differences in stress reactions.

Most often, stress has been defined as either stimulus or response. Stimulus definitions focus on events in the environment such as natural disasters, noxious conditions, illness, or being laid off from work. This approach assumes that certain situations are normatively stressful but does not allow for individual differences in the evaluation of events. Response definitions, which have been prevalent in biology and medicine, refer to a state of stress; the person is spoken of as reacting with stress, being under stress, and so on. Stimulus and response definitions have limited utility, because a stimulus gets defined as stressful only in terms of a stress response. Adequate rules are still needed to specify the conditions under which some stimuli are stressors.

The definition of stress here emphasizes the *relationship* between the person and the environment, which takes into account characteristics of the person on the one hand, and the nature of the environmental event on the other. This parallels the modern medical concept of illness, which is no longer seen as caused solely by an external organism; whether or not illness occurs depends also on the organism's susceptibility. Similarly, there is no objective way to predict psychological stress as a reaction without reference to properties of the person. Psychological stress, therefore, is a relationship between the person and the environment that is appraised by the person as taxing or exceeding his or her resources and endangering his or her well-being. The judgment that a particular person–environment relationship is stressful hinges on cognitive appraisal, which is the subject of the three subsequent chapters.

2

Cognitive Appraisal Processes

At the time of Lazarus's (1966) earliest full statement of his theory of psychological stress, mainstream psychology was still some distance from "the cognitive revolution" (Dember, 1974). Positivism, which regards mediating processes somewhat suspiciously, was the dominant outlook. Therefore, it was necessary at the time to dwell at length on why the concept of appraisal was essential to a theory of psychological stress and coping. Although the need is less pressing now, it is still worth taking the time to deal with this question. We shall begin our treatment of appraisal with a discussion of this issue and then examine some of the evidence. We then consider problems that are associated with a phenomenological approach, and conclude with a discussion of the concept of vulnerability, which is connected in important ways to cognitive appraisal.

Why Is a Concept of
Appraisal Necessary?

Although certain environmental demands and pressures produce stress in substantial numbers of people, *individual and group differences* in the degree and kind of reaction are always evident. People and groups differ in their sensitivity and vulnerability to certain types of events, as well as in their interpretations and reactions.

Under comparable conditions, for example, one person responds with anger, another with depression, yet another with anxiety or guilt; and still others feel challenged rather than threatened. Likewise, one individual uses denial to cope with terminal illness whereas another anxiously ruminates about the problem or is depressed. One individual handles an insult by ignoring it and another grows angry and plans revenge. Even in the most devastating of circumstances, such as the Nazi concentration camps, people differed as to how threatened, disorganized, and distressed they were. Their patterns of coping differed as well (Benner, Roskies, & Lazarus, 1980). In order to understand variations among individuals under comparable conditions, we must take into account the cognitive processes that intervene between the encounter and the reaction, and the factors that affect the nature of this mediation. If we do not consider these processes, we will be unable to understand human variation under comparable external conditions.

There is, as one might expect, a positivist counterargument, which is that individual differences occur because human environments are always different and therefore individual differences are not necessarily due to person characteristics. Strack and Coyne (1983) and Coyne and Gotlib (1983), for example, have noted that affective depression is not entirely explainable by people's tendencies to make cognitively inappropriate assumptions about themselves and to distort reality; to some extent they are responding accurately to their social environments. For example, people who are depressed generate feelings of distress in others, thus making themselves aversive. These depressed persons are therefore correct in perceiving that others are rejecting them. Moreover, to a considerable degree depressives may be responding to real losses in their lives. We agree that some portion of observed individual differences is the result of actual environmental differences, but this cannot be the whole story. Consistent with prior arguments by Lewin (1936) and others, we hold that what is important is the "psychological situation," which is a product of the interplay of both environment and person factors.

A second reason for understanding the appraisal process is that in order to survive and flourish people must distinguish between benign and dangerous situations. These distinctions are often subtle, complex, and abstract and depend on a highly versatile and efficient cognitive system made possible by the evolution of a brain capable of symbolic activity and powered by what we have learned about the world and ourselves through experience.

No one is surprised that plants have developed complex and essential protein discrimination mechanisms, or that animals have wired-in mechanisms for distinguishing dangerous predators (e.g., Tinbergen, 1951). Why then should it surprise anyone that a species as advanced neurologically as *Homo sapiens* should have developed a highly symbolic set of cognitive processes for distinguishing among experiences that harm, threaten, challenge, or nurture? Indeed, successful adaptation and the human sense of well-being rest on the ability to make such evaluative perceptions.

In humans, therefore, and to a lesser extent in other primates and mammals, cognitive appraisal processes of some sort mediate reactions and are essential for adequate psychological understanding. A cognitive appraisal reflects the unique and changing relationship taking place between a person with certain distinctive characteristics (values, commitments, styles of perceiving and thinking) and an environment whose characteristics must be predicted and interpreted.

The idea that how a person *construes* an event shapes the emotional and behavioral response has a long tradition in Western thought. Some two thousand years ago the Roman philosopher Epictetus stated ·(in the *Enchiridion*, 1979) that "Men are disturbed not by things, but by the views which they take of things" (p. 19). The same notion was more eloquently expressed by Shakespeare in the famous line from *Hamlet*, "There is nothing either good or bad, but thinking makes it so" (Act II, Scene 2, line 259). Perhaps the only thing that is new is the stubborn effort of behaviorist psychology over the past 75 or so years to demonstrate that it is unnecessary or even without scientific credibility to study internal mental events (see, for example, Bolles, 1974).

There is also a long tradition in psychology that emphasizes the importance of the subjective meaning of any situation. Murray (1938), for instance, distinguished between the properties of environmental objects as disclosed through objective inquiry (alpha press) and the significance of those objects as perceived or interpreted by the individual (beta press). Lewin (1936) also wrote:

> Even when from the standpoint of the physicist, the environment is identical or nearly identical for a child and for an adult, the psychological situation can be fundamentally different . . . the situation must be represented in the way in which it is "real" for the individual in question, that is, as it affects him. (pp. 24–25)

Many other current psychological theorists and researchers must be added to the list of those who adopt this stance (e.g.,

Bowers, 1973; Endler & Magnusson, 1976; Magnusson & Endler, 1977; Mischel, 1973; Murphy, 1966; Pervin & Lewis, 1978; Rotter, 1954, 1975; Sarason, 1977; see also many of the writers in Krohne & Laux, 1982, among others). All of these writers have urged that situations be considered in terms of their significance to the individual. This theme is found also in sociology, especially among symbolic interactionists (cf. Jessor, 1979). Ekehammar (1974) summarizes the implications of this position as follows:

> ... the person is a function of the situation, but also, and more importantly, ... the situation is a function of the person through the person's (a) cognitive construction of situations and (b) active selection and modification of situations. (p. 1035)

The Place of Cognitive Appraisal in Stress Theory

Many early writers in the field of psychological stress (e.g., Barber & Coules, 1959; Fritz & Mathewson, 1957; Janis, 1951; Shannon & Isbell, 1963; Wallace, 1956; Withey, 1962) made use of the concept of appraisal, although mostly in an unsystematic, informal way or by implication. It is stated directly in the work of Grinker and Spiegel (1945), who wrote "*appraisal* of the situation requires mental activity involving judgment, discrimination, and choice of activity, based largely on past experience" (p. 122, italics ours).

Arnold (1960, 1970) was the first to attempt a systematic treatment of the concept. She writes of appraisal as the cognitive determinant of emotion, describing it as a rapid, intuitive process that occurs automatically, as distinguished from slower, more abstract, reflective thought. She writes:

> It [appraisal] is immediate and indeliberate. If we see somebody stab at our eye with his finger, we avoid the threat instantly, even though we may know that he does not intend to hurt or even to touch us. Before we can make such an instant response, we must have estimated somehow that the stabbing finger could hurt. Since the movement is immediate, unwitting, or even contrary to our better knowledge, this appraisal of possible harm must be similarly immediate. (1960, p. 172)

Although we agree that appraisal determines emotion, and that an emotional reaction can be immediate, especially in response to strong auditory or visual stimuli, or even in response to more subtle or abstract cues such as facial expression, our emphasis is much more on complex, meaning-related cognitive activity. Appraisals go far beyond immediate and indeliberate cognitive-affective responses.

A fire alarm, for example, is a loud auditory stimulus that triggers automatic and instant arousal (fear). However, upon hearing a loud fire alarm in a building, unless we are panicked we are likely further to consider how realistic the perception of danger really is; if there is time, we localize the danger, assess its potency and, above all, consider how we might deal with it. New inputs and thoughts feed back to the original appraisal of threat, confirming it, enhancing it, or reducing it, depending on further evaluation of what is happening and what we can do. In short, the initial instant of fear experienced at the sound of the alarm initiates a whole chain of cognitive activity, some of it extending over a long period of time and involving complex thoughts, actions, and reactions, all of which make possible finely tuned and even sequential adaptational responses.

An immediate, intuitive appraisal such as Arnold speaks of does not exclude high-level cognitive activity at the outset. For example, in Mechanic's (1978b) study of students preparing for doctoral examinations, one student describes his reactions to a professor's words to him. The encounter took place while the examinations were being graded:

> "I guess I was pretty upset about my statistics and I was doing some statistics for [Doctor F] and we came across a problem. And he said, 'You work on this and see what you can do with it and, if you come up with a solution, I'll add two points to your statistics grade.' *Immediately, I started ruminating. What does he know about my statistics? Do I really need two points?* So I actually confronted him with these feelings later and he said it actually was just a figure of speech and that he hadn't heard anything." (p. 168, italics ours)

This student felt immediate threat, and his ruminations occurred so rapidly as to be considered virtually instantaneous. Nevertheless, they were the product of high-level cortical functioning and cannot readily be equated with the phylogenetically more primitive flight-fight type of response, or the sensory-based intuitive process Arnold refers to.

Although Janis and Mann (1977) do not describe their model of conflict and decision making in terms of appraisal, it is in fact heavily concerned with appraisal processes. They ask four questions about consequences, resources, and imminence, the answers to which determine the quality of information search and decision making: "Are the risks serious if I don't change? Are the risks serious if I do change? Is it realistic to hope to find a better solution? Is there sufficient time to search and deliberate?" (p. 70) These questions are all concerned with what we call appraisal in that they shape the person's evaluation of the event and consequent decision-making (coping) processes.

Janis and Mann's (1977) model is an excellent example of an appraisal-based theory, but it differs from ours in several respects. Our focus, for example, is broader. Whereas Janis and Mann are concerned with choices between courses of action, we are concerned with *any* event in which the person feels his or her adaptive resources to be taxed or exceeded. Also, Janis and Mann generally consider emotion primarily as an interference with information search and decision-making processes; we look at emotion not only with regard to its impact on information processing, but also as it is in turn shaped by such information (see Chapter 9). We cite this important work mainly to point up parallel stress-related formulations that hinge on cognitive mediational processes such as appraisal.

Despite this evidence of interest in cognitive appraisal, until recently stress research has been based largely on noncognitive theoretical models such as drive reinforcement and arousal or activation. Since these models have dominated so much of stress research, we think it is useful to review them briefly in order to highlight the distinctions between models such as these and the cognitive model that we advocate.

In the drive-reinforcement model, stress is typically regarded as a state of disequilibrium, a "perturbation of the organism." This perspective evolved from the view that in order to survive an animal had to learn to act adaptively to reduce tissue deficits (e.g., Dollard & Miller, 1950; Miller, 1948, 1959, 1980) or to discharge instinctual drives (Freud, 1953, 1955). Deficits or undischarged impulses resulted in tension or *drive states*. Even secondary or learned drives involving social behaviors such as affiliation and achievement were grafted onto primary or tissue-based drives through tension reduction (reinforcement).

An animal with unresolved drive tensions was also a physiologically *aroused* animal. Forty to 50 years ago, the concept of arousal was used synonymously with emotions; that is, emotion was assimilated into the concept of arousal or activation, and reduced to a simple, unidimensional construct which had behavioral and physiological manifestations (cf. Brown & Farber, 1951; Duffy, 1962; Malmo, 1959). Emotion as we know it in experience was written off as a psychological concept having no substance beyond the antecedent and consequent conditions that defined it. This view was also analogous to the physiologists' concept of equilibrium and its disruption, and fit well with Selye's General Adaptation Syndrome (see Chapter 7), which ignored the qualitative forms of emotion and the social and psychological factors that generated them.

The concept of drive, and the concurrent model of tension reduction, has lost favor, with evidence coming from a number of directions that general arousal theory is wrong or at least overstated. Studies in which more than one autonomic nervous system end-organ reaction was measured simultaneously have reported very low correlations (e.g., Lazarus, Speisman, Mordoff, & Davison 1962); this counters the notion of a generalized arousal state which implies that when one physiological indicator rises, the others will rise in concert. Actually, as Lacey (1967) demonstrated, when skin conductance rises, heart rate or blood pressure often falls. Lacey's impressive research on the specificity of automatic reactions in response to different stressful conditions weakened credibility in the simple concept of general activation. Research by Engel (1960), Engel and Bickford (1961), and others also demonstrated stimulus specificity, and Shapiro, Tursky, and Schwartz (1970) provided an effective demonstration of specificity by showing that heart rate could be conditioned to rise while blood pressure fell, and vice versa, as a result of biofeedback information. More recently, Ekman, Levenson, and Friesen (1983) have demonstrated emotion-specific autonomic nervous system activity in two ways: first, by having subjects construct facial prototypes of emotion by controlling specific muscle patterns; and second, by having subjects relive past emotional experiences. Not only could positive and negative emotions be distinguished in these ways, but differentiation also occurred within the category of negative emotions. This study provides one of the strongest empirical challenges to the idea of undifferentiated autonomic nervous system activity in emotional response.

The research of Mason (1974; Mason et al., 1976) also has provided evidence that the hormonal response varies with specific physical assaults such as heat, cold, fasting, and exercise, each creating a distinctive hormonal response pattern. Mason argues that a broad spectrum of hormones and endocrine systems, including the pituitary-gonadal, growth hormone, and insulin systems, along with the more commonly studied pituitary-adrenal cortical and sympathetic-adrenal medullary systems, respond selectively to diverse psychological processes. Mason (1975a) writes:

> It appears . . . the hormonal trend is a resultant of a balance of opposing and cooperative forces and can be predicted with increasing accuracy as the multiple factors involved, including affective states, defensive organization, social setting, prior experiential or developmental factors, and current activities, can all be evaluated in a psychodynamic perspective for each individual subject. (p. 149)

More recent psychophysiological research continues to support the idea that there is a specificity in the hormonal response to stressful and arousing conditions. For example, using an avoidance conditioning procedure with monkeys, Natelson, Krasnegor, and Holaday (1976) demonstrated that behavioral and cortisol measures of arousal both converged and diverged, depending on when during the stressful session they were measured. Early in the first avoidance session, when many electric shocks were being received and performance was poor, behavioral scores for arousal were high and cortisol secretion was elevated; later in the same session the behavioral score for arousal remained high but cortisol secretion was low, regardless of the monkey's ability to avoid shock. The authors suggest that changes in the cortisol response are the result of the monkey being able to control the impact of the shock, and that "steroids are of little general use as a neuroendocrine index of arousal" (p. 968).

Similarly, Frankenhaeuser et al. (1978) observed important gender differences in a number of adrenal cortical and adrenal medullary hormones in the response of students to an important school examination despite comparable performance. Frankenhaeuser et al. offer the interpretation that "the physiological cost involved in coping with the situation seems to have been lower for females than for males" (p. 341). Frankenhaeuser (1980) observes further, "challenging but controllable tasks are likely to induce effort without distress. On the physiological level this means that catecholamine secretion will rise, whereas cortisol secretion may be actively suppressed" (pp. 207–208). If coping is a major factor in the patterning of physiological response, as other studies by Frankenhaeuser and her colleagues suggest (see Frankenhaeuser, 1979, 1982, 1983), then a unidimensional concept of arousal must give way to the concept that different psychological conditions or processes will affect the physiological response pattern in different ways.

The above findings fail to support general drive-reinforcement or activation theory. They make untenable or at least grossly incomplete any psychophysiological theory of stress or emotion which views the response as unidimensional disequilibrium or arousal. The issue is also complicated by the fact that what is considered an optimal level of arousal is variable (see also Yerkes-Dodson law, 1908; and Janis, 1974). Zuckerman (1979), for example, argues that some people seek to increase their arousal by sensation-seeking rather than to reduce it. Theorists and researchers are now obliged to look for specific *patterns* of physiological response, and if understanding is to follow, they must attempt to learn the specific *cognitive-emotional* states that are associated with these diverse patterns. Once one distinguishes among fear, anxiety, anger, guilt, shame, envy, jealousy, disgust, joy, happiness, exhilaration—that is, whatever distinct emotions are considered part of the human repertoire—the possibilities for what is measured become far more complex. We will return to this point in Chapter 9, when we deal with cognitive theories of emotion.

A growing number of psychophysiological researchers are cognizant of the role of cognitive appraisal—with its significance for individual differences in meaning—as a factor in stress, although the cognizance does not mean that a cognitive-phenomenological approach will be used in interpreting findings. A good example is Levine, Weinberg, and Ursin (1978), who write:

> Before any further discussion of coping can occur it seems necessary to revise the stress theory prevalent in current medical and psychological literature where stress is still defined according to the early theories of Selye (1956). We believe that much of the controversy over stress theory can be eliminated by clarification of the "afferent limb," that is, by focusing on the nature of the stimuli that provoke physiological responses, rather than by focusing primarily on the physiological responses themselves. This requires an unusual intregation of physiology and psychology, disciplines that tend to be traditionally separated, and puts the emphasis on the psychological variables. However, even if we accept the hypothesis that psychological factors are the prepotent stimulators of the response to stress, we believe that there are, in fact, complicated psychological mechanisms involved in determining whether an individual does or does not respond to a specific situation. It appears that it is not just the stimuli or physical environment per se that determines the physiological response, but the individual's evaluation of these stimuli. This may be regarded as a filter or gating function. Thus, if the organism evaluates the situation as threatening and uncertain, there will be a continuing high level of activation. However, if the organism evaluates the situation as

being safe and one in which he can master the probable events, the result-ing physiological response will be diminished, if not absent, even though the situation itself had been extremely threatening. (p. 6)

This statement by Levine et al. (1978) goes a long way toward treating psychological stress in terms of cognitive mediation and permitting psychophysiological researchers to question unidimen-sional stress concepts such as arousal or activation. On the other hand, if one examines Levine's research on stress, coping, and con-trol, it is clear that what is said here is lip service rather than based on real conviction, a reluctant and cautious movement toward neo-behaviorism. The research models are all based on animal subjects and laboratory experiments, and therefore no direct effort is made to examine cognitive processes or to consider complex forms of coping and social and symbolic variables that are central in human adapta-tion. Yet the above quote reflects growing awareness of the signifi-cance of what we have been emphasizing in theory even if it is not always honored in actual research practice.

Basic Forms of Cognitive Appraisal

Cognitive appraisal can be most readily understood as the process of categorizing an encounter, and its various facets, with respect to its significance for well-being. It is not information processing per se, in the sense used by Mandler (1975), Erdelyi (1974), and others, al-though it partakes of such processing. Rather, it is largely *evaluative*, focused on meaning or significance, and takes place continuously during waking life.

In all previous accounts of appraisal theory, we have made a basic distinction between *primary appraisal* and *secondary appraisal*, identifying the two main evaluative issues of appraisal, namely, "Am I in trouble or being benefited, now or in the future, and in what way?" and "What if anything can be done about it?" The choice of terminology, "primary" and "secondary," was unfortunate for two reasons. First, these terms suggest, erroneously, that one is more important (i.e., primary) than the other, or that one precedes the other in time. Neither of these meanings is intended. Second, these terms give no hint about the content of each form of appraisal. It is awkward to try to change terms after they have found a place in the literature, however, so we think it is wise not to replace "pri-mary" and "secondary" with connotatively more accurate terms.

Primary Appraisal

Three kinds of primary appraisal can be distinguished: (1) irrelevant, (2) benign-positive, and (3) stressful. When an encounter with the environment carries no implication for a person's well-being, it falls within the category of *irrelevant*. The person has no investment in the possible outcomes, which is another way of saying that it impinges on no value, need, or commitment; nothing is to be lost or gained in the transaction.

Psychologists concerned with the orienting reflex recognize that an animal will respond to any stimulus with a "What is it?" reaction, but will habituate through repeated exposure until it no longer responds. This is a similar notion to what we mean by irrelevance. Make a noise at a dog whose eyes are closed and it will react automatically and prick up its ears; eventually, however, this response will fade when the dog discovers that nothing relevant is happening. It is highly adaptive for humans to distinguish among relevant and irrelevant cues so that they will mobilize for action only when it is desirable or necessary. Although appraisals of irrelevance are not themselves of great interest adaptationally, what is of interest is the cognitive process through which events are so appraised.

Benign-positive appraisals occur if the outcome of an encounter is construed as positive, that is, if it preserves or enhances well-being or promises to do so. These appraisals are characterized by pleasurable emotions such as joy, love, happiness, exhilaration, or peacefulness. Totally benign-positive appraisals that are without some degree of apprehension may be rare, however. For some people there is always the prospect that the desirable state will sour, and for those who believe that one must ultimately pay for feeling good with some later harm, benign appraisals can generate guilt or anxiety. These illustrations anticipate the idea that appraisals can be complex and mixed, depending on person factors and the situational context.

Stress appraisals include harm/loss, threat, and challenge. In *harm/loss*, some damage to the person has already been sustained, as in an incapacitating injury or illness, recognition of some damage to self- or social esteem, or loss of a loved or valued person. The most damaging life events are those in which central and extensive commitments are lost.

Threat concerns harms or losses that have not yet taken place but are anticipated. Even when a harm/loss has occurred, it is always fused with threat because every loss is also pregnant with negative implications for the future. The severely burned patients studied by Hamburg, Hamburg, and deGoza (1953), and the victims of polio studied by Visotsky, Hamburg, Goss, and Lebovits (1961) were not only severely incapacitated in the present but also had to face a host of related threats about their future functioning. The primary adaptational significance of threat, as distinguished from harm/loss, is that it permits anticipatory coping. To the extent that humans can anticipate the future, they can plan for it and work through some of the difficulties in advance, as in anticipatory grief work.

The third kind of stress appraisal, *challenge,* has much in common with threat in that it too calls for the mobilization of coping efforts. The main difference is that challenge appraisals focus on the potential for gain or growth inherent in an encounter and they are characterized by pleasurable emotions such as eagerness, excitement, and exhilaration, whereas threat centers on the potential harms and is characterized by negative emotions such as fear, anxiety, and anger.

Threat and challenge are not necessarily mutually exclusive. A job promotion, for example, is likely to be appraised as holding the potential for gains in knowledge and skills, responsibility, recognition, and financial reward. At the same time, it entails the risk of the person being swamped by new demands and not performing as well as expected. Therefore, the promotion is likely to be appraised as both a challenge and a threat. Although threat and challenge appraisals are distinguished from one another by their cognitive component (the judgment of potential harm or loss versus mastery or gain) and their affective component (negative versus positive emotions), they can occur simultaneously. For example, as part of a study about examination stress (Folkman & Lazarus, in press), students were asked to indicate the extent to which they experienced each of a number of threat emotions such as fear, worry, and anxiety, and challenge emotions such as hopefulness, eagerness and confidence, two days before a midterm examination. Ninety-four percent of the students reported feeling both threat and challenge emotions.

We want to emphasize that we do not view threat and challenge appraisals as poles of a single continuum. As we stated above, threat and challenge can occur simultaneously, and must be considered as separate, although often related, constructs. Moreover, the relationship between threat and challenge appraisals can shift as an encounter unfolds. A situation that is appraised as more threatening than challenging can come to be appraised as more challenging than threatening because of cognitive coping efforts which enable the person to view the episode in a more positive light (see Chapter 6), or through changes in the environment that alter the troubled person–environment relationship for the better.

Challenge, as opposed to threat, has important implications for adaptation. For example, people who are disposed or encouraged by their circumstances to feel challenged probably have advantages over easily threatened people in morale, quality of functioning, and somatic health. Challenged persons are more likely to have better morale, because to be challenged means feeling positive about demanding encounters, as reflected in the pleasurable emotions accompanying challenge. The quality of functioning is apt to be better in challenge because the person feels more confident, less emotionally overwhelmed, and more capable of drawing on available resources than the person who is inhibited or blocked. Finally, it is possible that the physiological stress response to challenge is different from that in threat, so that diseases of adaptation are less likely to occur (see also Chapter 7).

Although these speculations are plausible and agree with anecdotal observation, empirical evidence about challenge (as opposed to threat) and functioning and somatic outcomes is sparse, perhaps because only recently have researchers concerned with behavioral medicine become interested in challenge. A study by Schlegal, Wellwood, Copps, Gruchow, and Sharratt (1980) provides some encouragement for the basic thesis. Type A and Type B survivors of myocardial infarction were compared on reported symptoms and subjective fatigue during a bicycle ergometer exercise task and over a two-week period of daily living. The subjects were divided into those who scored high or low in perceived challenge in the course of daily living. Type A's and Type B's did not differ on the ergometer task, but those Type A's who scored high on perceived challenge in the course of daily living reported fewer symptoms (e.g., shortness of breath, pain, nausea) than those scoring low, whereas a positive correlation was found for Type B's. It is not possible to say whether these findings reflect suppression of symptoms by Type A's, greater indifference to symptoms, or, least likely, actual functional differences (see Chapter 5 for a more complete discussion of the Type A phenomenon).

Frankenhaeuser (1982, 1983) and her colleagues have been providing findings for short-run psychophysiological patterns in threat and challenge that appear promising. And Fish (1983) had developed a method of assessing challenge versus threat appraisals and has demonstrated that performance outcomes differ in the expected direction in a stressful encounter involving public speaking. The hypotheses about threat and challenge and short- and long-run adaptational outcomes seem worth investigating more closely in controlled studies.

Secondary Appraisal

When we are in jeopardy, whether it be a threat or a challenge, something must be done to manage the situation. In that case, a further form of appraisal becomes salient, that of evaluating what might and can be done, which we call secondary appraisal. Secondary appraisal activity is a crucial feature of every stressful encounter because the outcome depends on what, if anything, can be done, as well as on what is at stake.

Secondary appraisal is more than a mere intellectual exercise in spotting all the things that might be done. It is a complex evaluative process that takes into account which coping options are available, the likelihood that a given coping option will accomplish what it is supposed to, and the likelihood that one can apply a particular strategy or set of strategies effectively. Bandura (1977a, 1982) emphasizes the distinction between these two expectancies. He uses the term *outcome expectancy* to refer to the person's evaluation that a given behavior will lead to certain outcomes and *efficacy expectation* to refer to the person's conviction that he or she can successfully execute the behavior required to produce the outcomes. In addition, the appraisal of coping options includes an evaluation of the consequences of using a particular strategy or set of strategies vis-à-vis other internal and/or external demands that might be occurring simultaneously.

Secondary appraisals of coping options and primary appraisals of what is at stake interact with each other in shaping the degree of stress and the strength and quality (or content) of the emotional reaction. This interplay can be quite complex, although our understanding here is still rudimentary. For example, other things being equal, if the person is helpless to deal with a demand, stress will be relatively great because the harm/loss cannot be overcome or prevented. If the person has a high stake in the outcome, meaning that it touches a strong commitment, helplessness is potentially devastating. Even when people believe they have considerable power to control the outcome of an encounter, if the stakes are high any doubt can produce considerable stress.

Challenge appraisals are more likely to occur when the person has a sense of control over the troubled person–environment relationship. Challenge will not occur, however, if what must be done does not call for substantial efforts. The joy of challenge is that one pits oneself against the odds.

We need to look closely at what it means to speak of a sense of control in a stressful encounter with respect to challenge. There are numerous situations in which there seems to be little opportunity to enhance a value or commitment and/or in which the person feels helpless. Yet people can appraise these situations as challenges because challenges can also be defined as controlling oneself in the face of adversity, and even transcending adversity. An example is a life-threatening, incapacitating illness or a severe loss in which the person reports being challenged by the task of maintaining a positive outlook, or tolerating pain and distress without falling apart. Thus, we must use our broadened definition of control, as developed in Chapter 3, in which we speak of control over oneself and one's emotions, as well as control over environmental conditions, to understand how people can feel challenged even under the bleakest conditions.

Secondary appraisal of coping options has been discussed in an article by Lazarus and Launier (1978). The following quotations describe a series of interrelated, imaginary scenarios in which the threat is rejection in an upcoming job interview. Each scenario portrays a slightly different pattern of appraisal, as to both stakes and coping options, which has a strong impact on coping and emotion.

1. "As things stand now, I will probably be rejected. This is a very damaging outcome because I have no other job opportunities. If I had the ability to deal effectively with the interview, I could be hired, but I don't have the ability. Moreover, there is no one to help me. The situation is hopeless."

2. "As things stand now, I will probably be rejected. This is a very damaging outcome because I have no other job opportunities. If I had the ability to deal effectively with the interview, I could be hired. I believe I do have such ability and I must think out what would make me an attractive candidate, rehearse, and take a tranquilizer two hours before the interview to control my nervousness."

3. "As things stand now, I will probably be rejected. This is a very damaging outcome because I have no other job opportunities. If I had the ability to deal effectively with the interview, I could be hired, but I don't. However, I have a good friend who knows the personnel manager, and I think he will help me."

4. "As things stand now, I will probably be rejected. This would be too bad because I need a job and this one looks very attractive. However, there are other possibilities, so if I am not hired I can try those."

5. "As things stand now, I will probably be rejected. This is a very damaging outcome because I have no other job opportunities. I never get a fair shake in life because I am (black, a Jew, a foreigner, ugly, a woman, etc.; or because of the policy of affirmative action, which puts me at a disadvantage). It is a corrupt world." (pp. 306–307)

The authors briefly analyze the cognitive appraisal process in each scenario. For example, in Scenario 1 the coping-centered appraisal reinforces and enhances the threat (the stakes are high) and treats the situation as hopeless. Depression is a likely state of mind, and the person might not bother to show up for the interview. In Scenario 2 the person goes from threat and anxiety (high stakes) to finding reasons for hope in light of coping options, and the appraisal that emerges is more one of challenge than of threat. In Scenario 3 the sequence and emotional impact seem similar except that the person relies on a well-placed friend rather than on personal resources. We can visualize complications here, as when getting such help assaults conflicting personal values. In Scenario 4 the stakes are low because the person has other options; stress will also be low. In Scenario 5 blame is externalized, the appraisal is one of anticipated harm/loss, and the emotional reaction is one of anger rather than the depression in Scenario 1.

In the above scenarios, appraisal processes in different combinations illustrate the cognitive mediation of the stress reaction and the coping process. Each kind of emotional reaction depends on a particular cognitive appraisal process. For example, the anger in Scenario 5 stemmed from the externalization of blame for the problem, whereas the depression in Scenario 1 stemmed from an appraisal of hopelessness. That is, we can turn the reasoning about cognitive appraisal around and argue backwards from a particular kind of emotion, say anger, depression, anxiety, guilt, envy, jealousy, and so on, to the particular pattern of appraisal that produced it. For instance, a sense of imminent but ambiguous and symbolic harm should result in anxiety, and a judgment that one has been demeaned arbitrarily yields anger. We shall discuss this more fully in Chapter 9, where we talk at greater length about cognitive-phenomenological approaches to emotion.

Reappraisal

Reappraisal refers to a changed appraisal on the basis of new information from the environment, which may resist or nourish pressures on the person, and/or information from the person's own reactions. For example, while overt anger affects the other person, it is also noted and reacted to by its initiator. As such, it may result in guilt or shame, or it may generate a feeling of righteousness or even fear. Mediating these complex two-way transactions between the person and the environment are cognitive appraisal processes. In instances of this type of feedback, threat can be reappraised as unwarranted or, conversely, a benign appraisal may turn into one of threat, creating a succession of changing emotions and appraisals. A reappraisal is simply an appraisal that follows an earlier appraisal in the same encounter and modifies it. In essence, appraisal and reappraisal do not differ.

There is another form of reappraisal which we have called *defensive reappraisal.* It should be mentioned only in passing here because it properly belongs under the rubric of cognitive coping. A defensive reappraisal consists of any effort made to reinterpret the past more positively, or to deal with present harms and threats by viewing them in less damaging and/or threatening ways.

Theoretically, what distinguishes defensive reappraisal from other reappraisals is that the former are self-generated; they arise from needs within the person rather than from environmental pressures. Empirically, defensive reappraisals are distinguished from ordinary, information-based appraisals in the same ways that defenses themselves are assessed clinically, namely, by their compulsivity, by contradictions among verbal, behavioral, and somatic indicators or from one time to the next, and by obvious gaps between such appraisals and environmental evidence.

Research on Cognitive Appraisal

Most of the early field observations and anecdotes about cognitive processes in stress came from studies of war, natural disasters, and life-threatening or incapacitating illness. The ideas of primary and secondary appraisal were often implicit in these discussions. For example, of their research on the threat of combat in World War II, Grinker and Spiegel (1945) wrote that "The reactions to the stimuli of combat depend upon the meaning given to these stimuli and in terms of recognizing them as a threat and of feeling confident of the ability to neutralize the threat" (p. 122). For a full review of early field and laboratory research that demonstrates the role of cognitive mediation in stress, see Lazarus (1966).

In the 1960s, Lazarus and his colleagues (see Lazarus, 1966, 1968; Lazarus, Averill, & Opton, 1970, for reviews) embarked on a systematic effort to study cognitive mediation using motion picture films to create a quasi-naturalistic way of generating stress. This approach relied on people's tendencies to react vicariously with stress to viewing the plight of others. In this extensive research program, subjective distress as well as autonomic disturbances (skin conductance and heart rate) were monitored while subjects watched films that showed people being mutilated in primitive rites of passage, experiencing accidents in a woodworking shop, and so on. Four methods were used to study the cognitive appraisal process:

1. Appraisal was manipulated by encouraging subjects to interpret the filmed events as damaging and painful or benign (through denial-like processes), or to view them in a detached fashion (through a kind of distancing or intellectualization). It was found that by influencing appraisal through soundtracks and statements provided before the film, it was possible to affect both physiological and subjective stress response levels (e.g., Folkins, Lawson, Opton, & Lazarus, 1968; Lazarus & Alfert, 1964; Lazarus, Opton, Nomikos, & Rankin, 1965; Speisman, Lazarus, Mordkoff, & Davison, 1964).

2. Conditions on which the appraisal process depended were also manipulated, including the amount of time the subject waited for an anticipated source of pain or harm, and the uncertainty about whether and when the harm would occur. In these experiments it was found that even though the actual harm did not change, the amount of time the subject waited for the anticipated harm affected its stressful impact. Slightly longer brief anticipation periods produced greater stress reaction levels than very short ones; yet if sufficient time was allowed for thinking about and reappraising the situation—say, three to five minutes—subjects could considerably mitigate the stress effects (Folkins, 1970; Nomikos, Opton, Averill, & Lazarus, 1968). What made the difference was what the subjects thought about, or had time to think about, while awaiting the harm. The experimentally manipu-

lated conditions affected the appraisal and coping process and thereby also affected the levels of stress response.

3. Cognitive appraisal was also studied by seeking retrospective reports about what subjects thought about and felt during the stressful experience. Through these reports it was possible to identify various cognitive coping strategies such as detachment or denial as well as the intensity and quality of the distress experienced. One study (Koriat, Melkman, Averill, & Lazarus, 1972) combined manipulations and assessments of cognitive activity by asking subjects either to strive for detachment from the emotional features of a stressful film or to increase their involvement; subjects were then asked about the strategies they employed, such as identifying with the victims or, conversely, dehumanizing them.

4. By selecting subjects on the basis of personality or cognitive styles, cognitive appraisal was further studied as a function of individual differences in ways of thinking and coping. In such research (e.g., Speisman et al., 1964), efforts were made to influence appraisal through denial or intellectualization. The success of these efforts in reducing stress response levels varied depending on whether or not they matched the mode of thought characteristic of the persons studied. There was evidence that denial-oriented influences worked best for people who were inclined to use denial-like modes of appraisal, and intellectualization was most effective with intellectualizers.

This extensive series of studies demonstrated that cognitive appraisal processes affected (mediated) stress response levels, and identified some of the personality characteristics and situation factors on which mediation depended. Taken as a whole, these studies left little doubt about the powerful role played by cognitive appraisal processes in the stress response to diverse stressors.

Since this research, other studies of the cognitive appraisal process in stress reactions have been reported. Most of the studies have been focused on the determinants of emotional response or other outcomes, although a few have concerned the determinants of appraisal itself. In our discussion of more recent research on the appraisal process, we include only studies in which appraisal has been manipulated or varied in some way and linked to coping and emotional outcomes; we leave consideration of research on the determinants of appraisal for Chapters 3 and 4. Our purpose here is to summarize further evidence that differing appraisals do indeed affect coping and emotion as immediate outcomes of a stressful transaction.

Geen, Stonner, and Kelley (1974) extended the earlier research on cognitive appraisal to anxiety associated with aggression. Subjects were made to deliver painful electric shocks to confederates of the experimenter who either remained silent (a control) or expressed their suffering. All subjects then watched a movie of one boxer brutally beating another. The cognitive appraisal manipulations either reminded subjects that the fight was fictitious—to generate denial-like detachment from the observed distress—or provided no options for amelioration. The film was appraised as less violent by those in the denial-like manipulation. To these subjects, the boxer seemed less distressed. More relevant, the denial-like strategy helped reduce aggression anxiety in the subjects themselves.

A series of studies by Holmes and his colleagues (Bennett & Holmes, 1975; Bloom, Houston, Holmes, & Burish, 1977; Holmes & Houston, 1974) continued the tradition of appraisal manipulation, although these researchers spoke of the process as redefinition of the stress situation, a form of reappraisal. Holmes and Houston threatened their subjects with a series of painful electric shocks, using as a control a group with no manipulated threat. The threatened subjects were also given two additional types of instruction: threat redefinition, in which they were told to reduce stress by thinking of the shock as interesting new physiological sensations; and threat isolation, in which they were told to reduce stress by remaining detached and uninvolved. Pulse rate, skin conductance, and self-reports of anxiety provided evidence of the levels of stress response. Holmes and Houston reported that subjects who used redefinition and isolation showed smaller increases in stress response levels over baseline and control conditions than control subjects not told to use these cognitive coping strategies. Here too, although one can think of the experimental treatments as providing modes of coping with stress, the process studied can just as readily be regarded as one of cognitive appraisal or reappraisal.

In a subsequent study, Bennett and Holmes (1975) found that redefinition was effective in lowering pulse rates in a failure threat situation only when it preceded the threat, not as a post-threat focus. This finding should not surprise us, for Bennett and Holmes were dealing with two different appraisal situations, threat and harm. We would expect cognitive coping or reappraisal efforts that are successful in regulating distress in anticipation of an event likely to differ from those that are effective in regulating distress after an event has occurred.

The third experiment in the series involved attention diversion rather than redefinition. In this study, Bloom et al. (1977) reported that encouraging subjects threatened with shock to think about something else was effective in reducing autonomically measured stress levels. Moreover, redefinition of the situation was more effective when no preliminary shock was given to acquaint subjects with the nature of the harm. Their findings suggest, interestingly, that when a preliminary shock has not been encountered, that is, when the threat is ambiguous, redefinition is easier for subjects to accomplish than when the nature of the threat has been established. This fits countless instances reported in the literature which suggest that allowing subjects to experience shock demystifies it and makes it far less threatening than when it has not yet been experienced. In later chapters we give much attention to ambiguity, since we regard it as one of the key determinants of appraisal in that it amplifies individual differences in how transactions are construed.

Additional experiments by Neufeld have added further to our understanding of the appraisal process and its consequences. In one study, Neufeld (1975) employed signal detection modes of analysis in a complex and carefully designed study to determine whether cognitive appraisal works by changing merely the tendency to report stress or by actually affecting felt stress. This issue has traditionally been of great interest to those who question whether defense processes alter the experience of the person or the response indicator of this experience, that is, the propensity to report. The stress stimuli were unretouched color photographs, taken in the morgue, of victims of crime and patients in advanced stages of severe skin disease. The core procedure had subjects rank the aversiveness of the photos under two conditions, one after listening to an intellectualization-denial tape designed to reduce the threat, and the other after a neutral, study habits tape. This attempt to modify cognitive appraisal in the direction of reducing threat was effective in lowering stress response measured autonomically (skin conductance) without affecting later ratings of aversiveness to a mixture of new photos and some of the original ones. In effect, threat levels were changed but the tendency to report stress was not. Thus, Neufeld argues, the actual appraisal of threat was changed rather than merely the tendency to report aversiveness. This is in accord with the earlier formulation of Lazarus and Alfert (1964) that benign cognitive appraisals actually short-circuit threat. Subjects following such appraisal now can look at the same threat stimuli without as much stress response (see also Neufeld, 1976).

Deliberate attempts to separately operationalize primary and secondary appraisal processes have been infrequent, although systematic efforts are now beginning to appear (cf. Folkman & Lazarus, in press). Dobson and Neufeld (1979) raise some doubt about the usefulness of separating primary and secondary appraisal in assessing how people construe the threatening nature of an encounter. In our view, primary and secondary appraisal cannot be considered as separate processes. Even though they derive from different sources within the same encounter, they are interdependent, and probably influence each other.

The recent experimental research cited above in which appraisal was manipulated in the laboratory suffers from a well-known limitation of laboratory study of psychodynamic processes (see Wachtel, 1980; Willems, 1969, and others, as well as our discussion in Chapter 10). Without direct measurements of changes in appraisal produced by experimental manipulation, one cannot tell to what extent the laboratory treatments actually modified the appraisal process. Subjects may have differed greatly in the extent of such effects, and in some instances, such as the research of Geen et al. (1974), the treatments may not have overriden existing appraisal tendencies, a difficulty sometimes recognized by the experimenters in their attempt to interpret equivocal findings. The use of a single methodological approach rather than two or more procedures that supplement each other in the same study leaves in some doubt the issue of what, if anything, is being varied (see Lazarus et al., 1970, and our discussion in Chapter 10, of various methods of tackling appraisal in research).

An impressive use of appraisal-related interpretations of field and laboratory findings has been made by Breznitz (1976) regarding the effects of false alarms. He notes that the effects of false alarms represent a rare instance in which experience is detrimental, because the person fails to take protective action when the danger is real. Breznitz offers a number of hypotheses about how this comes about. He suggests that the reduction of active coping with the danger is greater if the threat is imminent when it is canceled. Thus, a warning about a hurricane which proves false at the last moment before impact will produce a larger false alarm effect than one which is canceled early in the process. Second, a manipulation which intensifies the fear reaction to the initial threat magnifies the false alarm effect following the cancellation of the danger. More generally, the greater fear can be seen as an indicator of a greater investment or commitment, with an increase in the person's vulnerability. Third, anything that encourages discrimination between a future threat and a canceled one will reduce the false alarm effect. In other words, if the person is made to see that the cancellation has nothing to do with the next occasion of threat, the next one is less likely to be ignored. Fourth, the personal costs of the precautionary measures that must be taken are also relevant, the false alarm effect being greater when the costs of evading the harm are greater.

These hypotheses, some of which Breznitz was able to confirm in his research, directly implicate the cognitive appraisal process not only in affecting whether or not preventive measures are taken, but also the level of emotional distress experienced. Moreover, the false alarm effect itself, that is, the person responding by not doing anything precautionary, is a product of what the false alarm teaches the person about the credibility of the threat, in short, how it influences the cognitive appraisal of threat.

Two field studies of our own might also be noted. The first (Folkman & Lazarus, 1980) directly bears on the relationship between appraisal and coping. Descriptions of over a thousand specific coping episodes involving stressful encounters were obtained from 100 middle-aged men and women once a month for a period of a year. Subjects were asked to indicate on a checklist the things they thought and did to cope. In addition, they were asked to indicate which of several appraisals characterized the situation for them. The appraisals concerned whether the situation was one about which they could actually do something or, alternatively, one which they had to accept or get used to. Appraisal proved to be a potent predictor of whether coping was oriented toward emotion-regulation (emotion-focused coping) or doing something to relieve the problem (problem-focused coping). An encounter judged as requiring acceptance was associated with a greater emphasis on emotion-focused coping, whereas an encounter the person felt could be acted on was associated with a greater emphasis on problem-focused coping.

The second study (Folkman & Lazarus, in press) bears on the relationship between appraisal and emotion. The context of the study was the midterm examination mentioned earlier. Two days before the exam students were asked how difficult they expected it to be, what was at stake for them in its outcome, how much they felt in control, and their grade-point average (GPA). As noted above, the students were also asked the extent to which they were experiencing threat-related emotions including anxiety, worry, and fear. Two appraisal variables—how much the student had at stake and how difficult the exam was expected to be—proved to be important predictors of threat emotions. GPA, on the other hand, which is not a cognitive appraisal variable per se, did not predict threat.

Krantz (1983) too assessed secondary appraisal of cognitive coping strategies prior to an examination in a college student group and the perceived ease of implementing those strategies in case the grade they received proved disappointing. In addition, Krantz directly observed six coping behaviors on a second exam for those who received an unsatisfactory grade on the first exam: amount of study time, class attendance, review session attendance, contact with the instructor, discussions with peers about course material, and whether help or information was obtained from other sources. She found that secondary appraisal predicted coping behaviors but not actual exam performance. In effect, subjects actually did what they had said they would do in the event of poor performance; their actual coping behaviors on the second exam were consistent with their secondary appraisals of coping options. Krantz interpreted the failure to predict actual exam performance as indicating that other variables, such as academic ability, were more important than preparatory coping behaviors. An unpublished finding from our study of examination stress (Folkman & Lazarus, in press) lends support to this interpretation. The coping strategies reported by the students before the exam did not predict their grade, but GPA did.

Overall, we can see in the above accounts a pattern of research and observation that shows clearly that the way a person appraises an encounter strongly influences the coping process and how the person reacts emotionally. The theoretical perspective that cognitive appraisal is central in mediating subsequent thought, feeling, and action is not only logically necessary to an understanding of individual differences and, we believe, even normative patterns of reaction, but it also accords well with the observations of people in adaptationally relevant encounters. Taken as a whole, research resoundingly supports such a view.

Indeed, the concept of cognitive appraisal in one form or another has become firmly entrenched in research and theory on stress, coping, and emotion. A large literature has developed in which researchers employ this concept in accounting for the effects of antecedent variables on stress and emotional reactions (see Baum, Singer, & Baum, 1981). In our discussions above we have taken pains to examine only research in which the concept of appraisal was directly studied; we have ignored the many investigations in which appraisal was used solely as an explanatory construct.

Cognitive Appraisal
and Phenomenology

Because cognitive appraisal rests on the individual's subjective interpretation of a transaction, it is phenomenological. The basic idea of phenomenology is neither new nor unusual. It has its origins in ancient philosophical treatises, and in more recent times is reflected in the work of Jung, Adler, and Rank, and psychological theorists such as Lewin, Rogers, Murray, Tolman, Heider, and Kelly (see Weiner, 1974). Phenomenology has negative connotations that could throw into question certain aspects of our cognitive approach: first, that appraisal is a private, subjective process that has an uncertain relationship to the objective environment; and second, that the concept of appraisal is inevitably circular, because in order to predict the emotional or adaptational outcome we must ask the person how he or she construes events; in turn, the subjective appraisal itself can only be verified by reference to the very outcome we want to predict.

The first issue touches on a longstanding conflict in psychology concerning perception. Classical perception theory (see, for example, Allport, 1955; Vernon, 1962) had three characteristics: it was veridical, normative, and "cool." The veridical perspective is reflected in the basic question, "How is it that we are able to perceive the world as it really is in order to behave adaptively?" With respect to its normative quality, the focus is on how people in general perceive (i.e., individual differences are ignored or treated as error). Finally, classical theory and research paid little attention to perception tasks that are emotionally laden and of high salience to the person ("hot" contexts). Most of its observations were about perception of laboratory displays ("cold" contexts, to paraphrase William James).

A dissident movement emerged in the 1940s and 1950s, which was referred to as the "New Look." Many of its protagonists were personality and clinical psychologists primarily interested in what goes wrong in human adaptation. In contrast with classical perceptionists, who were concerned with normative issues, the New Look psychologists focused on individual differences and the role of personality factors such as needs and defenses in shaping perceptions and cognitions. A different question was asked: "How is it possible that different people, or the same person at different times, perceive a given stimulus array in different ways?" This emphasis on individual differences required rejection of the normative tradition of studying "people in general." Because the New Look psychologists were particularly concerned with adaptation and its failures, perception was studied in situations where the person had some important stake in what was being perceived, that is, in hot contexts.

The New Look movement had a close affinity with phenomenology in that its proponents emphasized that to some extent people perceived what they want to or need to rather than what is actually in the environmental display. This outlook, despite its documentation in research, was never integrated into classical perception theory. The tradition of the classical perception theorists is evident today in the field of information processing, which, though process-centered, is by and large normative, is concerned with veridicality, and deals largely with cold contexts. Ultimately any comprehensive theory of perception and cognition must find a way to integrate these seemingly contradictory outlooks.

Since phenomenology refers to private ways of thinking that have no necessary relationship with objective reality, one can readily see this concept as an extreme version of the New Look. There is no doubt that personality factors can shape and distort perception, especially under conditions of ambiguity or severe mental disorder. When the environmental display is unambiguous, however, for most people perception and appraisal follow the objective environment quite well. We see what is there, so to speak, and there is little opportunity for individual differences to manifest themselves except in what is attended to and in styles of responding. Furthermore, no one would question that the physical and social environments have a powerful impact on our reactions (see Proshansky, Ittelson, & Rivlin, 1970, for a vivid account of the physical environment in life crises such as physical disability, natural disasters, aging and relocation, and divorce). Much of our social existence is ambiguous, however, and personality factors can play a large role in perception and appraisal.

When we speak of cognitive appraisal, we are not referring strictly to need-centered or defensively based judgments, although commitments (motives) and defensive processes are always involved. Our premise is that people usually want to know what is happening and what it means for their well-being, while, at the same time, they usually prefer to put a positive light on things. This stance integrates the approaches of classical perception theory and the New Look in that we acknowledge that both the environment as it is, and what individuals want, interact to produce any given appraisal. Thus, to say that the reaction to demanding or hostile environments is mediated by cognitive processes is not to say that inner promptings *alone* shape appraisals, but that such promptings interact with the objective environment in generating cognitive appraisals.

Our phenomenology does not state that thinking something necessarily makes it so, or that every appraisal is subjective and private. Rather, people are normally constrained in what they perceive and appraise by what is actually the case, although their cognitions are not perfectly correlated with objective reality.

Another issue is that because of its phenomenological character, the concept of appraisal is inherently circular. An appraisal is inferred from what a person says: an individual is threatened because he or she reports being threatened or appears threatened to us. To get out of this circle we need to demonstrate that what we call appraisal has antecedents and consequences. The research described earlier, in which appraisal, as inferred from self-reports, experimental manipulations, and personality assessments, affects coping and emotion, goes a long way to dispel this criticism, since this research demonstrates that appraisal does indeed have predictable consequences for emotion and coping.

At the antecedent end, what is needed to break the tautology is to demonstrate that certain conditions derived from theory, within the person and in the situational context, determine interactively the mediating appraisal process which, in turn, affects in predictable ways the coping and emotional response.

A familiar example of an earlier tautology is the concept of instinct, which was out of favor for many years because it had become merely a label rather than a genuine explanation of the seemingly built-in patterns of behavior of species. When asked why animals did what they did, the answer was that they had the instinct to do so; when asked for evidence of the instinct process, the answer was to refer to the very behavior that instinct was supposed to explain. It was not until research such as that of Lehrman (1964) that knowledge moved outside the circle by establishing the specific environmental and internal conditions that interacted complexly, and in sequence, to produce so-called instinctual patterns. For example, Lehrman showed that each step of the reproductive behavior of female ring doves is governed by interactions between hormones and external stimuli, including those arising from seeing the behavior of the mate which, in turn, affected endocrine patterns regulating behaviors such as mating, building a nest, laying eggs, sitting on them, feeding the young, and so on, all in synchrony. Likewise, only when we can specify the person and environment antecedent factors determining the nature of the appraisal process, and how these appraisals affect the coping and emotional consequences, can cognitive appraisal theory go beyond pure description, which is itself a valuable first step, and contribute to prediction. Only then too can such a theory power practical interventions designed to affect adaptational outcomes such as health, morale, and effective functioning.

There still remains a problem, however—that of making the concept of appraisal independent in measurement from antecedent and consequent variables. This problem has been effectively described by Kasl (1978) in a discussion of epidemiological contributions to the study of work stress. He states it as follows:

> Unfortunately, this convergence of theoretical formulations [about the role of individual differences in appraisal] had led to a *self-serving methodological trap which has tended to trivialize a good deal of the research on work stress* or role stress: the measurement of the "independent" variable (e.g., role ambiguity, role conflict, quantitative overload, etc.) and the measurement of the "dependent" variable (work strain, distress, dissatisfaction) are sometimes so close operationally that they appear to be simply two similar measures of a single concept. (p. 13)

One example offered by Kasl is a report by Lyons (1971) of a correlation of −.59 between "role clarity" and an index of a job tension among staff registered nurses. The index of job tension is defined by questionnaire items such as being bothered by unclear responsibility, unclear evaluation by supervisor, and unclear expectations by others. Kasl trenchantly and somewhat sardonically concludes that the correlation between the two measures is

> . . . about as illuminating as correlating "How often do you have a headache?" type of item with "How often are you bothered by headaches?" form of item. Similarly, what is the meaning of an association between high qualitative overload and low self-esteem among university professors (Mueller, 1965), when the former (perceiving one's skills and abilities as not being good enough to meet job demands) and the latter (being dissatisfied with oneself and one's skills and abilities) both derive from one and the same perception of oneself? (p. 14)

Having, in effect, noted that often the measures of the objective (stressor) conditions overlap operationally with the subjective ones, that is, with appraisal, Kasl goes on to suggest that one solution would be to measure both the objective and the subjective separately in the same research whenever possible; another is to search for modifying effects of various characteristics of the person on the association between the independent and dependent variables, a strategy we described earlier. Kasl is of course quite correct in pointing out that if there is no operational difference between subjective (appraisal-centered) and objective measures of environmental events and their impact—at least in some cases or under some conditions—the cutting edge of the appraisal concept is dulled to the point of futility. Some of the research on appraisal discussed earlier is sound in this respect, whereas other research falls into the trap described by Kasl.

In Chapters 3 and 4 we will examine the antecedent side of the picture, the person and situation determinants of appraisal. To the extent that we can identify antecendents and consequences of appraisal, or develóp a set of principles for doing so, we break out of the tautology.

The Concept of Vulnerability

The term *vulnerability* is widely used in the conceptualization and study of psychological stress and human adaptation. Most often, it is conceptualized in terms of the adequacy of the individual's resources. For example, Murphy and Moriarty (1976) define vulnerability in children as the "equipment" of the child, by which they mean the child's physical, psychological, and social resources for dealing with adaptive demands. In his study of cancer patients, Weisman (1976) treats vulnerability as a faltering capacity to cope, and emotional distress associated with pessimistic attitudes about recovery and inadequate social support. Similarly, Zubin and Spring (1977) describe vulnerability in schizophrenics in terms of inborn and acquired resource deficiencies. Garmezy (1976) too employs the concept of vulnerability in arguing for genetic factors as primary in childhood schizophrenia. The invulnerable child, from his perspective, is biologically highly resistant to mental disorder.

There are circumstances in which it makes sense to speak of vulnerability solely in terms of resources. One instance is when vulnerability is physical—for example, a person whose ankle was recently sprained is vulnerable to further injury, and a traveler in a foreign country is vulnerable to organisms in the water to which his or her system is unaccustomed. It is also reasonable to speak of vulnerability in terms of resources when there is such an enormous deficit that the person is unable to function adequately in most situations, as is the case with schizophrenics.

Among ordinary, adequately functioning people, however, inadequacy of resources is a necessary but not sufficient condition for psychological vulnerability. A deficiency in resources makes a person psychologically vulnerable only when the deficit refers to something that matters. For example, the extent to which the *physical* vulnerabilities mentioned above have implications with respect to *psychological* vulnerability depends on the importance of the commitments that the physical disabilities threaten. For a dancer, a weakened ankle means the possibility of a fall on stage; for a person at a desk job, a weakened ankle is a minor inconvenience. Anticipated problems in an interpersonal relationship will create psychological vulnerability only if the relationship has meaning for its members. In short, psychological vulnerability is determined not just by a deficit in resources, but by *the relationship between the individual's pattern of commitments and his or her resources for warding off threats to those commitments.*

This relational definition of vulnerability parallels our relational definition of threat. Indeed, vulnerability can be thought of as *potential* threat that is transformed into active threat when that which is valued is actually put in jeopardy in a particular transaction. In this sense, vulnerability also refers to a susceptibility to react to broad classes of events with psychological stress that is shaped by a range of person factors, including commitments, beliefs, and resources.

An example of research that uses a relational concept of vulnerability is provided by Kaplan (1976). He developed a scale of "defenselessness/vulnerability" that reflects the combination of two characters: a high value placed on receiving approval (a value or commitment) and the inability to regulate feelings of distress about disapproval (a deficit in resources). Another example comes from Schlenker and Leary (1982). These authors suggest that people who are motivated to make a good impression on an audience and simultaneously expect an unsatisfactory evaluation from that audience are vulnerable to social anxiety. Here the vulnerability is created by a relationship between a commitment and an expectation.

We have more to say about person factors that influence vulnerability to psychological stress in Chapter 3 and situations that can trigger the transformation of vulnerability to threat in Chapter 4.

The Issue of Depth

Before leaving this theoretical account of cognitive appraisal we want to briefly address a problem that inheres in cognitive approaches to stress, emotion, and coping: the issue of surface and depth, or consciousness and unconsciousness.

Appraisal is often taken to be a conscious, rational, and deliberate process. We have argued, however, that an individual may be unaware of any or all of the basic elements of an appraisal (e.g., Lazarus, 1966, 1982, 1984). A threat appraisal can arise without the person clearly knowing the values and goals that are evaluated as endangered, the internal or environmental factors that contribute to the sense of danger, or even that threat has been appraised. This lack of awareness can result from the operation of defense mechanisms, or it can be based on nondefensive attentional processes.

Our position allows the concept of appraisal to be integrated with depth or psychoanalytic-type theories. For example, the Jungian notion of superior and inferior functions, where one function predominates while the other is submerged, implies that a suppressed tendency may emerge from time to time to influence thought (e.g., appraisal), emotion, and behavior. And of course Freudian thought gives mental activity that is inaccessible to consciousness a role in shaping thought, feeling, and action. Within the context of stress research per se, Weisman (1972) has used the term *middle knowledge* to describe the vague sense of the truth that can unexpectedly surface and color mood even when the individual is engaged in what seems like a firm denial, as when a patient denies the truth of a terminal illness.

Appraisal theory thus need not be restricted to personal agendas that are accessible and easily operationalized; less accessible agendas and processes, about which psychoanalytic theorists have been most vocal, are also fair game. Appraisal theory is in a sense neutral with respect to the specific personal agendas that are conceived to shape it. The reader should keep this feature of the concept of cognitive appraisal in mind in subsequent chapters where we discuss person factors that influence appraisal (Chapter 3), the coping process (Chapters 5 and 6), and cognitive theories of emotion (Chapter 9).

Summary

There is an old phenomenological tradition in psychology that the meaning of an event to the person shapes the emotional and behavioral response. Our concept of cognitive appraisal refers to evaluative cognitive processes that intervene between the encounter and the reaction. Through cognitive appraisal processes the person evaluates the significance of what is happening for his or her well-being. Traditionally, stress research has been based largely on non-cognitive models such as drive reinforcement and arousal or activation. However, the utility of these models has come into question. For one thing, the evidence is overwhelming that appraisal-related processes shape the reaction of people to any encounter. Moreover, emotional response is in fact specific to appraised meanings and differentiated as to quality as well as intensity. As a result, a growing number of psychophysiological researchers are beginning to incorporate cognitive mediation into their models.

Our cognitive theory of stress is phenomenological. Phenomenology has two negative connotations, the first of which concerns the veridicality of appraisals. It is our premise that although personality factors such as needs, commitments, and preferred styles of attention influence perception, appraisals are generally correlated with reality. A second problem with phenomenological approaches is that they are inherently circular; an appraisal of threat is inferred from what the person says. We can break out of the circularity to the extent that we can identify antecedents and consequences of appraisals.

We have identified three kinds of cognitive appraisal: primary, secondary, and reappraisal. Primary appraisal consists of the judgment that an encounter is irrelevant, benign-positive, or stressful. Stressful appraisals can take three forms: harm/loss, threat, and challenge. Harm/loss refers to damage the person has already sustained, threat refers to anticipated harms or losses, and challenge refers to events that hold the possibility for mastery or gain. Threat and challenge are not poles of a single continuum; they can occur simultaneously and must be considered as separate, although often related, constructs.

Secondary appraisal is a judgment concerning what might and can be done. It includes an evaluation about whether a given coping option will accomplish what it is supposed to, that one can apply a particular strategy or set of strategies effectively, and an evaluation of the consequences of using a particular strategy in the context of other internal and/or external demands and constraints.

Reappraisal refers to a changed appraisal based on new information from the environment and/or the person. A reappraisal differs from an appraisal only in that it follows an earlier appraisal. Sometimes reappraisals are the result of cognitive coping efforts; these are called defensive reappraisals and are often difficult to distinguish from reappraisals based on new information.

The concept of vulnerability is closely related to cognitive appraisal. Vulnerability is frequently conceptualized in terms of coping resources; a vulnerable person is one whose coping resources are deficient. Psychological vulnerability, however, is determined also by the significance of the commitments that are engaged or endangered in any encounter. As in our definition of stress, this view of vulnerability to stress is relational.

Cognitive appraisal processes are not necessarily conscious, nor are the agendas that shape appraisal always easily accessible. Cognitive appraisal may also be shaped by agendas that are below the person's awareness.

3

Person Factors Influencing Appraisal

In this chapter we discuss two person characteristics that are important determinants of appraisal: commitments and beliefs. These variables influence appraisal by (1) determining what is salient for well-being in a given encounter; (2) shaping the person's understanding of the event, and in consequence his or her emotions and coping efforts; and (3) providing the basis for evaluating outcomes (cf. Wrubel, Benner, & Lazarus, 1981). In the next chapter we will discuss situation characteristics that influence appraisal.

Although we treat person and situation variables in separate chapters, we view these variables as interdependent. Thus, our discussion of person factors includes references to situations, and our discussion of situation factors refers to person characteristics. For example, when we speak of commitment as a person factor that influences appraisal, there is always an implied "to"—that is, a commitment *to* a relationship, an objective, or an ideal—that is pertinent to a specific transaction between the person and the environment. For a commitment to influence appraisal, it has to be engaged by a particular encounter.

Yet there is no way to evaluate the person and situation variables that affect appraisal without measuring them separately. The division of our discussion of determinants of appraisal into two chapters is a recognition of the need to separate them for purposes of discussion. However, although these factors can be measured independently, they must be analyzed and interpreted interdependently. This perspective is based on the concept of transaction, which we discuss in Chapter 9.

Commitments

Commitments express what is important to the person, what has meaning for him or her. They determine what is at stake in a specific stressful encounter. Any encounter that involves a strongly held commitment will be evaluated as meaningful to the extent that the outcome harms or threatens the commitment or facilitates its expression. Commitments also underlie the choices people make or are prepared to make to maintain valued ideals and/or to achieve desired goals.

Although our definition of commitment contains cognitive components, in that it refers to choices, values, and/or goals, we do not wish to abandon its motivational implications of forward movement, intensity, persistence, affective salience, and direction (cf. Lazarus, Coyne, & Folkman, 1982). Other terms and related concepts have been used by psychologists to express the motivational aspects of human functioning, including drive, cathexis, motive, investment, need, plan, intention, and value-expectancy theory (e.g., Atkinson & Birch, 1978; Heckausen, 1977; Schönpflug, in press). These terms are all relevant, but they are laden with other conceptual baggage that we would prefer to avoid. We prefer the term commitment because it denotes the higher-order cognitive and social processes emphasized in cognitive appraisal theory, and it implies an enduring motivational quality.

In our usage, one is committed to something or some things in particular. We are thus likely to speak of patterns of commitment, meaning that there are some things to which there is strong commitment and others to which there is little or none. It is not simple to assess a person's pattern of commitments, since a pattern is not necessarily revealed by knowing a person's objective circumstances. Koenig (1973) and others (e.g., Conte, Weiner, & Plutchik, 1982; Diggory & Rothman, 1961) point out that even a commitment to life itself is not always the main concern of dying persons or those who fear death. Dependency, separation, isolation, pain, physical disfigurement, fear of abandonment, and not completing important life goals are some of the diverse commitments that concern dying people, and these vary strikingly in importance from person to person. We shall beg the complex question of assessment here, and assume that researchers can find suitable ways of assessing the patterns among diverse persons.

Mechanisms Through Which Commitments Influence Appraisal

Commitments determine appraisal through numerous mechanisms (cf. Wrubel et al., 1981). First, they guide people into and away from situations that can challenge or threaten, benefit or harm them. The athlete who is committed to winning will engage in rigorous training and forgo pleasures that would diminish his or her chances in competition. The child who wants to gain acceptance from peers will participate in activities that have peer approval and avoid those that do not.

The significance of this line of reasoning is illustrated in an interesting study by Slife and Rychlak (1982) on children's modeling of aggression as a function of their values regarding aggression. The children in this study were assessed with respect to their liking of violent and nonviolent toys prior to watching television vignettes that modeled aggression. The children did not merely copy what they saw on television; their preferences for the toys, which could be viewed as a reflection of their values, influenced their subsequent behavior.

Commitments also influence appraisal through the manner in which they shape cue-sensitivity. For example, King and Sorrentino (1983) show that the variability in the ways people evaluate situations is due in part to individual differences in the weights given to various facets of those situations, such as pleasant versus unpleasant, physical versus social, or intimate/involved versus nonintimate/uninvolved. The weights described by King and Sorrentino are reflections of values and commitments that shape the person's sensitivity to these particular facets of a transaction. This study is one of the few in which serious effort is made to consider the dimensions of situations on which appraisal patterns vary from person to person, or show stability across persons.

Mechanic (1962) refers to the heightened cue-sensitivity of students awaiting word as to whether they passed their doctoral examinations. When the exams ended and the faculty began grading, students became extremely sensitive to the expressions and behavior of the faculty. Such sensitivity to cues would not occur if the students did not have a commitment to passing or doing well. While we do not understand the underlying mechanisms through which commitments shape cue-sensitivity, we do know that this process can occur in response to fragmentary cues on a tacit or nonconscious level (see Polanyi, 1966). An example drawn from common experience is found in the sleeping mother's sensitivity to her infant's cries.

Klinger (1975) elaborates on the cue-sensitivity aspect of commitment in his discussion of depression. In his view, depression is a normal result of disengaging from commitments when they have become overpowering or untenable. When disengagement from a commitment is successful, relevant environmental aspects lose commitment-related meanings with which they had previously been infused. Through disengagement the person thus loses his or her sensitivity to cues related to that particular commitment. In the interim between disengagement and engagement with a new commitment, the person may experience "apathy, reduced instrumental striving, loss of concentration, and increased preoccupation with momentary cues . . ." (p. 8), or, in brief, depression.

The third and perhaps most important way commitments influence appraisal is through their relationship to psychological vulnerability. This relationship has a curious two-edged nature. On the one hand, the potential for an encounter to be psychologically harmful or threatening, or, for that matter, challenging, is directly related to the depth with which a commitment is held. The deeper a person's commitment, the greater the potential threat or harm. On the other hand, the very strength of commitment that creates vulnerability can also impel a person toward a course of action that can reduce the threat and help sustain coping efforts in the face of obstacles.

Commitment as a Factor in Vulnerability

In Chapter 2 we introduced the concept of vulnerability to psychological stress. We described it as representing potential threat, determined by a number of person and situation variables. The role played by commitment in shaping vulnerability is particularly interesting, and often overlooked.

The greater the strength of a commitment, the more vulnerable the person is to psychological stress in the area of that commitment. The relationship between commitment and vulnerability to threat is illustrated in a laboratory experiment by Vogel, Raymond, and Lazarus (1959). Subjects in this study were high school boys. Measurements were made of the relative strength of two kind of motivation (what we would call commitments): affiliation and achievement. On the basis of a number of behavioral and self-report measures, the extremes were selected and divided into two much smaller groups, one taken to be very high in achievement motivaton but low in affiliation, the other very high in affiliation but low in achievement.

The two groups were exposed to conditions designed to threaten either achievement or affiliation goals. Subjects were required to perform tasks superficially relevant to these goals. Measurements were made of skin conductance, blood pressure, and pulse to determine the degree of physiological stress reaction and, by inference, degree of threat. The authors found that the degree of threat was greatest when the threat stimulus dealt with the motive that was stronger, and it was lowest in the case of the motive that was weaker. Subjects predominantly oriented to achievement were most disturbed by achievement-related threat stimuli, whereas those oriented mainly to affiliation were most disturbed by affiliation threat.

And at the psychophysiological level, Bergman and Magnusson (1979) have shown that Swedish male high school overachievers (students who accomplished more than their intelligence scores suggested), and those rated by teachers as extremely ambitious, excreted more adrenalin in an achievement-demanding situation than other boys in their class.

These findings are not surprising. Indeed, they are what our everyday experience leads us to expect. A student who has had a long and deep commitment to becoming a doctor will experience a rejection from medical school as much more harmful than a student for whom medicine is only one of several interesting career possibilities. The inability to have children will be much more threatening to a couple who very much want a child than for a couple who are ambivalent. The difference in each case has to do in part with the degree of commitment.

One of the most striking features of this principle is that even the most severe crises can be differently appraised with respect to threat because of peculiarities of commitment patterns. Most of the evidence for this is anecdotal, but it is also persuasive. Major illness, for example, is for some people not only a threat to life but also an acceptable reason for avoiding aversive situations such as a stressful job, or for others provides a legitimate way of asking for or accepting help and attention (cf. Fiore, 1979). Such instances are traditionally spoken of as "secondary gain" from symptoms. They can also be interpreted as examples of the complex costs and benefits deriv-

ing from particular patterns of commitment that are ordinarily difficult to act on because of social constraints, but which illness legiti-
mizes. There is growing interest in analyzing the commitment-based
meanings of experiences such as illness and old age as factors in
stress appraisal (Williams, 1981a, b).

Research by Kasl, Evans, and Niederman (1979) has also demonstrated the importance of commitment (they use the term motivation)
as a risk factor for infectious mononucleosis among students. Four-
teen hundred West Point cadets were compared with respect to level
of academic motivation, family history of motivation, and academic
performance as prospective risk factors for the disease. They found
that the combination of high academic motivation and poor academic
performance interacted to predict clinical infectious mononucleosis.
Thus, when the students were performing poorly, commitment to
achievement significantly increased the likelihood of this illness. In
other words, commitment presumably made the students vulnerable
to greater debilitating stress in the event of poor performance.

Janis and Mann (1977) make the additional point that the more
public a commitment is, the more threatening it is to have it challenged. They discuss this point in the context of their conflict model
of decision making. Discussing the effects of social pressures with
regard to reversing a decision, Janis and Mann say that postdeci-
sional stability is "predicated upon commitment insofar as the person makes a 'contract,' or takes on an obligation in the eyes of other
people in his social network, to carry out a chosen course of action"
(p. 279).

> Following a public commitment, the decision maker realizes that others
> are affected by his decision and expect him to hold to it. The stigma of
> being known as erratic and unstable is in itself a powerful negative
> incentive that inhibits even discussing with others the possibility of
> reversing a decision. In general, the greater the number of those in the
> decision maker's social network who are aware of a decision, the more
> powerful the incentive to avoid the social disapproval that might result
> from its reversal. (p. 280)

Janis and Mann are concerned with decision making under
stressful circumstances. However, the principle is important in all
circumstances where a threat to a commitment has the capacity to
diminish self-esteem or arouse social criticism. The greater the number of people who know about the commitment, the greater the
potential for threat. An interesting sidelight of this principle is that

people who fear that they will give up on a demanding commitment such as writing an article, stopping smoking, or changing jobs often announce this commitment to others. By making this announcement, people put added pressure on themselves to carry through with the commitment by building up the threat of embarrassment were the decision to waver. It is as if such people trap themselves into doing what they are afraid they will not do.

The Role of Commitment in Warding Off Threat

As we noted earlier, the very strength of commitment that creates vulnerability can also impel a person toward a course of action that can reduce threat and help sustain coping efforts in the face of obstacles. The depth with which a commitment is held determines the amount of effort a person is willing to put forth to ward off threats to that commitment. Klinger (1975), for instance, states that commitments keep an organism "pursuing a goal despite many changes in drive states and environmental cues, even in the face of repeated obstacles" (p. 2).

Perhaps the most graphic illustrations of the motivating property of commitments are found in cases of life-threatening illness. The "will to live," for example, is often seen as critical for survival. The particular commitments that form a will to live vary from person to person. In one it may be a commitment to one's family, in another to unfinished work, and in still another a desire to "beat the odds." The commitment to life is sometimes evident in the patient's willingness to undertake aversive treatment regimens. Regardless of the pattern of commitment that forges a will to live or the mechanisms through which it has its effect, it is clear that without the will to live, a patient can die.

Accounts of life in Nazi concentration camps provide further support for the role of commitments in sustaining life under the most devastating of circumstances. In this regard, Benner et al. (1980) write:

> The most severe trauma of the concentration camps, however, lay in the fact that the suffering experienced there could not readily be given life-supporting meaning, either in terms of individual sins of omission or commission, or in terms of the grand design of the universe. From Job onwards (Bakan, 1968), human beings who have experienced harm and pain have sought to reassure themselves of the essential goodness

and meaning of life by finding explanations for the events that have befallen them. When such a bizarre, inhuman (or uniquely human) plan as genocide and enslavement is involved, however, not only does the specific situation become senseless, but one is forced to doubt the general purpose and meaning of life. One of the most central coping strategies is to seek meaning in suffering. . . . Suffering for a reason is easier to endure than suffering without cause, benefit, or meaning. Needless to say, the suffering inflicted by the Holocaust had no ultimate good, reward, or meaning inherent in it. In contrast to the behavior of believing Jews during past episodes of collective suffering, the inmates of the camp did not typically plead to God for forgiveness, or even cry out against the severity of His punishment. Instead, 45% of survivors relocated in Israel reported that they had lost their faith as a result of the camp experience (Eitinger, 1964). The camps came to exemplify not the wrath of God, but the fact that He was dead (cf. Rubenstein, 1966). The process here is analogous to, but in the opposite direction from, the rebirth experienced via conversion.

Despite their inability to find meaning in the suffering of the concentration camps, prisoners did struggle for meaning in their survival. Even though the camps were designed to remove any vestige of meaning, worth, autonomy, and control, almost all survivors report that finding some purpose to one's existence seemed to aid survival (Dimsdale, 1974; Frankl, 1959; Heimler, 1963). Here we are making a distinction between meaning in the suffering and meaning in existence or survival. Although the victims found no reasons, benefits, or ultimate purposes in their suffering, they were strengthened and sustained by their personal reasons for survival or for existence. Survivors report that they endured the suffering rather than give up for varying reasons: for the sake of their close relatives, in order to bear witness, in order to seek revenge, and so on. (pp. 223–224)

Although far less dramatic, laboratory experiments have also shown that commitment determines effort, over and above the presence of extrinsic incentives. For example, in a series of five studies examining the effects of monetary incentives on behavior, Locke, Bryan, and Kendall (1968) found that goals and intentions are the mechanisms by which monetary incentives influence behavior. In each study it was shown that if a goal or intentional level was controlled or partialed out, the amount of incentive did not affect behavior. The authors make several points that illustrate what we have been saying about the role of commitment:

Monetary incentives may affect the *degree of commitment* of an individual to his goal or behavioral intention. Commitment may be expected to influence the degree of persistence an individual will show in the face of difficulty and frustration, the degree to which he will retain the goal if it conflicts with other goals (e.g., to be liked by co-workers), and the probability of his abandoning the goal altogether and "leaving the field" in the face of alternatives.

It must be stressed that whatever the effects of monetary incentives on performance, their *ultimate* impact should be a function of the degree to which the individual *values* money as compared to other incentives and his perception of the degree to which a given course of action is seen as a *means* of attaining this value (i.e., the perceived *instrumentality* of behavior) in gaining the value (Vroom, 1964). (p. 120)

The centrality of commitments in psychological well-being has been discussed extensively with reference to bereavement (e.g., Bowlby, 1973) and depression (e.g., Klinger, 1975, 1977) and is a major focus of traditional psychoanalytic therapy. The purpose of such therapy is to resolve inner conflicts that impede the formation of commitments to family and work. The assumption is that the person who can make commitments will have a meaningful and productive life (see also Singer, 1974).

Commitments are not often given much attention in the context of psychological stress and coping. This is largely due to the trend away from motivational concepts, which we discussed in Chapter 2. Yet commitments are clearly important as determinants of psychological stress. In addition to their motivating quality, which helps sustain coping effort, they guide people to and away from situations that can harm, threaten, or challenge them, shape cue-sensitivity, and, most important, define areas of meaningfulness and thereby determine which encounters are relevant to well-being. Moreover, only by knowing a person's pattern of commitments can areas of vulnerability be identified. This last point has particular significance for predicting the circumstances under which a person will feel harmed, threatened, or challenged.

Beliefs

Beliefs are personally formed or culturally shared cognitive configurations (Wrubel et al., 1981). They are preexisting notions about reality which serve as a perceptual lens, or a "set," to use the term preferred by perception psychologists. In appraisal, beliefs determine what is fact, that is, "how things are" in the environment, and they shape the understanding of its meaning.

Bem's (1970) discussion of the cognitive foundations of beliefs is helpful in understanding at a formal level how beliefs operate in appraisal. Briefly, Bem distinguishes between primitive and higher-order beliefs. Primitive beliefs rest on premises that to the believer are not open to question (see also Rokeach, 1968). The most fundamental primitive beliefs are

> so taken for granted that we are apt not to notice that we hold them at all; we remain unaware of them until they are called to our attention or are brought into question by some bizarre circumstances in which they appear to be violated. For example, we believe that an object continues to exist even when we are not looking for it; we believe that objects remain the same size and shape as we move away from them even though their visual images change; . . . Our faith in the validity of our sensory experience is the most important primitive belief of all. (p. 5)

Primitive beliefs can also be based on external authority. "When mommy says that not brushing after every meal causes tooth decay, that is synonymous with the *fact* that not brushing after every meal causes tooth decay" (p. 7).

Higher-order beliefs are learned as we come to regard sensory experiences as potentially fallible and similarly learn to be more cautious in believing external authorities. "We begin . . . to insert an explicit and conscious premise about an authority's credibility between his word and our belief" (p. 10). Higher-order beliefs are also derived by reasoning inductively from experience. Over time, higher-order beliefs that are constructed from faith and experience can come to be held without any reference to evidence. At this point a belief cannot be challenged by appeal to reason, and the higher-order belief becomes a primitive belief.

Because beliefs usually operate at a tacit level to shape a person's perception of his or her relationship to the environment, we are generally unaware of their influence on appraisal. However, their impact on appraisal becomes evident when there is a sudden loss of belief or a conversion to a dramatically different belief system (cf. Paloutzian, 1981). When belief is lost, hope may be supplanted by hopelessness. In the case of conversion, that which previously might have been threatening can become benign and that which was considered benign can become threatening. In both instances, there is likely to be greater awareness on the part of the individual of his or her beliefs. If the loss of an old belief and/or the adoption of a new one causes a shift in the person's characteristic way of relating to others or to the environment, then observers are also likely to become aware of the person's changed beliefs and their influence. Thus, it is at times of dramatic changes that the function of beliefs in appraisal becomes explicit both for the actor and for the observer. The more a new belief system differs from the old one, and the more comprehensive it is, the more explicit the mechanisms through which it influences appraisal become.

For instance, since the early 1970s thousands of young people have been recruited into cults and persuaded to adopt a new belief system. The values, commitments, and goals that flow from the core set of beliefs for a particular cult cover every aspect of the member's life, including the disavowal of affection and loyalty to his or her family, using lying and deception to raise money and engage recruits, and working 18 to 20 hours a day with little food and no pay (Clark, 1979; Conway & Siegelman, 1978; Delgado, 1977; Edwards, 1979; Gosney, 1977; Post, 1976; Rice, 1976).

Changes in belief systems such as those accomplished by many cults are extreme; most people do not convert so dramatically. However, these conversions illustrate the point that people who adopt a deviant and comprehensive belief system change the way they appraise their relationship to the world at every level of being. What was benign is now malevolent (e.g., parents), and what was malevolent is now benign (e.g., yielding total control to a higher authority). In these extreme circumstances, the manner through which belief systems operate as a perceptual lens becomes clear.

Let us now talk about specific sets of beliefs that are relevant to appraisal. We have selected two major categories: beliefs that have to do with the personal control an individual believes he or she has over events, and beliefs that have to do with existential concerns such as God, fate, and justice. These two major categories hardly exhaust the possibilities. Our selection reflects the zeitgeist or current interest and thought as well as the indispensable presence of actual research that bears on these concepts.

Beliefs About Personal Control

A promising hypothesis is that the extent to which people feel confident of their powers of mastery over the environment or, alternatively, feel great vulnerability to harm in a world conceived as dangerous and hostile affects whether an encounter will produce threat or challenge appraisals (e.g., Averill, 1973; Lefcourt, 1976). David Levy's (1943, 1966) classic studies of maternal overprotection and underprotection (and related research by Ainsworth, Salter, & Wittig, 1967; Baumrind, 1975; Main & Weston, 1982) suggest that vulnerability and fearfulness can arise early when parents paint the world as dangerous and overdo efforts to protect the child. The other side of the issue is stated by Murphy and Moriarty (1976) in their longitudinal study of coping and resilience in childhood. They comment that "the expectation of being able to handle new challenges is a major contribution of the preschool years that helps to dispel self-distrust and anxiety about not being able to manage" (p. 288).

Beliefs about personal control have to do with feelings of mastery and confidence (see Carlson, 1982, for a review of four models of perceived control in the context of biofeedback). These beliefs have been discussed both as generalized ways of thinking and as situation-specific expectations. To speak of control as a generalized belief is to treat it as a stable personality disposition as distinguished from a contextualized judgment or appraisal of a specific encounter. The distinction is important both theoretically and in practical terms because one refers to a stable antecedent variable, the other to a process.

General beliefs about control. A general belief about control concerns the extent to which people assume they can control events and outcomes of importance. The best known formulation is Rotter's (1966) concept of internal versus external locus of control. An internal locus of control refers to the belief that events are contingent upon one's own behavior, and an external locus of control refers to the belief that events are not contingent upon one's actions, but upon luck, chance, fate, or powerful others.

Rotter (1966, 1975) conceived of generalized control expectancies as having their greatest influence when the situation is ambiguous and novel. Under conditions of ambiguity, which is used here to refer to lack of clarity in the environment, situational cues regarding the nature of the outcome and/or the extent to which it can be controlled are minimal. (See Chapter 4 for discussion of ambiguity.) Consequently, person factors (such as beliefs and dispositions) have more influence in determining the meaning of the environmental configuration.

If we apply this principle to general control expectancies, we would expect that under conditions of ambiguity a general expectancy would be translated into a control appraisal with respect to the specific situation. Thus, when a situation is highly ambiguous, a person with an internal locus of control might be expected to appraise the situation as controllable, whereas a person with an external locus of control might appraise it as uncontrollable. However, when a situation is not highly ambiguous, we would expect, as does Rotter (1966, 1975), that judgments about controllability would be influenced more by situational characteristics than by general beliefs.

A version of a general belief about control that has had a strong impact on the thinking of social epidemiologists and psychiatrists in behavioral medicine is Antonovsky's (1979) "sense of coherence," which he treats as a

> . . . global orientation that expresses the extent to which one has a pervasive, enduring though dynamic feeling of confidence that one's internal and external environments are predictable and that there is a high probability that things will work out as can reasonably be expected. (p. 123)

Antonovsky emphasizes integration and union of the self and the world, which is also reminiscent of the neo-Freudian writings of Rank (1952), Jung (1953), and Fromm (1955). The notion of coherence is akin to Kobasa's (1979) notion of the hardy personality style, to Kanungo's (1979) "involvement," which is the antithesis of alienation or anomie, and to related ideas such as positive self-esteem, authenticity, self-confidence, and the sense of mastery.

A sense of coherence or being at one with the world should indeed have emotionally supportive functions, as Antonovsky and others have suggested, and it is probably a positive factor in social and work functioning and health (see Chapter 7). A troubling feature of this concept is that it is apt to be treated solely as a person factor without regard to the society in which the person lives. The sense of coherence engages two interdependent systems, the person and the society, each having its own distinct properties that must be described and taken into account. For example, for many people in Nazi Germany, a sense of coherence depended on suppressing conflicting basic values in order to remain part of the social order. This kind of sense of coherence is attained at the cost of individuality and autonomy, yet it can still be a positive factor in health.

One of the difficulties created by a highly global and overarching concept about human beliefs such as a sense of coherence is that it implies a monolithic pattern of beliefs when in fact people often entertain many contradictory beliefs at the same time. A global concept like the sense of coherence suggests an image of a person with a unified or consistent belief system, which may be more fiction than fact. Whatever the urge to self-consistency, belief systems are too complex, rich, and contradictory to be massed into a simple unidimensional concept. The difficulties in using global concepts to predict behavior have long been a problem in personality research. Like traits, global terms are oversimplified and ignore the complex and changing relationship between people and their environments. (The reader might consult Block, 1982, for a careful dialectic analysis that applies Piaget's concepts of assimilation and accommodation to how the person changes when beliefs fail.)

For example, it is very common for people to be fearful about flying, while at the same time identifying this mode of travel as safe in the sense of statistical risk. Often these same people will feel secure in an automobile and yet acknowledge that the danger of being killed or maimed in a car crash is alarming compared with that of commercial flight. These people appear to have two contradictory beliefs: that they are safe in flight and at the same time that they are in grave danger. This is reminiscent of the story of a passenger who carries his own bomb onto a plane because the odds of there being two bombs are virtually nil. The humor lies in the all too human need to seek reassurance even if it means integrating two contradictory beliefs, and no matter how absurd the synthesis.

It is also common for people to believe that they are effective at what they do or are liked by others, but nonetheless react as if they also believe they are inadequate or disliked. Why their appraisals and the emotions generated are determined by one of these beliefs, often that of their vulnerability, is not clear. It may be that there is a natural hierarchy in which those beliefs that imply danger or the control of danger will normally have more salience when activated by circumstances than those beliefs that imply safety or security. There also may be individual differences in the way this hierarchy is organized.

This is not to say that general beliefs or expectations about control lack value as predictors of appraisals and their consequences in stress and coping research, but that it is very important to distinguish between a general disposition or belief about control, which could operate under certain circumstances such as high ambiguity, and an appraisal of control in a specific context. When researchers use expressions such as "self-efficacy," "illusion of control," or "the sense of control" as measured in a *specific context* (e.g., Bandura, 1977a; Langer, 1975; Lefcourt, 1973), they are often speaking of a coping-relevant appraisal; when researchers use the term *beliefs*, or cognate expressions such as the sense of control over one's life, they are often speaking of general dispositions, that is, the tendency to make certain attributions about control not in one context but many. It is often not easy to tell from the term itself; thus, belief about control could be a belief in a specific context *or* a general belief. The former is a cognitive appraisal, the latter a disposition carried to the situation by the person. This distinction is a variant of the larger state-trait distinction, which has long been of interest to personality and social psychologists (e.g., Allen & Potkay, 1981; Averill, & Opton, 1968).

In recent years many suggestions have been offered for making measures of general beliefs about control more specific in order to improve their predictive power. Numerous possibilities have been discussed in the literature, including making the concept specific to an activity or a context, for instance, to crowding (Schmidt & Keating, 1979), intellectual and academic achievement (Crandall, Katkovsky, & Crandall, 1965), economic outcomes (Gurin & Gurin, 1970), and health behavior (Hartke & Kunce, 1982; Wallston, Wallston, Kaplan, & Maides, 1976). Paulhus and Christie (1981) have developed a series of "sphere-specific" scales that focus on personal efficacy, interpersonal control, and sociopolitical control, which appear to be independent (Paulhus, 1983). (For other examples, see Lefcourt, 1981.) The more restrictions placed on the definition of general control expectancies, the more closely they begin to resemble situational control expectancies or appraisals.

Situational control appraisals. These appraisals refer to the extent to which a person believes that he or she can shape or influence a particular stressful person–environment relationship. They are products of the individual's evaluations of the demands of the situation, as well as his or her coping resources and options and ability to implement the needed coping strategies. In the latter respects, situational appraisals of control parallel Bandura's concept of self-efficacy. We have already noted (see Chaper 2) that Bandura (1977a) distinguishes between an efficacy expectancy, which is the conviction that one can successfully execute the behavior required to produce an outcome, and an outcome expectancy, which is defined as a person's estimate that a given behavior will lead to certain outcomes. Bandura makes this distinction because

> . . . individuals can believe that a particular course of action will produce certain outcomes, but if they entertain serious doubts about whether they can perform the necessary activities such information does not influence their behavior. (p. 193)

Efficacy expectancies can differ in magnitude, generality, and strength. Magnitude refers to the level of difficulty of a specific task. Generality refers to the extent to which an experience creates circumscribed or general expectations, and strength refers to the extent to which an expectation is extinguishable by disconfirming experience.

Efficacy expectancies are given a central role by Bandura in determining a person's choice of activities. "People fear and tend to avoid threatening situations they believe exceed their coping skills, whereas they get involved in activities and behave assuredly when they judge themselves capable of handling situations that would otherwise be intimidating" (1977a, p. 194). In addition, efficacy expectancies also affect the person's willingness to persist in the face of obstacles and aversive experiences. Bandura also makes the important point that efficacy expectancies by themselves will not produce coping unless there are incentives.

In the above statements, Bandura is saying that efficacy expectancies affect the extent to which a person feels threatened and, in the presence of incentives, influence coping behavior. To couch Bandura's ideas in our frame of reference, we would say that efficacy expectancies are part of secondary appraisal, which also includes an evaluation of alternative coping options. These appraisals influence emotion and coping. Efficacy expectancies and incentives (stakes) enter into the person's total evaluation of a situation; it is the evaluated *relationship* between the two factors, and not *independent* efficacy and incentive factors, that determines emotion and coping.

This interpretation is implicit in Bandura's work. For example, one of the most consistent findings in the studies conducted by Bandura and his colleagues with phobics is that level of fear arousal varies with perceived coping efficacy (e.g., Bandura & Adams, 1977; Bandura, Adams, & Byer, 1977; Bandura, Adams, Hardy, & Howells, 1980). Perceived inefficacy was found to be accompanied by high anticipatory and performance fear arousal, but as strength of perceived efficacy increased, fear arousal declined.

Fear is the manifestation of a specific stressful appraisal. Changes in fear level indicate that there are changes in the way the person is appraising his or her relationship with the environment. As efficacy expectancies increase and the person judges his or her resources more adequate for satisfying task demands, the relationship is appraised as holding the potential for more control and therefore as less threatening. As a consequence, fear level decreases and coping behaviors are instituted. In other words, the coping behaviors are not instituted because of increased efficacy expectancies, but because of the effect of the efficacy expectancies on the person's appraised *relationship* with the environment.

Situational control appraisals are difficult to evaluate (Folkman, 1984). Part of the problem has to do with the question "Control over what?" In experimental studies the object of control is ususally a simple and clear aversive stimulus such as a shock, noise, or phobic object. In contrast, the object of control in real-life situations is generally complex, is frequently ambiguous, and often pertains not just to an external stimulus but to the person's internal state as well. In dealing with health-related stressors, for example, Moos and Tsu (1977) cite the following adaptive tasks, each of which can be viewed as involving an outcome or an object or target of control:

Illness-related:

1. Dealing with pain and incapacitation
2. Dealing with the hospital environment and special treatment procedures
3. Developing adequate relationships with professional staff

General:

4. Preserving a reasonable emotional balance
5. Preserving a satisfactory self-image
6. Preserving relationships with family and friends
7. Preparing for an uncertain future (p. 9)

A good overall outcome in a health-related source of stress thus requires numerous suboutcomes which vary in clarity and importance (see also Krantz & Schulz, 1980, for an analytic review dealing with cardiac rehabilitation in the elderly). Some pertain to changing environmental conditions, for example, installing wheelchair ramps, and others pertain to inner issues such as tolerating discomfort or maintaining a sense of adequacy or lovableness. Included among these inner issues is belief in the ability to control one's reactions. The person, knowing or fearful that not much or anything can be done to alter the harmful environmental factors (as in terminal illness), can still fall back on the belief in his or her capacity to exert control over feelings, public and private, and the ability to take whatever comes and keep up morale and a reason for living. To our knowledge, this belief has not been examined as an antecendent of stress and coping, emotion, or adaptational outcome. In real-life harms, threats, and challenges, then, the answer to the question "Control over what?" is likely to be multifaceted.

Outcomes also vary in controllability. A person might expect to control one aspect of a situation but not another. With respect to spinal cord injury patients, for example, Silver and Wortman (1980b) point out that a "person may believe that learning to get in and out of a bed to a wheelchair is in his control. However, he may feel that being able to walk again is only in the hands of God" (p. 4). That the targets of control or outcomes in a stressful encounter can vary in their degree of appraised controllability adds to the complexity of the secondary appraisal of coping options and to the overall appraisal of an event as threatening and/or challenging.

Moreover, as we have noted earlier, appraisals of control can shift as an encounter unfolds. Changes can come about as the result of new information from the environment and/or as the result of coping efforts. In his studies of efficacy expectancies in phobics, for example, Bandura (1982) notes:

> People register notable increase in self-efficacy when their experiences disconfirm misbeliefs about what they fear and when they gain new skills to manage threatening activities. . . . If in the course of completing a task, they discover something that appears intimidating about the undertaking, or suggests limitations to their mode of coping, they register a decline in self-efficaciousness despite their successful performance. (pp. 125–126)

The relationship between situational control appraisals and appraisals of threat and challenge is complex. Most theory and research on the relationship between control and stress is based on the assumption that having control is stress-reducing. Yet there are studies indicating that the obverse is sometimes true (for examples see reviews by Averill, 1973; Thompson, 1981). When might this be so?

Situational appraisals of control and their effects on stress are often examined in a laboratory setting in which the focal event is treated apart from other personal and environmental concerns. In real life, however, events are usually connected to other events, be they internal and/or external, psychological, physical, and/or social. The interrelated nature of events helps explain why the potential for control can be threat-inducing as well as threat-reducing. Consider the patient who is told that there is the potential for controlling a malignancy through chemotherapy. By exercising this control option, that is, by having chemotherapy, the malignancy may be contained, but often at additional cost of physical and psychological well-being (e.g., nausea, hair loss, and depression). A person with a coronary-prone Type A behavior pattern may be counseled to "control" his behavior by becoming less driven and competitive in order to reduce the risk of illness. But to do so may cause the person to act against strongly held values, with a consequent loss of self-esteem and productivity. In each of the above cases the potential for control presents a difficult choice. The person may value controlling the malignancy or the risk of myocardial infarction; yet the potential for control can generate distress because of its costs.

The same principle applies when having control is antagonistic to a preferred style such as avoidance (as opposed to confrontation) or dependence (as opposed to independence). A study by Averill, O'Brien, and DeWitt (1977) illustrates this point. In this shock-avoidance experiment, each subject could choose whether or not to listen for a warning that signaled an upcoming shock. The warning gave the subject potential control over the aversive stimulus in that it allowed the subject to try to switch off the shock. In each of 12 trials, the subject was informed as to how effective the switch was likely to be in preventing the shock; response effectiveness ranged from 0 to 100 percent. Vigilant subjects (those who preferred to listen for the warning) showed *less* evidence of distress as response effectiveness increased, whereas nonvigilant subjects (those who preferred not to listen for the warning) showed *increased* distress as effectiveness increased.

A study by Mills and Krantz (1979) also illustrates this idea. These investigators found that blood donors who were given information that would allow them to prepare for blood-drawing (thereby giving them the option for self-control) and the choice of which arm would be used (behavioral control) were more distressed than subjects who were given just one form of control. Mills and Krantz speculate that the combination of informational and behavioral control gave the donors more of a role in the blood-drawing procedures than they would have preferred. Citing Houston (1972), Mills and Krantz also suggest that when the individual prefers not to control, increased choice or participation may heighten stress. In studies by Shipley, Butt, and Horwitz (1979) and Shipley, Butt, Horwitz, and Farbry (1978) examining the relationship between repression-sensitization and stress, subjects were given information that allowed them to exercise self-control in response to an intrusive procedure (endoscopy). Repressors were more anxious than sensitizers when given this information. Presumably, those with a repressive style would have been less anxious if they had not been urged to think about the procedure. Similarly, S. Miller (1980) found that "blunters" (people who prefer to distract themselves from threat-relevant information) did better in a medical procedure when the amount of preparatory information they received was consistent with their preferred style. From these and earlier studies (e.g., Andrew, 1970; Delong, 1970), a clear pattern emerges indicating that exercising control can be stress-inducing when it opposes a preferred style.

Control can also have negative social consequences. Perhaps a person has the skills with which to exercise control over an aversive condition, but the exercise of those skills might result in damage to an important interpersonal relationship or in an embarrassing social interaction. In a study of the coping efforts of low-income mothers, for example, Dill, Feld, Martin, Beukema, and Belle (1980) describe how a woman was inhibited from addressing her child's behavior problems because to do so would likely involve "humiliating intrusions" from the school system, health and mental health services, or social workers.

Finally, on a more practical level, the possibility of heightened threat exists when the exercise of control requires material resources that are needed elsewhere. Thus, to cut down the aversive noise in the work environment may require money that is needed to buy new equipment. The potential practical, mundane consequences of control are too often overlooked in both laboratory and field settings (see also Antonovsky, 1979; Dill et al., 1980).

Situational appraisals of control and veridicality. Like primary appraisals of threat and challenge, secondary control appraisals are usually based only on selected facets of an encounter, attention to which is guided by person factors such as commitments and beliefs. Moreover, the evaluation of the controllability of those selected facets is itself subject to the influence of person factors. For these reasons, situational appraisals of control are not necessarily veridical and, in fact, probably seldom are.

Langer (1975) conducted a series of six studies in order to understand the conditions under which the *illusion of control* is induced. In each study she used completely chance-determined activities in the presence of stimuli associated with skill conditions. In one study, for example, she focused on *choice*, which is considered an important factor in a skill situation. Using a lottery as a vehicle, Langer predicted that subjects who were given their choice of lottery tickets would require a higher price for it. Findings supported the prediction. In another experiment *familiarity* was used to induce the illusion of control. Lottery tickets were either familiar (letters of the alphabet written on index cards) or unfamiliar (line drawings of novel symbols). Subjects were given the opportunity to keep their original ticket or to trade it in for a ticket in a lottery where the chances of winning were better. Again, findings offered evidence that an illusion of control had been induced. Other experiments induced the illusion of control through competitive behavior, and active and passive involvement. Overall, Langer found that the more similar a chance situation is to a skill situation, the more likely it is that people will approach the chance situation with a skill orientation.

Langer (1975) offers three reasons why people have a skill orientation (or an illusion of control) in chance situations. The first is that they are motivated to control their environment. She cites White's (1959) discussion of a need for competence, Hendrick's (1943) instinct to master, Adler's (1930) striving for superiority, and deCharms' (1968) striving for personal causation as examples of the widespread recognition that there is a motivation to master one's environment. Complete mastery would include the ability to control chance events. The second reason is the motivation to avoid the negative consequences that accompany the perception of having no control. For example, a review by Lefcourt (1973) shows that a nonveridical perception of control over an impending event reduces its aversiveness. Finally, Langer explains why people take on an illusion of control in chance situations in terms of their difficulty in discriminating between controllable and uncontrollable events. In all skills situations there is an element of chance, and in almost every chance situation there is an element of skill. Thus, not only are people motivated not to discriminate between skill and chance conditions, but there is often a real difficulty in making the discrimination.

The illusion of control refers to unrealistic control expectancies in chance situations. Its obverse is unrealistic feelings of helplessness in skill situations. A study by Garber and Hollon (1980) suggests that this particular form of helplessness is characteristic of depressives. Garber and Hollon point out that although helplessness has received a great deal of attention as a major correlate of depression (e.g., Beck, 1967; Bibring, 1953; Klein & Seligman, 1976; Melges & Bowlby, 1969; Miller & Seligman, 1975; Seligman, 1975), it is not clear whether depressives perceive the world to be a noncontingent place, in which case they would see skill situations to be essentially like chance situations, or whether depressives actually view skill tasks as contingent on skill, but believe that outcomes are independent of responses in their own repertoire. The latter view would mean that depressed individuals view themselves as personally helpless and incompetent in a skill situation, rather than viewing the situation as universally uncontrollable.

To test these interpretations, Garber and Hollon (1980) examined changes in expectancies following success and failure in skill and chance tasks in depressed and nondepressed subjects. Subjects were assigned to actor (performer) and observer (observing a confederate perform) groups. In the skill tasks, which ostensibly tested the subject's ability to raise a platform by pulling a string without letting a ball roll off the platform, depressed subjects showed significantly smaller changes in expectancy than nondepressed subjects when estimating the probability of their own success on repeated trials. In contrast, depressed and nondepressed subjects did not differ when estimating the probability of another person's success on the identical skill task.

The findings suggested that depressed and nondepressed individuals do not differ in their perception of skill tasks, but only in their belief about their own responses in the tasks. Depressed individuals view themselves as helpless in a skill situation, but do not view the situation itself as uncontrollable. Using Bandura's (1977a) distinction between efficacy and outcome expectancies, these findings suggest that depressives and nondepressives do not differ in outcome expectancies, that is, the belief that a particular course of action will produce certain outcomes, but rather in *efficacy* expectancies.

The work of Kahneman and Tversky (1971, 1973; Tversky & Kahneman, 1971, 1973, 1974) directed at identifying the heuristics people use to make predictions and judgments under conditions of uncertainty is relevant to this discussion. These heuristics sometimes yield reasonable judgments and sometimes lead to severe and systematic errors. We shall not discuss heuristics and biases in subjective probability estimates here, but it is important to keep in mind that subjective probability estimates do not necessarily correspond with objective estimates. (For an extensive review and discussion of sources of bias in subjective probability estimates and the conditions under which such biases are most likely to lead to error, see Nisbett & Ross, 1980.)

It is clear that beliefs about control, whether shaped more by person factors or situational contingencies, play a major role in determining the degree to which a person feels threatened or challenged in a stressful encounter. To the extent that a person's beliefs about control are general, they will color all appraisals, regardless of the situation. As we noted above, general expectancies of little or no control are strongly associated with depression. Less attention has been given to people who have general beliefs about being able to control most or all situations. In its extreme, such a belief would undoubtedly also give a characteristic tone to an individual's appraisals across all circumstances. A person holding such a belief might appear arrogant, smug, or possibly manic. The important point is that whether general or specific, illusory or realistic, one's *belief in one's ability to control an event* influences how that event is appraised and, through appraisal, subsequent coping activity.

Existential Beliefs

Existential beliefs, such as faith in God, fate, or some natural order in the universe, are general beliefs that enable people to create meaning out of life, even out of damaging experiences, and to maintain hope.

Earlier we discussed how commitments help sustain coping efforts. In this regard, commitments and existential beliefs appear similar. Yet, despite this overt similarity, commitments and existential beliefs are quite different. Beliefs concern what one thinks is true, whether or not one likes or approves of it, whereas commitments reflect values, that is, what one prefers or considers desirable (Wrubel et al., 1981). Commitments have a motivational-emotional quality, but beliefs are affectively neutral (Feather, 1975). They do not necessarily contain an emotional component.

This is not to say that beliefs have no relationship with emotion or commitment. Beliefs can give rise to stress emotions, as when they underlie threat appraisals (e.g., the world is hostile or dangerous), and they can be used to dampen or regulate an emotional response (e.g., belief that supportive others exist). In these instances, beliefs lead to or regulate emotions, but by themselves they are not emotional. They become emotional only when an encounter also involves a commitment to a value or an ideal, another person, or a goal, or when physical well-being is endangered.

The words of an inmate of a Nazi concentration camp show the convergence of beliefs and commitments that results in a belief serving to maintain hope, and thereby reducing threat. The speaker is a woman who was 20 at the time of her imprisonment.

I had a belief, a religious belief. I was convinced that all the wrong things had to change and we would be free. My mother put in me [the] belief that if someone is doing right, he will not always suffer . . . I knew to survive I had to believe, believe that such a bad thing cannot win. (Dimsdale, 1974, p. 793)

The key phrase is "I knew to survive . . ."; this indicates her will to live, her *commitment* to survive. Without this commitment, the belief would not be infused with emotion. One can be convinced that doing right will be rewarded, but unless the person wants to live, the belief will remain relatively free of affect.

Similarly, belief in some higher purpose enabled patients who had suffered spinal cord injuries to look for and see some benefit in the experiences to which they were subjected. To the question "Why me?" these patients' most frequent explanation was that God had a reason for their victimization (Bulman & Wortman, 1977). One respondent said, for example, "Could be that He had a reason for it. Maybe someboby else needs my leg more than I do." Another responded, "It's a learning experience. I see God's trying to put me in situations, help me to learn about Him and myself and also how I can help other people" (Bulman & Wortman, 1977, p. 358).

In these examples, individuals had been harmed; very real psychological as well as physical stakes were involved. The presence of these stakes caused the beliefs to become infused with emotion so that positive value or meaning was created in circumstances that might otherwise have been completely overwhelming.

Specific beliefs (e.g., in a physician, a particular medicine, an educational program) can also become charged with emotion and generate hope. The role of specific beliefs in appraisal processes differs from that of existential beliefs primarily in that the former are less general and are engaged only in specific situations where a relevant psychological or physical stake is at risk. Otherwise, these specific beliefs remain affectively neutral and are not likely to influence an appraisal. For example, a person might believe that a particular physician is a gifted surgeon. That belief will remain affectively neutral until the person or someone close to the person is scheduled for surgery with the physician. At that point, the person's belief in the doctor will take on a positive affect and generate confidence, hope, and perhaps relief from worry.

Commitments and beliefs, the two main person factors we have addressed in this chapter, can be brought together in a more general, overarching personality concept that many writers have called "self." Hilgard (1949), for example, pointed out that the concept of self is one instance of a unifying motivational principle in human affairs. The self, says Hilgard, is in part an organization of the largely interpersonal motives and attitudes that are of central importance to the person, and which persist and remain recognizable as the person ages. Thus, the commitments that characterize a person are reflections of and brought together under what personality psychologists treat as the self. A parallel idea is found in Epstein's (1976) self-theory. Epstein, as we do, regards emotions as indicators of what is important to the person, as organized in a person's self-theory. The implication is that in order to make sense out of the emotional life, we must know what is important to the person, in effect, the self-concept which organizes how the person thinks and what the person wants.

Our emphasis in this chapter has been on person factors that contribute to individual differences in appraisal, and we have stated that because of these person factors, primary and secondary appraisals are not necessarily based on veridical, isomorphic representations of what is going on in a stressful encounter. Nevertheless, if a person's appraisal of an encounter is to lead to adaptive coping and outcomes, the appraisal must be realistic; the person needs to focus on adaptationally significant aspects of an encounter and evaluate coping options in relation to the actual demands of the environment and his or her actual coping resources. We want to avoid suggesting, however, that in any given stressful encounter there is a *single* realistic primary or secondary appraisal. A person may generate several interpretations of an event depending on which facets of the encounter are attended to and the clarity or ambiguity of the available information concerning demands and coping resources. It is possible that any one of several appraisals could lead to an adaptive outcome, although some outcomes may be preferable to others. We will have more to say about the match between appraisals and the flow of events and adaptive outcomes in Chapter 7.

At the beginning of this chapter we said that person and situation factors *interdependently* influence appraisal. It is important not to lose sight of this principle, for only when the person perceives something in the environment that is relevant to his or her commitments and beliefs will these person characteristics selectively influence appraisal. In a sense, person and situation factors must hook each other in a particular encounter for an appraisal to occur. In the next chapter we will discuss certain situation characteristics that are likely to engage the person factors we have outlined here.

Summary

Among the most important person factors affecting cognitive appraisal are commitments and beliefs. Commitments are an expression of what is important to people, and they underlie the choices people make. They also contain a vital motivational quality. Commitments affect appraisal by guiding people into or away from situations that threaten, harm, or benefit them and by shaping cue-sensitivity. Commitments also influence appraisal through their impact on vulnerability. The deeper a person's commitment, the greater the potential for threat and challenge, yet at the same time, the depth of commitment can also push a person toward ameliorative action and help sustain hope.

Beliefs also determine how a person evaluates what is happening or is about to happen. They often operate on a tacit level, and as a consequence it may be difficult to observe their influence on appraisal. The impact of beliefs can be observed when there is a sudden loss of belief or a conversion to a different belief system.

Although many beliefs are relevant to appraisal, beliefs about personal control and existential beliefs are of particular interest in stress theory. Beliefs about personal control can be both general and situational. General beliefs about control, which concern the extent to which the person believes outcomes of importance can be controlled, are most likely to affect appraisal in ambiguous situations. The less ambiguity there is about a particular encounter, the more likely situational appraisals of control will affect emotion and coping. Situational appraisals of control are not restricted to expectations about the environment; they can also refer to expectations for controlling one's own response to the transaction.

In any given encounter there may be multiple outcomes varying in importance to evaluate with respect to controllability. Most research suggests that appraising an outcome as controllable is stress-reducing. An appraisal of controllability can also heighten threat, however, as when having control is contrary to a preferred style or conflicts with other commitments or goals. To the extent that situational appraisals of control are based on incomplete information and/or are influenced by person factors, they are less likely to be accurate. Regardless of their accuracy, however, situational appraisals of control, over the environment and/or one's self, influence emotion and coping.

Existential beliefs enable people to create meaning and maintain hope in difficult circumstances. They may be affectively neutral, but they can give rise to emotion when they converge with a strong commitment in a particular encounter.

By themselves, commitments and beliefs are not sufficient to explain appraisal. They work interdependently with situation factors (which we take up in Chapter 4) to determine the extent to which harm/loss, threat, or challenge will be experienced.

4

Situation Factors
Influencing Appraisal

In recent years there has been widespread interest in the properties of events that make them stressful. The most visible efforts have been in life events research, where a goal has been to scale various major events (e.g., death of a spouse, divorce, being fired, personal injury or illness, or retirement) on a dimension of the amount of readjustment required (Holmes & Rahe, 1967), desirability, anticipation, or control (see reviews by Fontana, Hughes, Marcus, & Dowds, 1979; Rabkin & Struening, 1976; Thoits, 1983). Metrics derived from these efforts treat events as *normatively* more or less stressful; a weight assigned to an event is assumed not only to reflect a population parameter, but individual preferences as well.

As we have emphasized in the previous chapters, however, even when a stimulus signals a clear and unambiguous threat of such magnitude that virtually everyone considers it dangerous or damaging, there remain great individual variations in the extent to which such events are appraised as stressful, and in their qualitative and quantitative response effects. These variations are no doubt due to factors the person brings to the event that shape its personal significance. (See Chapter 10 for discussion of the measurement of stress.) Nevertheless, the question of the situational component of the person–situation relationship must still be addressed. We need some way to identify those properties of situations that make them potentially harmful, dangerous, threatening (see Hansell, 1982), or for that matter challenging. The purpose of this chapter is to identify some of these properties.

Our approach to this task differs in fundamental ways from stimulus definitions of stress in which events are treated as normatively stressful. First, we shall be concerned with the *formal* properties of situations that create the potential for threat, harm, or challenge. We shall not deal with substantive issues concerning what a situation is actually about (e.g., being evaluated or disapproved, divorce, death, job loss, or moving). Second, we shall not generate a normative rank ordering of properties according to stressfulness. The extent to which any event is stressful is determined by a confluence of person and situation factors in a specific transaction; to rank situation properties without reference to person factors would be to ignore the role of person factors in determining appraisals. By identifying formal properties of situations, however, we hope to provide a taxonomy of those properties that are especially relevant to the person factors we have discussed, and hence to the appraisal processes through which threat, harm, and challenge are determined.

We shall first consider novelty, predictability, and event uncertainty, and then move on to the discussion of three temporal factors: imminence, duration, and temporal uncertainty. Finally, we shall discuss ambiguity and the timing of stressful events in the life cycle.

Novelty

Human beings inevitably find themselves in situations that are novel, by which we mean situations with which the person has not had previous experience. If a situation is *completely* novel and no aspect of it has previously been connected psychologically with harm, it will not result in an appraisal of threat. Similarly, if no aspect of the situation has previously been connected with mastery or gain, it will not result in an appraisal of challenge. The previous connections with harm or gain need not have been direct; the individual might have seen, read, heard, or otherwise inferred it, thus giving the relevant aspect of the situation the capacity to lead to a threat or challenge appraisal. In other words, a person does not have to have had a reaction to poison oak to know that it is dangerous. Conversations with friends or knowledge gained from reading is sufficient to connect the plant with danger. However, if the person has had no experience with poison oak, either direct or vicarious, he or she is likely to appraise the brilliantly colored leaves as benign and perhaps even be inspired to pick them to bring home. Alternatively, having heard only that poisonous leaves are shiny, the person might be indiscriminately wary of all plants with shiny leaves. Here the combination of novelty and inadequate information conspires to produce an appraisal that is generalized inappropriately.

Most situations are not *completely* novel. Certain facets will be familiar, or there will be a general resemblance between the situation and some other class of events. Even in the most novel situation, stimuli will be processed through preexisting systems of schematized and abstracted knowledge in an effort after understanding and meaning (Nisbett & Ross, 1980). This "general knowledge" (Schank & Abelson, 1977) enables one person to understand and interpret another's behavior simply because the other person has certain standard needs and lives in a world with certain standard methods of getting those needs fulfilled. Except in extreme circumstances, where one's preexisting knowledge has no relevance whatever (e.g., detainment in an unfriendly nation with no common language and no knowledge of the country's beliefs, values, customs, and legal systems), absolute novelty is quite rare. Usually the individual has some basis for inferring meaning from a situation that he or she has not confronted before. Thus, it is probably more useful to think of novelty as a relative rather than absolute property of situations (cf. Berlyne, 1960).

As we mentioned earlier, a novel situation is stressful only if there is a previous association with harm, danger, or mastery. In that case, novelty can itself become a source of threat. Furthermore, a novel situation is ambiguous to the extent that the person is not clear about the significance or meaning of the event. To make sense of the situation requires inference. The more inference required, the greater the possibility of an error in interpretation. If the person is aware of the increased risk of error that accompanies the interpretation of a novel, ambiguous situation, he or she is likely to experience a high degree of uncertainty and threat. We shall discuss ambiguity, uncertainty, and threat at length later in this chapter.

In addition, although general knowledge might be sufficient for interpreting a novel event, it may be inadequate for coping. Without direct or vicarious experience with the encountered demands, the person may not have had the opportunity to develop the specific coping skills required to deal with the demands (see Chapter 6). Awareness of this coping deficit will also increase threat.

Predictability

Predictability has been a major theme in stress research, especially in experimental studies of animals. Predictability implies that there are predictable environmental characteristics that can be discerned, discovered, or learned. Researchers have sometimes substituted the word *signaled* for predictable noxious stimulation, but the meaning is the same and refers to some type of warning that something painful or harmful is about to happen.

Weinberg and Levine (1980) reviewed an extensive literature on the role of predictability in promoting or reducing stress in animals and concluded that the findings are complex and confusing. A large body of evidence suggests that predictable shock is less aversive than unpredictable or unsignaled shock. For example, a study by Badia and Culbertson (1970) focused on the behavioral response of rats in a laboratory avoidance situation where a bar could be pressed to avoid shock. In the signaled condition the rats pressed the bar much less frequently and left the area of the bar more freely than rats in the unsignaled condition. Given a choice, the rats preferred the signaled condition over the unsignaled even when the shock was unavoidable and inescapable. In other animal studies (Badia, Culbertson, & Harsh, 1973), in fact, experimental animals chose signaled shock that was two to three times more intense and lasted four to nine times longer than unsignaled shock. Overall, these studies of infrahuman organisms including rats, pigeons, and fish show that the preference for predictable stimuli (usually shock) is robust: subjects prefer longer, stronger, and more dense signaled shock over shorter, weaker, and less dense unsignaled shock (for reviews see Badia, Harsh, & Abbott, 1979).

One explanation for the preference for signaled events is that they allow for the possibility of anticipatory coping, which is the essence of the *preparatory response hypothesis*. This hypothesis argues that a warning provides information permitting subjects to prepare in some way, thereby reducing the aversiveness of the stressor (e.g., Perkins, 1968).

An alternative explanation is offered by the *safety signal hypothesis*, which suggests that having a warning informs the subjects of when they are safe from a stressor. This knowledge could be useful because it provides periods during which they can relax. Both hypotheses seem to implicate two other factors in explaining the effects of predictability, namely, *control* over the environment and *feedback* from the transaction with the environment about what can or cannot be done and about the reliability of whatever environmental contingencies exist.

Weinberg and Levine (1980) point out that control and predictability are closely interrelated and often confounded in research. That is, the subject may not only be able to predict the aversive stimulus but also control it, although the latter may not be identified by the investigator as a parameter of the study. *One cannot control a situation that is not predictable; however, there may be predictability without control,* as when one is unable to influence whether shock will be experienced or how severe it will be. When animal subjects prefer predictable conditions, it is not possible to tell whether this is because of the control provided or because the signaled condition offers some other form of surcease, as implied by the safety signal hypothesis.

Feedback about the effects of a response has been shown, by Weiss (1971) and others (e.g., Coover, Ursin, & Levine, 1973) to have an ameliorative effect on stress responses in animals, including, for example, the development of gastric ulcers and pituitary-adrenal cortical activity. Indeed, Weinberg and Levine (1980) suggest that predictability of an aversive stimulus may reduce stress only when feedback about the environment is provided from .the animal's response. Thus, for example, an animal is able to "feel safe" (the safety signal hypothesis) when there is some reliable signal of shock that predicts shock-free periods (cf. Seligman, 1968). Weinberg and Levine (1980) say:

> . . . it appears that prediction of safety is more important, in terms of reducing an animal's stress responses, than prediction of shock. It may be that signaled shock is preferable and causes less stress only when the contingencies between warning and shock are such that the subject has an identifiable safe period and can therefore relax during the inter-shock interval. If the parameters of the task are such that a signal accurately predicts shock but provides the organism with little feedback or information about safety, then predictable shock may well be more aversive. (p. 56)

Levine and his associates (e.g., Levine, Goldman, & Coover, 1972) have also shown that after experimental animals learn to expect food or water, if the rewarding substance is removed or prevented from being consumed, there is a marked increase in plasma corticosteroids to a degree comparable with reactions to other noxious events. When the animals are able to view the food or water, or are allowed to consume it, however, there is rapid suppression of pituitary-adrenal hormonal activity. Levine suggests, therefore, that when established expectancies are no longer met—that is, when there is a loss of predictability—a corticosteroid stress response is generated until a new set of expectancies is created. In short, going from predictability to unpredictability is highly stressful and results in pituitary-adrenal cortical activity, whereas ambiguous conditions in which no expectations are violated do not produce hormone secretions.

Although theory and research concerning predictability and stress in animals have generated interesting hypotheses and relatively robust findings, the animal model is not sufficient for understanding psychological stress in humans. Animal studies are not concerned with individual differences in the ways subjects comprehend or respond to the situation. Such differences may not be significant in animals, whose cognitive and behavioral range is limited, but they are critical in studies of human stress.

The history of learned helplessness research, which is described in Chapter 7, provides a good illustration of the limitations of animal models for understanding stress in human beings. The concept of learned helplessness was developed in laboratory work with dogs and other animals to explain why animals that had previously been exposed to uncontrollable electric shock failed to avoid subsequent shock, even though an avoidance response was available (Overmeier & Seligman, 1967; Seligman & Maier, 1967). When the model was applied to humans, important and unpredicted individual differences in response became evident; not all people became passive and depressed after having been faced with uncontrollable conditions. The model has since been reformulated to include cognitive mediation in order to explain these individual differences in response (e.g., Abramson, Seligman, & Teasdale, 1978; Garber, Miller, & Abramson, 1980; Hollon & Garber, 1980). The newer versions bear less and less resemblance to the original model, which was based on experimental animal research.

Event Uncertainty

In order to help distinguish our cognitive model of research from animal models, we use the term *event uncertainty* rather than *predictability* to discuss how the likelihood of an event's occurrence influences appraisal. Event uncertainty introduces the notion of probability. For instance, a person might be given information that there is a 15 percent chance of a tumor recurring, an 85 percent chance of rain, or a 20 percent chance of being admitted to a particular college. This type of information is usually treated as a property of the stimulus. As noted in Chapter 3, however, subjective probability estimates often vary from the objective probabilities of occurrence because of the heuristics people use (Kahneman & Tversky, 1971, 1973; Parker, Brewer, & Spencer, 1980; Tversky & Kahneman, 1971, 1973, 1974). These heuristics make probabilistic judgments about events almost as much a property of the person as of the situation.

Laboratory investigations of event uncertainty in humans usually examine the effects of various levels of certainty on psychophysiological indicators of arousal, using actual probability levels of a noxious condition such as electric shock as the index of certainty. There are two alternative intuitive hypotheses. The first is that as certainty increases there will be a corresponding increase in arousal. The second hypothesis is that there is a curvilinear relationship between certainty and arousal, the peak occurring with maximum (.50) uncertainty. In these experimental designs, arousal is usually taken to be a sign of fear and/or threat.

Studies by Epstein and Roupenian (1970), Deane (1969), and Elliot (1966) indicate that the exact opposite of the first hypothesis is more often the case. They found that arousal was highest under conditions of lowest certainty of shock. Epstein and Roupenian think that this occurs because subjective probability estimates do not correspond to objective ones. Subjects in the 50 percent expectancy group made spontaneous comments that the likelihood of shock was high enough for them to assume they would get one, a strategy that reduced suspense and permitted only pleasant surprises. These subjects, in effect, increased their estimates of shock from an objective 50 percent to a subjective 95 percent. Epstein and Roupenian speculate further that subjects in the 5 percent shock expectancy group also raised their subjective probability level to 50 percent, or maximum uncertainty, through thoughts such as "At a chance of one in twenty, it's pretty certain that I won't get a shock, but what if I do?" (p. 26). They could therefore neither resign themselves to getting a shock nor dismiss the thought that they would get one. Nevertheless, Monat, Averill, and Lazarus (1972) found in a related experiment that the 5 percent, 50 percent, and 100 percent objective conditions of probability did not differentially affect changes in heart rate, skin conductance, or self-reported tension. However, most subjects preferred the 5 percent certainty condition the most and the 100 percent certainty condition the least.

On the other hand, Gaines, Smith, and Skolnick (1977) found support for the hypothesis that arousal (heart rate) would increase with increased certainty, but *only* for field-independent subjects (i.e., those whose perception is less subject to environmental influences; see Chapter 5). Field-dependent subjects, in contrast, were nearly as aroused in the 5 percent condition as in the 95 percent condition. Field-independent people are said to be better able to analyze and restructure a field than field-dependent people, which could explain these differences.

If stimulus factors *alone* caused arousal, the intuitive hypothesis that arousal (i.e., threat) is a function of degree of certainty or uncertainty would undoubtedly receive support: the more likely the event, the more threatening it is. The studies we have cited above, however, clearly indicate that stimulus factors alone do not predict arousal, and demonstrate the importance of considering a stimulus in relation to relevant person factors and strategies of coping.

The second intuitive hypothesis—that there is a curvilinear relationship between certainty and arousal—was adopted and tested in the research by Epstein and Roupenian. They cite extensive theoretical and research support for the idea that event uncertainty per se can be a source of anxiety and tension:

> Freud (1920) and others had distinguished the more disturbing state of anxiety from fear by attributing the former to an unknown source. Berlyne (1960) directly related uncertainty to conflict, and, therefore, to a state of heightened arousal. Fiske and Maddi (1961) state, as a basic proposition, that there is a direct relationship between expectedness and stimulus impact. The above positions suggest that uncertainty about receiving a noxious stimulus adds an increment of anxiety to that produced by direct concern over the noxious stimulus. Such a view receives support from a number of other studies that have varied uncertainty in one manner or another (cf. Berlyne, 1960; Deane, 1969; Elliot, 1966; Haggard, 1943; Zeaman & Smith, 1965). (Epstein and Roupenian, 1970, p. 21)

This hypothesis, like the other, produced contradictory findings. In one study (Gaines et al., 1977), maximum uncertainty (the 50 percent certainty–uncertainty condition) was even associated with the lowest level of arousal (for field-dependent subjects only).

It is possible, as Epstein and Roupenian suggest, that there is a general bias to inflate subjective probabilities, for example, a 5 percent probability is subjectively moved to a 50 percent probability, and a 50 percent objective probability to a 95 percent subjective probability. There is, indeed, research evidence for such psychological transformations.

We are inclined to believe, however, that in naturalistic circumstances conditions of maximum uncertainty are highly if not maximally stressful. Most studies of event uncertainty have been conducted in the laboratory, usually with psychology students. Even though subjects are warned of loud noises or shocks, they know that ethical considerations limit the degree of actual harm that can be created in a laboratory setting. Further, except for skeptical and/ or experiment-wise students who doubt explanations and instructions, most subjects have little reason not to believe what they are told about the probabilities of event occurrence. These conditions circumscribe the uncertainty of probability statements in laboratory experiments, and therefore mitigate the threatening effects of event uncertainty. Moreover, there has been little interest in what may be the most important mediating process affecting arousal or stress, namely, how people cope with the distress of uncertainty.

Event uncertainty in real life has a much greater potential for creating psychological stress than its counterpart in the laboratory. Most real life events are much more complex than laboratory events; there are more facets to the environmental configuration that have to be evaluated. In addition, the reliability or applicability of odds that are given about the occurrence of an event are often questionable. Previous inaccurate predictions and lack of faith in the reliability of instruments or in the person who is making the prediction are but a few of many reasons why proffered probabilities are not necessarily believed (cf. Breznitz, 1967; Janis & Mann, 1977; Nisbett & Ross, 1980). And, most important of all, real-life events are infinitely more meaningful than laboratory stressors. Even the simplest hassle in real life usually overshadows its laboratory counterpart in terms of its short- and long-term consequences. When major events are considered, there is no comparison with respect to their implications for well-being.

Perhaps nowhere is the role played by event uncertainty in generating threat more widely noted than in cases of physical illness and disability. Moos and Tsu (1977) and Cohen and Lazarus (1979), for example, in their comprehensive reviews of studies examining how people cope with the stresses of physical illness, cite dealing

with uncertainty as a major adaptive task. Mages and Mendelsohn (1979) state the problem cogently in their discussion of the effects of cancer on patients' lives:

> . . . one of the major problems posed by cancer is that the patient cannot be sure for many years whether or not a cure has been effected. This problem . . . involves not a single event or a series of events well marked in time, but rather a continuing, unremitting condition of uncertainty about potentially disastrous and poorly predictable future events. (p. 259)

Another example is found among women whose husbands are reported missing in action. These women suffer profound frustrations and uncertainties caused by not knowing whether their husbands are alive or dead. Hunter (1979) states that unresolved grief can effectively prevent one from getting on with living. Ambiguity as to marital status makes it difficult for these women to fit in with social groups or to have their own social lives, and as long as they expect or hope that their husbands will return home, it is difficult for them to make decisions about housing, employment, and their children's education.

Hunter and her colleagues were also concerned with the wives of men killed in action or taken prisoners of war. They compared four samples of Navy wives: a comparison group whose husbands returned from active duty in the Vietnam war, wives of men killed in action (KIA wives), prisoner of war (POW) wives, and missing in action (MIA) wives. The prediction was made that adjustment would decrease as uncertainty increased, going from wives whose husbands returned to KIA wives to POW wives to MIA wives. Comparisons among these groups on indices of physical and emotional health four years after the POWs were released supported the hypothesis. The greater the uncertainty, the poorer the adjustment. Among the MIA wives, those who acted more certain by "closing out" their husbands and taking over the behaviors associated with their husbands' roles were better adjusted than those who did not.

One of the most important reasons why event uncertainty in real life can be stressful is that it has an immobilizing effect on anticipatory coping processes. The coping strategies for anticipating an event's occurrence are often incompatible with strategies needed to anticipate the event's nonoccurrence. For example, one of the adaptive tasks in dealing with illnesses or disabilities which include significant losses such as sight, speech, or a part of the body is the acknowledgment and mourning of those losses (Mages & Mendel-sohn, 1979; Moos & Tsu, 1977). At the same time, new medical procedures raise hope for patients; thus, they must prepare for per-manent loss of function while maintaining the hope that functioning may be restored. Under these conditions, it is difficult to sustain both courses of action.

Another factor that often makes the preparation for alternative outcomes difficult, if not impossible, is the mental confusion that can result from having to consider first one possible outcome and then another. When one cannot decide on a path of action, and closure is unavailable, fear, excessive worrying and rumination, and eventually anxiety can result (cf. Breznitz, 1971). The heightened anxiety (threat) is itself likely to interfere with cognitive functioning, making it even more difficult to cope. In short, not knowing whether an event is going to occur can lead to a long, drawn-out process of appraisal and reappraisal generating conflicting thoughts, feelings, and behaviors which in turn create feelings of helplessness and eventual confusion. We would assume that the more meaning-ful the event, the more heightened these effects are likely to be, at least to the extent that they are not controlled by cognitive coping processes such as defenses.

Temporal Factors

McGrath (1970) and Appley and Trumbull (1967) point out that time may be one of the most important parameters of stressful situations, yet it has been one of the most neglected areas in stress research. In this section we focus on how temporal factors, including immi-nence, duration, and uncertainty, influence threat and challenge appraisals.

Imminence

Imminence refers to how much time there is before an event occurs. It is the interval during which an event is anticipated. Generally, the more imminent an event is, the more intense its appraisal becomes, especially if there are cues signaling harm, danger, or the opportu-nity for mastery or gain. Without these cues, imminence is not likely to affect appraisal. The less imminent an event in which these cues are present, the less urgent and more complex the appraisal pro-cesses become.

Janis and Mann (1977) examine the role of imminence within the context of decison-making processes in which the stakes have consequence. They state that the quality of decision making depends on the answer to the question "Is there sufficient time to make a careful search for an evaluation of information and advice?" (p. 59). If the answer to the question is yes, "the person is likely to make a thorough information search and to weigh carefully whatever he discovers concerning the pros and cons of each alternative before making his choice" (p. 75). This is a characteristic of high-level decision making.

On the other hand, if the person decides that there is not enough time to make a careful information search:

> . . . The decision maker will manifest a very high level of psychological stress. He will become frantically preoccupied with the threatened losses in store for him if he believes that a rapidly approaching deadline precludes an adequate search for a better solution, knowing that one or another set of undesirable consequences will soon materialize. (p. 74)

As a consequence, the person uses a hypervigilant decision-making style. In this pattern a person becomes

> . . . obsessed with nightmarish fantasies about all sorts of horrible things that might happen to him, and fails to notice evidence indicating the improbability of their actual occurrence. The person is constantly aware of pressure to take prompt action to avert catastrophic losses. He superficially scans the most obvious alternative open to him and may then resort to a crude form of satisficing, hastily choosing the first one that seems to hold the promise of escaping the worst danger. In doing so, he may overlook other serious consequences, such as drastic penalties for failing to live up to a prior commitment. (p. 74)

Janis and Mann do not discuss what happens when a deadline is distant rather than imminent. Is there, for example, an optimal amount of time which, if exceeded, would lead to reduced vigilance and poorer decision making? Janis and Mann imply that optimal decision making requires a certain amount of arousal. It seems reasonable that if a deadline were distant, the level of arousal necessary for vigilant information search and evaluation either would not be high enough initially to stimulate vigilance or would subside after an initial period of arousal, thereby reducing the quality of the decision-making process. Janis and Mann originally applied their model to emergency situations and later extended it to all decisions of consequence. Given the origins of their model, it is understandable how Janis and Mann would focus on the question of whether there is *enough* time to make a good decision. It would be interesting, however, to look at the question "Can there be *too much* time?"

Decreased imminence, that is, increased periods of time before an event, can bring greater complexity to appraisal processes, for, as we shall see, while longer time intervals before an event can sometimes lead to heightened threat, they can also lead to reduced threat.

Studies by Breznitz (1967, 1971) and Nomikos et al. (1968) shed light on how longer time intervals can lead to increased threat. Breznitz (1967) uses the concept "incubation of threat" to explain this phenomenon. He observed that when subjects were threatened with a severe electric shock at the end of 3, 6, and 12 minutes, the longer the interval, the faster was the heart rate immediately preceding the shock. Breznitz (1971) states that the degree of threat is not caused *directly* by the length of anticipaton time, but rather by the person's process of involvement, which incubates with time.

Breznitz (1971) has reported a study confirming the idea of incubation of threat, using a projective method in which subjects were asked to put themselves in another's place and guess that person's thoughts. Subjects were presented with a problem in which a person is waiting for another person to come. The other person, who is late, is very close to the one who is waiting. They were given a list of 14 possible thoughts that included four categories of response: the other will come soon; the other can't come; the other doesn't want to come; and aggression toward the other. The task was to guess which of the thoughts were more appropriate and write them down in the order that they entered the subject's mind. To prove that the incubation of threat had occurred, it was necessary that the more negative items should appear after the less negative items, in other words, "as the process of involvement goes on, subjects should advance along the various dimensions to more pessimistic thoughts" (p. 276). The findings on all four dimensions supported the idea of incubation of threat. "As the process of worrying develops in time, the subjects become more and more involved in the task, and choose items with intensively more negative implications" (p. 276).

An increase in threat as a function of anticipation time was also found in a laboratory experiment by Nomikos et al. (1968) that investigated psychophysiological reactions to a film-induced threat. The film depicted three wood-mill accidents, one in which the fingers of an operator are lacerated, a second where a finger is cut off, and a third in which an innocent bystander is killed when a flying board drives through his midsection. The viewer is led to anticipate the last two accidents through the techniques of flashback and suspense.

Two versions of the film were produced by editing the scenes that lead to one of the three filmed accidents. In the longer anticipation version, called "suspense," subjects were given about 20 and 26 seconds to wait for the accidents; in the shorter anticipation version, called "surprise," the periods of waiting were cut to about 4 and 7 seconds. Two major findings were obtained by comparing the stress effects of the two versions. First, the degree of stress response (heart rate and skin conductance increases) was far greater under suspense than surprise. Second, virtually all of the psychophysiological impact of the film was confined to the anticipatory period; the response was already in decline when the viewers were watching the actual mutilation and the horror on the faces of the victims and onlookers.

Although the above experiments indicate that time heightens threat, with an increasing amount of time there is also greater opportunity for the person to "think through" or reappraise the situation and bring to bear a variety of coping mechanisms by which the threat can be reduced or mastered. In such cases, a greater amount of anticipation time is associated with *lesser* rather than greater stress reactions. For example, the study by Nomikos et al. (1968) dealt with very brief anticipatory intervals, less than half a minute, giving little opportunity for the subject to mobilize his coping resources. Perhaps the positive relationship between anticipation time and stress reaction would be reversed if the time intervals were longer.

This possibility was examined by Folkins (1970), who made different groups of subjects await an electric shock for varying periods of time: 5 seconds, 30 seconds, 1 minute, 3 minutes, 5 minutes, or 20 minutes. It was found that although the objective harm (electric shock) was constant, there were marked differences in the autonomic and subjective levels of disturbance associated with the anticipatory intervals. As might be expected from the previously cited study by Nomikos et al. (1968), the level of stress reaction rose from a brief 5-second wait to a 30-second wait, reaching a maximum in the group that waited 1 minute for the shock. However, stress reaction fell sharply in groups waiting 3 and 5 minutes, and rose again slightly at 20 minutes.

Folkins interpreted these findings to mean that with only 5 seconds there was little opportunity for subjects to fully comprehend the nature of the impending harm; hence the level of stress was minimal. With slightly longer anticipation periods (30 seconds to 1 minute), there was enough time for subjects to grasp the significance of the threat, but not enough time to generate effective coping strategies. Ego-failure and panic-like reactions were the result. With 3 to 5 minutes to appraise the situation, subjects were better able to develop self-assuring coping responses, and hence displayed less stress. Reports by the subjects about their thoughts tended to confirm this. But what about the 20-minute interval, which was characterized by another rise in arousal? Perhaps there was increasing discomfort in being seated and confined with nothing to do for so long; alternatively, the long wait may have served as an ominous cue that something important, perhaps painful, was going to happen, in which case reassuring cognitions may ultimately have been rejected.

Rakover and Levita (1973) examined the relationship between anticipation time and arousal using rewarding tasks rather than aversive stimuli. They found a linear relationship between anticipation time and heart rate. Rakover and Levita's findings raise an interesting point regarding challenge and threat appraisals. By setting up a task for which subjects would be rewarded rather than punished, perhaps they created a *challenging* situation. Earlier (Chapter 2) we defined challenge as a stressful appraisal in which an opportunity for mastery or gain dominates, but with some sense of risk too. If, however, the threat associated with the risk is minimal, the person will have little reason to employ defensive strategies to regulate emotional and cognitive activity, a point made by Rakover and Levita. We suggest that the resulting linear relationship between time and arousal represents a physiological manifestation of a vigilant coping pattern that occurs in *challenge* appraisals. Threat appraisals, on the other hand, elicit more coping complexity—e.g., both avoidant and vigilant strategies—as shown in the curvilinear relationship between time and arousal that was found by Breznitz and Folkins. In other words, *challenge and threat appraisals have their own distinct patterns of coping*, but these patterns can be observed only when an event is distant enough in time to allow appraisal–coping–reappraisal processes to take place and when efforts are made to look at changes across time.

Mechanic's (1962) study of students preparing for doctoral examinations provides a real-life illustration of the cognitive complexity that can occur in appraisal processes when there is a relatively long interval during which an event is anticipated. As in the laboratory studies cited above, there is a curvilinear threat arousal pattern as the event grows more imminent. Students felt the first wave of anxiety during their first year, while observing second-year students prepare for qualifying examinations. The anxiety was largely due to "examination socialization," a function of the extent to which the stress experienced by the group taking examinations was visible to the younger students, and of communications from the faculty that referred to the examinations and legitimized their importance. After the initial exposure to the examination situation, however, the demands of other work made the examinations less salient for the students, and their anxiety abated. Mechanic began interviewing the students three months before their own exams, when the situation was again salient. He reports that anxiety was high and both vigilant and palliative coping strategies were evident. During the three months before their examinations

> . . . joking increased, and, while students still sought social support and talked a great deal about examinations, they began specifically to avoid certain people who aroused their anxiety. Stomach-aches, asthma, and a general feeling of weariness became common complaints, and other psychosomatic symptoms appeared. The use of tranquilizers and sleeping pills became more frequent. (p. 142)

About a month before the examinations, coping patterns that minimized the significance of the event became prominent, and there were fewer comments about physical stress response symptoms, which suggests a decrease in arousal.

Finally, the weekend before the examinations, arousal increased:

> . . . severe psychosomatic symptoms seemed to appear. A few students actually became sick, probably attributable in part to the increased vulnerability resulting from the physical and mental exhaustion that had accompanied study and from keeping late hours. Many students reported having stomach-aches, anxiety attacks, increased problems with asthma, and some rashes and allergies. Appetite and eating patterns also seemed affected, and a number of students reported difficulty in sleeping. (p. 162)

The morning of the examination:

> . . . most students reported stomach pains; a number reported diarrhea; and a few reported that they had been unable to hold their

breakfast. As one student said: "I was real scared, I never was so scared in my life. . . . I felt that I was going to fall apart." Most students reported considerable relief of anxiety once they got started on the first examination. . . . One student explained: *"Taking it is not as bad as anticipating it. It's not nearly so bad. . . . You don't have time to worry while you are doing it."* (pp. 162–163, italics ours)

Numerous coping strategies were used by students to regulate their emotions during the periods prior to the examinations, including seeking sócial support, avoiding people who aroused their anxiety, taking drugs, using reassuring self-statements, and lowering levels of aspiration, among others. Yet as the examinations approached, the palliative effects of these strategies wore off and there were psychological and somatic indications of heightened arousal. This rise in level of threat appeared universal among the students.

In short, the longer the anticipation time, the more potential there is for complexity in appraisal because of mediating coping processes. Given time, people can reflect, suffer, or grieve; they can also avoid the problem, think about it, take action, or make efforts to gain self-control. Each of these intervening coping processes will affect subsequent appraisals and their accompanying emotions. ·

By implication, the coping processes that are involved in any stressful encounter that is anticipated may be described in stages, involving different types of coping as the encounter progresses. The concept of stages of coping is employed by Horowitz (1982), Klinger (1977), Kübler-Ross (1969), Main (1977), Shontz (1975), and Wortman and Brehm (1975). We shall examine this concept more closely in our discussions of coping in Chapter 6.

Duration

Duration refers to how long a stressful event persists. It is closely related to imminence, differing in that imminence refers to the period *before* an event occurs, and duration to the period *during* which the event is occurring.

Duration is widely considered a major factor in disease and psychopathology, the assumption being that enduring or chronic stressors wear the person down psychologically and physically. Selye (e.g., 1950, 1956) has provided strong impetus for this line of thought with the development of his concept of the General Adaptation Syndrome.

Briefly, the General Adaptation Syndrome (GAS) refers to three stages of stress response: the initial alarm reaction, the stage of resistance, and exhaustion. The alarm reaction has two subordinate portions, the first of which, the "shock phase," represents the initial and immediate effect of the noxious agent on tissues. This is characterized, for example, by the reduction of body temperature and the lowering of blood pressure. The second portion of the alarm reaction is the "countershock phase," which appears to represent active defensive efforts on the part of the physiological system. It is reflected in an enlargement of the adrenal cortex and an increase in adrenal cortical secretions and produces a rise in blood pressure and often in body temperature. The stage of resistance follows. This is characterized primarily by an increased resistance to the stressor agent and a decreased resistance to other stimuli. This stage, more concretely, is identified by a triad of reactions: adrenal enlargement, shrinkage of the thymus gland and its associated reduction of lymphocytes, and gastrointestinal ulceration. Thus, adaptation to one agent appears to occur at the expense of resistance to other agents. Finally, following long exposure to severe stress, exhaustion occurs, and many of the symptoms of the alarm reaction reappear. The final phase produces what Selye calls "diseases of adaptation," such as anaphylactic shock and arthritis, and can be followed eventually by death.

Chronic stressors do not inevitably lead to Selye's exhaustion stage. The notion that we get used to chronic, repeated stressors has long been expressed in the concept of *habituation*, which refers to the lessening of behavioral or physiological stress response (or arousal) that occurs with repetition. The concept has been investigated more throughly in animals than in humans, but two of the issues raised in animal research are relevant.

One issue is whether the lessening of arousal is due to becoming used to the enduring source of stress or becoming worn down by it. In a series of shocks over 72 hours that had to be avoided, rhesus monkeys in a study by Hennessy and Levine (1979) showed a more substantial cortisol response—a product of adrenal cortex secretion—during the first or second series than later; by the time the monkeys experienced the third or fourth 72-hour series, there was no longer any cortisol elevation compared with baseline. They had evidently habituated to the chronic stressor. Similarly, Pollard, Basset, & Cairnscross (1976) found that corticosteroid, corticosterone, and pituitary changes in rats habituated after 20 days of exposure to prolonged stress. In reviewing some of this work with hormonal measures, however, Rose (1980) does not interpret this finding as evidence of habituation but rather as the "stage of exhaustion" of the General Adaptation Syndrome after prolonged exposure to stress and prolonged resistance.

Another issue has to do with the processes involved in habituation. For example, in his treatment of the arousal features initially generated by a novel stimulus, Sokolov (1963) spoke of the "orienting reaction," which involves a complex autonomic response (see Zimney & Keinstra, 1967, for a review). As the animal becomes habituated to the stimulus, it shows progressive reduction or cessation of this orienting reaction. To speak this way about habituation involves minimal theorizing about the nature of the processes involved.

It will come as no surprise that we conceptualize the process of habituation, even in animals, as a cognitive process in which information about the environment is evaluated. In the orienting reaction, for example, the dog lifts its ears, turns its head toward the stimulus, sniffs, and awaits information about what the stimulus means. This has been described as the "What is it?" reaction. Habituation to the stimulus then would mean that the animal concluded there is no need to pay attention, since nothing of adaptational relevance is being signaled. Mere repetition of the stimulus without anything of note happening reinforces the habituation. In short, it is the discovery, based on information or interpretation, that there is no adaptational significance to a stimulus (Harris, 1943; also Galbrecht, Dykman, Reese, & Suzuki, 1965).

Emotional habituation in humans involves the same basic evaluative appraisal process found in the habituation of the orienting reaction in animals. In humans, however, habituation can also result from coping, especially cognitive coping. The persistence of a chronic stressor can give the person the opportunity to learn to deal with its demands, or to deal with it by avoidance or distancing. New skills can be developed, commitments reordered, old goals abandoned, and new ones created (see also Schönpflug, 1983). The damaging effects of a chronic stressor can thus be mediated through coping and reappraisal, but these processes take time (see Stokols, 1977; Altman & Wohlwill, 1977). The initial degree of threat and its pattern over time in chronic persistent events will of course be determined in large part by the nature of the stressor. What is important to remember is that the appraisal of a chronic persistent event is not static; threat will fluctuate over the course of an event as a function of coping and reappraisal processes and as a function of changes in the environment.

In addition to chronic persistent events, there are also *chronic intermittent* events such as conflicts with in-laws, financial problems, or the weather, and *acute time-limited* events such as a parachute jump, an exam, or minor surgery. Each of these patterns of duration has different implications with respect to appraisal (cf. Cohen et al., 1982).

Presumably, a chronic intermittent pattern gives the individual time off to the extent that the event is put out of mind between occasions. A chronic persistent pattern, on the other hand, does not easily allow time off, and we would expect a more persistent level of threat, at least until coping and reappraisal processes intervene.

Another pattern is the kind of stress sequence occasioned by divorce, bereavement, parenthood, or a rigorous academic program. In these instances, the individual can anticipate a series of stressful situations that will endure for some time. Some people might not look too far ahead, and will deal with each set of problems only as they arise. In this case, the sequence is like a series of events, each more or less threatening depending on the stakes involved and the resources available for managing its demands. Others might see the sequence as one long event with different facets. This pattern might have effects more like a chronic persistent condition.

With the exception of studies about negative effects of chronic persistent stressors, there is virtually no research on duration as an antecedent variable in stress research. Given that duration is so important in disease and psychopathology, it is surprising that so little data are available as to its effects. We would like to see more systematic attention directed to this variable, in particular to assessing the effects of various patterns of duration on appraisal and coping processes.

Temporal Uncertainty

Temporal uncertainty refers to not knowing *when* an event is going to happen. A hurricane might be headed for your section of the Gulf Coast shoreline; the only question is when in the next 24 hours it will hit. A worker might be told a layoff is inevitable, but not when it will occur.

Very little research has been done on temporal uncertainty. One of the few studies that deals with this problem was carried out by Monat et al. (1972). This study is particularly interesting because it compared the relative stressfulness of temporal and event uncertainty.

Monat and his colleagues conducted two experiments with electric shock as the stressor. The first involved a between-subjects design in which each subject experienced only one of four possible conditions: time unknown with 100 percent event uncertainty, time known with 100 percent event uncertainty, time known with 50 percent event uncertainty, and time known with 50 percent event uncertainty but no shock. The second experiment employed a within-subjects design where each subject experienced four conditions: time unknown with 100 percent event certainty, time known with 100 percent event certainty, time known with 50 percent event uncertainty, and time known with 5 percent event certainty. Physiological arousal was assessed with heart rate, skin resistance level, galvanic skin response, and respiration. Self-reported affect was also recorded, and there were two measures of avoidant-like and vigilant coping. The second experiment also asked the subjects to rank their preferences for the treatment conditions.

The results of the two experiments were similar. Overall, temporal uncertainty was associated with heightened arousal at the outset of the experiment, and then, as the experiment went on, with lowered arousal. In contrast, the time-known event certainty conditions were associated with lowered arousal at the outset and heightened arousal at the conclusion. The conditions were also different with respect to coping. In both experiments, temporal uncertainty was associated with greater vigilance at the outset and more avoidant-like coping at the end, whereas when time was known, regardless of event uncertainty, the opposite pattern emerged. The authors made a link between arousal and coping:

> The main findings of these experiments indicate that although temporal uncertainty conditions initially may be appraised as more threatening than time-locked conditions, they allow a pattern of coping (attention deployment), which, in turn, may lead to a lowering of arousal (and presumably stress response, to express it differently). More specifically, under conditions in which a person knows exactly when the aversive event is to occur, and regardless of how certain or uncertain he is about whether it will occur, his thoughts turn increasingly toward vigilant examination of the anticipated event as it grows imminent; and this increased vigilance is accompanied by an increase in arousal. In contrast, under conditions in which the person does not know when the event is to occur, that is, temporal uncertainty, the person's thoughts tend increasingly toward avoidant-like modes of coping, and these coping strategies in turn lead to progressively lowered levels of affective arousal. (Monat et al., 1972, p. 250)

One can, of course, question whether the lowered levels of arousal were due to avoidant coping strategies used to deal with the threat, or simply to a lack of concern with the threat. The fact that subjects ranked the time-unknown conditions as significantly less preferable than any of the time-known conditions argues that coping associated with temporal uncertainty was, in this instance, an indication of the heightened threat associated with not knowing when the shock would occur. Being uncertain as to when an aversive event is going to occur does not mean that one is going to be in a perpetual state of threat. Temporal uncertainty is stressful only when a threatening cue indicates that the event is going to happen, in other words, only in the presence of imminence. Then the important question is, *how* imminent?

Ambiguity

We have discussed numerous formal properties of situations that influence appraisal, including novelty, event uncertainty, and temporal factors such as imminence, duration, and temporal uncertainty. Information about each of these contributes to the person's evaluation of what is at stake, its significance for well-being, and what, if anything, can be done. Unfortunately, in most human encounters the information to make these evaluations is unclear and/or insufficient with respect to at least one, if not all, of these factors. Rarely does a person know exactly what is going to happen *and* the likelihood of its occurrence (event uncertainty) *and* when it will happen (temporal uncertainty) *and* how long it will last (duration). Nor can the person predict what other demands are likely to be encountered. When the information necessary for appraisal is unclear or insufficient, we say that the environmental configuration is ambiguous. We make a distinction between ambiguity (lack of situational clarity) and uncertainty (the person's confusion about the meaning of the environmental configuration). Information from the environment can be unambiguous and yet a person can experience uncertainty. Such uncertainty can arise, for example, from conflicting values, commitments, and goals, and/or simply from not knowing what to do. On the other hand, even when there is ambiguity in the environment, a person can feel confident about what to do. This can happen when a person arbitrarily resolves the ambiguity by choosing an interpretation and acting upon it, refusing to acknowledge or attend to the lack of clarity in the information provided.

*The Reciprocity Between
Ambiguity and Personality*

Ambiguity creates the condition of projective tests whereby the person infers meanings based on personal dispositions, beliefs, or experiences. The greater the ambiguity, the more influence person factors have in determining the meaning of the environmental configuration. The ubiquitous nature of ambiguity, especially in stressful encounters, is one reason it is so difficult to identify *independent* situation characteristics; *whenever there is ambiguity, person factors shape the understanding of the situation, thereby making the interpretation of the situation more a function of the person than of objective stimulus constraints.*

The well-established principle that personality dispositions play a more influential role under conditions of ambiguity than under conditions of clarity has been demonstrated anew by Archer (1979), who studied the interaction of trait anxiety and expectancy of control in a shock-avoidance experiment. He used three conditions, two clearly defined (unambiguous) as to the method and degree of control subjects could exercise over shock, and an ambiguous-avoidance condition which provided few cues to subjects regarding the nature of the shock-avoidance task. The dependent variable was the subject's expectancy of control.

Under clearly defined conditions—whether chance or complex control—there were no significant differences in expectancies between subjects who were high and low in trait anxiety. Both groups had a relatively low expectancy of control under chance control conditions and high expectancy under complex control conditions. However, there was a significant difference in the ambiguous conditions. Persons with low trait anxiety reported a significantly greater expectancy of avoiding shock (control) than those with high trait anxiety. In other words, the personality trait variable (trait anxiety) was found to be influential in the ambiguously structured situation, but not in conditions containing clear and explicit situational cues regarding reinforcement contingencies.

A study by Lazarus, Eriksen, and Fonda (1951) also demonstrated the increased influence of person factors under conditions of ambiguity. A series of recorded sentences, some emotionally threatening and some neutral, were played against a background of noise that made them difficult for the subjects to hear without effort; usually they could make out only about 50 percent of the material. Two groups of neurotic patients were selected, varying in symptoms and in their characteristic mode of coping with emotionally disturbing experiences. One group was composed of hysterical neurotics, who are said to cope by repressing or avoiding threatening material. The other group was composed of obsessive-compulsives, whose characteristic way of handling such material is by vigilance—that is, by being extremely alert to anything that might be threatening—and then dampening its sting through detachment. Both groups wrote down what they heard. Hysterics turned out to be more accurate in transcribing the neutral sentences than those that were emotionally threatening, in keeping with their presumed tendency to handle threat by avoidance. Obsessive-compulsive patients were more accurate in their transcriptions of the emotionally threatening sentences than the neutral ones, in keeping with their presumed hypervigilant and intellectualized way of responding to threat.

Inferences about the meaning of environmental information are also based in large part on knowledge gained from experience. Earlier we mentioned what Schank and Abelson (1977) refer to as general knowledge, which permits a person to interpret events even if they have not been experienced before. Specific knowledge, in contrast, is used to interpret events that have been experienced often. Obviously, the amount of inference required is greater when there is little specific knowledge available.

Knowing a person's experiences, however, does not mean that we can predict the types of inferences a person will make. Even when people have had similar experiences, there are many ways that internal processes can influence the meaning of those experiences in memory, the information that is retrieved from memory, and how that information is utilized in making inferences or predictions. For example, a threatening or harmful experience can be diminished in memory through defensive processes that minimize or repress its disturbing aspects. This is a form of defensive reappraisal. On the other hand, the memory can become strengthened over time, as when a fuller understanding of what happened is admitted into awareness and with it comes an increased sense of threat and/or harm (see Horowitz, 1976). In either case, mediating internal processes regulate the information from experience that is available for inference.

The Dual Nature of Ambiguity

As in the case of event and temporal uncertainty, ambiguity can itself be a source of threat. In animals, high levels of excitation and disorganization can be generated in classical conditioning situations by presenting difficult discriminations and by disconfirming strongly established expectancies (e.g., Badia, McBane, Suter, & Lewis, 1966; Badia, Suter, & Lewis, 1967; Epstein & Clarke, 1970; Knapp, Kause, & Perkins, 1959). Indeed, "experimental neurosis" is a common phenomenon in laboratory animals (e.g., Lidell, 1964; Masserman, 1943).

In humans, ambiguity can intensify threat by limiting the individual's sense of control and/or increasing a sense of helplessness over the danger. Anxiety, for example, one of a number of threat emotions, is often associated with uncertainty about the nature of a threat, whether it will happen and when, and what might be done about it (Lazarus & Averill, 1972; May, 1950; Seligman, 1975).

Ambiguity, however, does not always result in threat (e.g., anxiety) in humans and in fact will do so only if the disposition exists to be threatened (e.g., if the person has a low tolerance for ambiguity [cf. Frenkel-Brunswik, 1949] or if there is some other cue present which leads the individual to anticipate harm). This was recognized by Lazarus (1966), and more recently by Kreitler and Kreitler (1976), who wrote:

> Normally fear and anxiety do not stem from the mere existence of open alternatives but from what some of these alternatives imply . . . as is well known to every dinner guest who is uncertain about the dessert, expecting either his beloved strawberry shortcake or his adored peach melba. . . . This is evident when one considers, for instance, the following pair of alternatives: "either dessert will be served or burglars will interrupt the dinner party." Conversely, even very precise information does not necessarily—through its precision and adequacy—stabilize the system and reduce fear and anxiety, as is psychologically evident from the information "Tomorrow you will be executed." This demonstrates that the core concepts of information theory, namely, the number of alternatives, their respective probabilities, and their eventual reduction to bits of information, have far less psychological relevance than their actual meanings. (pp. 16–17)

Even in situations where there are cues signaling harm or danger, ambiguity can be used to reduce threat by allowing alternative—perhaps reassuring—interpretations of the meaning of the situation. The dual nature of ambiguity is recognized in political situations where it is sometimes judged useful to perpetuate ambiguity in order to temporize and let emotions cool down. Weisman of the *New York Times* reflects on this in an analysis of the crisis caused by Iranian students holding Americans hostage during the fall of 1979:

> Some officials noted that the coverage of the Iranian crisis reflected a classic difference in perspective between government and journalism. State Department aides are interested in keeping Iran's positions ambiguous or fluid, so that either they or other diplomats could negotiate. Journalists, on the other hand, tend to ask questions with the aim of eliminating ambiguity.
>
> Several times recently, for example, journalists asked the Iranians on television whether executions of the hostages was possible. The question made State Department officials cringe. (*San Francisco Chronicle,* December 12, 1979, p. 16, "Iran Siege Puts TV in the News")

At the conclusion of the 14-month ordeal, an editorial in the *New York Times* pointed out how the Reagan administration felt free to "drown the affair in ambiguity":

> Ambiguity surrounded the consequences Iran might suffer. Mr. Reagan could accept Jimmy Carter's deal with Iran but also leave room for legal maneuver. He could promise future terrorists "swift and effective retribution" but let his Secretary of State point out that "retaliatory action is sometimes not only constrained but uncertain." (February 1, 1981, p. 22EY, "Through the Night, with the Light")

Sometimes people even seek ambiguity rather than clarity, a theme that was studied by Gibbons and Wright (1981). They exposed high and low sex guilt male and female subjects to erotic materials so that the subjects were either sexually aroused or led to believe they were sexually aroused. In addition to viewing the erotic stimuli, subjects were provided with an alternative bogus source to which they could attribute their arousal. High-guilt subjects attributed their arousal to the bogus source more than low-guilt subjects, thereby creating ambiguity as to the actual nature and cause of their arousal. Gibbons and Wright interpreted attributions to the bogus source as a defensive process; for high-guilt subjects it was less threatening not to be clear about the cause of their arousal. These findings fit with our assertion that ambiguity is not always more threatenting than clarity, and that the latter can sometimes be psychologically more aversive.

In sum, ambiguity is present in one form or another in practically every type of human encounter and ensures that person factors will play an important role in creating individual variations in the appraisal of what is happening. In many instances ambiguity can be threatening, and the individual will seek to reduce it by searching for more information, or with inferential processes or arbitrary judgments. On the other hand, there are times when ambiguity appears advantageous, as when it permits the maintenance of hope or prevents premature closure.

The Timing of Stressful Events in Relation to the Life Cycle

A stressful event does not occur in a vacuum, but in the context of the individual's life cycle and in relation to other events, be they distant, recent, or concurrent (see Hultsch & Plemons, 1979). These specific contextual properties define an event's *timing*. The timing of an event sheds light on puzzling questions as to why events that most people presumably welcome, such as a promotion, marriage, and grandparenthood, or events usually considered merely bothersome, such as receiving a parking ticket, waiting an hour in a dentist's office, and having a flat tire, can take on great significance; or, conversely, why normally distressing events do not take on major significance.

Neugarten has written thoughtfully and extensively about this aspect of timing (e.g., Neugarten, 1968a, 1970, 1977, 1979; Neugarten, Moore, & Lowe, 1968). She points out that people have a concept of the normal life cycle which includes expectations that certain events will occur at certain times. They readily report their timetable for finishing school, marrying, having a child, starting a job, advancing in the job, becoming a grandparent, and retiring. She states that people have a mental clock telling them whether they are "on time" or "off time" in the life cycle. From this point of view, she argues that many normal and expectable life events are not themselves life crises. Whether or not such events produce crises depends on their timing. "For instance, for the majority of middle-aged women the departure of children is not a crisis. It is, instead, when children do *not* leave home on time that a crisis is created for both parent and child" (1979, p. 889).

Blau (1973), for example, found that young widows are more stressed than older ones, and Bourque and Back (1977) report that the departure of children and retirement are perceived as more disruptive if they occur off time than on time. Lowenthal, Thurnher, and Chiriboga (1975) found also the absence of an expectable event—a "nonevent"—a source of stress in occupational, family, and parental contexts (see also Stewart, Sokol, Healy, Chester, & Weinstock-Savoy, 1982). These findings point up the importance of eliciting information about expectable events that do not occur as well as events that do occur in assessing sources of stress.

What makes an event that is off time more threatening? *Having an event happen too early or too late can mean that one is deprived of the support of compatible peers.* Consider a woman whose first child is born when she is 38. The new mothers with whom she might hope to share information about child care, from whom she might seek emotional support regarding the demands of a new baby, or with whom she might like to spend time while walking the baby in the park are likely to be 15 years younger than she. How comfortable will she feel with them and they with her?

Being off time can mean that one is deprived of a full sense of pride and satisfaction that would accompany an event had it been on time. What is the meaning of a promotion that has been wanted for 10 years when it is given the year before retirement? Does it indicate significant accomplishment, or does it feel like an empty gesture on the part of management to recognize many years of service? During the period when the event has not yet occurred the person might feel deprived of a "union card" in his or her peer group. For those who are waiting for the promotion, its absence sets them apart from those who are moving ahead.

Having an event occur too early can deprive a person of the chance to prepare for a new role. Consider the young adult who suddenly has to take over the family business, the young widow who is faced with supporting a family and finding her way in a society where most of her friends are couples, or a dancer whose injury prematurely terminates a career. These events might have been faced with relative equanimity or at least only moderate distress had they occurred at age-appropriate times. In these cases, people find themselves inadequately prepared, and the event is therefore more threatening.

Timetables for expectable events differ from generation to generation, and from group to group within generations (cf. Elder, 1980). Increased longevity, added years of education, fewer children per family, and the increased cost of housing are among some of the obvious factors that have changed timetables over the last 50 years. For example, as a result of added years of education, today's young adults expect to begin full-time work later than people did 50 years ago. Differences within generations are a function of many factors, although the most prominent one seems to be social status (cf. Elder, 1974; Neugarten, 1977; Neugarten et al., 1968). For instance, Neugarten found that the upper-middle-class business executive is likely to consider a man at the "prime of his life" at age

40, middle-aged at 50, and not old until 70, whereas the unskilled worker views a man as middle-aged by 40 and old by 60. Also, upper-middle-class men view the period of young adulthood—up to about age 30—as a period of exploration, of finding one's way in marriage and job or careers, whereas working-class men view this as a period to get settled and take on the responsibilities of job, marriage, and children.

The events we have been discussing are limited to life experiences that are largely age-related, socially recognized, well labeled, and normative. Such events comprise but a few of the many that are likely to happen during the course of living. As Brim and Ryff (1980), Pearlin and Lieberman (1979), Lazarus and Cohen (1977), and others point out, there are numerous events not related to normative life transitions that must also be considered. These include work disabilities, loss of reputation, the sudden rise and fall of fortunes, chronic unremitting stressors in the work place, and natural disasters. It is important to examine these events in relation to relevant life cycle dimensions. A freezing winter will affect an elderly couple more severely than a middle-aged couple. A failed examination will be more serious for a graduating senior than for a junior. The death of a father will have a different impact on a 5-year-old than on a 13-year-old.

In a study on the effects of the Great Depression, Elder (1974) found that younger middle-class males were placed at greater risk of impaired life changes and development than older counterparts; the younger men were just beginning their careers, whereas the older men were more established. In contrast, lower-class males fared better in the long run if they were younger rather than older at the time of the Depression.

Brim and Ryff (1980) urge us to consider yet another category of events—*hidden events*. These are nameless experiences, events for which no concept has been invented. As an example, Brim and Ryff note that advances through the working career are not as well marked as are transitions through the family career. They point out that it has only been in the past decade that the event of reaching the top of one's achievement, or "plateauing," in a career has received any serious attention, and it still does not have any well-accepted name equivalent to, say, marriage or widowhood. Another hidden event is associated with male hormonal changes during adulthood, which is presently called by analogy "the male menopause."

Brim and Ryff suggest several criteria for classifying hidden events, for example, whether they are age-correlated or not, likely to be experienced by many or few, and socially deviant or acceptable. Incidentally, with the exception of the last criterion, these properties are used by Brim and Ryff to classify, not only hidden events, but all events. Their scheme is interesting and deserves attention by those interested in life events and life span research.

Another aspect of timing is the relationship between a major stressful event and other events that have occurred. The Holmes-Rahe Schedule of Recent Experience, perhaps the best known measure of stress, evaluates stress in terms of the cumulated life events that have happened to a person within a specified time. Events are weighted according to the amount of social readjustment they require. The respondent checks off those events that occurred during the specified period and a stress score is calculated by summing the weights of the events (cf. Holmes & Masuda, 1974; Holmes & Rahe, 1967).

Aside from major problems having to do with ignoring the valence or the meaning of the event to the individual (see Chapter 10), simple additive models such as the Schedule of Recent Experience do not do justice to the impact of timing. In their study of depression among women, for example, Brown and Harris (1978) found that the stressfulness of an event varied according to its relationship to other proximal events. If a woman had separated from her husband, the birth of a child some months later was rated as severely threatening. Had there been no separation, the birth would not have been rated as severe. Their findings indicate that for "related" events, as in the case of the separation and birth, only one event is important in producing depression. In other words, related events do not sum, which is understandable, since Brown and Harris's measurement approach builds in the meaning of the event in terms of its impact on other events. Unrelated events do appear to sum to a limited degree. However, Brown and Harris believe that "mechanically" adding events is unlikely to have much relevance to the outcome of concern to them—depression. They postulate three other ways in which events might sum, each of which takes the meaning of an event into account.

The first way involves summing distress by means of a *general appraisal:*

"Oh God, yet another thing" is the final cause of the breakdown. Here we have in mind a series of quite distinct events—learning a son has been diagnosed dyslexic, a friend moving away, and a husband losing his job—although such a response might also occur in response to events forming part of a series—a husband's second heart attack. It is as though the proverbial camel's back would not break unless he realized that the load was too heavy. (Brown & Harris, 1978, p. 110)

Similarly, we would suggest that the occurrence of a major, pervasive, and intrusive stress experience might increase the capacity of other stressful experiences to generate distress. Thus, when lovers fall out, many other problems (e.g., work responsibilities, bad economic or political news) might all gain in their power to cause psychological disturbance.

The second way events might sum involves an appraisal of the specific implications of an event that add weight. The example of the baby's birth given above illustrates this form of appraisal. The event is severe because of its implications for a woman living alone.

The third possibility is similar to the second in that it considers links between events, but the links are no longer direct and obvious. Brown and Harris offer the following as an example:

One of the patients developed a severe depression a few weeks after the birth of her first child. Several weeks earlier her father had died. His death was in no way part of the context of the birth in the sense we have used this concept—he, for instance, was not supporting her financially. But, for the woman, his death appeared to have been an ever-present part of the significance of having her first child; she could not stop thinking of how she had looked forward to him seeing his first grandchild and now he could not see it. It is possible that without the birth she might have weathered the death without a breakdown and that the poignancy of the combination of the two was crucial. (p. 110)

We would like to add another illustration to this last category in which the links between events are not necessarily obvious. When people are confronted with a series of events, even minor ones, they can begin to question their general competence or luck. "Am I having these mishaps because I'm inept? Am I unable to manage my life well, ineffective in managing problems? Are my social skills such that I create problems for myself?" Others might ask, "Am I unlucky? Am I destined to be touched by fate in an unfavorable way?" If the answers to these questions are yes, each additional event can take on added significance in that it is used to confirm the proposition. Then a flat tire is not simply a nuisance; it is an indicator of ineptness or bad luck.

Brown and Harris have melded situation and person characteristics in their three additive models. Their proposals for summing events require that the *meaning* of the event be considered in the context of the person's overall functioning, and in relation to what else is going on in the person's life. This approach is very different from mechanically adding normatively weighted events.

There is no question that methods such as those suggested by Brown and Harris pose difficult methodological problems. For example, if events are related, are we in fact speaking about just one event? What are the boundaries for the context of an event? Are they defined by time, other events, by the person, or by the researchers? Despite these problems, we believe that the method suggested by Brown and Harris has great potential for uncovering some of the mechanisms through which *timing* adds to distress.

We would like to give some attention to another side of this issue—when it is that recent or concurrent events might not add to distress. If two important goals are thwarted in close order, we would ordinarily assume that the person would feel an enormous drain on his or her resources. Consider a man whose wife is hospitalized with a life-threatening illness at the same time a crisis occurs in his business. Under such circumstances, however, rather than dealing with both sets of demands and concerns, one event might be put aside, at least temporarily. The husband might well decide that his wife's recovery is of such overriding importance that nothing else matters, and his business crisis recedes in significance. Thus, the second event does not add in the expected way to his level of distress.

Moreover, many people dealing with crises seem to tap previously unrealized resources and cope heroically with enormous physical and psychological demands. Anecdotal accounts of the ways people cope with natural disasters, disability, bereavement, and illness attest to this phenomenon. Under conditions of increased resources, will the person feel as threatened or harmed? Indeed, might he or she not experience some positive emotions associated with the awareness of effectively managing the self, the environment, or both? It is thus possible that under the taxing condition of two or more difficult events going on at the same time, the events might not have an additive effect and in fact might in some subtle ways combine to reduce distress. These possibilities need to be examined empirically.

It seems almost self-evident that the timing of events, in relation both to the life cycle and to other events, affects their appraisal. Nevertheless, this topic has received little systematic attention, perhaps because of issues surrounding the definition of events. Expectable life transitions are relatively easy to identify. Unexpected minor and major events, too, can be identified, although it is not always easy to learn when minor events might at first seem insignificant (e.g., waiting in the dentist's office). They take on significance only when they have special meaning to the person. Nonevents—expectable events that do *not* occur—must also be considered, as must Brim and Ryff's (1980) "hidden" events. Obviously, the question of how to define an event has implications for stress research that extend well beyond the issue of timing. The question of definition is, however, particularly relevant to timing, since without definitions, the investigation of timing cannot proceed.

A Comment on the Selection and Treatment of Variables

In these last two chapters we have selected a few of the many person and situation factors that we think have particular relevance to appraisal. We emphasized person factors that confer meaning on an event, and situation factors that have potential for creating threat. These variables were chosen because a case can be made for their importance in determining the significance of an encounter for the person's well-being.

The person and situation factors were all treated as interdependent components of a dynamic person–situation relationship. They can be considered antecedents of appraisal, but only in terms of their meaning with respect to the balance between demands and resources within the person, within the environment, and between the person and the environment. If person and situation factors are considered independently, they lose much of their usefulness as predictors of appraisal.

Further, these factors must always be considered in combinations. Only in the laboratory, and rarely even there, can a single variable be manipulated while holding all the others constant. In real life, commitments and beliefs intermingle to shape the person component of the transaction; and the nature of the event, its certainty, its temporal properties, its ambiguity, and its timing all affect how the environment will enter into the transaction. Thus, *processes within the person and within the environment combine to determine the relationship between the two.*

Finally, many if not all person and situation factors have the potential to both contribute to *and* diminish threat. These dual capacities were brought out in our discussions of commitments, beliefs, event uncertainty, temporal factors, ambiguity, and timing. It is extremely important to keep this characteristic in mind in any examination of person and situation antecedents of appraisal.

Summary

In this chapter formal properties of encounters that create the potential for threat, harm, or challenge were discussed. First, novelty, predictability, and event uncertainty were dealt with. A completely novel situation will result in an appraisal of threat only if some aspect of it has been previously connected with harm. Novelty encourages appraisal inferences based on related previous experience or on general knowledge. Predictability has been studied extensively in animals, and the findings indicate a preference for predictable stimuli. However, the animal model, which has most commonly been employed for this situation variable, is not adequate for understanding psychological stress in humans, partly because it is not concerned with individual differences in appraisal or coping. The analogous construct in human behavior is event uncertainty, which introduces the notion of probability. Laboratory research indicates that the relationship between uncertainty and arousal is complex, due perhaps to subjective biases in probability estimates. In real-life events, anecdotal observations suggest that maximum uncertainty is often extremely stressful; it can have an immobilizing effect on anticipatory coping processes and cause mental confusion.

Three temporal situational factors were considered: imminence, duration, and temporal uncertainty. Generally, the more imminent an event, the more urgent and intense the appraisal. The less imminent an event, the more complex the appraisal process becomes. Although the passage of time can heighten threat, it can also allow the person to manage threat through cognitive coping, in which case increased anticipation time can lead to the reduction of stress reactions. There is some evidence that the relationship between imminence and arousal is different for threat and challenge; threat elicits greater coping complexity than challenge.

Duration refers to the length of time during which an event is occurring. Much of the research on duration has been influenced by Selye's concept of the General Adaptation Syndrome, which includes an alarm reaction, a stage of resistance, and exhaustion. Not all enduring stressors lead to exhaustion; animals, for example, often habituate, resulting in a diminished stress response. Emotional habituation occurs in humans, and it may arise through the same evaluative mechanisms as discerned in animals, and/or through coping.

Temporal uncertainty refers to not knowing when an event will occur. Little research has been done on this important temporal factor, but the existing evidence suggests that temporal uncertainty generates coping activity that reduces stress reactions.

Ambiguity is characteristic of many if not most real-life encounters. The greater the ambiguity, the more person factors shape the meaning of the situation. Ambiguity can intensify threat if the disposition exists to be threatened or if there is some other cue present that indicates potential harm. Ambiguity can also reduce threat by allowing alternative interpretations of the significance of an encounter.

The timing of stressful events over the life cycle can also affect appraisal. Neugarten has pointed out that many normal life events are stressful crises only if they occur "off time." Off time events are more threatening because they are not expected and therefore deprive the person of the support of compatible peers, a full sense of satisfaction that would accompany an event had it been on time, or the opportunity to prepare or engage in anticipatory coping. Hidden stressful events, which mainly comprise experiences for which concepts are lacking (e.g., male menopause) or are suppressed in thought, are also relevant to a life cycle view of stress and coping. The timing of events in relation to other events was also considered; the effects of a given event may be heightened or even suppressed if it occurs in juxtaposition to other events, resulting in its having different personal significance.

Finally, one must remember that situation and person factors are always interdependent, and their significance for stress and coping derives from the operation of cognitive processes that give weight to one in the context of the other.

5

The Concept
of Coping

The concept of coping has been important in psychology for well over 40 years. It provided an organizing theme in clinical description and evaluation in the 1940s and 1950s and is currently the focus of an array of psychotherapies and educational programs which have as their goal the development of coping skills. The subject of coping has also received widespread lay attention, as can be seen by scanning any magazine rack, best-seller list, or broadcast schedule. Indeed, coping is as much a colloquial term as a scientific one. Despite the rich history and current popularity associated with coping, however, there is little coherence in theory, research, and understanding. Even the most cursory inspection of readings selected from scholarly and lay publications reveals confusion as to what is meant by coping and how it functions in the process of adaptation.

Traditional Approaches

The concept of coping is found in two very different theoretical/research literatures, one derived from the tradition of animal experimentation, the other from psychoanalytic ego psychology. We have already discussed some of the research based on the animal model of stress and control. This approach is heavily influenced by

Darwinian thought, according to which survival hinges on the animal discovering what is predictable and controllable in the environment in order to avoid, escape, or overcome noxious agents. The animal is dependent on its nervous system to make the necessary survival-related discrimination.

Within the animal model, coping is frequently defined as acts that control aversive environmental conditions, thereby lowering psychophysiological disturbance. N. E. Miller (1980) says, for example, that coping consists of the learned behavioral responses that are successful in lowering arousal by neutralizing a dangerous or noxious condition. Similarly, Ursin (1980) states that "The gradual development of a response decrement in the animal experiments as well as the human experiments is coping. The animal is learning to cope through the lowering of drive tension by positive reinforcement" (p. 264).

Some of the most interesting research on the psychophysiology of coping and cardiovascular responses has been done by Obrist (1981) and his colleagues, in particular their work on the concept of active, as contrasted to passive, coping. This research suggests strongly that active coping is an important mediator of sympathetically controlled cardiovascular changes.

It will come as no surprise that overall we consider the animal model of coping simplistic and lacking in the cognitive-emotional richness and complexity that is an integral part of human functioning. The central theme of the animal model, for example, is the unidimensional concept of drive or arousal, and research centers largely on avoidance and escape behavior. With this emphasis little can be learned about strategies that are so important in human affairs, such as cognitive coping and defense.

In the psychoanalytic ego psychology model, coping is defined as realistic and flexible thoughts and acts that solve problems and thereby reduce stress. The main difference between the treatment of coping in this model compared to the animal model is the focus on ways of perceiving and thinking about the person's relationship with the environment. Although behavior is not ignored, it is treated as less important than cognition.

Another difference between the models is that the psychoanalytic ego psychology approach differentiates among a number of processes that people use to handle person–environment relationships. For example, Menninger (1963), Haan (1969, 1977), and Vaillant (1977) each offer a hierarchy in which coping refers to the highest and most advanced or mature ego processes, followed by defenses, which refer to neurotic modes of adaptation, also hierarchically arranged, and finally, at the bottom, processes that Haan calls fragmentation or ego-failure and Menninger refers to as regressive or psychotic levels of ego functioning.

Menninger, in one of the earliest formulations, identifies five orders of regulatory devices that are ranked according to the level of internal disorganization they indicate. At the top of this hierarchy are strategies for reducing tensions caused by stressful episodes in the course of ordinary living. These strategies are called coping devices, and include self-control, humor, crying, swearing, weeping, boasting, talking it out, thinking through, and working off energy. They are regarded as normal or, at worst, as idiosyncratic characteristics. If these strategies are used inappropriately or to an extreme, however, as when a person talks too much, laughs too easily, loses his or her temper frequently, or seems restless and erratic, they lose their status as coping devices and become symptoms indicating a degree of dyscontrol and threatened disequilibration. The greater the internal disorganization, the more primitive the regulatory devices become. For example, second-order devices include withdrawal by dissociation (narcolepsy, amnesia, depersonalization), withdrawal by displacement of aggression (e.g., aversion, prejudice, phobias, counterphobic attitudes), substitution of symbols and modalities for more frankly hostile discharge (e.g., compulsions, rituals), and substitution of the self or a part of the self as an object of displaced aggression (self-imposed restriction and abasement, self-intoxication or narcotization). Third-order devices are represented by episodic, explosive outbursts of aggressive energy, more or less disorganized, including assaultive violence, convulsions, and panic attacks. The fourth order represents increased disorganization, and the fifth order is total disintegration of the ego. In this system, coping devices are those that indicate minimal disruption and disorganization. Any device that indicates dyscontrol or disequilibration is by definition not a coping device.

Vaillant (1977) groups defenses in four levels progressing from psychotic mechanisms (e.g., denial of external reality, distortion, and delusional projection) through immature mechanisms (e.g., fantasy, projection, hypochondriasis, passive-aggressive behavior), neurotic mechanisms (e.g., intellectualization, repression, and reaction-formation), to the highest level, mature mechanisms (e.g., sublimation, altruism, suppression, anticipation, and humor).

Like Menninger (1963) and Vaillant (1977), Haan (1969, 1977) also uses a hierarchical system for classifying ego processes. She proposes a tripartite hierarchical arrangement—coping, defending, and fragmentation—and identifies the modes by the manner in which an underlying generic ego process is expressed. For example, the generic process, means-end symbolization, is expressed as logical analysis in coping, rationalization in defense, and confabulation in fragmentation. Sensitivity is expressed as empathy in coping, projection in defense, and delusion in fragmentation. The major criterion Haan uses to define processes in the coping mode is adherence to reality. If a person distorts "intersubjective" reality, he or she is not coping, ". . . [T]he person's accuracy is the hallmark of coping, whether or not he is actually situationally successful" (1977, p. 164). The underlying presumptive value is that:

> it is better to know one's intrasubjective and intersubjective situations accurately and to act in that framework, than it is to distort or negate one's appraisals and actions. The value is then one of accuracy in . . . interpersonal interchange, and to know that value is to match social and personal reality as it is defined by common, practical agreements about the nature of our mutual experiences.
>
> All the properties of coping . . . —choice of action, flexibility, and reality adherence—rest on the value of accuracy and can be deduced from it. (p. 80)

Coping Traits and Styles

The psychoanalytic ego psychology models that have dominated coping theory have also dominated coping measurement. The measurement purpose to which these models have been applied, however, has generally been limited to classifying people in order to make predictions about how they will cope with some or all types of stressful encounters. This application of the psychoanalytic ego psychology model results in viewing coping structurally as a style or trait rather than as a dynamic ego process. For example, a person may be classified as a conformist or conscientious, obsessive-compulsive, or as a suppressor, repressor, or sublimator (cf. Loevinger, 1976; Shapiro, 1965; Vaillant, 1977).

A coping style differs from a trait primarily in degree, and usually refers to broad, pervasive, encompassing ways of relating to particular types of people such as the powerful or the powerless, the friendly or the hostile, the controlling or the permissive, or to particular types of situations such as ambiguous or clear, imminent or distant, temporary or chronic, evaluative or nonevaluative. Traits, which are regarded as properties of persons that dispose them to react in certain ways in given classes of situations, are usually narrower in scope. Examples of traits that have been identified with coping include repression-sensitization (e.g., Krohne & Rogner, 1982; Shipley et al., 1978, 1979), "anger-in" and "anger-out" (e.g., Funkenstein, King, & Drolette, 1957; Harburg, Blakelock, & Roeper, 1979), coping-avoiding (e.g, Goldstein, 1959, 1973), or monitoring-blunting (e.g., S. Miller, 1980). (For a comprehensive review of trait measures, see Moos, 1974.)

Some of the richest descriptions of coping styles based on the ego psychology model can be found in case reports, as in the work of Vaillant (1977). Vaillant examined data on male college graduates that had been gathered over a 30-year period and then interviewed each subject. He put together his impressions with those of the investigators who had preceded him and evolved comprehensive descriptions of each subject. In addition, behaviors that occurred at time of crisis and conflict were interpreted by raters as to the defense mechanisms they suggested. Vaillant presents approximately half these subjects in case studies that are graphic and effective in conveying the styles with which these men managed their relationships with other people, troubling events, and the pursuit of commitments and goals. From these analyses he also distills what he calls the "adaptive style" that best characterizes the way these men manage their lives in general.

Unfortunately, descriptions of coping styles that are based on case analyses tend to be idiographic portraits rather than examples of common coping styles. As such, the utility of this approach is limited in that it does not facilitate interpersonal comparisons and group analysis. Furthermore, case studies used in research have the practical drawback of requiring enormous amounts of time and money for data gathering and analysis.

Type A as a Coping Style

The conceptualizations of coping style we described above grew out of the ego psychology tradition. The concept of the Type A pattern focuses more on behavior than ego processes and has an entirely different flavor.

We have already touched on the Type A phenomenon in Chapter 1 with a quote from Sir William Osler showing that the suspicion that certain life styles increase the risk of coronary heart disease goes back a long way in the history of medicine. This suspicion was supported empirically by the goundbreaking research of Friedman and Rosenman (1974), who define the Type A pattern as a "chronic, incessant struggle to achieve more and more in less and less time, and if required to do so, against the opposing efforts of other things or persons" (p. 67). We will not cover the enormous Type A literature. Given the interest in the relationship between Type A and health outcomes, however, we should at least consider briefly whether the Type A phenomenon could be regarded as a coping style.

The Type A pattern is a constellation of three interrelated concepts—a set of beliefs about oneself and the world; a set of values converging in a pattern of motivation or commitment (e.g., striving or job involvement); and a behavioral life style (e.g., time-urgent and competitive)—that operates in a wide variety of social contexts. Although writers and researchers have emphasized one or another of these concepts, they should be regarded as interdependent psychological facets of the same phenomenon.

Glass (1977a, b) has provided us with one of the most influential theories about the nature of Type A and how it works to increase cardiovascular risk. He characterizes Type A persons as having a strong commitment to control situations, which makes them particularly vulnerable to the loss or absence of control. When control is threatened or frustrated, Type A's are said to become highly emotional, perhaps alternating between excessive striving to strengthen control and despair over their lack of control. According to Glass, this leads to surges of catecholamine secretion, and possibly other psychophysiological changes relevant to cardiovascular functioning such as increased lipids or changes in blood clotting time. Efforts are being made to test this idea by manipulating task or stress conditions and examining psychophysiological reactions that could be implicated in immediate cardiovascular risk (as in sudden cardiac death) and risk over the long run (as in atherosclerosis). Other research gives some qualified support to this concept (e.g., Pittner, Houston, & Spiridigliozzi, 1983; Rhodewalt & Davison, 1983).

With respect to a motivational or commitment-centered interpretation, Type A persons compared with Type B's have been characterized as obtaining their rewards more from achievement and ambition than from socializing (Ditto, 1982; Jenkins, Zyzanski, Ryan, Flessas, & Tannenbaum, 1977). The research of Gastorf and Teevan (1980) and Gastorf, Suls, and Sanders (1980) diverges slightly in its emphasis by characterizing Type A's as having a fear-of-failure orientation. Alternatively, one could think of this concern with failure as a belief in one's own limitations or inadequacies, a vulnerable self-esteem, without greatly changing the meaning of the inferred differences in personality.

To researchers in behavioral medicine, an important issue is whether, to what extent, and by what psychophysiological mechanisms the psychological constellation of Type A influences somatic health and, more broadly, morale and social and work functioning. For example, the primary concern of a panel selected to examine Type A theory and research (see the report of the Review Panel on Coronary-prone Behavior and Cornary Heart Disease, 1981) was the psychophysiological mechanisms through which the Type A pattern influences health. These mechanisms are also the focus of research by Sherwitz et al. (1983), Kahn, Kornfeld, Frank, Heller, & Hoar, 1980; Kahn et al., 1982, Van Egeren, Frabrega, and Thornton (1983), Williams and his associates, who have emphasized hostility as a key factor (e.g., Williams et al., 1982; Williams et al., 1980), Krantz, Arabian, Davia, and Parker (1982), Jennings and Choi (1981), and McCranie, Simpson, and Stevens (1981), among others.

It is this influence on health that, after all, mobilizes interest in Type A, so much so that many writers have substituted the term "coronary prone behavior" for Type A. In our view this is a circular approach and helps to obscure a central feature of the psychophysiological issue, which is the nature of the psychological pattern that increases cardiovascular risk and the physiological changes that contribute to it. It should be noted too that since empirical research on Type A has focused mainly on cardiovascular disorder, we know little about whether and to what extent the same behavioral pattern might affect all-cause mortality, that is, diseases other than cardiovascular. "Coronary-prone behavior" may not, in effect, be unique in its impact on heart disease, but may represent a more general illness-disposing life style.

Psychometric issues are also of concern to researchers of Type A. It is not clear whether Type A is best regarded as a typology or a dimension from extreme Type A to extreme Type B. This general issue of typologies versus dimensions has been debated by personality assessment researchers (see exchange between Mendelsohn, [1979], who questions the value of typologies, and Block [1982], who defends them). Another psychometric issue concerns the best way to measure Type A. In an extensive review, Matthews (1982) identifies three types of measurements: the Jenkins Activity Survey, the Framingham Type A Scale, and the structured interview. The first two are self-report questionnaires, and the third a procedure used by Friedman and his colleagues emphasizing ratings of speech and social behaviors, as well as the content of the person's answers to questions. Matthews points out that the three measures produce results that have "only the slightest margin of overlap" (p. 296).

From our standpoint, the most fundamental and intriguing research issues concern identifying the psychological properties of Type A that increase the risk of coronary heart disease, how Type A works psychophysiologically, and whether it should be regarded as a stable trait or a situationally generated reaction.

The search for understanding of the psychological properties of Type A behaviors has led researchers to expose people varying in Type A-B characteristics to diverse stressful tasks and to study how they react (e.g., Diamond, 1982; Lovallo & Pishkin, 1980; Pittner & Houston, 1980; Yarnold & Grimm, 1982). Some researchers, such as Vickers, Hervig, Rahe, and Rosenman (1981), have searched for a link between Type A and ego-defense activity. They found that the structured interview measure was not related to defense, but that the questionnaire measure of "job involvement" correlated with high scores on coping and low scores on defense, leading them to the interesting hypothesis that increased cardiovascular risk occurs only when Type A is combined with low coping skills.

This suggestion fits nicely with Frankenhaeuser's (1980) findings that Type A persons selected a faster work pace and hence a heavier work load, but that they also coped with it better than Type B's with a lighter work load. Moreover, their superior performance did not have greater physiological costs (e.g., increased catecholamines), although they may have taken longer to unwind and return to baseline (Rissler, 1977). Frankenhaeuser states, "We interpret our results as showing that the Type A person, when in control of the situation, sets his or her standards high, copes effectively with the self-selected heavy load, and does so without mobilizing excessive physiological resources" (p. 210). Citing Lundberg's (1982) data that persons with high job involvement had a relatively low incidence of coronary heart disease, Frankenhaeuser suggests that "conditions calling for effort may be potentially harmful primarily when they evoke feelings of distress, whereas conditions characterized by effort point to controllability as a major key to coping without distress" (p. 211). Thus it is by no means unreasonable to suggest that the issue may be less a matter of Type A and more a matter of Type A's who are poor copers and who view what they are doing as threatening in some way.

Can the Type A pattern be regarded as a coping style that includes a number of interdependent behavioral, cognitive-affective, and motivational facets? Most assuredly, the behaviors displayed in Type A research include what we consider coping, for example, redoubling efforts to achieve more control, and strategies that lead to accepting the lack of control without distress. However, except for Vickers et al. (1981), investigators have generally not tried to measure coping thoughts and acts explicitly, since their emphasis has been on task performance. Therefore, to speak of Type A as a coping style is an interpretation, our interpretation to be sure, but one that we think is justified.

Moreover, a theory such as Glass's (1977a, b) seems to imply a personality trait or set of traits that makes the person vulnerable to psychological stress under conditions that endanger his or her need for control, or perhaps those that generate feelings of inadequacy in a person who usually struggles for control. This view requires two elements in order for distress to be generated: the disposition to be threatened or mobilized under certain conditions—or what we have called vulnerability in Chaper 2—and the environmental conditions that activate it. This kind of analysis is also consonant with our transactional formulation of psychological stress and emotion (see Chapter 9).

Ironically, the research that exists seems to tell us that Type A's behave as prescribed only in certain contexts, yet it is assumed, in seeming contradiction, that Type A is a broad, stable trait or style. There is a dearth of ipsative or longitudinal studies that compare the same individuals over time or across more than simply two experimental conditions. Such research is necessary to test the stability of Type A behavior and to determine the social contexts on which it might depend in given persons or types of persons. Type A would have to be a stable trait or style if the conditions necessary to produce disease are to be satisfied, namely, that a person reacts pathogenically over a long period of time, long enough in this case to produce atherosclerosis.

Thus, our assumption that Type A can be regarded as a coping style, as well as a stable pattern of commitments and beliefs, is reasonable and perhaps necessary in order to understand its role in cardiovascular disease. This assumption has not been adequately tested, however, nor have the psychodynamics of Type A been adequately revealed. In our view, Type A probably arises developmentally through the internalizing of certain socially desired, rewarded, or demanded values that are more or less characteristic of industrialized, technological societies. Lawler, Allen, Critcher, and Standard (1981) and Matthews and Siegel (1983), for example, have already demonstrated that the Type A–Type B distinction is behaviorally and physiologically observable in children as young as 11. The child comes to have certain beliefs about having an impact on the world, or about achievement and control, and goes about striving accordingly, probably selecting environments that reward the pattern. Later, in interaction with the social contexts that potentiate this cognitive-affective-motivational constellation, the susceptible person reacts with the speedy, urgent, and competitive Type A coping behaviors. Given the health implications of this pattern, it may be that Type A, seen as a system of beliefs, commitments, and coping styles, promises to be important and fruitful in the study of stress, coping, and adaptation.

Speaking more broadly, coping styles in general have great theoretical potential. A taxonomy of coping styles that captures in summary form the richness and complexity of coping processes can be used to help systematize the investigation of the relationship between coping and adaptational outcomes, not only in the context of illness, but within the contexts of family and work as well. The careful development of such a taxonomy would be an important contribution to stress research.

Cognitive Styles

The ego psychology model also spawned a body of theory and research on cognitive styles. Cognitive styles refer to automatic rather than effortful responses, and therefore we do not consider them as coping or coping styles. (We will discuss the issue of automatic versus effortful coping responses below.) Nevertheless, cognitive styles serve as control mechanisms and in their effect bear some resemblance to what is sometimes meant by coping style.

Cognitive controls. Gardner, Holzman, Klein, Linton, and Spence (1959) developed the concept of cognitive controls to describe the attributes of perceptual and memory apparatuses in the relatively conflict-free spheres of ego functioning. Cognitive controls are forms of cognitive styles that are assumed to be mediating variables accounting for individual consistency in attitudes and orientations. They are seen as directed, adaptive operations of ego structures that function to bring about an equilibrium between inner strivings and the demands of reality.

One cognitive control that has been identified is *leveling-sharp-*

ening, which is relevant to individual consistencies between new stimuli and memories experienced previously. *Leveling* is the tendency to see things in terms of their sameness or similarity. *Sharpening* is a way of seeing things in terms of their differences. Other cognitive controls include: *focusing or scanning,* relevant to the extent of spontaneous attention deployment in a variety of situations; *equivalence range,* relevant to judgmental preferences concerning similarity and difference; *flexible and constricted control,* relevant to response in the face of perceived incongruity; and *tolerance for unrealistic experiences,* relevant to response in situations that defy or abrogate one's usual assumptions concerning external reality (Gardner et al., 1959).

Field dependence–independence. The global-analytic dimension developed by Witkin and his colleagues is a good example of another cognitive style with its roots in perception as well as in ego psychology (for review see Witkin, Goodenough, & Oltman, 1979). This work began with the examination of field-dependent and field-independent tendencies (cf. Witkin, Dyk, Faterson, Goodenough, & Karp, 1962). A rod and frame apparatus is widely used to identify field-dependent and field-independent types. In this test, the subjects sit in a darkened room in sight of a movable luminous frame and rod. The frame is tilted by the experimenter and the subject is asked to bring the rod to a position perpendicular to the ground. A large tilt of the rod indicates an adherence to visual cues, whereas a vertical rod indicates independence of the visual field and reliance on bodily posture. The purpose of this test is to examine the extent to which subjects use the external visual field or the body itself as the main referent for locating the upright.

The manner of locating the upright was found to be related to relative ease of disembedding a figure from its field, and the latter was in turn found to be related to disembedding ability in intellectual activities. In later research and writing this dimension has been referred to as "psychological differentiation" (cf. Witkin et al., 1979). The field-dependent/independent dimension was extended to describe structuring competence in both domains, called an articulated versus global field approach, and designated a cognitive style. Since 1962 an active program of research has confirmed the picture of self-consistency in cognitive functioning established in the earlier field-dependent/independent studies. In general, field-independent people are better able to restructure the components of a stimulus array than field-dependent people. The relevance of this dimension to stress and coping is shown in the study by Gaines, Smith, and Skolnick (1977), mentioned in Chapter 4. Compared with undifferentiated subjects, differentiated or field-independent subjects reacted with greater increases in heart rate as the probability of hearing an uncomfortably loud noise increased. Heart rate change was viewed as a function of active preparation for the stressor, and psychological differentiation as a personality disposition that affects appraisal and coping.

Limitations and Defects of Traditional Approaches

A number of problems limit the usefulness of the traditional approaches to coping and the trait and style dimensions they have spawned. Some of these problems are not necessary consequences of existing theories, but arise from how theories have been expressed in operational measures of coping. We see four major issues: the treatment of coping as a structural trait or style; the failure to distinguish coping from automatized adaptive behavior; the confounding of coping with outcome; and the equation of coping with mastery.

The Treatment of Coping as Trait or Style

Traditional models of coping tend to emphasize traits or styles, that is, achieved ego-structures that, once created, presumably operate as stable dispositions to cope in this or that way over the life course. Even if such a static, structural perspective is not mandated by the theoretical formulation, in practice and research structural concepts take center stage, as in the trait–style concepts we discussed earlier in this chapter. We end up speaking of people who are repressors or vigilants, people who are field-dependent or -independent, people who are deniers, and so on.

If the assessment of coping traits really allowed us to predict what a person would actually do to cope in a specific stressful encounter, research would be a simple matter, since for all intents and purposes, traits could stand for process. If a person coped with threat by avoidance, whenever he or she felt threatened we would expect avoidance to occur. The assessment of coping traits, however, has had very modest predictive value with respect to actual coping processes.

The problem with traits as predictors is well illustrated by Cohen and Lazarus's (1973) research on coping with the threat of surgery. Surgical patients were interviewed in the hospital the evening before their operation and an assessment was made of how much they knew about their illness and its treatment and how much interest they had in learning more. This procedure assessed what the person thought and did in a specific threat context, as it was happening, something that trait measures do not provide. Patients varied from the extreme of avoidant coping, characterized by knowing little and not wanting to know, to the other extreme of vigilant coping in which they had much information and welcomed still more. Along with this direct assessment of coping with the threat of surgery, a standard trait measure with a similar theoretical rationale, the Byrne (1964) repression-sensitization scale, was also administered. No correlation was found between the trait measure and the process measure, and the process measure alone predicted the speed and ease of recovery from surgery: avoiders did better in this regard than vigilants. Most important to the issue being addressed here, the trait measure did not predict how people actually coped with the threat as it occurred.

Trait conceptualizations and measures of coping underestimate the complexity and variability of actual coping efforts. Most trait measures evaluate coping along a single dimension such as repression-sensitization (Byrne, 1964; Welsh, 1956) or coping-avoiding (Goldstein, 1959, 1973). The unidimensional quality of most trait measures does not adequately reflect the multidimensional quality of coping processes used to deal with real-life situations. Naturalistic observation (e.g., Mechanic, 1962; Murphy, 1974; Visotsky et al., 1961) indicates that coping is a complex amalgam of thoughts and behaviors. Moos and Tsu (1977), for example, point out that in coping with physical illness a patient must deal with many sources of stress, including pain and incapacitation, hospital environments, and the demands imposed by the professional staff and special treatment procedures. At the same time, the patient must preserve emotional balance, a satisfactory self-image, and good relationships with family and friends. These multiple tasks require an array of coping strategies whose complexity cannot be captured in a unidimensional measure.

We are of course not arguing that there are no stabilities in coping or that people do not have preferred modes of coping with the same or similar sources of psychological stress over time. Gorzynski et al. (1980), for example, located 30 patients who had been studied earlier by Katz, Weiner, Gallagher, and Hellman (1970) with respect to coping with the threat of breast biopsy. These patients were reevaluated using the same assessment techniques as earlier, including interview ratings of coping and cortisol secretion rates. Gorzynski et al. found that the "psychological defense patterns" were stable over time, remaining unchanged in 9 out of 10 subjects, and that hormonal secretions were also more or less stable, with a correlation across occasions of .64.

Other studies also suggest consistencies in coping (e.g., Kobasa, 1979), although in most cases coping per se has not been assessed directly but has been inferred from some other variable. As Moskowitz (1982) has argued, improvements in the design and methodology of cross-situational studies of traits, using multiple references, situations, and observations, could well increase the evidence of cross-situational generality. Findings on this issue are clearly mixed, especially in children, and rather than argue for only a process-centered as opposed to a structural, trait-centered approach, we should recognize that there is both stability and change in coping, but that the research emphasis has been overwhelmingly on stable traits compared with coping as a process. Our message here is that in seeking to understand coping or its antecedent and consequent correlates there is no substitute for direct assessment of coping acts and how they change with the changing demands of the situations as these are appraised by the person. We shall argue for a process-centered approach to coping in the next chapter.

Coping Versus Automatized Adaptive Behavior

There is an important distinction that is not made in many traditional approaches to coping, namely, between automatized and effortful responses. The skills that humans need to get along must be learned through experience. One useful idea about human adaptation is that the more quickly people can apply these skills automatically, the more effectively and efficiently they can manage their relationships with the environment. We see an important difference between the early stages of skill acquisition, which require enormous effort and concentration, and the later stages, in which the skills become automatized.

For example, experienced drivers are not ordinarily conscious of using the clutch and brake, steering, stopping for traffic signals, and so on, nor is there much special effort involved. We do these things so automatically that we can think about a problem at work while engaging in all the complex acts needed to get us there. These acts are adaptive but they should not be called coping. If they were, coping would consist of almost everything we do. When there is a nonroutine occurrence, however, such as a road closed for repairs that requires a decision as to an alternative route, or a flat tire that needs changing, effort is required. In these circumstances coping *efforts* are clearly distinguishable from the automatic adaptive behaviors that occur in routine driving situations.

The distinction between coping and automatized responses is not always clear. When a situation is novel, responses are not likely to be automatic, but if that situation should be encountered again and again, it is likely that the responses will become increasingly automatized through learning. Consider the student driver's first hours behind the wheel of a car. He or she concentrates intensely on the operation of the car and its location in traffic, and probably wonders how other people manage to drive so easily (i.e., automatically). Gradually, the need for intense concentration wanes, and responses are made with less deliberation and effort. As the driver becomes experienced, the behaviors become automatized. At the beginning of this process coping is required; at the end the behaviors are no longer coping by our definition. The transition is gradual, and it would be difficult to say when the behaviors become automatized and can no longer be considered coping. That most people deal with many of the demands of daily living in ways that do not tax or exceed their resources is evidence that many coping responses become automatized as learning takes place. However, at one point most such demands do tax or exceed available resources and therefore require coping.

Murphy (1974), who also views coping as a process that involves effort, makes an additional distinction between coping and ready-made adaptational devices such as reflexes. She views ready-made, phylogenetically more primitive devices at one end of a continuum which has at its center coping efforts, and at its other end, complete and automatized mastery. Her concern with primitive responses evolves from her observations of infants and children, whose early responses to stressful situations depend primarily on instinctual, wired-in protective mechanisms. As the infant evolves into a more mature organism whose capacity for cognitive manipulations and symbolic reasoning becomes increasingly important for functioning, the role played by primitive mechanisms becomes less significant in relation to the role played by coping.

Similarly, we distinguish between cognitive style, which involves an automatized response, and coping, although the distinction is often difficult to pinpoint in real-life contexts. For example, in extreme circumstances such as the concentration camp, there is often a tunneling of vision or a restriction of perspective (see Frankl, 1963). Rather than focusing on the meaning of imprisonment and the omnipresent threats to survival, attention may be focused on small segments of reality.

Friedman, Chodoff, Mason, and Hamburg (1963) report that for parents of leukemic children, long-range hopes for the child's well-being and happiness were gradually replaced, as the child moved closer to death, by the immediate, limited concern of a pain-free day. A similar reaction was observed in mothers of severely deformed thalidomide children, who insisted that they could continue to function only by forgetting the painful past, ignoring the uncertain future, and instead concentrating on living "day to day" (Roskies, 1972). Mages and Mendelsohn (1979) observed that cancer patients "who felt overwhelmed by the multiple physical, emotional, and practical burdens of their illness often narrowed their interests to create a smaller and more manageable world" (p. 260).

When the tunneling of vision or restriction of perspective illustrated above is an automatic response, we would say it is due to the person's cognitive control mechanisms; when it is purposeful and requires effort, we would classify it as coping. The extent to which the above individuals reduced their focus automatically or purposefully could only be known by interviewing each subject about the situation.

Put differently, not all adaptive processes are coping. Coping is a subset of adaptational activities that involves effort and does not include everything that we do in relating to the environment. From this point of view, the cognitive styles we discussed above may be adaptive processes, but not coping. Klein and his colleagues (Gardner et al., 1959) have suggested, in fact, that cognitive styles emerge developmentally from the child's struggle to discharge drive or instinctual impulses safely and effectively in the face of environmental obstacles and dangers. They were originally defense mechanisms that later could be said to have become automatized. Piaget (1952) held a similar view of the development of intelligence as a product of the processes of assimilation and accommodation in transactions with the environment. It is the struggle to adapt that ultimately results in automatic styles of perceiving, thinking, and acting. Klein also noted that, alternatively, defenses could be the product of modes of thought that are characteristic of a given time of life. The direction of effect here remains one of the unsettled theoretical issues of cognitive and defensive development.

The Confounding of Coping with Outcome

In both the animal and psychoanalytic ego psychology models, coping is equated with adaptational success, which is also the popular meaning of the term. In the vernacular, to say a person coped with the demands of a particular situation suggests that the demands were successfully overcome; to say a person did not cope suggests ineffectiveness or inadequacy.

In the three psychoanalytic ego psychology models we described earlier, there is a hierarchy of coping and defense such that some processes are automatically considered superior to others. For Menninger the hierarchy represents the degree of disorganization or primitivization which, in turn, informs us about the severity of stress, a quite circular analysis. For Haan, coping reflects a strong and well-functioning ego, whereas defense is neurotic, and ego-failure or fragmentation represents the most disorganized functioning.

When efficacy is implied by coping and inefficacy by defense, there is an inevitable confounding between the process of coping and the outcome of coping. These conceptual systems are not appropriate to the investigation of the relationship between coping and outcome, and we must abandon the hierarchical assumption and manage to keep the study of process and outcome independent. In order to determine the effectiveness of coping and defense processes, one must be open-minded to the possibility that both can work well or badly in particular persons, contexts, or occasions.

The analytic and interpretive problems posed by hierarchies of coping and defense can be illustrated by the major study reported by Vaillant (1977), who defines coping as the adaptive application of defense mechanisms. Earlier we described this research on coping and defense in 94 men followed for many years in which each man was ranked according to the relative maturity and pathological import of his characteristic defenses. In this study it is not surprising that an association was found between level of defense and lifetime adjustment. The raters were given a life-style summary of each subject to assist them in assigning a defense level score to each behavior observed in times of conflict and crisis. Using information about a subject's overall functioning to help score a behavior as indicative of one or another level of defense creates a tautology; in effect, defense and outcome are totally confounded.

Kahn et al. (1964) also point out the importance of defining coping independently of outcome, adding that the study of coping behavior should include failures as well as successes:

The concept of coping is defined by the behaviors subsumed under it, not by the success of those behaviors. It may even prove profitable to concentrate upon those behaviors which are intended to cope with stress but which fail to do so. The psychoanalytic study of defense mechanisms would have been seriously retarded had it confined itself to the observation of conspicuously successful defenses. It is often in situations of failure where the ramifications of a particular coping mechanism or defense can be seen most vividly. (p. 385)

Definitions of coping must include *efforts* to manage stressful demands, regardless of outcome. This means that no one strategy is considered inherently better than any other. The goodness (efficacy, appropriateness) of a strategy is determined only by its effects in a given encounter and its effects in the long term. This contrasts with the conceptualizations of coping in which predetermined criteria having to do with degree of disorganization or level of maturity are used to classify strategies on an evaluative dimension, based on ideas about pathology and health derived from the traditions of Freud and ego psychology. Heavy weight is given to the extent to which a strategy adheres to reality and indicates emotional equilibrium. We noted earlier that Haan's approach depends on assessing the accuracy of the person's intersubjective reality. This is difficult to ascertain. Much research in psychology (e.g., the New Look Movement in the 1950s) has been concerned with individual differences in intersubjective (objective) reality (see review by Erdelyi, 1974), and few answers have emerged about how to define such a reality (see also Watzlawick, 1976). Without a technique to do so, studies of ego hierarchies are seriously handicapped.

Predetermined ideas as to the inherent quality of ego processes prejudice us against the possibilities of strategies ranked high in a hierarchy being maladaptive and low-ranked strategies being adaptive. Denial is a case in point; it is usually ranked toward the bottom of ego hierarchies as indicating disorganization, primitivization, or distortion of reality and is considered inherently maladaptive. This line of thinking can be seen in research stemming from Janis's (1958) observations on the "work of worrying" (see also Lindemann's [1944] concept of "grief work"). The central theme of this research is that people who use denial, or even avoidance, as a mode of coping with stressful encounters will experience greater emotional ease on the first occasion but will pay for that ease by continued vulnerability on subsequent occasions. On the other hand, people who vigilantly face a threat will be more distressed at the outset, but on subsequent occasions they will experience less distress because they will be better prepared to handle the demands.

In Janis's initial studies, patients who displayed little or no apprehension prior to surgery showed excessive distress postsurgically compared with those who displayed normal vigilance and anxiety. This finding suggested that because these patients put off thoughts about the expectable pain and indignity of the recovery period, they were unprepared to face its distressing realities. Later experimental studies by Goldstein and his colleagues (Goldstein, 1973) supported the argument. However, subsequent work produced mixed findings. One can now speak of a box score of studies with contradictory results, some showing that those who deny or avoid threats are worse off than those who address them, and other studies in which denial is associated with positive outcomes.*

Denial or avoidance in the context of illness is considered ineffective because the person fails to engage in appropriate problem-focused coping (e.g., seeking medical attention or adhering to a medical regimen) that would decrease the actual danger or damage of illness. This drawback is different from that implied by psycho-analytically oriented conceptualizations. According to the latter, a person using denial to cope with a threat is vulnerable to disconfirmations by evidence to the contrary and is therefore forced to narrow his or her attention to only confirmatory experiences. Denial closes the mind to whatever *could* be threatening. People who

---

*A large number of studies discuss denial-like processes and their consequences. Below are some striking current examples in which there were negative or positive outcomes. Negative outcomes include: Andrew (1970); Auerbach (1973); Delong (1970); Hitchcock (1982); Katz, Weiner, Gallagher, and Hellman (1970); Lindemann (1944); and Staudenmayer, Kinsman, Kirks, Spector, and Wangaard (1979). Positive outcomes include: Cohen and Lazarus (1973); George, Scott, Turner, and Gregg (1980); Hackett, Cassem, and Wishnie (1968); Hamburg and Adams (1967); Levine and Zigler (1975); Stern, Pascale, and McLoone (1976); Rosenstiel and Roth (1981); and Bean, Cooper, Alpert, and Kipnis (1980). Additional articles in which denial was associated with mixed or inconclusive outcomes, or was merely discussed, include Sackheim (in press); Yanagida, Streltzer, and Seimsen (1981); Spinetta and Maloney (1978); Billing, Lindell, Sederholm, and Theorell (1980); Beisser (1979) and Knight et al. (1979). There is also the older research of Wolff, Friedman, Hofer, and Mason (1964) in which denial-like processes prior to the loss of an ill child to leukemia were associated with lowered adrenocortical hormonal output (stress responses). However, this was followed up by a later finding by Hofer, Wolff, Friedman, and Mason (1972) in which parents who had used denial-like processes for coping before the child's death showed higher physiological stress responses two years after the child's death compared with an opposite pattern for those who had confronted the tragedy without denial-like coping.

defend themselves in this way must remain forever on guard, involved with "silent internal tasks" (Fenichel, 1945), and may experience depleted energy or even depression. This psychoanalytic interpretation of the costs of denial is difficult to operationalize in research, and the issue remains unsettled as to whether or not denial operates in this manner.

A major methodological problem has to do with the meaning of denial, which is usually defined as the disavowal of reality. The first serious difficulty with this definition has to do with its breadth. Some actions that are considered to be behavioral exemplars of denial, such as not talking to others about an ailment or condition of life (e.g., in Hackett & Cassem's, 1974, denial rating scale for postcoronary patients), are more akin to avoidance than the disavowal of reality (Dansak & Cordes, 1978–1979). The patient who is reluctant to talk about a terminal illness such as advanced cancer, and who tries to keep it out of mind as much as possible, may readily acknowledge the reality of the illness and its attendant distress when asked directly. Other cognitive coping processes that have been classified as denial may be better regarded as efforts at positive thinking, or minimization, to use Lipowski's (1970–1971) term. These processes are capable of sustaining morale and constructive efforts to cope, and, again, do not disavow reality.

Breznitz (1983a) has identified seven different kinds of denial in an analysis that accords nicely with our concerns about the definition of denial and the diverse coping processes commonly included under its rubric. He distinguishes denial of information, threatening information, personal relevance, urgency, vulnerability-responsibility, affect, and affect relevance. These types of denial are arranged hierarchically, with the assumption that only when a higher form of denial fails does the individual proceed to the next one down. Thus, Breznitz offers a kind of stage model, with each level implying a progressively more severe challenge to coping. The use of any form of denial, moreover, implies helplessness to change the objective situation. For readers interested in the topic of denial, we recommend a book edited by Breznitz (1983b) which contains the above material as well as discussions of other aspects of the problem such as the relations between denial and hope, and denial and religion.

Aside from definitional problems, support can be found for both the costs and the benefits of denial and denial-like processes. What is needed, therefore, are principles that specify the conditions under which denial and denial-like forms of coping might have favorable or unfavorable outcomes. We offer the following as possibilities:

1. When there is nothing constructive that people can do to overcome a harm or threat, that is, when there is no direct action that is relevant, denial and denial-like processes contain the potential for alleviating distress without altering functioning or producing additional harm.

2. Denial and denial-like processes may be adaptive with respect to certain facets of the situation, but not the whole. Patients with diabetes can deny the seriousness of the situation as long as they also continue to give vigilant attention to diet, activity level, and insulin.

    The distinction made by Weisman (1972) between denial of fact and denial of implication is also relevant here. For example, it is probably more dangerous to deny that one *has* cancer than to deny that the diagnosis implies a death sentence. Denial of implication may be more akin to illusion, positive thinking, or hopefulness—which all of us experience and the capacity for which may be a valuable psychological resource—than to distortion of reality.

3. S. Miller (1980) points out that in situations that are subject to change, that is, from uncontrollable to controllable, the optimal strategy may be one that reduces arousal without completely impeding the processing of external threat-relevant information. However, in chronically uncontrollable (and unchangeable) situations, the strategy of choice may be one that effectively reduces both arousal and concomitant processing of information from the environment.

4. The timing of denial and denial-like forms of coping may be a major significance. Denial may be less damaging and more effective in the early stages of a crisis, such as sudden illness, incapacitation, or loss of a loved one, when the situation cannot yet be faced in its entirety, than in later stages. Hackett and Cassem (1975) and Hackett, Cassem, and Wishnie (1968), for example, observed both positive and negative effects of denial and avoidance depending on when their observations were made. During a heart attack these cognitive coping processes were damaging because they obstructed the effort to get medical help. After a heart attack, however, the same coping processes facilitated recovery and resulted in fewer deaths from subsequent attacks. Cohen and Lazarus (1983) reviewed other studies in which the same principle seemed to apply, that is, denial-like coping processes that proved helpful while the patient was still in the hospital

seemed to have negative consequences when used after leaving the hospital.

We have used denial and denial-like processes to illustrate that (1) no strategy should be labeled as inherently good or bad; (2) the context must be taken into account in judging coping; and (3) principles must be developed with which to judge whether a particular coping process fits with both personal and situational aspects of the transaction. This approach should be used not only for denial, but for virtually every form of coping.

Menninger (1963), Haan (1977), and Vaillant (1977) all acknowledge the importance of evaluating an ego process within the situational context. Vaillant states, "We cannot evaluate the choice of a defense without considering the circumstances that call it forth and how it affects relationships with other people" (pp. 85–86). Lipowski (1970–1971), too, notes that the evaluation of denial must always include a consideration of what is denied, in what situation, and by whom. The hierarchic nature of these systems of ego processes, however, militates against such situational evaluations. A process ranked on the lower end of a hierarchy has an onus that is difficult to remove even when the strategy is effective, appropriate, and successful according to situational criteria. Denial is bad unless proved otherwise, and even then it is suspect.

In Chapter 7 we discuss the question of coping effectiveness and the outcomes of coping at length. Here our purpose has been to explain why we define coping as *all efforts* to manage taxing demands, without regard to their efficacy or inherent value.

The Equation of Coping with Mastery Over the Environment

There is an implicit corollary to those definitions of coping that consider certain strategies inherently better or more useful than others, namely, that the best coping is that which changes the person–environment relationship for the better. In keeping with deeply ingrained Western values regarding individualism and mastery, and the Darwinian impact on psychological thought, these definitions tend to venerate mastery over the environment as the coping ideal. Coping is viewed as tantamount to solving problems by acting effectively to obviate them.

The problem here is not that solving problems is undesirable, but that not all sources of stress in living are amenable to mastery, or even fit within a problem-solving framework. Examples include natural disasters, inevitable losses, aging and disease, and the ubiquitous conflicts which abnormal psychology and psychiatry have long addressed, all normal features of the human condition. Emphasizing problem solving and mastery devalues other functions of coping that are concerned with managing emotions and maintaining self-esteem and a positive outlook, especially in the face of irremediable situations. Coping processes that are used to tolerate such difficulties, or to minimize, accept, or ignore them, are just as important in the person's adaptational armamentarium as problem-solving strategies that aim to master the environment.

Having reviewed the main, traditional approaches to coping and considered their limitations and defects, we are now ready to spell out our own process definition and conceptualization of coping, in which we seek to avoid the pitfalls of the past.

Summary

Traditional approaches to coping emerged from two separate and distinct literatures, animal experimentation and psychoanalytic ego psychology. The animal model focused on the concept of drive (or arousal, or activation), and coping is usually defined as acts that control aversive conditions and thereby lower drive or activation. The emphasis is largely on avoidance and escape behavior. In our view, what can be learned from this model about human coping, which includes cognitive coping and defense, is only modest.

When the concept of coping is formulated within the tradition of psychoanalytic ego psychology, it is centrally concerned with cognition, differentiating among a number of processes people use to manage troubled relationships. Systems of coping based on the ego psychology model generally conceive of a hierarchy of strategies that progress from immature or primitive mechanisms, which distort reality, to mature mechanisms.

Measurement approaches based on the ego psychology model have tended to assess coping traits and styles rather than processes. "Coping traits" refers to properties of persons that dispose them to react in certain ways. Styles are similar, differing primarily in degree; they refer to broad ways of relating to particular types of people or situations.

The Type A behavior pattern, which grew out of clinical observation rather than ego psychology, can be thought of as a coping style that includes behavioral, motivational, and cognitive properties. Research is needed to determine the stability of Type A behavior and to understand its role as a coping style in disease outcomes.

The ego psychology model spawned much research and thought on what have been called cognitive styles or cognitive controls. They are related to and can influence coping activity, although they cannot explicitly be considered coping styles.

The trait and style approach to coping is inevitably incomplete. Measures of coping traits and styles are not good predictors of actual coping processes; they underestimate both the complexity and the variability of the ways people actually cope.

Coping activity also must be distinguished from automatized adaptive behavior. Coping implies effort, whereas automatized adaptive behaviors do not, as the word *automatized* implies. Many behaviors are originally effortful and hence reflect coping, but become automatized through learning processes.

Coping as a concept is typically equated with adaptational success, especially in the ego psychology models, wherein unsuccessful or less successful efforts to deal with stress are called defense. This results in a confounding of coping and its outcome. If progress is to be made in understanding the relationship between coping and outcome, that is, what helps or hurts the person and in what ways, coping must be viewed as efforts to manage stressful demands regardless of outcome. Accordingly, no strategy should be considered inherently better or worse than any other; judgments as to the adaptiveness of a strategy must be made contextually. Denial or denial-like behaviors, for example, may be adaptive in some sense in certain situations and/or at certain stages of an encounter. Principles are also needed to guide the evaluation of the adaptiveness of coping strategies.

Finally, coping should not be equated with mastery over the environment; many sources of stress cannot be mastered, and effective coping under these conditions is that which allows the person to tolerate, minimize, accept, or ignore what cannot be mastered.

6

The Coping Process:
An Alternative to
Traditional Formulations

In this second chapter on coping, we present our own definition and conceptualization, being careful to address the limitations and defects of the traditional approaches discussed in Chapter 5. The core of the chapter consists of discussions of coping as a process, its multiple functions, and the influences of the context of stressful encounters on the coping process. Later in the chapter we discuss the differences between control as an appraisal and control as coping, and coping over the life span. We end by considering some of the difficulties and uncertanties in our approach.

Definition of Coping

We define coping as *constantly changing cognitive and behavioral efforts to manage specific external and/or internal demands that are appraised as taxing or exceeding the resources of the person.* This definition addresses limitations of traditional approaches as follows:

First, it is process-oriented rather than trait-oriented, as reflected in the words *constantly changing* and *specific* demands and conflicts. We shall elaborate on this below.

Second, this definition implies a *distinction between coping and automatized adaptive behavior* by limiting coping to demands that are appraised as taxing or exceeding a person's resources. In effect, this limits coping to conditions of psychological stress, which requires mobilization and excludes automatized behaviors and thoughts that do not require effort.

Third, the problem of *confounding coping with outcome* is addressed by defining coping as *efforts* to manage, which permits coping to include anything that the person does or thinks, regardless of how well or badly it works.

Fourth, by using the word *manage*, we also avoid equating coping with mastery. Managing can include minimizing, avoiding, tolerating, and accepting the stressful conditions as well as attempts to master the environment.

Coping as a Process

A process approach to coping has three main features. First, observations and assessment are concerned with what the person *actually* thinks or does, in contrast to what the person usually does, would do, or should do, which is the concern of the trait approach. Second, what the person actually thinks or does is examined within a *specific context*. Coping thoughts and actions are always directed toward particular conditions. To understand coping, and to evaluate it, we need to know what the person is coping with. The more narrowly defined the context, the easier it is to link a particular coping thought or act to a contextual demand. Third, to speak of a coping process means speaking of *change* in coping thoughts and acts as a stressful encounter unfolds. Coping is thus a shifting process in which a person must, at certain times, rely more heavily on one form of coping, say defensive strategies, and at other times on problem-solving strategies, as the status of the person–environment relationship changes. It is difficult to see how the unfolding nature of most stressful encounters, and the concomitant changes in coping, could be adequately described by a *static* measure of a general trait or personality disposition.

The dynamics and change that characterize coping as a process are not random; they are a function of continuous appraisals and reappraisals of the shifting person–environment relationship. Shifts may be the result of coping efforts directed at changing the environment, or coping directed inward that changes the meaning of the event or increases understanding. They may also be the result of changes in the environment that are independent of the person and his or her coping activity. Regardless of its source, any shift in the person–environment relationship will lead to a reevaluation of what is happening, its significance, and what can be done. The reevaluation process, or reappraisal, in turn influences subsequent coping efforts. The coping process is thus continuously mediated by cognitive reappraisals which, as we noted in Chapter 2, differ from appraisals primarily in that they follow and modify an earlier appraisal.

The meaning of coping as a process can be seen in the long duration of grief work and the changes that take place over time, beginning with the moment of loss. Initially, for example, in the loss of a loved one, there may be shock and disbelief, or efforts to deny the death. There may also be frantic activity, tearfulness, or brave struggles to carry on socially or at work. Later stages often involve temporary disengagement and depression, followed ultimately by acceptance of the loss, reengagement, and even attachment to other persons. The entire process may last several years and be characterized by multiple ways of coping and emotional difficulties, or it may last only for months. To an observer, the process will appear to be quite different at different stages. For full discussions of grieving, see also the classic work by Lindemann (1944), Bowlby (1961, 1969, 1973, 1980), Rochlin (1965), and Schoenberg et al. (Schoenberg, Carr, Peretz, & Kutschen, 1970; Schoenberg, Carr, Kutschen, Peretz, & Goldberg, 1974; Schoenberg et al., 1975), among others, including many psychoanalytic treatments.

The above account of coping as a process applies to all stressful encounters. Changes in coping and other aspects of the psychological state as the encounter unfolds may occur within a few moments, as in an argument that is quickly resolved, or may continue to occur for hours, days, weeks, or even years, as in grieving. In both short- and long-term cases there is an unfolding, shifting pattern of cognitive appraisal and reappraisal, coping, and emotional processes.

Stages in the Coping Process

Those researchers who discuss coping in terms of stages are employing a process view of coping, either explicitly or implicitly. For example, Main (1977) has suggested the presence of stages of coping over time in her work on the separation of the young child and its mother. Main used the Ainsworth and Wittig (1970) strange situation experimental design, which calls for repeatedly separating mother and child, each time returning the child to the mother after several minutes or more. Careful observations are made about how the child reacts to the reunion behaviorally and emotionally. If the separation is long enough, the mother may be persistently avoided at reunion and treated as a stranger. According to Main (see also Robertson & Bowlby, 1952), the child proceeds through three separate stages—protest, despair, and detachment—all viewed as ways of coping with the stressful experience.

A number of explanations have been offered for this pattern (see, for example, Main & Weston, 1982). Main sees the avoidance behavior as a way for the child to protect itself from the disorganizing consequences of the conflict between anger toward the mother and the need for reasserting attachment. Heinicke and Westheimer (1965) suggest that the chlid's initial avoidant response to reunion is best understood as a defense that permits the child to maintain control over anger that has grown severe and disruptive. Most explanations of this behavior are ethological and phylogenetic in character and seem to avoid inferences about what the child is thinking and feeling, except perhaps in the recognition of the anger that seems inherent in the separation situation.

The stress and coping concepts embedded in the child's response to the strange situation are stated normatively, but one must recognize that there are major variations among children in whether or not, or how much, the child will respond to the reunion in the pattern described. Thus, we must also understand individual vulnerabilities in the child and what it is in the mother–child relationship that contributes to variation. For example, Main reasons that mothers who were dealt with coldly or in a hostile fashion by their mothers repeat this pattern with their own childen, generating in them the stages of protest, despair, and detachment.

Several other writers have been sensitive to the temporal aspects of coping. Klinger (1977), for example, suggests that loss or threatened loss of a commitment is first responded to with increased *effort* and level of *concentration*. With continued thwarting, *frustration and anger* also increase, the immediate consequences being primitivity, protest, and stereotypical actions in the fashion illustrated in a classic study with children by Barker, Dembo, and Lewin (1941). Ultimately, failure to achieve the goal or to make progress toward it leads to *depression*, which is characterized by pessimism and apathy. Klinger regards this sequence as the normal stages of coping; in his view, disengagement and depression are initially an adaptive way to cope (cf. Lazarus & DeLongis, 1983).

Ultimately, there is a psychological recovery from the loss, and intrusive thoughts about it also dissipate, an outlook consonant with Horowitz's (1974, 1976, 1982) picture of the person as cycling back and forth between two stages or syndromes of stress response: *denial* and *vigilance.*

Shontz (1975) has proposed that when people are dealing with serious physical illness or disability they will proceed through a series of coping stages from the point of initial discovery. For Shontz, the first stage is *shock*, which is especially prominent when the crisis occurs without warning. This stage is manifested by a feeling of detachment and sometimes remarkable clarity and efficiency of thought and action. There follows an *encounter* phase, an extremely intense period in which the person is apt to experience helplessness, panic, and disorganization. This is followed by a third stage of *retreat*, which seems to correspond to the denial, numbing phase discussed by Horowitz (1976). In Shontz's treatment, however, retreat is gradually abandoned in favor of increasing *reality testing.* The coping process involves continual shifting back and forth between confrontation or struggle and retreat or denial/avoidance and, as with Klinger's analysis, the retreat phase is viewed as an important, natural means of preventing breakdown by allowing temporary withdrawal into safety. When the coping process has been successfully completed, the cycles occur less frequently and virtually disappear. The coping process outlined above is considered by Shontz to be a necessary precursor to psychological growth, in which there is a renewed sense of personal worth, a greater sense of satisfaction, and a lessening of anxiety.

Finally, Wortman and Brehm (1975) also propose a stage model, based in part on Brehm's (1966) concept of *reactance*, in an effort to explain why people do not necessarily give up when they discover that they are helpless, as the learned helplessness model originally argued (Seligman, Maier, & Solomon, 1971; see also our Chapter 7). Reactance means that when behavior is restricted, people respond with anger and increased motivation to overcome the resistance to their freedom of action. Wortman and Brehm propose that such increased motivation, and efforts to regain control, are apt to be the initial reaction to uncontrollable outcomes, but that continued unsuccessful efforts will lead ultimately to lowered motivation, increased passivity, and depression. This sequence of reactions is described as invigoration-depression, a stage-like pattern not unlike those proposed by Klinger, by Horowitz, and by Shontz.

What is seen above is that the process of coping becomes more or less a stage concept, much as Kübler-Ross (1969) speaks of the stages of dying. We must be concerned, however, about whether such stages are assumed to be invariant in sequence, as in Piaget's stages of cognitive development, or merely a convenient way to describe certain cognitive-affective-behavioral patterns that are momentarily ascendant depending on when in the total process one makes observations. Wortman and Brehm (1975), for example, point out that in their model the sequence does not necessarily move from invigoration to depression.

One reason for being wary of formulations that propose invariant sequences of stages is that clinically one sees that the sequence can be variable. Life-threatening illnesses such as cancer present patients with markedly different demands from one point in the illness to another. Mendelsohn (1979; see also Mages & Mendelsohn, 1979) has observed such changes from the initial discovery and diagnosis of cancer through the later stages as the illness either progresses or seems halted. What is observed is not a necessary progression derived from some inexorable maturational process, but patterns that reflect what is actually happening to the person. What are called stages of coping may refer as much to the progression of physical or external demands and threats as to internally stimulated or required sequences. Mendelsohn also observed great individual variation both in terms of how the significance of the disease is appraised and how it is coped with. "Each patient," says Mendelsohn, "faces a particular set of circumstances within the context of a unique personal history" (p. 67), and to understand the personal significance of the disease one needs to place the illness crisis in the context of that life history.

Silver and Wortman (1980a) reviewed research and theory relevant to stages of coping and noted a paucity of adequate observational studies with which to resolve the problem. They conclude that the limited data do not clearly fit a stage model of emotional reactions and coping with life crises; in fact, they point to evidence for great variability among persons rather than evidence for a normative pattern.

Further, a stage model creates expectations in both the person and those involved with the person with respect to appropriate feelings and actions. Those who adopt the Kübler-Ross stage concept of dying, for example, may inadvertently exert pressure on patients to comply with the expected stages (Lazarus, in press). When their response deviates from the norm, patients might question the normality, health, or suitability of their reactions. One might then label

Dylan Thomas's stirring exhortation to "rage against the dying of the light" as pathology-inducing.

Although some patterns may be more common than others because of shared cultural ways of responding, we doubt that there is a dominant pattern of coping stages. But even more important than whether there are universal or common sequences of coping, there is a great need for information about whether some coping patterns are more serviceable than others in given types of people, for given types of psychological stress, at certain times, and under given known conditions. As with coping in general, researchers have barely scratched the surface of this set of issues.

The disaster literature (e.g., Baker & Chapman, 1962) highlights stages of events rather than stages of coping. Three stages are usually defined: anticipatory or warning, impact or confrontation, and postimpact or postconfrontation. Our cognitive-phenomenological approach to the problem is that the significance of the encounter for well-being is appraised differently at different stages and calls for different modes of coping (see also Lazarus, 1966). We assume, for example, that the period of anticipation, the period of impact or confrontation, and the postimpact period each provides its own characteristic significance.

During *anticipation*, for example, the event has not yet occurred and the paramount issues to be appraised include whether it will happen, when it will happen, and what will happen. The cognitive appraisal process also evaluates whether, to what extent, and how the person can manage the threat, a secondary appraisal process relevant to the sense of control. Can it be prevented? In what ways? What can be done to prepare for it to minimize or prevent the damage? Can some damage be prevented while other damage must be endured? If it cannot be prevented, can it be endured, and if so, how? Can it be postponed? What are the costs of anticipatory coping? While people await an anticipated threat, their thoughts about these matters affect stress reactions and coping, as Folkins (1970), Monat, Averill, and Lazarus (1972), and Monat (1976) have shown. They use coping strategies such as distancing themselves psychologically, avoiding thoughts about the threat, denying its implications, looking for information that might reveal something relevant on which other coping strategies might be predicated, and seeking and responding to feedback from actions and thoughts already entertained or acted on.

During the *impact* period, many of the thoughts and actions relevant to the sense of control are no longer relevant, since the harmful event has already begun or ended. As its full character reveals itself, the person begins to realize whether it is as bad as or worse than anticipated, and in what ways. In some stressful encounters mental energy is so focused on acting and reacting that it may take considerable time to sort out what has happened and to assess its significance. Unexpected differences in control over the unfolding event may mean that the person must reassess its significance. We call these cognitions *reappraisals;* others have used the term *situational redefinition.*

These cognitive processes that begin during the impact period often persist in the *postimpact* period. In addition, a host of new considerations and tasks emerges. How can one mop up, psychologically and materially, after the damage? What is the personal meaning or significance of what has happened? What new demands, threats, and challenges does it impose? Can one return to the *status quo ante*, or have things changed appreciably?

Although the stressful encounter has ended, it brings in its wake a new set of anticipatory processes. Even the impact or confrontational period contains a set of appraisal and coping processes addressed not only to the past and the present, but also to the future. Damage or harms that have already occurred also contain elements of threat in the anticipatory sense of the term, and it is never possible to fully separate, except for convenience of analysis and communication, the cognitive and coping processes associated with each stage of a stressful encounter.

During the encounter the person is discovering the realities of what is happening and what can be done about it, and this affects coping. For example, learning that one lacks control over the most significant aspects of the situation will encourage the use of strategies for regulating emotions; direct actions on the environment may have to await suitable opportunities. Conversely, changes in the person's relationship with the environment brought about by actions taken during a stressful encounter may obviate the need for regulating emotions or indicate that such regulation is even more necessary.

The Multiple Functions of Coping

An important feature of our conceptualization is that coping involves much more than problem solving and that effective coping serves other functions as well. We do not want to confuse coping functions with coping outcomes. A coping function refers to the purpose a strategy serves; outcome refers to the effect a strategy has. A strategy can have a given function, for example, avoidance, but not result in avoidance. In other words, functions are not defined in terms of outcomes, although we can expect that given functions will have given outcomes. This distinction is consistent with our definition of coping in that it is independent of outcome.

The definition of coping functions depends on the theoretical framework (if there is one) in which coping is conceptualized, and/ or on the context in which coping is examined. For example, when coping is formulated within systems of ego processes such as those discussed in Chapter 5, its central function is the reduction of tension and the restoration of equilibrium. In contrast, the maintenance of equilibrium is not a background concern for Janis and Mann (1977), who formulate coping functions within a decision-making framework. In their model, the primary functions of coping have to do with decision making, particularly the search for and the evaluation of information.

Several writers identify multiple coping functions. Working within an ego psychology framework, White (1974) cites three:

> (1) to keep securing adequate information about the environment, (2) maintain satisfactory internal conditions both for action and for processing information, and (3) maintain . . . autonomy or freedom of movement, freedom to use [one's] repertoire in a flexible fashion. (p. 55)

Mechanic (1974), who has a social-psychological perspective, also cites three coping functions: dealing with social and environmental demands, creating the motivation to meet those demands, and maintaining a state of psychological equilibrium in order to direct energy and skill toward external demands. Pearlin and Schooler (1978) name changing the situation out of which strainful experiences arise, controlling the meaning of such experiences before they become stressful, and controlling stress itself after is has emerged.

Finally, there are coping functions that pertain to specific contexts such as health/illness (reviews in Cohen & Lazarus, 1979; Moos, 1977), exam taking (Mechanic, 1962), political crises (George, 1974), parachute jumping (Epstein, 1962), the welfare system (Dill et al., 1980), and changes in institutional residence (Aldrich & Mendkoff, 1963). Coping functions defined within specific contexts are less general and more situation-specific than those derived from larger theoretical perspectives.

Common to the coping functions described above is a distinction that we believe is of overriding importance, namely, between coping that is directed at managing or altering the problem causing the distress and coping that is directed at regulating emotional response to the problem. We refer to the former as *problem-focused coping* and the latter as *emotion-focused coping* (Folkman & Lazarus, 1980). These two major functions of coping have been noted by George (1974), Kahn et al. (1964), Mechanic (1962), Murphy (1974), and Murphy and Moriarty (1976) and are implicit in the models suggested by Mechanic (1974), Pearlin and Schooler (1978), Pearlin, Menaghan, Lieberman, and Mullan (1981), and White (1974).

In general, emotion-focused forms of coping are more likely to occur when there has been an appraisal that nothing can be done to modify harmful, threatening, or challenging environmental conditions. Problem-focused forms of coping, on the other hand, are more probable when such conditions are appraised as amenable to change (Folkman & Lazarus, 1980, in press).

Emotion-focused Forms of Coping

A wide range of emotion-focused forms of coping is found in the literature. One large group consists of cognitive processes directed at lessening emotional distress and includes strategies such as avoidance, minimization, distancing, selective attention, positive comparisons, and wresting positive value from negative events. Many of these strategies derive from theory and research on defensive processes and are used in virtually every type of stressful encounter. A smaller group of cognitive strategies is directed at *increasing* emotional distress. Some individuals need to feel worse before they can feel better; in order to get relief they first need to experience their distress acutely and to this end engage in self-blame or some other form of self-punishment. In still other instances, individuals deliberately increase their emotional distress in order to mobilize themselves for action, as when athletes "psych themselves up" for a competition.

Certain cognitive forms of emotion-focused coping lead to a change in the way an encounter is construed without changing the objective situation. These strategies are equivalent to *reappraisal*. Consider the following cognitive maneuvers that are commonly used to reduce threat: "I decided there are more important things to worry about"; "I considered how much worse things could be"; "I decided I didn't need him nearly as much as I thought." In each case, threat is diminished by changing the meaning of the situation—a coping effort qua reappraisal.

Elsewhere, we have referred to these cognitive coping efforts as "defensive reappraisals" (Lazarus, 1966). However, the word *defensive* implies a concern with reality and its distortion, an issue which we choose not to incorporate into our definition of coping. Not all reappraisals are defensive. Positive comparisons or wresting value from negative situations, for example, do not necessarily require that reality be distorted. Furthermore, not all reappraisals are targeted at the regulation of emotion; as we shall see below, some reappraisals are focused on the problem itself. For all these reasons, we choose to refer to cognitive maneuvers that change the meaning of a situation without changing it objectively as *cognitive reappraisals*, whether the changed construal is based on a realistic interpretation of cues or a distortion of reality.

Other emotion-focused coping strategies do not change the meaning of an event directly, as do cognitive reappraisals. For example, whether selective attention or avoidance changes meaning depends on what is attended to, or what is being avoided. The meaning of an encounter can remain the same even if some of its aspects are screened out, or thoughts about the encounter are put aside temporarily. Similarly, behavioral strategies such as engaging in physical exercise to get one's minds off a problem, meditating, having a drink, venting anger, and seeking emotional support can lead to reappraisals but are not themselves reappraisals. We make this point because we do not want emotion-focused coping to be taken as synonymous with reappraisal. Certain forms of emotion-focused coping are reappraisals, other forms are not, and still others sometimes are and sometimes are not.

Although emotion-focused processes may change the meaning of a stressful transaction without distorting reality, we must still consider the issue of self-deception, which is always a potential feature of this type of coping process. We use emotion-focused coping to maintain hope and optimism, to deny both fact and implication, to refuse to acknowledge the worst, to act as if what happened did not matter, and so on. These processes lend themselves to an interpretation of self-deception or reality distortion.

One cannot successfully deceive onself, however, and simultaneously be aware that one is doing so, since the awareness renders self-deception ineffective. Successful self-deception must therefore occur without consciousness (see also Suls, 1983). The issue of lack of awareness or unconsciousness fits with our assertion that cognitive appraisal processes need not be conscious (see Chapter 2). As long recognized (e.g., Eriksen, 1962a), it is difficult if not impossible to empirically define lack of awareness without being tautological.

Clinicians have typically looked for one of three kinds of contradictions to infer unconscious process: between what is said and done, between what is said at one moment and another, and between what is said and what is felt. These criteria help anchor the inference of unconsciousness in observables; however, they cannot serve as *proof* of self-deception (see Sarbin, 1981, for a further discussion of self-deception).

We are inclined to argue that self-deception extends on a continuum from personal or social illusions to major distortions, with no sharp dividing line between so-called healthy and pathological forms. We must be aware of the contexts in which self-deception occurs, and the short- and long-term costs and benefits that accrue from it (see Chapter 5). Confusion and misunderstanding lie in wait for anyone who dichotomizes self-deception into the healthy or pathogenic and who fails to take into account the place of cognitive forms of emotion-focused coping in the overall psychological economy of the person.

Problem-focused Forms of Coping

Problem-focused coping strategies are similar to strategies used for problem solving. As such, problem-focused efforts are often directed at defining the problem, generating alternative solutions, weighting the alternatives in terms of their costs and benefits, choosing among them, and acting. However, problem-focused coping embraces a wider array of problem-oriented strategies than problem solving alone. Problem-solving implies an objective, analytic process that is focused primarily on the environment; *problem-focused coping* also includes strategies that are directed inward.

This point is made by Kahn et al. (1964), who speak of two major groups of problem-oriented strategies—those directed at the environment and those directed at the self. Included in the former are strategies for altering environmental pressures, barriers, resources, procedures, and the like. The latter includes strategies that are directed at motivational or cognitive changes such as shifting the level of aspiration, reducing ego involvement, finding alternative channels of gratification, developing new standards of behavior, or learning new skills and procedures. The strategies named by Kahn et al. as directed toward the self would not be called typical problem-solving techniques, yet they are indeed directed at helping the person manage or solve the problem. With the exception of developing new behavior or learning new skills and procedures, we would call the inward-directed strategies named by Kahn et al. *cognitive reappraisals* that are problem-focused.

The number of problem-focused forms of coping that are applicable across diverse situations seems relatively limited compared to the vast array of emotion-focused strategies discussed in the literature. The more situation-specific the research domain is, however, the greater the proliferation of problem-focused strategies. For example, if asked about the strategies used to resolve problems on the job, a secretary will undoubtedly list a large number that have to do with specific tasks to be accomplished, obstacles that impede progress, resources available in the office for overcoming those obstacles, and so on. The list will differ from that of a salesperson, who has different tasks, obstacles, resources, and therefore different specific coping strategies. That the definition of problem-focused coping strategies is to a certain extent dependent on the types of problems being dealt with means that transsituational comparisons of problem-focused coping strategies are more difficult than transsituational comparisons of emotion-focused strategies. Nevertheless, efforts should be made to evaluate problem-focused coping, for reasons that will be made clear later in this chapter.

The Relationship between Problem- and Emotion-focused Coping Functions

Theoretically, problem- and emotion-focused coping can both facilitate and impede each other in the coping process. Consider the following examples in which the two forms of coping are mutually facilitative:

A. A woman experiences anxiety as she steps to the podium to give a paper. She does some deep breathing and gives herself comforting messages to regulate the anxiety. These devices allow her to engage in problem-focused forms of coping, for example, glancing over her notes or rehearsing an opening line, that will facilitate her delivery (cf. S. Miller, 1980).

B. A student beginning a major exam experiences great anxiety. The anxiety abates when attention is turned to taking the exam. In this instance, turning to the task (problem-focused coping) results in a reduction of emotional distress. This dynamic is illustrated in Mechanic's (1962) study of students taking doctoral examinations that we described in Chapter 4.

In the following examples, the two forms of coping impede each other:

A. A person suffering over having to make a difficult decision finds the emotional distress unbearable, and in order to reduce the distress makes a premature decision. Such decisions, say Janis and Mann (1977), are likely to be characterized by "lack of vigilant search, selective inattention, selective forgetting, distortion of the meaning of warning messages and construction of wishful rationalizations that minimize negative consequences" (p. 50). In this instance, the strategy used to reduce emotional distress interfered with problem-focused efforts.

B. A person with a recently diagnosed illness perseveres in gathering and evaluating information, the acquisition of which contributes to uncertainty and increased anxiety. He gets trapped in a cycle of problem-focused coping (information-gathering and -evaluating) which exacerbates his emotional distress and interferes with mechanisms such as avoidance that might otherwise be used to reduce distress (cf. Breznitz, 1971).

Anecdotal Examples

Problem- and emotion-focused forms of coping are not explicitly identified in most naturalistic descriptions. Nevertheless, both forms are usually evident, and in many instances we can see the extent to which they facilitate and/or impede each other. Consider the following discussion by Goldstein (1980):

> . . . "uncooperative" behaviors employed by [seriously ill] patients are viewed as attempts to minimize or avoid the recognition of one's tenuous hold on life by "proving" to themselves and others that life-threatening treatments are not required, and therefore, that they are not as critically ill as others might fear. However, by denying the severity of their condition and the need for treatment, such patients risk their lives through noncompliance with the treatment regimen. . . . (p. 90)

Emotion-focused coping strategies in the above account include those "designed to make life more bearable by avoiding realities which might prove to be overwhelming if directly confronted" (p. 90), which Goldstein labels as minimization and avoidance. These strategies interfere with the treatment regimen, which in this context comprises the problem-focused function.

Hay and Oken (1972) note that strategies such as distancing and avoidance seemed to decrease the distress of nurses in an intensive care unit, which in turn helped them to pursue their patient care tasks more effectively. An interesting by-product of this combination of emotion- and problem-focused coping is that the same techniques used by the nurses to regulate emotion that facilitated their delivery of health care probably also made them appear detached and mechanical to their patients, perhaps frustrating the patients' needs for warmth and emotional support.

Another example is provided by Kahn et al. (1964) in a study of organizational stress. They describe an incident in which an employee is accused by his peer of not carrying out a particular procedure. The interviewer asks, "What did you do when that happened?" The response:

> "Well, it burned me up. . . . My immediate first reaction was to confirm . . . that what he was saying was not true, that everything [letters] had gone out. There's always a chance you might be wrong so I checked first. Then I told him. No, everything had gone out. My immediate reaction was to call him on the carpet first. He doesn't have any right to call me on something like this. Then I gave it a second thought and decided that that wouldn't help the situation." (pp. 301–302)

The first strategies this man used were directed at the problem itself. He confirmed that everything had gone out. He also inhibited an impulse to express his anger, and "to call him on the carpet first." He decided that an expression of anger would interfere with a solution. In other words, he regulated his emotional distress in order to facilitate problem-focused coping.

Another point that is illustrated in these accounts is that emotion- and problem-focused coping often occur concurrently. It seems likely, for example, that the employee experienced anger and inhibited its expression at the same time that he took action to confirm whether the letters had gone out. However, if we were to look at a longer period, as in recovery from traumas, we might see a clearer pattern of sequence of strategies. For instance, descriptions of recovery from traumatic events such as spinal cord injury or the death of a loved one show a common pattern in which a period of denial or minimization (emotion-focused coping) occurs immediately after the event, to be gradually replaced by problem-focused concerns having to do with treatment programs, accommodating to the limitations imposed by the trauma, restoring, maintaining, or developing relationships, and in general getting on with one's life (for examples, see Andreason, Noyes, & Hartford, 1972; Hamburg et al., 1953; Kübler-Ross, 1969; Moos, 1977; Visotsky et al., 1961).

Empirical Evidence

There is also substantial empirical support for these distinctions between problem- and emotion-focused coping. Mechanic (1962) uses
similar distinctions in his rich and systematic study of graduate students preparing for doctoral examinations. His term *coping behavior*
refers to thoughts and behaviors relevant to "defining, attacking,
and meeting the task" (p. 51). *Defense* refers to the maintenance of
the integration of personality and the control of feeling states. In
other words, Mechanic uses *coping* for what we call problem-focused
coping, and *defense* for emotion-focused coping.

Problem-focused strategies related to meeting the task include
selecting content areas to study, preparing, and allocating time for
studying and for developing approaches to questions. Strategies
used to regulate emotion include seeking comforting information
from the environment that was consistent with the attitudes and
hopes the student held about the examinations, joking and humor,
being a member of a select group, magical practices, hostility, seeking support, avoiding other students, finding acceptable possible
reasons should they fail, tranquilizers, and externalizing responsibility. This list was not constrained by traditional notions of defense
and concern with reality and ego functioning. Instead, Mechanic
examined all ways—behavioral as well as cognitive—that can be
used to regulate feeling states. He also referred to the interplay
between task- and emotion-related devices. He pointed out, for example, that students who looked at old examination questions as a
preparation technique found that the old questions made them anxious, leading some to reduce or discontinue the practice. "This indicates that the students do compromise between their coping and
defense needs" (p. 93).

The ubiquity of problem- and emotion-focused functions is
clearly demonstrated in our empirical work on coping (Folkman &
Lazarus, 1980). Data were gathered on the ways 100 middle-aged,
community-residing adults coped with the stressful events of daily
living during the course of a year. Each subject reported approximately 14 stressful episodes, which ranged from minor concerns
with house repairs or family celebrations to concerns with aging
parents, life-threatening illness, and death. Subjects reported the
thoughts and behaviors they used to deal with the demands of these
events on a 68-item Ways of Coping checklist. The items on the
checklist were drawn from the domains of defensive coping, information seeking, problem solving, palliation, inhibition of action, di-

rect action, and magical thinking. Each item was classified (using both rational and empirical procedures) under the general rubric of emotion-focused or problem-focused. Emotion-focused strategies included such items as "looked for the silver lining, tried to look on the bright side of things"; "accepted sympathy and understanding from someone"; and "tried to forget the whole thing." Examples of problem-focused strategies included "got the person responsible to change his or her mind"; "made a plan of action and followed it"; and "stood your ground and fought for what you wanted."

Findings indicated that both functions were used by everyone in virtually every stressful encounter: of the 1,332 episodes included in the analysis, there were only 18 in which only one function was used. This finding points up that people use *both* problem- and emotion-focused coping strategies to deal with the internal and/or external demands posed by real-life stressful situations.

Further, several of the types of emotion-focused coping mentioned earlier were found in a factor analysis of the coping data from this field study. Included were the categories of wishful thinking, interpreting events as opportunities for personal growth, minimizing threat, seeking social support, and blaming self. There was also one problem-focused category, and another that was a mixture of information-seeking problem-focused coping and avoidant emotion-focused coping (Aldwin, Folkman, Schaefer, Coyne, & Lazarus, 1980). These more narrowly defined coping functions proved to be differentially related to outcome. We shall discuss these findings in Chapter 7. We found a similar array of coping factors in two subsequent studies (Folkman & Lazarus, in press). The important point is that it is useful to look within the larger functions for various types of problem- and emotion-focused coping. It is also important, however, to keep the two major functions in mind to ensure that both are evaluated.

Coping Resources

We have stated that coping is determined by cognitive appraisal. In earlier chapters we focused on primary appraisal as well as the properties of the person and environment that influence the judgment that something of importance is at stake in an encounter. In this chapter we consider secondary appraisal, which addresses the question "What can I do?" The answer to this question is a key determinant of what the person will actually do. Although many features of the person and environment that were described in Chapters 3 and 4 affect secondary appraisal, the ways people actually cope also depend heavily on the resources that are available to them and the constraints that inhibit use of these resources in the context of the specific encounter.

To say that a person is resourceful means that he or she has many resources and/or is clever in finding ways of using them to counter demands. These meanings share the idea that resources are something one draws upon, whether they are readily available to the person (e.g., money, tools, people to help, relevant skills) or whether they exist as competencies for finding resources that are needed but not available. Both meanings are relevant to our discussion.

Antonovsky (1979) has used the term *generalized resistance resources* to describe characteristics that facilitate the management of stress. These characteristics can be physical, biochemical, artifactual-material, cognitive, emotional, attitudinal, interpersonal, and macro-sociocultural. Antonovsky's approach differs from ours in that he is concerned with factors that contribute to *resistance* to stress, whereas we are concerned with the resources which a person *draws on in order to cope.* This difference in orientation is reflected in Antonovsky's inclusion of coping as a resistance resource, whereas we see coping as a process that evolves from resources. In other words, Antonovsky sees resources as buffers of stress, and we see them as factors that precede and influence coping, which in turn mediates stress.

The extent to which resources by themselves buffer the effects of stress as compared to actual coping processes was examined empirically by Pearlin and Schooler (1978). Pearlin and Schooler looked at mastery and self-esteem and at the relationship between these characteristics and coping responses and reduction of emotional distress in four role areas: household economics, job, parenting, and marriage. They found that in the close interpersonal context of marriage, and to a lesser extent in parenting, it is the specific things people do that more closely determine whether or not they will experience emotional distress, whereas possessing the "right" resources is somewhat more effective in dealing with relatively impersonal problems. Pearlin and Schooler suggest that resources are

> more helpful in sustaining people facing strains arising out of conditions over which they may have little direct control—finances and job. But where one is dealing with problems residing in close interpersonal relationships, it is the things one does that make the most difference. (p. 13)

It would be impossible to catalogue all of the resources upon which people draw in order to cope with the myriad demands of living. Instead, we shall identify major categories of resources. Our purpose is not to be exhaustive, but to illustrate the multidimensionality of coping resources and the various levels of abstraction at which several of these dimensions can be considered. We shall begin with resources that are primarily properties of the person. These include health and energy (a physical resource), positive beliefs (a psychological resource), and problem-solving and social skills (competencies). The remaining categories are more environmental and include social and material resources.

Health and Energy

These are among the most pervasive resources in that they are relevant to coping in many, if not all, stressful encounters. A person who is frail, sick, tired, or otherwise debilitated has less energy to expend on coping than a healthy, robust person. The important role played by physical well-being is particularly evident in enduring problems and in stressful transactions demanding extreme mobilization.

One can, of course, overstate the importance of health and energy for coping. Much research (e.g., Bulman & Wortman, 1977; Dimsdale, 1974; Hamburg & Adams, 1967; Hamburg et al., 1953; Visotsky et al., 1961) suggests that people are capable of coping surprisingly well despite poor health and depleted energy. Thus, whereas health and energy certainly facilitate coping efforts—it is easier to cope when one is feeling well than when one is not—people who are ill and enervated can usually mobilize sufficiently to cope when the stakes are high enough.

Positive Beliefs

Viewing oneself positively can also be regarded as a very important psychological resource for coping. We include in this category those general and specific beliefs that serve as a basis for hope and that sustain coping efforts in the face of the most adverse conditions. As we noted in Chapter 3, hope can be encouraged by the generalized belief that outcomes are controllable, that one has the power to affect such outcomes, that a particular person (e.g., a doctor) or program (e.g., treatment) is efficacious, or by positive beliefs about justice, free will, or God. Hope can exist only when such beliefs make a positive outcome seem possible, if not probable.

The view of positive beliefs as a coping resource is in the tradition of "inspirational" writers such as Norman Vincent Peale, who claim functional powers for positive thinking and the capacity to put a good light on experiences. What is not clear is whether there are costs to positive thinking, and whether people who do not engage in it can be influenced to do so. It may be that those who most need to cultivate this capacity are the least able to. We think it is important to study positive thinking, including the conditions that encourage it, its costs and benefits, and the extent to which it can be developed through interventions.

Not all beliefs serve as coping resources. Indeed, some beliefs can dampen or inhibit coping efforts. For instance, a belief in a punitive God can lead a person to accept a distressing situation as punishment and to do nothing about mastering or managing the situational demands. A belief in fate (an external locus of control) can lead to an appraisal of helplessness that in turn discourages relevant problem-focused coping. Similarly, a negative belief about one's capacity to have any control in a situation, or about the efficacy of a particular strategem to which one is committed, can discourage essential problem-focused coping efforts.

The extent to which a given belief system is generalized also influences its role as a resource. As we noted in Chapter 3, belief systems vary from those that apply to virtually every environmental context to those that have a very narrow range of applicability. A belief in a paternal God may permeate a person's appraisal in practically all stressful encounters and influence coping activity in both direction and strength, whereas beliefs about personal control and mastery may be limited to selected situations. A belief that one has poorer control over outcomes at work than at home can discourage problem-focused coping in the former context. Thus, both the nature of a belief system and the extent to which it is generalized determine its value as a resource or liability in the appraisal and coping process.

Despite its theoretical importance as a resource, little research has been done on how beliefs are actually manifested in coping processes. Of the beliefs that we have posited above as coping resources, those that pertain to control have received the most research attention. For example, a general belief about an internal locus of control (usually measured by the Rotter scale) yields more effort and persistence in achievement situations (for review see Lefcourt, 1976) than belief in an external locus. Likewise, as we noted in Chapter 3, positive appraisals of control in a specific encounter, which Bandura (1977a) refers to as efficacy expectancies, also determine coping effort and persistence (see also Bandura, 1982).

Several studies also suggest that general control expectancies are related to the *type* of coping activity. In her review of research on internal–external locus of control expectancies and health attitudes and behaviors, Strickland (1978) cites studies indicating that people who believe that outcomes are dependent on their own behavior cope differently with health problems than people who see outcomes to be the result of luck, chance, fate, or powers beyond their personal control. Those with an internal locus of control are more likely to collect information about disease and health maintenance when alerted to possible hazards, such as hypertension (e.g., Wallston, Maides, & Wallston, 1976; Wallston, Wallston et al., 1976); are more likely to take action to improve their health habits (e.g., James, Woodruff, & Werner, 1965; Mlott & Mlott, 1975; Steffy, Meichenbaum, & Best, 1970; Straits & Sechrest, 1963; Williams, 1973); engage in preventive dental care (Williams, 1972); and practice birth control effectively (MacDonald, 1970). (See also Lau, 1982; and Lau & Ware, 1982, for a health-specific locus of control scale.)

Anderson (1977) examined the relationship between locus of control and coping behaviors among 102 owner-managers of small businesses during the 3½-year period following a flood. He found that people with an internal locus of control used more task-related coping behaviors than those with an external locus of control and that people with an external locus of control responded with more defensiveness than those with an internal locus of control. Examples of task-oriented coping behavior included problem-solving efforts such as obtaining aid to deal with the initial loss. Behavior directed at managing emotional or anxiety reactions included withdrawal, group affiliation, hostility, and aggression.

Rothbaum, Wolfer, and Visintainer (1979) report a relationship between coping behavior and locus of control in children. Their findings suggest that *inward behavior* (e.g., helplessness) is related to external locus of control, and *outward behavior* (e.g., aggression) is related to internal locus of control. However, their study is limited by its measure of coping, which is heavily oriented toward pathology, and seems to be more a list of stress responses than coping behaviors. For instance, *inward* items include: not responsive to others; curled up or hunched over; stomach aches or headaches. *Outward* items include: yelling or screaming; disobedient; overactive, hitting or breaking things (p. 123).

The discussions by Anderson (1977) and Strickland (1978) suggest that general beliefs about locus of control do influence coping: internals seem to use more problem-focused forms of coping, and externals more emotion-focused forms. Data from our study of 45-to-65-year-olds provide mixed findings (Folkman, Aldwin, & Lazarus, 1981). General beliefs about locus of control were not related to coping; contrary to what might be expected, internals did not use more problem-focused coping than did externals.

On the other hand, situational control appraisals, which were reported by each subject for each event, were strongly related to coping, as we noted in Chapter 3. Situations appraised as holding the possibility for change (control) were associated with more problem-focused coping than those having to be accepted. Conversely, situations that had to be accepted were associated with more emotion-focused coping than those appraised as changeable. Similarly, in our study of emotions and coping during a midterm exam (Folkman & Lazarus, in press), problem-focused coping was used more than emotion-focused coping during the period of preparation for the exam. After the exam, while students were waiting for grades to be announced and nothing more could be done to affect the outcome of the exam, emotion-focused coping increased and problem-focused coping decreased.

In Chapter 3 we also discussed the two-sided nature of *commitments,* pointing out that the more deeply held the commitment, the more vulnerable the person is to threat but at the same time the more motivated to ward off any threats and harms to that commitment. The motivational property of commitments is an important resource because the person is impelled toward coping activity and is more apt to sustain it. Thus, the motivational quality of commitments has an effect similar to positive beliefs that generate hope: both help sustain coping effort in the face of obstacles. (See also Chapter 8 for discussion of involvement and alienation.)

Problem-solving Skills

Problem-solving skills include the ability to search for information, analyze situations for the purpose of identifying the problem in order to generate alternative courses of action, weigh alternative courses of action, weigh alternatives with respect to desired or anticipated outcomes, and select and implement an appropriate plan of action (Janis, 1974; Janis & Mann, 1977); they are also important resources for coping. Such general, abstract skills are ultimately expressed in specific acts, such as changing a flat tire, presenting oneself to a prospective employer, preparing for an examination, and so on. Some writers conceptualize skills in broad terms, such as dealing with moral dilemmas (Schwartz, 1970), emergency situations (for reviews see Appley & Trumbull, 1967; Baker & Chapman, 1962; Coelho et al., 1974; Janis, 1958; Lazarus, 1966), role conflict, marital conflict (Levinger, 1966; Parsons & Bales, 1955), or ambiguity (Haan, 1977). Others favor narrower definitions such as one might find in training manuals (Meichenbaum, 1977; Rogers, 1977; Yates, 1976). Problem-solving skills are themselves drawn from other resources— a wide range of experiences, the person's store of knowledge, his or her cognitive/intellectual ability to use that knowledge, and the capacity for self-control (e.g., Rosenbaum, 1980a, b, in press).

Social Skills

Social skills are an important coping resource because of the pervasive role of social functioning in human adaptation. They refer to the ability to communicate and behave with others in ways that are socially appropriate and effective. Social skills facilitate problem-solving in conjunction with other people, increase the likelihood of being able to enlist their cooperation or support, and in general give the individual greater control over social interactions.

The importance of social skills as a resource is evident in many areas, including therapeutic programs that help the individual better manage the problems of daily living and organizational training programs to improve interpersonal communications skills. The movement within organizations to teach communications skills reflects a trend in which solutions to problems are less likely to depend on individual action than on the ability to work out solutions involving group action (Mechanic, 1974). The more pronounced this trend becomes, the more important social skills will be in working in cooperative relationships with others.

Attempts to conceptualize and assess the social skills of both children and adults are now proliferating (e.g., Bond & Rosen, 1980; Kent & Rolf, 1979; Zigler & Trickett, 1978). McFall (1982) provides a thoughtful review of measurement approaches in this area. He identifies two major models, a trait model, which treats social skills as a general, underlying personality characteristic or response predisposition, and what he calls a molecular model, in which social skills are construed in terms of specific, observable units of behavior. In general, measures based on the trait model are psychometrically weak and have not related to performance in criterion situations. Measurements based on the molecular model pose a different set of problems such as uncertaintly about the size and scope of units of analysis, and whether or not to include in the assessment the behavior of the other person involved in the interaction. McFall suggests that neither the trait nor the molecular model is adequate and proposes an alternative two-tiered model based on an information-processing approach.

Most attempts to evaluate social skills have the practical objective of improving those skills in what has been referred to as the primary prevention of psychopathology (e.g., Cowan, 1980). Although not based on clinical intervention, the work of Murphy (Murphy & Moriarty, 1976; Murphy & associates, 1962), which involves observations of how children gain coping competence through struggles with the ordinary stresses of living and growing up, is also highly relevant.

Social Support

Having people from whom one receives emotional, informational, and/or tangible support has been receiving growing attention as a coping resource in stress research, behavioral medicine, and social epidemiology (e.g., Antonovsky, 1972, 1979; Berkman & Syme, 1979; Cassel, 1976; Cobb, 1976; Kaplan, Cassel, & Gore, 1977; Nuckolls, Cassel, & Kaplan, 1972). We discuss this resource at length in Chapter 8, and therefore we need only note it here without elaboration.

Material Resources

This refers to money and the goods and services that money can buy. This obvious resource is rarely mentioned in discussions of coping (see also Antonovsky, 1979), although its importance is implied in discussions of the strong relationships that are found among economic status, stress, and adaptation (cf. Antonovsky, 1979; House, 1979; Syme & Berkman, 1976). People with money, especially if they have the skills to use it effectively, generally fare much better than those without. Obviously, monetary resources greatly increase the coping options in almost any stressful transaction; they provide easier and often more effective access to legal, medical, financial, and other professional assistance. Simply having money, even if it is not drawn upon, may reduce the person's vulnerability to threat and in this way also facilitate effective coping.

Constraints Against
Utilizing Coping Resources

The novelty and complexity of many stressful encounters create demands that often exceed the person's resources. For many occasions, however, resources are in fact adequate, but the person does not use them to their fullest because to do so might create additional conflict and distress. The factors that restrict the ways an individual deals with the environment may be called constraints, some of which arise from personal agendas, others of which are environmental.

Personal Constraints

Personal constraints refer to internalized cultural values and beliefs that proscribe certain types of action or feeling, and psychological deficits that are a product of the person's unique development. We also call these personal constraints personal agendas. Culturally derived values and beliefs serve as norms that determine when certain behaviors and feelings are appropriate and when they are not. Humor may be an appropriate and effective device for reducing tension in an escalating argument, but it would be inappropriate and indeed tension-provoking at a funeral. In an investigation by Klass (1981), women students who felt a high sense of guilt over assertive behavior reported being less assertive in social contexts than women with low guilt. The measure of guilt suggests a personal constraint, presumably derived from their process of socialization. Undoubtedly, there are some situations where an individual will be more influenced by cultural norms, depending in part on what is at stake and the consequences for violating them. Also, individuals differ in the extent to which they comply with norms. Nevertheless, even allowing for a wide range of situational and individual differences, culturally derived values, beliefs, and norms operate as important constraints.

For example, people may have at their disposal many forms of social support in a crisis but be unable to use them because of how they construe this support. They may decline proffered help because it implies that they are needy or helpless; or they may not want to feel under obligation or perhaps they distrust the motive behind the help. Analyses of the reactions of recipients of help who are handicapped suggest that they are commonly offered help tactlessly or without an understanding of what is really needed, in which case they might find it difficult or demeaning to accept.

Similarly, as we noted above, Mechanic (1974) states that the solution to certain problems is likely to depend on the ability and willingness of people to work together. He writes that individuals

> who may be adaptive and effective persons from a psychological perspective may be unfitted because of their values and individual orientations for the kinds of group cooperation that are necessary in developing solutions to particular kinds of community problems. Thus, many effective copers may become impotent in influencing their environment because of their resistance or inability to submerge themselves into cooperative organized relationships with others. (pp. 36–37)

There are many other examples of personal agendas that can constrain coping. One is tolerance of ambiguity (Frenkel-Brunswik, 1949), which we discussed in Chapter 3. The premature closure that characterizes this personality disposition can seriously constrain the exent to which the person fully utilizes resources. Other possibilities include fear of failure and fear of success (e.g., Atkinson, 1964; Horner, 1972), which can interfere with coping in situations where outcomes are likely to be evaluated. Problems with authority figures, dependency needs, and preferred styles of doing things can also figure prominently as constraints. (For discussions of how preferred styles can constrain coping, see pp. 73–74, Chapter 3.)

Environmental Constraints

Constraints exist as much in the environment as they do in the person. For instance, there can be competing demands for the same resources. Since many resources are finite—especially material resources such as money—choices have to be made as to how to allocate them. In other instances, the environment thwarts the effective use of resources, which is illustrated in the study by Dill et al. (1980) of stress and coping in low-income working mothers that we mentioned in Chapter 3. Their respondents provided numerous examples of how public institutions were unresponsive to their efforts to cope with adverse situations. One respondent, for example, through no failure of effort or imagination on her part, was unsuccessful in getting her dyslexic and emotionally disturbed child into a Big Brother program or after-school day care or a special school for the learning disabled. Other women were equally unsuccessful in obtaining needed and appropriate assistance, and they often evaluated the environmental response as a reflection of their own incompetence, even though they had very little objective control over those institutional forces. Dill et al. conclude that environments may differ in the nature and frequency of threats posed to the individual and in the breadth of options available for addressing threatening situations, and that the environment may respond to people's coping efforts in ways which negate their strategies.

The thrust of this discussion has been to view constraints as inhibitors of the effective use of coping resources. However, constraints can also be facilitative. A graphic example has been provided by Lucas (1969) in a detailed study of group behavior in a mine disaster. Trapped by an explosion, a group of six men ran out of water while awaiting rescue and had to confront the possibility of imminent death. In this case, social constraints helped maintain hope. Crying and other expressions of despair were gently restrained by one or another of the group members. The following vignette illustrates this process:

> "I [also] had tears in my eyes—but I said, 'Don't cry; we need all our strength.' That's what I said. And I said, 'I think I got strength enough yet for a couple more days and maybe more.' So he said, 'All right . . . I'll stop crying.' And we talked there quite a while." (pp. 273–274)

Whether or not such a purposive group function (here, to maintain hope) is a reasonable inference (see Merton, 1957, for an excellent critique of the errors of functional interpretation), there seems little doubt that such efforts did help the group members cope. Most important from the present standpoint, the example illustrates how social constraints facilitated individual and group coping.

Level of Threat

Threat appraisals can range from minimal, where little stress is experienced, to extreme, characterized by intense negative emotion such as fear. Along with resources and constraints, the level of threat the person experiences plays a role in determining coping. Here we get caught in some circularity. The extent to which a person feels threatened is in part a function of his or her evaluation of coping resources with respect to internal and external demands in a particular situation, as well as the constraints inhibiting their use. Level of threat, in turn, influences the extent to which available resources can be used for coping. Let us arbitrarily break this circularity by considering the effects of threat on coping.

The greater the threat, the more primitive, desperate, or regressive emotion-focused forms of coping tend to be and the more limited the range of problem-focused forms of coping. With respect to emotion-focused forms of coping, Menninger (1954) writes:

> Minor stresses are usually handled by relatively "normal" or "healthy" devices. Greater stresses or prolonged stress excite the ego to increasingly energetic and expansive activity in the interests of homeostatic maintenance." (p. 280)

Wheaton (1959), in a study of the effects of isolation, notes that as threats (such as hunger, thirst, injury, illness, or physical discomforts) were added to the experience of isolation, extreme pathological symptoms and "regression to a childlike type of emotional lability and behavior pattern" (p. 41) became more likely. He points out that the absence of any workable alternatives for coping encourages primitive defense activity.

Excessive threat interferes with problem-focused forms of coping through its effects on cognitive functioning and the capacity for information processing. The point is central in Janis and Mann's (1977) conflict model of decision making in which excessive threat leads to ineffective information gathering and evaluation, which they call hypervigilance. Hypervigilance is characterized by obsessive fantasies, constricted cognitive functioning, and premature closure (see Easterbrook, 1959; Hamilton, 1975; Korchin, 1964; Sarason, 1975). The reduction in information-processing and problem-solving capacity due to high threat is, for example, recognized by physicians when they give patients bad news. A patient's ability to hear what the physician has to say about prognosis, procedures, and treatment can be critically impaired by the high level of threat engendered by the diagnosis. The perceptive physician recognizes that the patient needs time to adjust to the diagnosis before information about treatment and procedure can be absorbed. Notice that we are not speaking here of denial, which also often characterizes the response to threatening information, but the reduction in cognitive functioning, and thereby access to problem-solving resources, caused by threat.

The study by Anderson (1977) of owner-managers whose businesses were damaged by floods, mentioned earlier, is particularly interesting in that it examines the effects of stress on both problem- and emotion-focused forms of coping. The situation was characterized by both harm/loss and threat. The harm/loss occurred at the time of the flooding, and the threat concerned its consequences.

Problem- and emotion-focused forms of coping were used with different frequencies depending on the level of perceived stress. For subjects perceiving relatively low degrees of stress, the two forms of coping appeared with similar frequency. At moderate ranges of perceived stress, problem-focused mechanisms, for example, taking action to recover the damage to their businesses, were the dominant coping response. At high levels of stress, emotion-focused forms of coping began to predominate, with subjects exhibiting a greater frequency of emotional or defensive behavior. Anderson concludes that "anxiety associated with high stress leads to overconcentration on emotional and defensive coping mechanisms and insufficient attention to problem-solving coping mechanisms, resulting in lower levels of performance" (pp. 33–34).

It is important to note that high levels of threat do not *necessarily* mean that either or both forms of coping will diminish in quality. Numerous anecdotal examples in the literature, especially in accounts of individuals coping with the stress of physical illness and disability and in extreme circumstances such as warfare or plane crashes, illustrate high-level emotional and cognitive functioning under the most difficult circumstances. Coping behavior is multidetermined; level of threat is only one of the determining factors.

It is also important to recognize that in some situations there are few, if any, options for problem solving. In such cases the absence of problem-focused coping should not be interpreted as primitivization, but rather as a function of the situation. Janoff-Bulman and Brickman (1982), for example, point out that adaptive coping includes knowing when to stop trying to achieve a goal that is unattainable.

An interesting line of investigation would be to examine the conditions under which problem- and emotion-focused coping are differentially affected by high degrees of threat. It is possible that high-level cognitive functioning can be sustained in a high-threat situation while at the same time emotion-focused coping becomes more primitivized. Denial, for instance, is considered a primitive defense. Are there not situations where the use of denial enables the person to preserve the emotional balance needed to engage in problem-solving activity? The converse, that is, restricted problem-solving activity in the presence of "mature" emotion-focused coping, seems less likely, unless, of course, such restrictions are a function of limited resources.

We conclude this section by pointing out why knowledge of a person's resources is not sufficient to predict coping. We have argued that the relationship between resources and coping is mediated by personal and environmental constraints and level of threat. Furthermore, coping resources are usually not constant over time; they are likely to expand and contract, some more erratically than others, as a function of experience, time of life, and the requirements of adaptation associated with different periods in the life course. Therefore, the presence of a given resource at a given time does not imply that it will be available for the same person to the same extent at another time.

We are not saying that resources should not be measured. On the contrary, we believe that information about resources can contribute to an understanding of why some people seem to be challenged more often than threatened, and fare better than others over the course of numerous stressful encounters. However, rather than listing resources and identifying personal and environmental constraints and the level of threat that mediates their use, we urge that greater attention be given to the actual coping processes through which the person manages the demands of a stressful encounter. By focusing on processes rather than resources and the factors that determine their use, we can more easily identify the mechanisms through which the stress–outcome relationship is mediated.

Control as Appraisal; Control as Coping

Intuitively it would seem that to cope with a situation is to attempt to control it—whether by altering the environment, changing the meaning of the situation, and/or managing one's emotions and behaviors. Indeed, when control refers to cognitive or behavioral *efforts* to deal with a stressful encounter, we see coping and control as synonymous and different from general and/or situational *beliefs* about control that influence cognitive appraisals of threat and challenge. The distinction between control as a belief that influences appraisal and control as coping is a subtle but important one if there is to be clarity about how control operates in stress and coping processes.

Rothbaum, Weisz, and Snyder (1982), for example, suggest a two-category taxonomy of control: *primary control*, the attempt to change the environment; and *secondary control,* the attempt to fit in with the environment or "flow with the current" (p. 8). The key word here is *attempt,* which places these concepts in the category of coping rather than belief or appraisal, though they actually seem to be speaking of a kind of appraisal. For example, they differentiate four subordinate modes of secondary control, namely, *predictive control,* the prediction of aversive events in the service of avoiding disappointment; *illusory control,* in which the person aligns with the forces of chance to share in the control exerted by those powerful forces; *vicarious control,* achieved by associating with powerful others; and *interpretive control,* the ability to interpret events so as to better understand them.

Averill (1973) also implicates effort in his discussion of control. For example, he identifies *behavioral control,* which involves direct action on the environment that presumably involves effort. He also speaks of *cognitive control,* which refers to the way a potentially harmful event is interpreted; and *decisional control,* which is the range of choice or number of options open to the individual. The latter forms of control suggest effort, although they could also operate as beliefs.

Thompson's (1981) taxonomy at first glance appears similar to Averill's (1973) in that she speaks of behavioral, cognitive, informational, and retrospective control. However, these forms of control are described as beliefs, not as efforts. Behavioral control, for example, is a "belief that one has a behavioral response available that can affect the aversiveness of an event" (Thompson, 1981, p. 90).

Clearly, the concept of control has become multipurpose, and this leads to inevitable analytic confusion. By disaggregating the concept of control with respect to its appraisal and coping functions, we are better able to define the pathways through which control affects the outcomes of stressful encounters and short- and long-term adaptational outcomes, as will be seen in the next chapter. Further, in order to be clear about definitions, when control implies effort we will use the language of coping rather than control, even though the terms are then synonymous.

Coping Over the Life Course

It has long been assumed that coping changes from childhood to old age. Changes are certainly evident in early development as the young child comes to understand the world and learn complex problem- and emotion-focused ways of coping. Lois Murphy and her colleagues (1962, 1974; Murphy & Moriarty, 1976) have suggested that despite changes in the details of coping, from primitive modes of reacting to complex, cognitive processes, the biological base for shutting out, exploring, and aggressing come into being very early and remain a constant factor in coping. Nevertheless, the course of coping from childhood to adulthood remains to be charted.

Whether or not coping changes from early adulthood to old age is controversial. That it does change has been suggested by Jung (1933, 1953), who is virtually the only psychodynamic thinker of Freud's era who paid much attention to later-life phenomena. Erikson's (1963) stage theory of the life course has many Freudian features and clearly implies that what we would call coping changes at various periods of life. However, this analysis is stated more in terms of the basic conflicts or psychological tasks of each period and is not easily connected with the concepts of problem-focused and emotion-focused coping that we have been emphasizing here.

Research by Gutmann (1974) suggests that as people age they move from active mastery, that is, aggressive controlling modes of coping, to more passive modes, and ultimately to a regressive· reliance on magical modes. Vaillant (1977) and Pfeiffer (1977) also state that coping changes with age, but in different directions than suggested by Gutmann. Vaillant and Pfeiffer say that coping becomes more effective and realistic with age. There is less dependence on immature mechanisms such as projection and acting out and more use of mature mechanisms such as altruism, humor, and suppression. Field studies such as those of Lowenthal et al. (1975) provide some evidence that the social roles of men and women become more similar during middle age, and accordingly men become more dependent, while women more aggressive and domineering. Our findings on life events and hassles strongly suggest that sources of stress change with age (see also Estes & Wilensky, 1978). This theme is also emphasized theoretically by Hultsch and Plemons (1979) and Brim and Ryff (1980). Perhaps the best generalization regarding changes in coping over the life span, therefore, is that as sources of stress in living change with stage of life, coping will change in response.

That coping changes in basic ways, regardless of changes in sources of stress, is subject to doubt at the present time. With respect to problem- and emotion-focused coping, the evidence of systematic change for people in general is mostly negative. We found no clear differences in coping pattern from 45 to 64 years of age in a white middle-class sample (Folkman & Lazarus, 1980). A study by McCrae (1982), which employed our Ways of Coping checklist, produced similar findings. McCrae states:

> In most respects older people in these studies cope in much the same way as younger people; though they employ different mechanisms, it appears largely to be a function of the different types of stress they face; and in the two cases that showed consistent evidence of age differences unrelated to type of stress, middle-aged and older individuals were less inclined than younger men and women to rely on the theoretically immature mechanisms of hostile reaction and escapist fantasy. (p. 459)

The sample studied by McCrae was characterized by subjects generally in good mental and physical health, and economically well off. It is still possible, therefore, that the ailing and economically deprived elderly are forced by the loss of psychological, social, and material resources to cope differently than those who are healthier and economically more secure. Perhaps they emphasize problem-focused forms of coping less and address life's assaults more passively (see also Lieberman, 1975).

Elsewhere (Lazarus & DeLongis, 1983) we have argued, as do McCrae (1982) and Elder (1974), that changes in coping over the life span cannot be addressed solely by cross-sectional research. The reseacher cannot observe coping change with age in given individuals, as would be possible in longitudinal research. Furthermore, changes in beliefs and commitments as a means of coping with role loss and changes in physical resources (cf. Pearlin, 1980a, b; Rosow, 1963, 1967) will occur in different people at different times and in different ways over the adult course. (See Bandura, 1981; Lowenthal, 1977; Sarason, 1977; and Thomae, 1976, for further discussions of these developmental issues.) When we limit ourselves to averaging what people face and do within age groups, as in cross-sectional research, we are in danger of not being able to see the very changes in which we are interested. At this stage of knowledge, and without better evidence, it seems best to assume that aging per se brings no changes in coping; it is when people are faced with deteriorioating environmental conditions and impaired physical and mental resources that they display regression to the more dependent, helpless period of infancy and early childhood.

Prospects for the Study of Coping Styles

In moving toward a process definition and conceptualization of coping, we have gradually been forced to deal more and more with context and microanalysis. Coping thoughts and actions differ according to which situational demands are being attended to at any one time. If a patient with cancer is asked, "How are you coping with your cancer?" we do not know whether the thoughts and acts that are reported refer to managing pain, the side effects of treatment, or uncertain prognosis, the threat of death, or troubled interpersonal relationships generated by the illness—in effect, which aspects of the illness the person is dealing with at that moment. Similarly, because coping changes from the anticipatory to the outcome stages of a stressful encounter, we cannot understand coping without reference to the point in the encounter at which it is observed.

This process-oriented approach has an important drawback. Although it enables us to describe the process of coping in a specific encounter, including the particular situational demands, resources, and constraints that affect it, this emphasis on the specific context draws our attention away from the person's general coping style. The process approach is useful for studying the short-run consequences of stressful encounters; the difficulty is in characterizing the person's coping style over the long run. This handicaps our search for understanding how coping affects long-range outcomes such as somatic health, social functioning, and morale.

One of our options is to study a sufficient number and range of stressful encounters and coping patterns in the same persons and somehow to aggregate them in order to provide a picture of the typical pattern (or style) across encounters. Two formal aspects of the coping process might be considered as dimensions on which to examine coping over many encounters: complexity and flexibility. Complexity refers to the range of coping strategies used by the person at any given time and across times in dealing with a stressful situation. Does the person typically try just one strategy (a simple style), or does he or she use multiple strategies (a complex style)? Flexibility refers to whether the individual uses the same strategy or set of strategies in different situations, or even in similar situations, or instead varies them. White (1974) regards flexibility as phylogenetically crucial to survival.

There are indications that these formal dimensions are related to coping efficacy and functioning. Pearlin and Schooler (1978), for example, report a relationship between size of coping repertoire (complexity) and reduction of distress. On the other hand, Coyne, Aldwin, and Lazarus (1981) report that the use of a large number of strategies is associated with depression. The measures of coping used in the two studies are not comparable, and therefore these apparently contradictory findings cannot easily be interpreted, although it may be that there is a curvilinear relationship between coping complexity and adaptational outcome. The only conclusion one can safely draw is that the complexity of coping and its relationship to outcomes is interesting and warrants serious investigation.

The evidence is clearer favoring flexible versus rigid coping styles. Flexibility is associated with high levels of ego development (cf. Loevinger, 1976), "mature" ego processes (Haan, 1977; Vaillant, 1977), high-quality decision making (Janis & Mann, 1977), and resilience (Murphy & Moriarty, 1976; see also Block & Block, 1980, for discussion of the concepts of ego control and ego resiliency). Rigidity, on the other hand, is associated with low levels of ego functioning and, in its extreme, pathology (cf. Menninger, 1963; Shapiro, 1965).

Substantive characteristics of coping should also be considered, for example, what the person actually thinks or does to cope, underlying meaning systems that give coherence to diverse coping strategies, and the functions that coping strategies serve.

Although focusing on coping *behavior* has certain advantages—it can often be observed or self-reported—it also has limitations. First, there is the problem of the sheer number of such behaviors. Second, even if patterns of behaviors can be observed, they are *styles* only if they are used consistently. A high degree of consistency at the behavioral level, however, is not common in ordinary populations. For example, Pearlin and Schooler (1978) report that certain types of strategies are used consistently across the four role areas of marriage, parenting, household economics, and work, whereas other strategies are not. People consistently used selective perception and positive comparisons across all role areas, but strategies such as negotiation and substitution of rewards were used primarily in only the contexts of marriage and work, respectively. Ilfeld (1980), in an analysis of the same data set, reported a similar mixture of variability and stability. And our study of coping in a middle-aged population (Folkman & Lazarus, 1980) examined the extent to which people were intraindividually consistent or variable in relative proportions of problem- and emotion-focused coping. Our findings indicated that although there was a wide range of individual difference on this dimension, on the whole people were more variable than consistent in their use of the two forms of coping. These studies suggest that in coping with situations in day-to-day living, people are both consistent and variable in their coping.

Variability and consistency are difficult to interpret. Does it mean that situational factors are influencing coping? Or is coping varying in some sort of systematic way according to underlying person factors such as roles, patterns of commitments, goals, or beliefs? This problem plagues early efforts to study consistency at the behavioral level in personality psychology, as can be seen in the classic study by Hartshorne and co-workers (Hartshorne & May, 1928; Hartshorne, May, & Maller, 1929; Hartshorne, May, Maller, & Shuttleworth, 1930). This study asked whether moral character resided within a person independent of the circumstances. A large number of preadolescent children were studied under a variety of circumstances that permitted them to act honestly or dishonestly. Results indicated only slight consistency in behavior (an average correlation of about .30) from one situation to another. Arguing from these results, the authors propounded the doctrine of specificity, stipulating that honesty was not a character trait of the individual, but rather that there were only honest acts in response to particular situations.

The major limitation of this study is that the investigators defined consistency in a behavioral sense only, in that they asked whether honest or dishonest behavior would be repeated from situation to situation. They did not consider the underlying reasons that determined the behavior. For example, brighter children had less reason to cheat because they knew their work and were confident of doing well. Furthermore, the children were probably not all motivated to succeed in the same degree. Thus, although a child may have behaved inconsistently from situation to situation, the underlying reasons for the behavior were probably characteristics of the child's personality—and therefore consistent. A child who was highly motivated to succeed and knew the material well in one test situation might not cheat, but given a test that threatened the child with failure, he or she might behave dishonestly. The superficial behavior might be different from situation to situation, but the underlying structure, say, the child's pattern of motivation or general interpretations (appraisals) of the relationship between self and world, might be very stable in spite of changes in the external conditions (Lazarus, 1961).

The importance of underlying patterns of motivation and meaning systems in determining coping is, of course, one of the major themes of this book. We devoted Chapter 3 to a discussion of the ways such factors influence appraisal, and hence coping. Lipowski (1970–1971) makes a similar point in his discussion of coping styles, coping strategies, and illness:

> It is the writer's thesis that coping strategies are directly related to the individual's personal meaning or an attitude towards his illness, injury or disability. . . . It [the given meaning] functions as a cognitive nucleus which influences emotional and motivational responses to illness and thus the coping strategies. (p. 98)

Lipowski described common categories of the meaning of illness and disease that reflect the past personal experiences, knowledge, cultural background, and beliefs of the sick people. For example:

> (1) Illness as challenge. This common view of illness inspires active and generally adaptive coping strategies. Disease or disability is seen as any other life situation which imposes specific demands and tasks to be mastered and which is accomplished by any means available. The related attitudes and coping patterns tend to be flexible and rational. . . . Timely seeking of medical advice, cooperation, information seeking . . . , rationally modulated activity and passivity, finding substitute gratifications—these are some of the related and desirable coping strategies.
>
> (2) Illness as enemy. Disease is viewed as an invasion by inimical forces, internal or external. Our language clearly reflects this attitude when we talk of "combating" illness or "conquest" or disease. The usual emotional concomitants of this meaning are anxiety, fear and/or anger. These feelings inspire the readiness to flight or fight or helpless surrender, depending on the current appraisal by the subject of his capacity to resist. In its extreme pathological form this attitude may be frankly paranoid and others may be blamed for having caused or aggravated the illness (Orback & Bieber, 1957). Free-floating anxiety or hostility may appear. Coping strategies reflect this attitude and take various forms of defense against danger and attack. Some degree of denial and projection are common, although regressive dependency and passivity may express a sense of helplessness and readiness to surrender. (p. 98)

Our recognition of beliefs such as these brings coherence and consistency to coping behaviors which might otherwise appear inconsistent and difficult to explain in relation to the demands posed by an illness.

We also suggested above that coping styles could be defined at the substantive level in terms of the functions coping strategies serve, for example, to avoid, confront, or analyze. We believe that such functions should be drawn from the problem-managing *and* emotion-regulating domains. Most coping styles are defined in terms of the emotion-regulating functions (e.g., repression-sensitization). To confine a coping style to just the regulation of emotion—and just one dimension of it at that—is to exclude the important problem-solving functions of coping, a point we discussed at length earlier in this chapter.

Thus, our criticism of the structural or trait-style approach to coping is not based on the claim that it is inappropriate, unimportant, or unnecessary in order to locate stable patterns of coping, but rather on the impression that previous efforts have not been successful. As we noted earlier, these attempts grossly simplify complex patterns of coping into unidimensional schemes such as repression-sensitization which have little explanatory and predictive value for what the person actually does in particular contexts. The problem of assessing stable patterns cannot be dismissed, whether or not we will ultimately succeed in building them out of the details of how the person handled numerous specific stressful encounters.

It remains to be seen whether a microanalytic process-oriented approach to coping will take us further toward understanding the coping process and explaining adaptational outcomes from the global, structural approaches that have thus far dominated coping theory and research.

Summary

In this chapter we have presented our own conceptualization of coping. We defined coping as constantly changing cognitive and behavioral efforts to manage specific external and/or internal demands that are appraised as taxing or exceeding the resources of the person. This definition is process- rather than trait-oriented in that it is concerned with what the person actually thinks or does in a specific context, and with changes in these thoughts and actions across encounters or as an encounter unfolds. The definition also distinguishes between coping efforts and automatized adaptive behaviors, and it avoids the problem of confounding coping with outcomes by defining coping as all efforts to manage regardless of outcome.

Changes in coping are often conceptualized as occurring in

stages. There are reasons to be wary of stage formulations when they imply an invariant sequence; evidence suggests substantial variations among persons in the ordering and duration of different kinds of coping across and even within particular types of stressful encounters. Moreover, what sometimes looks like self-generated stages of coping may actually represent a sequence of external demands, as in the concepts of anticipation (or warnings), confrontation, and postconfrontation in disaster research.

Coping serves two overriding functions: managing or altering the problem with the environment causing distress (problem-focused coping), and regulating the emotional response to the problem (emotion-focused coping). Support for these two functions of coping comes from anecdotal accounts and empirical research. Problem- and emotion-focused coping influence each other throughout a stressful encounter; they can both facilitate and impede each other.

The way a person copes is determined in part by his or her resources, which include health and energy; existential beliefs, e.g., about God, or general beliefs about control; commitments, which have a motivational property that can help sustain coping; problem-solving skills; social skills; social support; and material resources.

Coping is also determined by constraints that mitigate the use of resources. Personal constraints include internalized cultural values and beliefs that proscribe certain ways of behaving and psychological deficits. Environmental constraints include demands that compete for the same resources and agencies or institutions that thwart coping efforts. High levels of threat can also prevent a person from using coping resources effectively.

Efforts to exercise control are synonymous with coping. On the other hand, control in the sense of general and/or situational beliefs operates as appraisal dispositions or processes. The distinction between control as coping and control as appraisal is essential if there is to be clarity about these important concepts in stress and coping theory and research.

Although it has long been assumed that coping per se changes over the life course, the case has not been made empirically. Current research suggests that sources of stress change as people age, and as a consequence coping changes to meet the new demands. Longitudinal research is needed to address this question.

Our process approach to coping, which requires a contextual analysis of stressful encounters, makes it difficult to conceptualize and assess a person's overall coping style. A process approach might lead to a study of coping styles only if a sufficient number of encounters from a person's day-to-day life are examined. Two formal dimensions of style that might be considered are complexity and flexibility, as well as substantive aspects of coping such as distancing, confronting, and minimizing. Efforts should be made to identify the appraised meaning of situations, which underlies the ways a person copes, since this could help explain variability in coping in specific contexts or classes of contexts. It remains to be seen whether or not a process approach to coping such as ours can be used to describe coping styles.

7

Appraisal, Coping, and Adaptational Outcomes

Regardless of how they are defined or conceptualized, the prime importance of appraisal and coping processes is that they affect adaptational outcomes. The three basic kinds of outcome are functioning in work and social living, morale or life satisfaction, and somatic health. Simply put, the quality of life and what we usually mean by mental and physical health are tied up with the ways people evaluate and cope with the stresses of living. The task of this chapter is to spell out the mechanisms through which appraisal and coping might affect adaptational outcomes in individuals.

In laying the groundwork for our discussion, we want to emphasize that we do not view stress as inherently maladaptive and deleterious. Major stress—what is sometimes referred to as a crisis—causes some people to draw upon adaptive resources they never thought they had. Such people can gain strength from stress that can be used in subsequent crises; they seem to *grow* from stress. By the same token, people who as children are protected from certain kinds of stress are likely to be all the more vulnerable to stress later because they fail to learn coping skills that are needed for day-to-day living (cf. Murphy & Moriarty, 1976). We know too that life without stress would be an exercise in boredom, which has its own negative somatic consequences (cf. Frankenhaeuser, 1976). Indeed, people often seek stress, although we have at best only a rudimentary understanding of this (see Klausner, 1968; Zuckerman, 1979); they take high risks, such as diving from airplanes, pitting themselves against the elements, and engaging in a host of other activities that belie a strictly tension-reduction view of human activity. Thus, the question should not be whether stress is good or bad, but rather how much, what kinds, at which times during the life course, and under what social and personal conditions it is harmful or helpful.

The same distinction between positive and negative applies to emotion. The concept of adaptation in biology refers to the capacity of a species, and an individual animal, to survive and flourish. Through natural selection, successfully functioning biological forms emerged able to extract a livelihood from the physical and social environment. Among mammals, emotions presumably played a positive, adaptive role in this evolutionary process. For example, anger involves impulses to assault the environment, thereby to bring down an adversary, make the adversary back off or retreat, or otherwise to change for the better a damaging relationship with the environment. Fear often serves a valuable function in survival by galvanizing escape or avoidance. Even depression has been analyzed from this standpoint in Bowlby's (1969, 1973) work on separation and loss and in Averill's (1968) analysis of grief. While these adaptive emotions and their impulses may overshoot the mark and create their own ailments, as in the "diseases of adaptation," without them it is questionable whether species now surviving and flourishing, including humans, would have evolved successfully. We must not be misled by the negative consequences of these and other emotions into understating their positive functions in human adaptation.

We also want to emphasize that we are concerned with all aspects of health—physical, psychological, and social. Too often one aspect of adaptational outcome is emphasized without regard to the others. The emerging field of behavioral medicine, for instance, is overly preoccupied with somatic illness and too little concerned with other critieria of adaptational soundness such as social functioning (e.g., in the family and at work) and morale or life satisfaction. Studies by Tobin and Lieberman (1976) and Rosow (1967) demonstrate, for example, that many old people who are physically ill and moderately incapacitated appraise their health status and life circumstances quite positively. They are happy and function well. A distorted picture of adaptational status would have been created in the above research if only somatic criteria had been considered.

Each of the three major long-term adaptational outcomes with which we are concerned—social functioning, morale, and somatic health—has its counterpart in the short-term outcomes of stressful encounters: social functioning in the effectiveness with which the demands of a specific encounter are managed; morale in the positive and negative affect a person experiences during and after an encounter; and somatic health in the physiological changes that are generated by a stressful encounter. Both the short- and long-term outcomes of stressful encounters can thus be understood as including effective, affective, and physiological components.

The parallelism between short- and long-term outcomes does not mean there is a one-to-one relationship between the outcome of any given encounter and its long-term counterpart. Dissatisfaction and negative affect in a single person–environment transaction say little or nothing about whether the person is generally dissatisfied. Similarly, to speak of a person as having functioned effectively in a specific encounter does not provide sufficient evidence of good overall social functioning. For example, the child who can handle the social environment of an inner-city ghetto may lack the understanding and resources for functioning well in a middle-class work context. The person must be observed again and again in a variety of contexts in order for us to judge general properties such as morale and functioning.

To understand how appraisal and coping processes ultimately affect long-term adaptational outcomes, therefore, we must first understand how these processes affect the short-term outcomes of stressful encounters. Accordingly, we will discuss each of the major adaptational outcomes in the context of both the short-term stressful encounter with its adaptive outcomes and over the long term.

Social Functioning

Social functioning is often conceptualized from a sociological perspective as the manner in which the individual fulfills his or her various roles, for example, as a parent, spouse, job-holder, or community member. Less frequently social functioning is defined psychologically as satisfaction with interpersonal relationships and/or in terms of requisite dispositions and skills. In our view each of these perspectives is limited with respect to understanding social functioning as an adaptational outcome, yet each sheds understanding on this particularly complex concept.

With respect to the sociological perspective, for example, there is no single uniform set of cultural expectations with any one role; instead, multiple expectations exist (Platt, 1981). This point is illustrated in a study by Gross, Mason, and McEachern (1958) which shows that different audiences or reference groups have heterogeneous and often conflicting expectations concerning the school superintendent's role. Role expectations also vary according to the other roles (or positions) occupied by the individual. A husband's expectation for his wife's behavior may vary depending on whether she is a working mother or a housewife mother, and a wife's expectations for her husband's behavior may vary depending on the amount of time he spends on the job.

Little theory exists about social functioning from the psychological perspective, although its importance seems universally recognized. Alfred Adler (see Ansbacher & Ansbacher, 1956) first suggested that the motives for social connections arose from the long period of childhood dependency. Adler's position was echoed by associative reinforcement learning theorists who presumed that the child learned to want social approval, for example, by the association of reduced primary drive tensions (e.g., hunger, thirst) to the supportive presence of the mother. Adler later changed his argument, stating that "social interest" was an inborn species characteristic, a stance not dissimlar to the modern ethological conviction that forming social bonds has survival value and evolved in higher species. Erikson (1963), in his treatment of the stages of psychological development, emphasized that the emerging adult must struggle for a sense of individual identity, which depends on achieving a place in the worlds of work, relationships with others, and social institutions. From this standpoint, feeling a part of the social world is an essential psychological theme in all our lives. Therefore, the quality of social and work functioning must be known in part through the eyes of individuals in the form of satisfaction with their social relationships, for example, rather than just through the eyes of others in the society (see also Renne, 1974).

Social functioning is thus influenced by many factors, including the person's history with its implications regarding dependency, autonomy, trust, intimacy, and so on, on the one hand, and, on the other, cultural values and expectations regarding social roles and how they should be enacted. These enduring characteristics of the person and the person's environment play a major role in determining with whom the individual will have relationships, the functions of these relationships, and how these relationships will be subjectively experienced and expressed in behavior.

Although personal and cultural factors impel a person toward a particular constellation of social roles and relationships, however, they are developed, altered, and maintained through the encounters of daily living. The effectiveness with which these day-to-day events are managed is a major determinant of the overall quality of the person's social functioning.

Effectiveness in the
Specific Encounter

The traditional view of coping effectiveness is trait-centered or dispositional and involves person properties that define *competence*, usually without reference to the particular situations with which that person must deal or the actions through which his or her goals are realized. An alternative to the dominant trait approach is to view the environment as providing a set of resources, constraints, and demands to be used or responded to by the person or the society (cf. Klausner, 1971; S. B. Sarason, 1977). This latter perspective is reflected in the research on environmental pressures by Lawton (1977, 1980) and Moos (1975) and in efforts to direct corrective or preventive interventions toward environmental systems (e.g., Stokols, 1977). Scheidt (1976), for example, observes that a taxonomy of attributes of environmental situations the elderly might be expected to encounter is required to assess their competence.

Neither a trait nor an environmental perspective alone is adequate to the study of effectiveness, since effective coping depends on the relationships among the demands of the situation and the person's resources (Schönpflug, in press) and on the appraisal and coping processes that stand between these and the outcome of the encounter. The central issue that emerges from this formulation is: What constitutes effective appraisal and coping?

In Chapter 5 we argued that coping strategies are not inherently good or bad. A strategy that is effective in one situation can be ineffective in another, and vice versa. The effectiveness of a coping strategy depends on the extent to which it is appropriate to the internal and/or external demands of the situation. The same point applies to appraisal. Threat, harm/loss, or challenge appraisals, or irrelevant or benign appraisals, are not in and of themselves appropriate or inappropriate, effective or ineffective. Their appropriateness and effectiveness depend on what is actually going on, and any judgments must always be made in the context of the encounter. We can, however, identify some fundamental characteristics of appraisal and coping processes that should form the basis of evaluations of appropriateness and efficacy.

Appraisal effectiveness. In any encounter with the environment, the key problem for the person is to make a series of realistic judgments about its implications for his or her well-being. An appraisal that leads to appropriate and effective outcomes must match or at least approximate the flow of events. The mismatch between appraisal and what is actually happening can take two basic forms: either the person will appraise harm, threat, or challenge in instances and ways in which they do not apply; or the appraisal will reflect the failure to recognize harm, threat, or challenge in instances where they should be recognized (cf. Caplan, 1983; French, Rodgers, & Cobb, 1975; Van Harrison, 1978).

Mechanic's (1962) study of students preparing for doctoral examinations, described earlier, provides an example of the former error. Mechanic, it will be remembered, pointed out that as the examination neared and stress mounted, students responded with heightened anxiety to a variety of communications that were in fact neutral. For example, a mention by a faculty member that a particular book might be worth reading sent them into a frantic search for the book, and after the exam, but before the results were known, less than cheerful greetings from the faculty as they passed in the halls were interpreted as signaling a poor performance and possibly failure.

Lucas's (1969) study of coal miners illustrates the type of error in which there is a failure to recognize harm or threat. Reports of the miners interviewed after the rescue from a mine explosion and subsequent entrapment indicated that they failed to recognize the danger of running out of water and the need to conserve it while they searched for an exit. Although cut off, the miners apparently did not foresee the possibility of being trapped for a long period. After two days of searching for an exit, their water supply was exhausted and they were forced to drink their urine in order to survive.

Coping effectiveness depends also on the match between secondary appraisal of resources and the flow of events. In her description of a middle-aged subject in the field study of stress and coping in 45- to 64-year-olds mentioned previously, Benner (1982) provides an illustration of what can happen when a secondary appraisal is faulty. This subject was not promoted as he had hoped. Instead, the position was filled by a woman who had been his peer, and his great disappointment and anger at this affront were evident in monthly interviews over the course of a year. Although the primary appraisal in this instance seemed more or less appropriate and understandable (i.e., he had indeed been passed over), a faulty secondary appraisal led this man to a hopeless coping strategy. Instead of finding a way of accepting the inevitable or taking another job, he set out to embarrass his female competitor at every opportunity, with the result that he repeatedly discredited himself and thus perpetuated the problem and its corollary of anger and disappointment. During the entire year no improvement was observed in the way he coped and in the emotional and behavioral outcomes of his attempts. At the conclusion of the study, the work situation had deteriorated to the point where it was no longer possible for him to remain.

In extreme instances, the mismatch between a primary and a secondary appraisal and the actual flow of events can be clear and obvious. For instance, a paranoid person who sees threat where there is none and takes action in accordance with that appraisal is likely to cause harm to others. Conversely, a woman with a breast lump who sees no threat or danger may cause harm to herself. Most mismatches, however, are not extreme and are difficult to identify. Moreover, it is likely that most appraisals do not match the flow of events perfectly. Two characteristics of stressful encounters—ambiguity and the person's patterns of commitments and hence selective vulnerability—lead us to this principle.

Most stressful situations are ambiguous to one extent or another; either information is missing, or that which is present is unclear, or both. The miners described by Lucas, for example, were operating without full information about their entrapment. Given the men's backgrounds and what they had heard from past accounts of mine disasters, their initial appraisal was reasonable. Only when they had more complete information regarding the extent to which they were trapped did they recognize that they might run out of water. In general, the greater the ambiguity, the more room there is for a mismatch between an appraisal and what eventually transpires.

Vulnerability also affects the match between appraisal and the flow of events. Vulnerability is the readiness of the person to react to certain types of situations as stressful. As we pointed out in Chapter 3, vulnerability goes hand in hand with commitment; the stronger a commitment, that is, the more a person cares, the more vulnerable he or she is to a particular threat. One person is readily distressed by being evaluated by others, another by the withdrawal of approval or support. Still another is distressed by a demand from a superior, or by having to evaluate others, and so on. In each case, the vulnerability is a function of a strongly held value or commitment. Even in situations that should not ordinarily call for distress, the vulnerable person is more likely to appraise threat because of these values and commitments. Benner (1982), for example, describes another man, aged 52, who experienced continuing psychological stress at his job. For him, the source of vulnerability was his fragile sense of competence, which led him to appraise almost every work demand as threatening. Every incident on the job was a personal test on which he could not afford to make any errors, despite the fact that he did his job in an exemplary fashion, judging from commendations he had received, objective criteria of performance, and an offer of a more responsible position at another location (which he declined).

Because ambiguity and vulnerability are so much a part of stressful encounters, mismatches between the appraisal process and the actual flow of events are pervasive. The critical question concerns the *degree* of mismatch and its implications for coping, the outcome of the encounter, and, if there is a tendency to repeat the unrealistic appraisals, the person's adaptation over the long term.

Coping effectiveness. In Chapter 6 we discussed two coping functions that are of overriding importance in nearly every type of stressful encounter: the regulation of distress (emotion-focused coping) and the management of the problem that is causing the distress (problem-focused coping). Coping effectiveness in a specific encounter is based on both functions. A person who manages a problem effectively but at great emotional cost cannot be said to be coping effectively (cf. Schönpflug, in press). For example, the decision to place an aged parent in an institution may be made effectively according to Janis and Mann's (1977) criteria for good decision making, yet the son or daughter who is responsible for the move can be left with feelings of loss, guilt, and despair. Effective coping includes the management of these negative feelings. Note that effective coping in this instance does not mean that positive feelings will occur, only that negative feelings will be managed.

Similarly, a person who regulates his or her emotions successfully but does not deal with the source of the problem cannot be said to be coping effectively. A growing body of research, for example, tells us that one of the functions of alcohol is to reduce emotional distress (e.g., Levenson, Sher, Grossman, Newman, & Newlin, 1980; Sher & Levenson, 1982). This form of coping carries with it a high risk of alcoholism and is likely to impede problem-focused efforts and over the long run can damage health and increase depressive affect (see Anehensel & Huba, 1983). Moreover, one may cope effectively and handle emotions adequately in one context, for example, military combat, but pay a price with emotional disturbances later in a different context, as when repatriated veterans suffer "impacted grief" (Shatan, 1974).

Not every encounter, of course, holds the potential for being coped with effectively. As we have noted many times in this volume, the problems that underlie certain types of stressful encounters are not amenable to change. Therefore, if people are prevented from coping effectively in a particular instance, it does not necessarily signify that they are ineffective copers. Pearlin and Schooler (1978) comment:

> There are important human problems, such as those that we have seen in occupation, that are not responsive to individual coping responses. Coping with these may require interventions by collectivities rather than by individuals. Many of the problems stemming from arrangements deeply rooted in social and economic organizations may exert a powerful effect on personal life but be impervious to personal efforts to change them. . . . Coping failures, therefore, do not necessarily reflect the shortcomings of individuals; in a real sense they may represent the failure of social systems in which individuals are enmeshed. (p. 18)

For coping to be effective, there must also be a good match or fit between coping efforts and other agendas. These agendas refer to values, goals, commitments, beliefs, and preferred styles of coping that cause conflict if the requisite coping strategies in a particular encounter are implemented. These agendas were identified in Chapter 6 as constraints that shape actual coping processes. When coping strategies that are acted out are in conflict with strongly held personal values, for example, they present the person with new sources of stress. Moreover, strategies that are incongruent with such values or goals are likely to be used reluctantly or without conviction and are likely to fail.

That effective coping is in part a function of a good match between coping options and other agendas in the person's life is becoming more widely recognized among therapists with a behavioral orientation. Teaching a person to behave differently in order to increase coping skillfulness, however, is not sufficient to reduce stress if the new behavior causes conflict. Many therapists now attempt to alter those beliefs that constrain the behavior of their clients, so that behavioral change is accompanied by a change in the underlying values (see Chapter 11).

The significance of a match between the way a person actually copes and his or her preferred style of coping was discussed in

Chapter 3. There, for example, we pointed out that for people who prefer avoidance, to be given information or a role in their treatment can increase distress, and, conversely, not involving them in a situation can increase distress for those who prefer vigilance or confrontation. A mismatch between a preferred style of coping and the coping that is actually used in a particular situation is likely to reduce coping effectiveness in much the same way as the mismatch between coping and other agendas in that such strategies may be applied reluctantly and/or ineptly (cf. Speisman et al., 1964).

If we are to accurately evaluate coping within each encounter, we also need a system for classifying the various possibilities concerned with outcome. Ideally, the processes used will lead to a permanent resolution without generating additional conflicts. This type of resolution will be marked by cessation of effort and mobilization as well as a positive affective state marked by emotions such as relief, pleasure, contentment, or joy. Ideal outcomes, however, in which the problem is resolved and there are no residual negative emotions, are probably not typical, thus making the evaluation of coping efficacy even more complex.

We need also to differentiate between the outcomes of one-time-only encounters initiated by some adventitious circumstance and encounters that result from a chronic or repeated conflict. For example, it is not full resolution when a husband and wife settle an argument about task sharing before they leave home for work if the underlying conflict has not been resolved. They may have decided in this instance that one or the other would do the grocery shopping or stop at the bank on the way home, but the same argument is likely to resurface at another time if the broader questions about task sharing, beliefs about role behavior, and so on, have not been settled. This pattern, in which the same stressful encounter is replayed again and again, points up one reason why apparent effectiveness in one encounter may not indicate good overall functioning.

Social Functioning Over the Long Term

Social functioning over the long term is clearly an extension of the idea of coping effectiveness, and indeed differs little from that notion except in the level of abstraction or generalizability that is implied by the term *adaptational outcome*. For example, to achieve good overall functioning, the way a person generally appraises events must at least tend to match the flow of events. Many relationships can withstand occasional errors of appraisal, but any relationship will be put to a severe test if inappropriate appraisals are frequent. Because of the social context, there will be, not only a pattern of poor problem-focused coping, but misunderstandings and hurt feelings as well.

Even when appraisals do a relatively good job of matching the flow of events over time, the person who tends to be consistently threatened more than challenged is likely to have problems with social functioning. Threat can encourage withdrawal or defensive operations that turn the person inward or encourage hostile, aggressive behavior. Either response hinders effective social functioning. Challenge, on the other hand, encourages venture and openness and increases the possibility of good communication and problem solving. Both of the above principles also apply to functioning at work, which we include under the rubric of social functioning.

From a broader, more sociological perspective, we can ask about the relationships among roles and how functioning in one social role might be affected by functioning in another. There are a number of interesting questions having to do with the direction of such efforts. Does functioning in the family affect job functioning or does functioning on the job affect family functioning (Kanter, 1977; Macoby, 1976; Seidenberg, 1973), and/or does the family serve as a resource for buffering the effects of job stress (Burke & Weir, 1979; House, 1979)?

Methodological problems. In general, the criteria that are used to evaluate social functioning are arbitrary and of questionable ecological validity (cf. Platt, 1981). For example, social adjustment is operationally defined on the Normative Social Adjustment Scale (NSAS) (Barrabee, Barrabee, & Finesinger, 1955) as the extent to which the person's performance matches an "ideal" norm, explained as "what we ought to do." On the Structured and Scaled Interview to Assess Maladjustment (SSIAM) (Gurland, Yorkston, Stone, & Frank, 1974), social adjustment is defined as the extent to which the subject's performance reaches a "reasonable" adjustment, a state that would not require treatment. And on the Social Adjustment Scale (SAS) (Weissman & Paykel, 1974), adjustment is considered the extent to which the subject's performance attains the "ideal" or "statistical" norms. The "ideals," "norms," and "levels" of reasonable adjustment" are derived in the case of the NSAS from social scientific studies and the researchers' own experience; in the case of the SSIAM, from norms established by four practicing psychotherapists; and on the SAS from the authors' expectation of an average rating for the general population. (For a comprehensive critical review of these instruments, see Platt, 1981.)

None of the norms takes into account the expectations of the subject's reference group regarding the appropriateness of the role(s) or how the role should be performed. For example, the "ideal" norms that are used on the NSAS in the area of employment entirely disregard the circumstances in which the person works. A change of job for a poorer one is thus automatically rated at the maladjusted end of the job change subscale, regardless of whether or not the change was a free choice or based on extenuating circumstances. Similarly, the expression of dissatisfaction with one's job is considered evidence of "malajustment" regardless of whether the expression is reasonable or unreasonable, commonly held by others, and so on. On the SSIAM a person is rated as maladjusted or deviant if he or she has terminated a job in the four months prior to the interview. And on the SAS, as Platt (1981) succinctly puts it:

> . . . the ideal world is characterized by harmony, happiness and consensus, and inhabited by men and women who are consistently interested, active, friendly, adequate, guilt-free, nondistressed, and so on. If they show anything less than interest in their work they are maladjusted. (p. 106)

Group norms, the bases of which are themselves questionable, are used to judge *individual* performance, regardless of the context.

The issues that are involved in the definition and evaluation of social functioning echo those discussed in Chapter 5 regarding coping. There we stated that coping must be defined independently of its outcome if it is to be used to predict outcome. So too social functioning needs to be defined independently of an outcome (i.e., "good" or "bad" functioning). Platt (1981) points out that several researchers are becoming more aware of the problems of confounding social functioning with its outcome and are attempting to develop instruments that describe (but not evaluatively) social functioning (e.g., Platt, Weyman, Hirsch, & Hewett, 1980; Remington & Tyrer, 1979). Whether social functioning is good or bad, adaptive or maladaptive, high quality of poor quality, can be judged only by taking into account the social context in which the person is operating, including the multiple roles or positions that person occupies and the expectations of significant others with respect to his or her behavior.

Extensive efforts to analyze and assess social functioning have been made by the Rand Health Insurance Experiment Series (Donald & Ware, 1982) in which 11 questionnaire items provided three separate measures predictive of what is called "positive well-being." The 11 items were grouped into two subscales, social contacts and group participation. Positive well-being, the criterion variable, consisted of ratings of physical and mental health, positive affective states, and general satisfaction with life. An important conclusion from this work is that these facets of health are distinct conceptually and empirically, and that social well-being is separable from physical and mental health. Moreover, social well-being is multidimensional; frequency of social contacts must be distinguished from social resources and subjective evaluations of social relationships. The authors point out, for example, that measures of social resources predict mental health better than do measures of social contacts. The above cautions accord with our own concerns about the complex concept of social functioning. Further, little if any effort is made to examine the processes of social functioning and to evaluate how well these processes work except indirectly in a static measure of social contacts and resources, an approach somewhat akin to the examination of social networks. We shall have more to say about social networks and supports in Chapter 8.

Status of empirical research. The perspective we have offered for thinking about long-range social functioning touches a number of empirical questions that have been little studied. The first question concerns the stability of individual differences in functioning, the second the effects of major life stresses on long-range functioning, and the third the effects of mediating person variables on appraisal and coping and thereby on long-range functioning.

The finding that people who function well (or poorly) in crises also functioned well (or poorly) previously is the most common, but unimpressive, finding relevant to the stability of functioning. A case in point are observations that mental patients with a previous history of good functioning have the best prognosis for improvement and release (cf. Phillips, 1968), as are findings by Andreason et al. (1972) that patients who showed a poor adjustment to the crisis of severe burns—that is, demonstrated regressive behavior, severe depression, delirium, and unmanageable behavior—had had a history of physical problems and psychopathology. Thus, there appears to be a fair degree of stability in functioning over the long term. Such findings, however, do not help us decipher what it is about the well-functioning person that accounts for continuing positive outcomes. Nor do such findings help us intervene to prevent bad outcomes.

The conditions that differentiate stressful events that scar the individual from those that produce increased strength or resiliency remain unclear. Possibilities include the severity of stress, its timing developmentally, its type, and the presence or absence of a host of personal and social resources. With respect to timing, for example, Koocher, O'Malley, Gogan, and Foster (1980) observed the destructive effects of having had cancer before the age of 18. Many psychological sequelae remained, possibly because of the uncertainty about the future that this particular illness seems to generate. Koocher et al. also found that those who were better adjusted functioned better socially and had more self-help skills and better intellectual functioning than those rated as poorly adjusted. Setting aside for the moment the potential tautologies involved in the measures of adjustment and personal and social resources, we again see the theme that people who seem to be well put together do better in handling potentially traumatic life experiences than those whose resources are less adequate.

Several studies have considered properties that influence functioning when there is stress. Reviewing a large number of studies about how people appraise and handle failure in achievement settings such as the schoolroom, Dweck and Wortman (1982) observe that some people consistently seem to make maladaptive responses to failure, whereas others react adaptively. The former are characterized by a high fear of failure, high test anxiety, and a general sense of helplessness; the latter respond to failure as a signal to change their coping strategy rather than viewing the failure as a sign of their incompetence or inadequacy. Along similar lines, Gilmore (1978), reviewing studies on locus of control and adaptive behavior in children and adolescents, suggests that internals, compared with externals, function in a more positive, effective, and adaptive manner in both achievement and nonachievement situations.

Morale

Morale is concerned with how people feel about themselves and their conditions of life. It is related in a somewhat unclear way to avowed happiness (McDowell & Praught, 1982; Wilson, 1967), satisfaction (Campbell, Converse, & Rodgers, 1976), and subjective well-being (Bradburn, 1969; Costa & McCrae, 1980; Diener, in press). All these terms have been used more or less interchangeably, and they all pertain to morale. The multidimensional quality of this concept is reflected in a report by Bryant and Veroff (1982) on the structure of psychological well-being. Using a confirmatory factor analysis of the data from two very large nationwide representative samples, the authors identified three major dimensions of psychological well-being: unhappiness, strain, and personal inadequacy. The dimensions touch on all the above definitions, namely, avowed happiness, satisfaction, and subjective well-being.

Although definitions of morale, or whatever one calls it, are highly variable, divergent approaches appear to have overlapping meanings (Costa & McCrae, 1980), most of which relate closely to affect or emotion. It is crucial, however, to distinguish between the emotions and sense of well-being a person experiences in a stressful encounter and morale over the long term. The positive and negative emotions that are experienced during a stressful encounter are reflections of the person's momentary evaluation of his or her well-being. To the extent that these evaluations are based on dimensions such as satisfaction/dissatisfaction, happiness/unhappiness, or hope/fear, the affect that is experienced in the encounter parallels the affect that is experienced when one speaks of long-term morale. Yet there are differences. Affect in a specific encounter is likely to be very much in the foreground and to shift as the encounter unfolds (Folkman & Lazarus, in press); morale over the long term is likely to be more of a backgrond affective state that is relatively enduring. Costa and McCrae (1980), who distinguish as we do between momentary happiness and happiness in the long run, view the difference in terms of the relative contribution of person and situation factors. Citing Epstein (1977), they write:

> Few would argue against the position that, for normal people, the major determinant of *momentary* happiness is the specific situation in which the individual finds himself. Social slights hurt our feelings, toothaches make us miserable, compliments raise our spirits, eating a good meal leaves us satisfied. The contribution of personality to any one of these feelings is doubtless small. Yet over time, the small but persistent effects of traits emerge as a systematic source of variation in happiness, whereas situational determinants that vary more or less randomly tend to cancel each other out. (p. 699)

From the perspective of stress and coping theory, the key questions concern how appraisal and coping processes affect positive and negative emotion, or subjective well-being, in a specific stressful encounter, as well as the relationship between well-being in the short-run encounter and morale over the long run.

Emotion and Well-being in the Short Run

Emotions and judgments about well-being in the short run must be viewed from a process-oriented perspective: emotions and appraisals are dynamic and change at each stage of an encounter. At the outset, a person is likely to experience a variety of seemingly contradictory positive and negative emotions (see also Chapter 9). A challenge appraisal will be positively toned, but still contain some threat emotion; eagerness may be mixed with fear, confidence with doubt. Conversely, a threat appraisal is likely to involve some positive emotion as well; dread may be softened by some hope, sadness by comfort.

As the stressful encounter unfolds, coping becomes extremely important as the mechanisms through which a positive sense of well-being can be sustained in the face of adverse conditions. Mechanic's (1962) "comforting cognitions," which we described in Chapter 6, are a good example of strategies that help boost spirits. Positive comparisons (e.g., Pearlin & Schooler, 1978; Taylor, 1983) are another good example. Taylor, for instance, describes how cancer victims use positive comparisons to put a good face on a bad situation (see also Bulman & Wortman, 1977; Dunkel-Schetter & Wortman, 1982). The author cites statements from three women, each of whom finds different reasons for not feeling as bad as she might about her malignancy. One states, "I had a comparatively small amount of surgery [lumpectomy rather than mastectomy]. How awful it must be for women who have a mastectomy. I just can't imagine, it would seem it would be so difficult." Another says, "The people I really feel sorry for are these young gals. To lose a breast when you're so young must be awful. I'm 73, what do I need a breast for?" The third says, "If I hadn't been married, I think this thing would have really gotten to me. I can't imagine dating or whatever knowing you have this thing and not knowing how to tell some man about it" (p. 1166).

Appraisals of the outcome of an encounter involve judgments about how successfully desired goals were achieved and how satisfied the person is with his or her performance. With respect to well-being, the central issue is the relationship between expectations and the encounter outcome.

Linsenmeier and Brickman (1980) provide an elaborate and comprehensive review of research on the role of expectations in the sense of satisfaction with one's performance. They argue that although performing well is generally more satisfying than performing badly, the lower the expectations, the more satisfied the person will be. They suggest, in short, that people will be satisfied with themselves and what they accomplish to the extent that their accomplishment exceeds what they had expected to achieve, and disappointed if it falls short of what they had expected. They cite much research supporting this position, and quote Bertrand Russell (1968) as saying that people who underestimate themselves are apt to be continually surprised by success, whereas those who overestimate themselves are apt to be just as often surprised by failure. The former kind of surprise is pleasant, the latter unpleasant.

In effect, satisfaction depends on more than the performance outcome; it depends also on *expectations* regarding the performance outcome. People with lower expectations are more likely to view their performance with satisfaction than people with higher expectations. Too high expectations are likely to sour the person's appraisal of his or her performance and short-circuit good feelings that might otherwise be derived from it.

The Relationship Between Short-term Well-being and Long-term Morale

Costa and McCrae (1980) point out a longstanding dilemma with respect to morale, namely, that correlations between a person's objective conditions of life, for example, financial status and health, and subjective happiness are low and inconsistent. Drawing on adaptation level theory (Helson, 1959), they suggest that the subjective experience of an event depends on the discrepancy between present and past levels of input rather than on the absolute level. Thus, habituation would make extreme conditions such as wealth or poverty seem normal to the person, which leads these conditions to be taken for granted or at least tolerated. This implies that a person will evaluate the existing conditions of life, those that are positive as well as negative, on the basis of a personal norm rather than evaluating them on an absolute or objective basis. This may be why older people who are in poor physical condition may see themselves as healthy (e.g., Tobin & Lieberman, 1976) and take satisfaction in their health despite having serious ailments. This analysis, of course, implicates coping, since the tendency to put a positive light on things is best regarded from the standpoint of defensive reappraisal, a form of emotion-focused coping.

The power of immediate events to affect morale may also depend heavily on how they tie into background factors such as life goals, long-range commitments, and belief systems (cf. Lefcourt, Miller, Ware, & Schenk, 1981). Psychologists concerned with emotion have often been greatly concerned with mood factors as the background against which immediate events are juxtaposed. One reason why the laboratory is so unsatisfactory in the study of emotion is that one can rarely take into account the interpenetration of the stimulus "figure" and the mood or commitment "ground" in assessing the stimulus condition as a factor in the emotional response (cf. Klos & Singer, 1981).

In the long rún, however, positive morale must depend on a consistent tendency to appraise encounters as challenges, or to appraise harms and threats as manageable and even productive of growth, and to tolerate negative experiences (once called frustration tolerance; e.g., Rosenzweig, 1944). One obstacle to research on this topic has been that what Norman Vincent Peale called the power of positive thinking has traditionally seemed defensive and pathogenic to psychiatrists and clinical psychologists. This prejudice is one of the reasons that there has also been little serious study of the role of religious commitment in overall adaptation.

Morale must also depend on being effective in coping across the widest range of encounters. People who are competent copers should experience less stress or be less oppressed by the ordinary stresses of living, because they handle situations in such a way as to prevent stress or mitigate it when it occurs. To the exent that people are effective in most contexts, the frequency and intensity of required mobilization should be less, and they should experience less drain on their energy. This should contribute to more satisfaction, because personal goals are more readily realized, and less dissatisfaction than if the coping exacted a high toll. A qualification to the notion that competent copers experience less stress than incompetent ones is that the former, being highly capable, may tackle more than the latter (e.g., "When you want something done, ask a busy person"). This is the expectation issue raised by Linsenmeier and Brickman (1980). On the other hand, it is a reasonable hypothesis that competent copers will experience more satisfaction through the greater actualizaton of personal goals and the greater range of reinforcements they receive.

Methodological problems. In addition to the above issues, there are numerous methodological problems surrounding the assessment of morale. First, even when separated, most measures of morale summate divergent emotions into a single positive and a single negative affective index, leaving unsettled what part is played by different specific emotion qualities and intensities. Whether a person's predominant negative emotion is anger, sadness/depression, or guilt may matter greatly in assessing overall morale in addition to how well he or she addresses the problems of living. Second, it is difficult to determine to what extent statements by informants about their emotional state can be taken at face value, and to what extent they might reflect defensive reappraisals. Third, over what period of life should an assessment of morale be made, and how stable will this assessment be during the period and across periods? To the extent that the reported state reflects stable personality attributes, there will be some degree of stability; to the extent that changing conditions of life are significant factors, or that relevant personality changes occur over the life course, an assessment at one period of life should diverge in some degree from that at another period. Fourth, since terms such as satisfaction, happiness, positive feeling, morale, and so on, have many connotations that vary with culture, ideology, and religion, we are left uncertain about the terms that should be employed in assessing morale and the extent to which some of the variation in response is a product of these diverse connotations. Researchers who hope to assess morale or life satisfaction must be concerned with such issues (see Bradburn, 1969; Campbell, 1976; Costa & McCrae, 1980; Wilson, 1967; Zautra & Goodhart, 1979).

Learned helplessness: a special case. In Chapter 1 we pointed out that control expectancies can be treated as the outcome of a stressful encounter or a series of such encounters. Learned helplessness is a special case of this type of outcome. It is therefore important to include it within our discussion of the effects of stress and coping on morale, since depression, which is traditionally viewed as a consequence of helplessness, is a relatively long-term state of dissatisfaction or low morale. Because of the volume of work on learned helplessness, it would be futile and counterproductive to offer a review. (For reviews and critiques see Abramson et al., 1978; Buchwald, Coyne, & Cole, 1978; Costello, 1978; Garber & Seligman, 1980; *Journal of Abnormal Psychology*, 1978, 87, No. 1; Overmeier, Patterson, & Wielkiewicz, 1980; Wolpe, 1979; Wortman & Brehm, 1975; Wortman & Dintzer, 1978.) Our purpose here is to analyze the core issues from the standpoint of stress and coping theory.

The theory of learned helplessness had its origins in laboratory work with dogs and other infrahuman animals that failed to avoid electric shock, even though an avoidance response of jumping to safety was readily available (Overmeier & Seligman, 1967; Seligman & Maier, 1967). This "performance deficit," as it was later termed, could be interpreted in a number of ways, including neurophysiologically (cf. Weiss, Glazer, & Pohorecky, 1976), but the one of interest to us is the cognitive interpretation: the animals had learned through prior conditioning that they were helpless in the face of "uncontrollable" shock, and so gave up trying to cope behaviorally and instead passively cowered in the cage.

The concept of learned helplessness was then offered as an explanation of human depression (Seligman, 1975). When the model was tested with humans, however, the findings seemed inconsistent and inconclusive. Uncontrollable conditions did not always result in passivity, depressed mood, and performance decrements, but sometimes generated anxiety and invigorated effort. Depressed subjects did not display the sorts of cognitions or attributions that were hypothesized from the theory. There is now a proliferation of studies on the cognitive correlates of depression, many of which report findings that are not consistent with existing learned helplessness formulations (e.g., Cutrona, 1983; Dobson & Shaw, 1981; Gong-Guy & Hammen, 1980; Gotlib & Asarnow, 1979; Hammen & Cochran, 1981; Hammen & deMayo, 1982; Hammen, Krantz, & Cochran, 1981; Lewinsohn, Mischel, Chaplin, & Barton, 1980; Miller, Klee, & Norman, 1982; Peterson, Schwartz, & Seligman, 1981; Zuroff, 1981).

The laboratory research design from which the concept of learned helplessness arose (Seligman, 1974, 1975) used a shuttlebox, which has two compartments separated by a barrier. The floor is an electrified grid through which shock can be administered on either side. After being exposed to one of three conditions—controllable shock, uncontrollable shock, or a no-treatment control condition—the animal is given an opportunity to avoid shock, which is signaled by a conditioned stimulus. The animal that jumps over the barrier into the other compartment avoids the shock or escapes it if the jump is made after the shock has begun. On a subsequent trial the animal must jump back over the barrier to avoid or escape the shock.

An inexperienced dog runs around frantically when the shock begins until it accidentally jumps the barrier and escapes the shock. In subsequent trials the dog escapes more quickly, until it learns to avoid the shock completely when it is signaled. Dogs that have had prior training with inescapable shock behave very differently than dogs exposed to other treatments. They soon stop running and howling when shock is given before avoidance training and sit or lie whining until the shock is ended. They do not cross the barrier to escape but seem to give up and passively accept the shock. According to the theory of learned helplessness, the dogs have learned that termination of the shock is not contingent on their behavior. They have learned that they are helpless, and this negative expectation continues to operate even when they could successfully make an avoidance or escape response.

The original formulation of learned helplessness had a deceptive elegance and simplicity as an account of human depression and the failure to cope. Stemming from a drive-reinforcement learning paradigm, the basic premise was that frequent or continual experience with lack of contingency between action and outcome—the basic condition of being helpless—produces a general belief that a person is helpless to deal with the world, which results in depression. The elegance of the idea is that a history of this type of experience leads to depression. The process could be described as the conditioning of a belief which has profound implications for later behavior and emotion.

What is deceptive about this simplicity and elegance is that there is no way to examine the reinforcement history of the person who is depressed compared with someone who is not depressed. The early animal studies with a single instance of helplessness were said to be an analogue of the history of learned helplessness in human depression. The premise had to fail, because it required us to believe that it is simply a matter of the summation of the negative experience of lack of contingency between effort and outcome that produces the belief in one's own helplessness.

What was not considered was that many people who have a history of negative experience or conditioning remain optimistic and committed, whereas many with a positive history become depressed. As we noted earlier, the paradox of life satisfaction research is that there is little relation between living under objectively favorable or unfavorable conditions and satisfaction (cf. Costa & McCrae, 1980). The simple, now all but discarded, concept of learned helplessness is parochial, seductive in its elegance but not in touch with other literatures and observations. From a cognitive standpoint, it is not merely a person's history that counts but how events are construed. The critical factors shaping processes were not addressed by learned helplessness theory, nor are they known today, despite some attempts at speculation (e.g., Silver & Wortman, 1980a; Wortman, 1976; Wortman & Dintzer, 1978).

It seems to be the fate of all extreme attempts at elegance, simplicity, and positivism in psychology to crumble in the face of human complexity and to require modification to accommodate to multiple determinants. This was precisely what happened to the original learned helplessness theory; the current reformulations of the theory bear little resemblance to the original (e.g., Abramson et al., 1978; Garber et al., 1980; Hollon & Garber, 1980). These reformulations lean heavily on attribution theory, which is unabashedly cognitive and built on the premise that a person construes in a seemingly idiosyncratic fashion the factors responsible for events and outcomes. In the reformulated theory, the person discovers that certain responses and their outcomes are independent, which leads to attributions about the causes of what happened. These attributions then determine whether the future expectation is that there will also be noncontingency, and to what extent it will be chronic, that is, generalized to a variety of contexts.

Learned helplessness theorists are now saying, in concert with traditional attributional analysis of emotion (cf. Weiner, 1974, 1980; Weiner, Graham, & Chandler, 1982; Weiner, Russell, & Lerman, 1978, 1979), that when a negative outcome is thought to be a product of the person's effort (internality), there will be a loss of self-esteem and a greater likelihood of depression than if the outcome is seen as the result of external factors. If such attribution is viewed as the result of stable person factors, the costs of uncontrollability will be chronic as well. There is, moreover, an added attributional factor of "globality," that is, a generalization of helplessness from a specific context to the overall life context (Abramson, Garber, & Seligman, 1980).

The more a person expects not to have control, the greater will be the cognitive, emotional, and motivational deficits leading to nonadaptive behavior and depression. The *cognitive deficit* is that the person fails to notice that his or her coping response might be connected to a favorable outcome. The *motivational deficit* refers to passivity in the face of a condition of helplessness. The *emotional deficit* is no longer simply depression, as in the original formulation, but can be anxiety; now only when the person sees the situation as *hopeless* is there depression (Garber et al., 1980). This theme makes the revised theory more consonant with those stage theorists who argue that noncontingency can temporarily increase the vigor of effort (e.g., Horowitz, 1976; Klinger, 1977; Shontz, 1975; Wortman & Brehm, 1975). What creates hopelessness, however, is far from clear in any of the cognitive approaches to depression (e.g., Beck, 1967).

These reformulations still fall short as explanations of morale in uncontrollable situations in three important ways. First, attribution analysis of helplessness cannot be linked to outcome until the meanings of such attributions as interpreted from the standpoint of the person's well-being are taken into account. This point is discussed further in Chapter 9.

Second, the revised formulations of learned helplessness pay little attention to coping. Successful coping in the face of loss of control over outcomes may require the very cognitive and behavioral processes that are regarded as pathological or pathogenic in some contexts and which, in many instances, look much like the emotional and motivational deficits of concern to the theory of learned helplessness. What learned helplessness theorists regard as helplessness-induced passivity, that is, the motivational deficit—and depression, the emotional deficit—may well be an adaptive accommodation to lack of control over the environment or, as we would put it, the troubled person–environment relationship. Included within this accommodation are the self-same cognitive coping processes we treat under emotion-focused coping, the processes ego psychologists speak of as ego defenses.

For example, one option available to the person coping with an uncontrollable environment is to do what Pearlin (1980b), cited earlier, suggested, namely, give up unserviceable commitments and reorder priorities. Pearlin says:

> The control of meaning typically relies heavily on the selective use of socially valued goals and activities. . . . If a man is exposed to intense strain in his work, he may avoid distress by relegating work to a marginal place in his life, committing himself instead, for example, to being a good husband or father. Thus, adults not infrequently will move those roles in which there is painful experience to the periphery of importance, making more central those that are comparatively free of hardship. In rearranging their priorities, people temper stress by demeaning the importance of areas in which failure and conflict are occurring. (p. 185)

Wortman and Dintzer (1978), too, write:

> We believe that many of the behaviors associated with helplessness (giving up, losing interest in the outcome, and/or motivation to pursue it) are maladaptive only when the outcome in question is controllable or modifiable. If the outcome is truly uncontrollable, these behaviors may be highly functional (cf. Weiss, 1971). (p. 87)

People can live under extremely negative conditions that are refractory to effective control and yet remain sanguine and involved. They find ways of rationalizing their condition, sometimes even retaining hope that things will change or will not be as bad as feared. Janoff-Bulman and Brickman's (1982) interesting discussion of the reactions of European Jews in the 1930s who passed up the chance to escape from Nazi Germany is a case in point. From the learned helplessness perspective, this behavior might look like helplessness and giving up. However, this same behavior could just as easily be regarded as cognitive coping efforts to accommodate to what seemed like a temporary aberration, with the interpretation that the highly advanced German culture would not abandon a civilized outlook—in effect, a benign, stress-regulating interpretation which sustained hope.

Third, most writers tend to treat emotion, especially helplessness, hopelessness, and depression, as the final stage in an adaptational sequence that can reflect maladaptation. If one takes a larger—and longer—view, however, depression and other emotions are usually a step on the way to other states and processes. As Klinger (1977) notes, depression is usually temporary, as are anger, guilt, anxiety, and so on. Even positive feelings after the achievement of some long sought-after goal are usually restricted in duration and intensity, because such achievement proves to be merely a way-station to something else. Thus one often sees graduate students who react with mild depression after having obtained their doctorate. The degree had been overestimated as an end point and turns out to be only a temporary source of satisfaction to be followed by the next step of beginning a career (Lazarus, Kanner, & Folkman, 1980).

Wortman and Brehm (1975), seeking an integration of "reactance" theory with learned helplessness theory, also postulate a two-stage process of managing uncontrollable conditions and outcomes, namely, *invigoration* and *depression*. They do not, however, assume that this sequence is invariant, but suggest that either can occur initially depending on specific conditions and history. As in most social learning views, their analysis of the process is thus tied to the twin factors of value and expectancy.

Reviewing Garber and Seligman's (1980) book, Synder (1982) states that ". . . we still lack an adequate understanding of the consequences of experience with uncontrollable outcomes" (p. 11). Indeed, we do not yet know how to predict how a person will cope with the conditions that bring these outcomes about, nor with the outcomes themselves, in both the short and long run. These are crucial research questions for the future if we are to come to terms with the problem of control or lack of control over the environment and its relationship to outcomes such as morale. (For critiques of the revised learned helplessness concept in its attributional form see Coyne, 1982; Coyne & Gotlib, 1983; Zuroff, 1980.)

Somatic Health

An essential theme of the analysis of stress, coping, and health that dominates thinking in behavioral medicine is that emotional states of all kinds and intensities accompany appraisals of harm, threat, and challenge. The link with illness is the conventional one that massive bodily changes are associated with emotions, especially strong, negative ones such as fear and anger. It is this theme that has given Selye's (1956, 1976) work on the physiology of stress great influence in behavioral medicine and psychosomatics.

That stress, emotion, and coping are causal factors in illness is still only a premise, albeit widely assumed (see Plaut & Friedman, 1981). Belief in this premise led to the extraordinary growth of research during the 1960s and 1970s that attempted to link life events with illness. The empirical case needed to be made, and life events measures offered the promise of an objective assessment of stress. By and large, we accept the premise that stress, emotion, and coping are causally tied to illness, although evidence is less clear and less fully spelled out than is generally realized. Most people working within psychosomatic medicine, behavioral medicine, health psychology, and related fields also accept this premise to a greater or lesser degree, since it largely defines these fields (see also Engel, 1974, 1977). A review of research on psychosocial factors and susceptibility to infectious disease by Jemmott and Locke (1984) presents a fairly strong empirical case that this premise is sound, at least with respect to the mediating role played by immune competency in the stress-infection relationship.

Without challenging the premise, medical sociologists have dealt with one of the methodological dilemmas in making the empirical case for the connection between illness, stress, emotion, and coping by examining what is called illness behavior—the tendency to seek or avoid medical care for symptoms, or to exaggerate or understate their importance. Illness behavior is an interesting phenomenon in its own right; patterns vary, for example, among cultures, and subcultures, as a function of sociodemographic variables, and among individuals (see, for example, Mechanic, 1978, for a representative account, and work by Rundall & Wheeler, 1979). From our perspective the facts of illness behavior pose a problem. If complaining about symptoms, or failing to complain, depends on values, beliefs, and personal patterns of coping rather than on the illness itself, then the actual behavior of the patient is a source of noise in the system, making it more difficult to disentangle whether what is being viewed is illness or only an outward, behavioral manifestation of values, beliefs, and coping activity whose relationship to the illness is variable.

Generality Vesus Specificity

The theoretical controversy that today dominates thinking about psychological and social factors in health and illness concerns two overarching ways of viewing the role of emotion or stress in illness, one emphasizing *generality*, the other *specificity*. The generality position, which is the more widely advocated, arose as an antidote to the failure of specificity theories, popular from about 1920 to 1940 (see Lipowski, 1977, for a brief historical overview), to support proposed relationships between largely unconscious and conflict-centered psychodynamic processes and particular diseases such as ulcers, colitis, asthma, and migraine (e.g., Alexander, 1950; Alexander, French, & Pollack, 1968).

Selye's concept of the General Adaptation Syndrome provided the impetus for generality theories because he argued for a uniform bodily defensive response to *any* kind of environmental demand, including psychosocial. The hormones secreted in this syndrome were demonstrated to have massive effects on tissue systems and on the activity of every cell in the body, and these effects could easily explain an increased general susceptibility to a wide assortment of illnesses. This emphasis on a common bodily reaction to diverse environmental demands made it easy to move toward a concept of disease in which the specific nature of the demand, in effect, its psycho- or sociodynamics, did not really matter. With a sustained outpouring of catabolic stress hormones, the body's resistance would be weakened enough to increase the probability of infection and tissue damage, or what Selye called the diseases of adaptation. The reason one disease rather than another occurred depended on individual differences in past psychological conditioning or on genetic or constitutionally based vulnerabilities.

Generality theories are, in effect, built around two concepts that have to do with demands on the one hand and responses on the other: (1) All demands are more or less qualitatively equivalent in producing physiological mobilization—a built-in defense mechanism that is part of our phylogenetic inheritance—which comes into being when bodily equilibrium is disturbed (this flows from the earlier work of the French physiologist Claude Bernard; see Cannon, 1932); and (2) that this defensive mobilization, or response, increased general susceptibility to all diseases, not specific ones. In sum, if a person is continuously bombarded with stressful demands, the body's defensive response will increase the risk of any and all disease processes; and if there is no surcease allowing restoration of the cellular conditions necessary for health, the person will ultimately succumb.

In the main, Selye and other physiologists treat the eliciting stimulus conditions or demands of the environment—what Selye called "stressors"—without detailed reference to mediating psychosocial processes. Thus, generality theories of disease susceptibility typically cast the problem in terms of stressors such as life events or chronic demands of daily living that generate the stress or emotional response. The psychological processes that create the emotional response out of environmental demands (see also Chapters 2 and 9) are rarely discussed.

The movement toward generality theory in the 1940s and 1950s had a counterpart in the psychophysiology of emotions. As we noted in Chapter 2, the concept of emotion was subsumed by concepts of arousal and drive, making emotion at best a simple, unidimensional concept ranging from high to low intensity in which the idea of different kinds of emotions was all but abandoned. This approach was compatible with generality theory about psychosocial factors in disease in that the quality of an emotion and its psychodynamics did not count in the processes involved in emotion-based disorders. All that mattered was a sustained state of excessive arousal, in short, disturbed homeostasis.

More recently, the General Adaptation Syndrome, like the general arousal concept, has begun to show serious deficiencies as a way of understanding emotion or stress, stress disorders, and their psychosocial components. We have addressed research on this issue in Chapter 2. As we noted there, research by Mason and his colleagues (Mason, 1975a; Mason et al., 1976) with hormonal patterns has presented a major challenge to the generality position. First, when they removed threat as a confound, monkeys and people showed markedly divergent patterns of hormonal secretions to diverse physical stressors such as fasting, heat, cold, and exercise; second, the adrenal corticosteroid response may be sensitive mainly or only to psychological threat, a factor usually confounded with physically noxious stimuli, rather than to physical assaults on homeostasis. Moreover, Mason's evidence gives some support to the idea that each emotion—anger, fear, etc.—has its own particular hormonal response pattern. Difficulties of research methods, particularly those that make it difficult to distinguish one emotion quality from another, perpetuate the controversy about generality versus specificity. The issue is still far from resolved (see, for example, Ekman et al., 1983; Ursin, 1980).

We would argue, however, that general arousal or mobilization is not adequate as the sole interpretive concept underlying the causal relationship between emotions (and the conditions bringing them about) and somatic illness. Selye's (1974) assertions about eustress and distress (see also Lazarus, 1976) also imply that the bodily response to different emotional states may well be critically different as it affects adaptational outcomes.

Many present-day social epidemiologists (e.g., Antonovsky, 1979; Cassel, 1976; Syme, in press) espouse the idea that stressful experiences work by increasing a person's general susceptibility to disease. This version of the generality theory shifts the concept of disease causation from the ideas of Koch, Pasteur, and Lister that specific bacterial agents are implicated in specific diseases. We have since learned that the mere presence of a noxious environmental agent often does not produce illness. Becoming ill depends also on the physical state of the animal, often called "host resistance," which can be affected by stress or emotional disturbances. The notion of the ability of the organism to ward off illness is clearly a sound one, but to interpret all disease onset in terms of host resistance is to ask too much of the concept of general susceptibility. "General" has become too broad a term and fails to take into account the distinctive psychophysiological processes distinguishing heart disease, say, from cancer, colitis, infection, or hypertension.

We can illustrate the major defects of the generality model with the classic finding that smoking cigarettes increases all-cause mortality, that is, death from a variety of ailments such as lung cancer, emphysema, cardiovascular disease, liver and kidney disorder, and respiratory infections, which in turn increase the chance of flu or pneumonia, and so on. The data unequivocally show that those who smoke are more likely than those who do not to die from one or another of these ailments. Aggregating all illness outcomes creates a strong case for smoking as a cause but ignores the diverse routes through which it increases the risk of premature death.

These diverse routes are essential to understanding because they affect the kinds of illnesses people get and the likelihood of getting them. One person who smokes is presumably susceptible to malignancy, whereas another is susceptible to emphysema, or to hypertension, with its danger of stroke or coronary occlusion. Still other people seem to have no measurable health effects from smoking. We cannot understand these variations with a generality model, or with its counterpart in epidemiology, the general susceptibility model, because the mechanisms of illness vary from person to person and thus implicate specific individual or group variables which are not described by these models.

The concept of general susceptibility might be greatly improved by placing diseases into broad classes, such as infections, broken bones or head injuries resulting from accidents, cardiovascular disease, and cancers of different types. For example, although evidence is as yet weak and controversial, one type of cancer might result from defects in the process of immune surveillance whereas another might be generated or aggravated by defects in the immune response to foreign agents once they have been detected (e.g., Schwartz, 1975).

The classification of disease outcomes, however, can provide only part of the answer. Attention must be given to the processes involved in major disease causation beginning with social variables, proceeding to the psychological and ultimately to each stage of the physiological level. This is, indeed, what the specificity theorists were trying to do at the psychological level with their psychodynamic formulations, but this effort never proceeded to a reasonable analysis at the physiological level; their concepts were too limited, as will be seen shortly, and their data base was deficient. Thus, it is still possible that anger might create a different pattern of susceptibility to illness than other emotions, as is suggested in the case of hypertension. But even distinguishing among emotions is insufficient, since it leaves out the varying patterns of coping employed under stress, each of which has quite different consequences for somatic illness.

The original doctrine of specificity in the etiology of diseases focused on the environment as a causal influence. A major factor in this doctrine was the 19th century discovery that particular forms of bacteria caused particular illnesses. As we pointed out in Chapter 1, we now know that the host's condition also influences susceptibility to pneumonia, tuberculosis, and other illnesses that bacteria and viruses produce (cf. Dubos, 1959). The idea that disease depends, not only on an invasion of hostile environmental forces, but also on the total condition of the person, is expressed in terms such as illness-proneness, host-resistance, resistance resources (Antonovsky, 1979), or wellness (Bakan, 1968).

The psychoanalytic version of the specificity doctrine referred not merely to a specific environmental cause, but to the generation of complex states and processes involving different emotional patterns and coping in a particular person in a particular environment. This view is similar to the original doctrine of specificity in that specific emotions, such as anger or fear, or particular patterns of coping, generate their own special disease risks. For example, a common hypothesis about hypertension is that it is related to the way anger is handled. The psychoanalytic view differs from the original doctrine of specificity in that the causal agent is not seen as strictly environmental, but as an interaction between a person with particular proclivities (personal agendas, special vulnerabilities, styles of coping) and an environment that imposes constant or recurring demands and constraints relevant to those proclivities.

Despite a loss of confidence among theorists and researchers in the old-fashioned versions of psychosomatic specificity which looked for an ulcer personality, a migraine personality, and the like, some explanations of certain diseases still draw on the concept of specificity in the form of hypotheses about broad, overarching problems such as dependency or helplessness (e.g., Weisman, 1956). For example, a broadened application of specificity may be found in Engel's (1968) thesis that many diseases derive from personal loss or bereavement in the context of the psychological predisposition to be highly dependent on others. In these cases, the loss will be interpreted as a central threat to security. These persons feel abandoned, helpless, and hopeless, which leads them to give up trying to come to terms with the circumstances of their lives (see also Schmale, 1972; and Schmale & Iker, 1966, who see cancer as a product of this type of psychodynamic). It is not merely the loss itself that is critical; in our terms, its impact also depends on the disposition of the person to appraise it as a significant threat to his or her well-being, and/or to cope in a particular way. Those theorists, for example, who see this psychological vulnerability as an important factor in cancer (or in depression, if we consider morale rather than somatic illness) have adopted a variant of the specificity hypothesis in a broader form.

Appraisal. Depue, Monroe, and Schachman (1979) have made a searching analysis of generality and specificity concepts and argue that the idea of appraisal offers an effective way of viewing psychosocial factors in disease from a very general standpoint without sacrificing individual patterns of psychological vulnerability. The psychological disposition toward dependency as the basis of illness is unnecessarily restrictive, they state, since a wider range of events may be appraised as stressful, depending on a person's tendency to evaluate transactions as threatening. The tendency to appraise events as threatening could, indeed, be related to dependency needs; nevertheless, any one of a large number of vulnerabilities, which differ from person to person because of their diverse histories and agendas, could have a similar emotional impact. Specificity, therefore, lies in the person factors that lead to a common process, namely, cognitive appraisal. Summing up this position, Depue et al. write:

> Therefore, the appraisal process may provide the final common pathway for a host of person and psychosocial variables that modify the impact of the psychosocial environment. In applying this model to the initiation of disease, the factor unifying all of these variables is the appraisal process as it modifies the intensity and duration of the psychological response to a threat in the environment. The unifying factor is viewed in terms of psychological threat as it is this response that initiates what is, for some theorists, the major mediator of the psychosocial environment—emotions and their biological concomitants. (p. 16)

In this statement, Depue et al. have made emotions a central mediator of somatic illness, although they do not speculate on the relationships between specific emotions and illnesses. They go on to suggest that threat appraisals lead to coping patterns which, in turn, may have their own specific ties with particular diseases or groups of diseases. In our view, the latter emphasis is even more crucial in the psychosociobiological etiology of illness.

Coping and Health Outcomes

Let us now shift the focus from threat appraisals and emotions as disturbers of bodily equilibrium and precursors of disease to the coping efforts that they stimulate and how these efforts affect health over the long run. Note that we are not asking how people cope with illness. We are asking about the diverse routes through which the ways people cope with the events of daily living can affect their health.

There is a dearth of systematic studies that address this question directly; it is usually considered indirectly by *inferring* coping as the mediator of the relationship between antecedent variables and health. Those few studies that examine the relationship between coping and health generally fall short of the goal in that they do not consider the pathways through which coping affects health.

The use of inference in identifying coping as a mediator of the relationship between antecedent variables and health can be illustrated by the work of Kobasa and associates on the personality construct of hardiness as a moderator of the effects of life stress on illness (see especially Kobasa, 1979; Kobasa, Maddi, & Courington, 1981; Kobasa, Maddi, & Kahn, 1982). The basic design of this research was to compare two groups, one with high stress, as measured by the Holmes and Rahe life events list, that had fallen ill, the other with high stress but free of illness. Hardiness as a personality construct was measured by a number of scales which were interpreted as tapping three personality characteristics: commitment, the tendency to appraise demands as challenging rather than threatening, and having a sense of control over one's fate. Together these traits were considered to constitute the variable of hardiness. It was found in these studies that people characterized as hardy were less prone to develop illness under stress.

Problems with this series of studies can be illustrated by Kobasa's 1979 article. Here she infers coping processes or styles on the basis of the personality measures that distinguished a high-hardiness group of executives from a low-hardiness group. She suggests, for example, that the hardy executive will throw himself actively into a new situation. However, Kobasa offers no data describing the actual coping processes of the two groups. The basis for inference is especially shaky because of questions concerning the validity of the personality scales used to measure hardiness. Commitment, for example, is measured negatively in terms of alienation: a low score on the alienation scale is considered the equivalent of commitment. Similarly, challenge is measured negatively by a security scale. Are these scales measuring commitment and challenge, or are they best thought of as measuring alienation and security? And to what extent are the illness outcome measures confounded with emotional indicators of alienation? These questions are all the more troubling in the absence of observational data that might support the author's interpretations. The same pattern with even more extensive speculation about coping is evident in a later analysis (Kobasa & Puccetti, 1983).

Another group of studies comes closer to examining the relationships between coping and health more directly. For example, an oft-cited study by Aldrich and Mendkoff (1963) suggests strongly that how elderly people who are moved from one situation to another cope with the stressful experience influences their mortality. Those who responded philosophically showed a minimal death rate, followed closely by those who responded with anger. The elderly with the poorest outcomes, that is, high postdislocation mortality, reacted with denial and depression or had been functioning before and after relocation at a psychotic level, which in this case probably means they were senile. Although this study did not explain how the coping process actually affected mortality rates, it nevertheless strongly implicated coping.

A later study (Janoff-Bulman & Marshall, 1982), although severely lacking in detail, reported that institutionalized aged subjects who had appraised their situation favorably, as indicated by their positive reports of well-being, had a higher mortality rate three years later compared with subjects who had expressed strongly negative evaluations of their well-being in the initial assessment. This finding seems parallel to the observation of Aldrich and Mendkoff that angry aged people had a lower death rate than those who used denial or reacted with depression. In a related study with terminal cancer patients, Weisman and Worden (1975) reported shorter survival rates for patients who responded with withdrawal, alienation, and depression compared with those who preserved and used social relationships with friends and family. A growing set of studies is beginning to suggest that passive acceptance, helplessness, and depression result in a poorer outlook for survival in old age than anger, complaining, or fighting to stay alive or to control one's circumstances (see Lieberman & Tobin, 1983; Turner, Tobin, & Lieberman, 1972; and Derogatis, Abeloff, & Melisaratos, 1979, on cancer survival). The above research suggests that mortality, obviously the ultimate in somatic illness, may indeed be subject to the mediating effects of the dominant type of emotion and coping.

On a lesser scale of illness severity, we note the work of Weiner, Singer, and Reiser (1962) in which hypertensives appeared to deal with the emotionally disturbing features of a diagnostic interview by telling uninvolved, unemotional stories to the interviewer and displaying minimal cardiovascular responses, compared with normotensives, who were far more reactive. This finding led the researchers to propose that the hypertensives coped with the stress of the interview by controlling or suppressing its threatening aspects, thereby protecting themselves. A later study by Sapira,

Scheib, Moriarty, and Shapiro (1971) confirmed this finding with the observation that hypertensives tended to deny the emotional significance of events viewed in a movie that depicted either the warm behavior of a doctor to a patient or cold, rude behavior.

The two studies above appear to suggest that hypertensives display a style of suppressing or denying emotionally significant material that might raise their blood pressure. This interpretation is paradoxical, for if they succeed in this coping style, as they appear to be doing, why then are they hypertensive? One explanation is that the hypertensives do not suppress or deny all the time, although they did use these coping strategies in the two experiments reported. This explanation could not be tested, since the patients were seen on only one occasion, and it was not possible to examine ups and downs in blood pressure as a function of experimental manipulations. Another explanation, which draws on a hydraulic model, is that a persistent pattern of denying and suppressing could lead to a build-up of unreleased anger that ultimately causes chronically elevated blood pressure. This explanation has been widely discredited in recent years, however, in favor of a cognitive-environmental feedback explanation: consistent failure to express anger and hence to deal with an affront keeps the person experiencing recurrent anger-generating relationships. Alternatively, the consistent expression of anger even when it is counterproductive produces negative interpersonal outcomes and makes it difficult to resolve troubled relationships, which then recur. The findings could also be the result of artifacts of measurement. For example, it might be that blood pressure did not change for the hypertensives merely because their baseline blood pressure was already about as high as it could go, an instance of the law of initial values in psychophysiology. And so we must be wary about generalizing from these studies, which are derived from a single assessment with fairly primitive procedures for evaluating psychophysiological effects.

A much sounder study, by Harburg et al. (1979), implicates the control of anger or anger-inducing conditions in hypertension. Interview-based questionnaire data were obtained on how subjects would handle work-related anger in response to an angry boss; in addition, blood pressure was sampled several times during the interview. The coping styles included "anger-in" ("just walk away from the situation"), "anger-out" ("protest to him directly"; "report him to the union"), and "reflective" ("talk to him about it after he has cooled down"). The findings suggest that a reflective style, in which the person analyzes an arbitrary attack by the boss and either delays response for later discussion or tries to reason at the time, is associated with lower blood pressure. Impulsive strategies such as ignoring or denying the meaning of the attack (anger-in) or attacking or protesting to higher-ups (anger-out), on the other hand, appear to be associated with higher blood pressure.

These studies on anger, anger-control, and hypertension are just a few examples of how emotion and coping could be implicated in illness. This research, which overlaps somewhat with research on Type A behavior, also has important substantive and methodological implications for stress, coping, and illness more broadly considered. For example, the study by Harburg et al. (1979) leaves us with the unanswered question of how the subjects actually cope in an encounter with an angry boss. The way the study was designed, we can only know how they *think* they would respond. The reader will recognize this theme; it was elaborated in Chapter 6 and is discussed further in Chapter 9. If we are to understand the stress-coping-illness relationship, we must look at the ongoing processes whereby people react to and manage stressful encounters. (For related discussions see, for example, a review by Diamond, 1982; and also research by Barefoot, Dahlstrom, & Williams, 1983; Long, Lynch, Machiran, Thomas, & Malinow, 1982; Shekelle, Gale, Ostfeld, & Ogelsby, 1983; Williams et al., 1980; and Williams et al., 1982.)

A second, broader question emerges from a consideration of the above studies and others dealing with hypertension and other illnesses. What are the routes through which coping might adversely affect somatic health? We offer three possibilities:

First, coping can influence the frequency, intensity, duration, and patterning of neurochemical stress reactions (1) by failing to prevent or ameliorate environmentally noxious or damaging conditions; (2) by failing to regulate emotional distress in the face of uncontrollable harms or threats; and (3) by expressing a set of values and a corresponding life style and/or coping style that in itself is consistently mobilizing in a harmful way.

Failures to prevent or ameliorate environmentally damaging conditions—(1) above—refer to the inadequacy of problem-focused coping. Such failures may be due to the intractability of the environment and/or to a deficit in problem-focused coping resources. Regardless of the reason, failures in problem-focused coping may even increase the aversiveness of the situation, thereby exacerbating the neurochemical stress reactions.

Failing to regulate emotional distress in the face of uncontrollable harms or threats—(2) above—refers to emotion-focused coping. The possibilities for failure here include ineffectiveness of strategies such as distancing or detaching that have as their goal a reduction in mobilization, or use of strategies such as self-blame that are likely to maintain or even increase mobilization.

Type A is an example of a set of values and a corresponding life style that can adversely affect neurochemical stress reactions—(3) above. As we noted in Chapter 5, Type A can also be viewed as a coping style. In effect, the person responds to (copes with) external pressures and incentives to be effective, ambitious, competitive, and successful by cultivating an appropriate life style and internalizing it. The risk of heart attack is increased (e.g., Haynes, Feinleib, & Kannel, 1980) through particular mediating physiological mechanisms such as elevated blood pressure (a relationship now controversial in light of findings by Rose, Jenkins, & Hurst, 1978), serum cholesterol and other lipids, and changes in platelets and fibrinogen that result in more rapid blood clotting. Although such bodily changes might also increase the risk of other illneses, they seem particularly important in heart disease.

Another example of a potentially maladaptive style of appraisal and coping is suggested by Linden and Feurstein (1981), who describe a tendency of hypertensives to be disposed toward threat appraisals and aggressive or angry behavior in social situations. They conceptualize this style as a deficit in social competence. Glass (1977a; Glass et al., 1980) has argued that a style which alternates between intense efforts to control stressful transactions and helplessness when coping efforts fail is associated with fluctuations in catecholamines sufficiently dramatic to influence the pathogenesis of coronary heart disease (Holroyd & Lazarus, 1982).

In addition, some people complain excessively of symptoms and illness (as in "sick role" behavior, or modes of appraisal and coping that reflect cultural values) or, conversely, minimize symptoms or avoid medical care (see Mechanic, 1966b; Zborowski, 1969). A colorful language has emerged for describing these patterns, for example, "the worried well" and "help-rejecting complainers."

Second, coping can affect health negatively, increasing the risk of mortality and morbidity, when it involves excessive use of injurious substances such as alcohol, drugs, and tobacco, or when it involves the person in activities of high risk to life and limb. A person might smoke, drink, or take drugs to reduce stress but in so doing increase the risk of illness. For example, men at risk for coronary heart disease may initiate or aggravate disease processes if they increase their smoking in response to stress (Horowitz et al., 1979). Conversely, people can use behaviors to reduce stress that do not exacerbate illness (e.g., judicious exercise); in these instances, coping should not increase somatic problems and might even reduce them. Research by Belloc (1973) and Belloc and Breslow (1972), for example, shows that there is a strong relationship between a number of common health habits—e.g., eating and exercising regularly, controlling weight, getting sufficient sleep, not smoking, and using moderation in drinking—and long-term health. They found that average life expectancy and general health were much better for people who reported six or seven of these practices than for people who reported fewer than four. Although the cause-effect relationship is not clearly demonstrated, there is nonetheless a strong implication that supports this hypothesized route. In fact, it may well be that the third route described below might depend more on actual health-related practices than on the neurochemical stress reactions described in the first route, which is commonly assumed to be important by those who argue for the operation of stress and other psychosocial factors in health outcomes.

Third, emotion-focused forms of coping can impair health by impeding adaptive health/illness-related behavior. This point was discussed in terms of denial or avoidance, which can succeed in lowering emotional distress but simultaneously prevent the person from realistically addressing a problem that is responsive to suitable action. This pattern is described in a study by Katz et al. (1970). Through the use of denial-like processes, the women in this study were able to minimize the significance of a breast lump and thus reduce their psychological distress, but these very processes delayed their seeking important medical attention. A similar type of concern has been expressed by Kinsman, Dirks, Jones, and Dahlem (1980) about efforts at anxiety-reduction in asthma. They note that when asthmatics focused their anxiety directly on breathing, adaptive coping was facilitated, whereas the absence of anxiety may reduce the mobilization needed to cope with the dangerous symptoms. Farberow's (1980) observations on indirect self-destructive behavior in diabetics, and Goldstein's (1980) on hemodialysis patients, are also illustrative. The patient tries to deny the serious implications of the disease, which are terrifying, and therefore fails to do what is prescribed. In order to survive and live well, the diabetic and kidney failure patient, among others, must remain actively responsible for a multitude of difficult, self-managed activities such as diet, exercise, medication, and treatment (Surwit, Feinglos, & Scovern, 1983).

In Figure 7.1, we have tried to summarize and contrast the essential features of the generality and specificity models. In examining this figure, the reader should keep in mind that in the generality model illness can be produced via the effects of physiological disequilibrium on the immune process or the metabolic consequences of stress hormones in the fashion argued by Selye. Similarly, in the specificity model, illness can be produced via the particular patterns of physiological disturbance associated with different emotional patterns of response in the fashion implied by Depue et al. (1970) cited earlier, and/or by the direct behavioral effects of coping under routes (2) and (3) discussed above. In the figure the details of such routes are ignored in favor of making the point that coping can directly affect health via ways other than physiological disequilibrium.

Methodological problems. We conclude the discussion of somatic health with some comments on the measurement of health status, which contains as many difficulties as are inherent in the measurement of the two preceding adaptational outcomes, morale and social functioning. Only when the criterion is mortality are most of the problems of measurement obviated, although this extreme criterion gives us little information about the disease processes themselves. Three difficulties stand out in health status measurement. The first concerns the use of self-reports of health and functioning, or disease history, versus the use of laboratory and clinical evidence; the second concerns how to estimate the seriousness of a disease with respect to two often independent values, namely, impact on functioning and risk for mortality; and the third concerns the variability and stability of health.

Most research on health status is based on what a person reports as his or her disease history, present symptoms, and functioning. One reason for the use of self-report is the high cost of doing a full medical examination, which, as is widely recognized, is itself not a reliable basis for the estimation of health. Many insidious physiological processes leading sooner or later to actual clinical disease are missed in such examinations. Also, even the objective tests in medical examinations depend heavily on verbal reports of recent or past illnesses and symptom patterns. In the main, the physician's diagnosis of actual illness requires the convergence of both what the person says about his or her functioning and symptoms and clinical or laboratory evidence.

Estimates of health status based on verbal reports and healthcare utilization typically have a bad press. This is based realistically on the awareness of inaccuracies that result from distortions in

The Generality Model of Illness

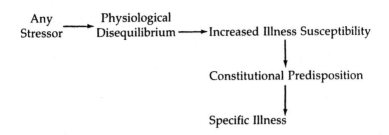

The Specificity Model of Illness

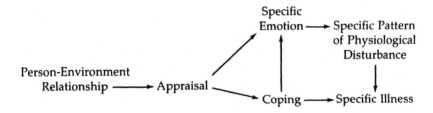

Figure 7.1.

memory and from divergent personal and cultural values and belief systems about symptoms and medical care. As we noted earlier, some people exaggerate difficulties of functioning, feelings, and symptoms and worry needlessly about them, whereas others treat them stoically and understate them, sometimes even when they are sick.

Regardless of these shortcomings, all recognized indexes of health status (e.g., Belloc & Breslow, 1972, which is one of the most widely respected; Belloc, Breslow, & Hochstim, 1971; and Ware, Brook, & Davies-Avery, 1980) of necessity draw heavily on verbal self-reports about functioning, disease history, symptoms, subjective evaluations, and affective states. In validational studies of the Belloc and Breslow index, Meltzer and Hochstim (1970) found the measure, which was used in survey studies of health practices and health status by the Alameda County Human Population Laboratory, reasonably reliable, in good accord with objective medical records, and predictive of health status and mortality nearly a decade later (Wingard, 1980). These findings do not eliminate legitimate concerns about the measurement of health status, but suggest that with all its problems, we can assume the measure has a reasonable degree of validity.

The second issue, the seriousness of an illness, has been given little attention. Some ailments, such as hypertension, are relatively silent with respect to their effects on functioning or in their subjective impact, but they greatly increase the risk of death. Other ailments, such as mucous colitis, can cause suffering and severely limit normal functioning yet have no measurable effect on mortality. The two values, namely, how comfortably or effectively people can function in their daily lives and how long they will live, are typically not separated or given weightings related to their consequences. There must be greater interest in assessing functioning as part of the measurement of health status (e.g., Rosow & Breslau, 1966).

The third issue concerns variability and stability of health. To the extent that a person's health is stable, the possibilities for the study of stress and coping factors in health are limited to correlates or predictors of interindividual differences in health. On the other hand, if there is much variability within individuals over time or across conditions of life, we can examine the covariation between stress and coping factors, such as ups and downs of stress and patterns of coping, and the varying symptoms of ill health. This approach would be important in determining the causal significance of stress and coping factors in intraindividual health variations. If health stability within a given time frame is modest, then it is possible to apply both strategies.

The studies by Belloc (1973) and Belloc and Breslow (1972) cited above suggest that there must be a fair degree of stability in health status over a considerable period; otherwise there would not be such a strong relationship between health habits, health status, and mortality. Moreover, Bayer, Whissel-Buechy, and Honzik (1980) have studied both the stability and health status and the personality correlates of health over many decades in a sample that was followed from childhood to middle age. They found moderate stability, with ratings of health in later life modestly predictable from childhood ratings, and more so from the adolescent years. A number of personality measures were also moderately predictive of health status in later life. The traits that predicted health had to do with self-control, conformity, and good feelings about oneself. Thus, a good guess is that people who are controlled and conforming may be the same kinds of people Belloc and Breslow found to follow good reliable health habits and who in addition perhaps experience less distress. Not surprisingly, personality factors proved a better predictor of health status when the latter was variable rather than stable.

When we consider the consequences of stress and coping processes for long-term health outcomes, we must keep the above issues in mind: the problems inherent in present methods of assessing health status, the divergent implications of relatively unimpaired functioning on the one hand and risk of mortality on the other, and the issue of variability or stability of health within individuals. These issues are relevant to theory-building about how stress and coping affect health outcomes, and also to the price that people might have to pay for certain life styles that relate to or flow from stress and coping processes. The greatest significance these issues have, however, is with respect to empirical research and whether and how stress and coping affect health. Just as measurement problems plague the assessment of stress and coping and therefore limit the quality of research, so inadequacies in the measurement of long-range health outcomes introduce limitations in the reliance we can place on generalizations about the role of stress and coping in health.

Concluding Comments

More than once in this chapter we have spoken of the complex relationships among morale, social functioning, and somatic health. The most common assumption is that these adaptational outcomes are somehow intertwined and compose a general trait of good or poor adaptation: if you function well, you have good morale and somatic health. It is important, however, to allow for the possibility that the relationships among these outcomes may be more complex and that a good outcome in one sphere may be bought at the expense of another.

For example, the current preoccupation with Type A behavior and life styles that increase the risk of cardiovascular disease (see Chapter 5) adopts as its main value that this increased risk is medically or epidemiologically unsupportable, and that every effort should be made to lower it by abandoning or modifying such styles. Indeed, to most people somatic health is an overriding value on which other values rest. Although we have no quarrel with the desirability of lowering medical risk, too little attention has been paid to the social and psychological values associated with Type A behavior and to the conflict among somatic, social, and psychological values that can be created by modifying it. A fast-moving, competitive man can be taught to move more slowly, be less compulsive about time, and act less competitively, but what will be the effect on his morale if he values speed and competiton as personally and socially desirable?

We have also seen in Chapter 5 that there are complicated costs and benefits associated with various ways of coping such as denial-like processes or distancing. The control of affective distress may be bought at the expense of costly delays in seeking medical attention (e.g., Hackett & Cassem, 1975; Katz et al., 1970; Staudenmayer et al., 1979). In these instances and many others, one value, somatic health, is potentially compromised by another value, maintaining morale by minimizing distress.

The point we wish to emphasize here is that when we consider the consequences of coping we must take into account not a single adaptational outcome, but multiple outcomes. The major adaptational outcome of any transaction that has involved coping often depends on a complicated trade-off of costs and benefits, or divergent values about what is positive and negative, important and unimportant. The empirical issues growing out of this position concern the relationships among the various outcomes, the choices people make, and the social, cultural, and psychological conditions affecting those choices. Surprisingly little attention has been directed at this question by workers in the intersecting field of somatic, social, and psychological adaptational outcomes. Behavioral and psychosomatic medicine and health psychology will remain parochial and limited to the extent that they continue to restrict their concerns to somatic health without regard to social functioning and morale.

The material we have discussed in this chapter contains, so far, the most important practical implications of our stress and coping theory because it attempts to relate cognitive appraisal and coping processes to health outcomes. It is ironic that although a central issue in health psychology and behavioral medicine today is the relationship between stress and health, little attention has been given to how the appraisal and coping processes that mediate stress might affect health in all its short- and long-term manifestations, social as well as psychological. Our analysis suggests that there are a number of ways appraisal and coping, each with its own sets of antecedent and mediating psychological and behavioral variables, could influence health outcomes. We must go beyond the simplistic concept that has been at the center of thinking for quite some time, namely, physiological disequilibrium and its restoration, and view the person more broadly in physiological, social, and psychological terms.

Summary

An issue of great concern to researchers in this field is how appraisal and coping affect three major classes of adaptational outcomes— social functioning, morale, and somatic health. To understand the relationships between appraisal, coping, and these long-term adaptational outcomes, however, we must first understand how these processes affect the short-term outcomes of stressful encounters.

Social functioning can be defined as the ways the individual fulfills his or her various roles, as satisfaction with interpersonal relationships, or in terms of the skills necessary for maintaining roles and relationships. A person's overall social functioning is largely determined by the effectiveness with which he or she appraises and copes with the events of day-to-day living. The effectiveness of appraisal within a specific encounter is determined in part by its match with the flow of events. Ambiguity and vulnerability, which are present in most encounters, can make this match difficult to achieve. Effective coping in an encounter also depends on a match between secondary appraisal, that is, of coping options and actual coping demands, and between a selected coping strategy and other personal agendas. In effective coping, problem- and emotion-focused forms of coping will work in a complementary fashion and not impede each other.

Social functioning over the long term is an extension of coping effectiveness in many specific encounters over the life course. Problems exist in the assessment of social functioning, many of which have to do with value judgments as to what constitutes good social functioning. Important empirical issues that have been little examined include the stability of social functioning, the effects of major life stresses on functioning, and the influence of person variables.

The long-term outcome of *morale* parallels the short-term outcome of emotions generated in a specific encounter. Emotions in a specific encounter vary as the encounter unfolds and, at the outcome of an encounter, reflect appraisals about how well goals were achieved and how satisfied the person is with his or her performance. Morale over the long run probably depends on a tendency to appraise encounters as challenges, to cope with negative outcomes by putting them in a positive light, and, overall, effectively managing a wide range of demands. The assessment of morale tends to focus on general negative and positive emotion; researchers have not addressed the part played by specific emotions. There are also other methodological problems concerning self-report data and the connotative meaning of the words used to describe morale.

Learned helplessness and the depression it is said to generate is relevant to the issue of morale. The original model, which was based on animal experimentation, could not explain observed individual differences in human emotions in response to uncontrollable events. Reformulations have introduced cognitive mediators, but they are still incomplete in that they do not take into account the meaning of helplessness, and they pay little attention to coping.

It is widely assumed that stress, emotion, and coping are causal factors in *somatic illness*. The major controversy is not whether this assumption is true, but whether there is generality or specificity in the relationship between stress, emotion, and somatic illness. Generality theories, for which Selye's General Adaptation Syndrome provided the impetus, hold that all demands are more or less qualitatively equivalent in producing physiological mobilization and that this mobilization increases general susceptibility to all diseases. An epidemiological version of the generality theory is the concept of "host resistance." Generality models cannot easily explain individual differences in physiological response patterns and disease outcomes, however, and specificity models, some of which incorporate cognitive appraisal and coping, are gaining prominence. Appraisal processes provide a common pathway through which person and environment variables modify psychological response, and hence emotions and their biological concomitants.

Studies of coping suggest that different styles of coping are related to specific health outcomes; control of anger, for example, has been implicated in hypertension. Three routes through which coping can affect health include influencing the frequency, intensity, duration, and patterning of neurochemical stress reactions; using injurious substances or carrying out activities that put the person at risk; and impeding adaptive health/illness-related behavior.

The measurement of health status as an outcome has many of the same problems as the measurement of social functioning and morale, including issues of self-report and judgment as to the definition of the quality of health.

Overall, the relationships among morale, social functioning, and somatic health are complex. It is important to recognize that good functioning in one sphere may be directly related to poor functioning in another and that good functioning in one area does not necessarily mean that the person is functioning well in all areas.

8

The Individual and Society

The social sciences are concerned primarily with the relationship between the individual and society. As Gerth and Mills (1953) have observed, "The sociologist . . . tries to 'locate' the human being and his conduct in various institutions, never isolating the individual or the working of his mind from his social and historical setting" (p. 3). With respect to stress and emotion, society is viewed as making stressful demands on the individual and as imposing constraints on the ways such an individual might deal with these demands (e.g., Goldschmidt, 1974; Mechanic, 1974). Society is also used by the individual or group to prevent stress or anxiety. Finally, stress or anxiety can be viewed also as a factor that influences culture or that is even conducive to social order.

We begin this chapter with a brief treatment of society as a factor in adaptation, proceed with an in-depth examination of its role in individual stress and coping, and conclude with the problems of social change.

Three Perspectives

As we implied above, the relationship between stress and society can be viewed from several perspectives, each of which is in some sense valid. Society can be a means through which people adapt to nature, and it can also be a shaper of persons and groups as well as a product of the individuals and groups who create, influence, and struggle to change it.

Society as a Means of Adaptation

Different environments clearly impose different adaptational demands; for example, the inhabitants of a warm, humid climate will obviously expend greater effort to keep their food from spoiling than those who live in severe cold. Behavior and society are, in some degree, a response to conditions of the physical environment, specifically, to the survival-related *demands* these impose, the constraints on how and where people live and travel, and the resources that can be used to live and function well. When there have been arguments about this, they have been over how peremptory these demands and constraints are in shaping human thought, action, and emotions and in shaping the evolution of the social systems. In turn, a social system that does not help people adapt to the natural environment must fail. Mechanic (1974), for example, stated that "Man's abilities to cope with the environment depend on the efficacy of the solutions that his culture provides, and the skills he develops are dependent on the adequacy of the preparatory institutions to which he has been exposed" (p. 33).

Few would argue, however, that individual variations in personality, psychodynamics, and behavior are fully encompassed within a view of society as an adaptation to the natural environment. The overarching problem is how best to understand the relationships between the individual and society and the disturbances of that relationship that fall under the heading of stress.

Society as a Shaper of Persons and Groups

We live in the midst of a complex web of human relationships, ranging from intimate family groups to large social entities. Few of us are aware of how elaborate the social rules are that regulate these relationships (Goffman, 1971). These rules serve as constraints on us, much as the demands of the natural environment do. We follow complex rules of pedestrian traffic on busy streets and accepted ways of behaving in a crowded elevator or in formal settings such as a classroom, wedding, or funeral, and we reveal delicate nuances of meaning through culturally shared patterns of conversation and body gestures.

Equally important, even the values and commitments that shape our emotions and behavior are derived in part from social rules and institutions such as those that determine patterns of authority and status (cf. Kemper, 1978). These began long ago as matters of convenience or necessity, but once established they persisted as social patterns handed down from one generation to the next (Berger & Luckmann, 1966). For a child born into a society, or a subculture within it, they constitute *the* social world, especially in the formative years when family, peers, and TV play key roles in the socialization process and in the internalization of the social world in the development of personality. To utilize the perspective of society as a shaper of persons, we must move from the "macro" level of the large and complex social system to the "micro" level of the individual's actual life context and ask how the former influences the latter.

Culture versus social structure. House (1981) points out that the earliest tradition for thinking about how persons and groups are shaped by the social system was to emphasize *cultural forces*, that is, the values and beliefs that are shared by members of a social system and passed from generation to generation. More recently, the emphasis has been shifting to *social structural variables*, that is, the more detailed patterns of social relationships among people who occupy roles and statuses within a social system. These components of the social system "imply quite different types of proximal stimuli and interactions through which macrosocial phenomena affect the individual" (p. 547).

Although cultural and social structural variables are closely interrelated, each influencing the other, their correspondence is imperfect, just as they are selectively influential on and internalized by the individual members of a social system. Social scientists do not yet have a clear grasp of the relative importance of these variables in affecting the thoughts, feelings, and actions of people, and thereby the harmonies and disharmonies of a person's relationship with the social system.

The *cultural component* of a social system has been shown to have major impact on the individual's emotional life. The shaping of an emotional reaction, as well as how it is expressed or managed, hinges on the meaning and significance the culture gives to human transactions with the environment (Gordon, 1981). The same events may be fear-inducing in one culture, anger-inducing in a second, and benign in a third. There are marked cultural differences in the psychophysiological and emotional response to pain, as demonstrated for example by Tursky and Sternbach (1967), Mechanic

(1966a, b), and Zborowski (1969). The influence of the culture is even more obvious when emotions are elicited in response to abstract, symbolic stimuli such as occur in interpersonal transactions. Since emotion is the product of interpretations of the personal significance or meaning of a transaction, then culturally based systems of judgment about what is important, desirable, damaging, or ennobling will play a large role in determining the conditions under which particular emotions will occur.

Similar principles apply to the expression and management of emotion (Hochschild, 1983). There appears to be considerable cultural variability in the conditions under which it is appropriate to express feelings and in the patterns of their outward expression (such as crying and laughing). This is not to deny that many patterns of expression also transcend culture and are recognizable from one culture to another (Ekman, 1972). Recent research on the expressive aspects of emotion, particularly as shown in the face, has emphasized the universality of certain patterns of expression for common feeling states such as happiness and anger, patterns which are not completely overwhelmed by cultural variability (cf. Darwin, 1872).

Striking variations among cultures are also to be found in conventional patterns of emotional behavior such as those manifested in mourning rites, courting and marriage rituals, and institutionalized forms of aggression in athletics and warfare. The dividing line between social custom and individual emotional experience and expression is difficult to draw, because one often cannot tell whether people are merely acting out prescribed social patterns or expressing true feelings. Even the extent of "appropriate" grief varies within the same society according to ethnicity, social class, role, and so forth (cf. Caine, 1964).

The *social structural component* is emphasized by Kohn (1969, 1976; see also Kohn & Schooler, 1973, 1978; Pearlin & Kohn, 1966), whose research suggests that self-direction, which varies with occupation, is a powerful determinant of values in oneself and one's children. In effect, Kohn suggests that work conditions shape values, although values can also affect work conditions reciprocally. Thus, in this view, class differences in values and behavior can better be interpreted structurally than culturally. Moreover, according to Kohn, what is most important about social class is its relationship to the expectation that one's decisions and actions have consequences. A higher-class position is associated with the expectation that one's actions can make an important difference, while a lower-class expectation is that one is at the mercy of people and forces beyond one's control or even one's understanding. It is noteworthy that this interpretation of the essence of class differences is psychological. Social psychologists and personality psychologists today, especially those working in stress and coping, have increasingly centered their attention on the sense of personal control over events (see Chapters 3, 6, and 7).

Bearing more directly on the issue of stress and emotion is Goffman's (1971, 1974) work on impression management, which also centers on social rules that operate in the context of social interaction. Such rules have more to do with the management of the outward expression of emotion than with its experience per se. Except for convenience and analytic clarity, however, it is probably a distortion to separate the shaping of the experience of emotion from its outward expression. Hochschild (1979) has effectively argued that Goffman's account of "cold" impression management in conformity to social norms tells only part of the story of the emotion process in social transactions. She argues that emotion management is also "emotion work," that is, the process of shaping the person's inner feelings as well as their social expression in accordance with "feeling rules" that are indigenous to the social system. Lazarus (1975b) has argued similarly with respect to the regulation of emotion. In the natural social context the generation of feeling and the management of its expression are normally integrated (see also Lazarus et al., 1982).

Hochschild (1979) points to a variety of verbal expressions in our language that reflect the effort to adjust one's actual feelings—as distinguished from their visible expression—to what is called for in a specific situation. People "psych themselves up," "squash down their anger," "try to feel grateful," "let themselves feel sad." Feeling rules express themselves, according to Hochschild, especially when we feel we should be sad when instead we feel happy, and vice versa; when we should feel worse or better than we do; or when we feel something for a shorter or longer time than is appropriate. Feeling rules are often implicit rather than explicit, but they nevertheless operate as powerful sanctions on our feelings and their social expression. As we noted earlier, such rules are part of the social fabric into which we are born and in which we live. Just as we tailor our behavior to fit social rules, we also internalize these rules and think something is amiss when we do not conform to them in our actual feelings.

How social influences can be understood. In order to move from macrosocial concepts such as the social system to the individual (micro) level, not only is it essential to distinguish among various components of the system, but we must also distinguish between their proximal and distal features. The proximal–distal dimension refers to the ordering of various environments according to their conceptual proximity "to experience, to perception, to interpretation, or to psychological response" (Jessor, 1979, p. 6; see also Asch, 1952; Janis, 1972; Newcomb, 1943; Schachter, 1951; Sherif, 1935). The most distal environments are without specific functional significance for the person; they are generally described in nonpsychological language. The most proximal environments usually involve personal meanings. Geographic, biological, and social environments, especially social institutions of the macro type, would be more distal, while the most proximal environment would be the perceived environment of immediate significance to the actor. Social structures are *distal* concepts whose effects on an individual depend on how they are manifested in the *immediate* context of thought, feeling, and action, or, stated differently, in the *proximal* social experiences of a person's life.

Jessor treats the sociodemographic variables used in sociological analysis as considerably more distal than subjective variables such as the ways individuals perceive themselves and the world, and he presents data suggesting that problem behavior (use of drugs, for example) can better be predicted through subjective variables than through sociodemographic variables such as social class, age, gender, and the like. While there is a statistical tendency for members of the same gender, class, or age to share some common psychological characteristics, variations among persons within a group are often as great or greater than between groups, a problem that led social psychologists in the past to distinguish between membership groups and reference groups, the latter being the social group by which people define themselves.

In short, the psychological importance of distal variables such as class hinges on their correspondence to proximal variables including individual perceptions and expectations. To understand the way the social environment, whether structural or cultural, affects a person always requires reference to psychological mediation, which House refers to as the "psychological principle," and Jessor as the environment as perceived by the actor. We refer to "cognitive appraisal" as the psychological variable mediating the person and the environment.

The issue of individual differences. The above brings us to what is one of the most deceptive issues in the social sciences. Although there is no doubt that both culture and social structure markedly affect and shape our thoughts, feelings, and behaviors—our very self-definitions—we do not come out as duplicates of each other. The social template, as Kemper (1978) refers to this shaping, to some extent represents a shared social reality, yet each of us also has a private identity, a subjective world that is never completely opened to others. We have our own private thoughts, feelings, wishes, and goals, and for that matter our own consciousness and unconscious. What each of us knows is not exactly what anyone else knows, and therefore the way social reality is constructed differs from individual to individual. And, by extension, similarities that we note among Japanese, Americans, or Germans, for example, are generalizations that apply only in the most gross statistical sense. Similarly, too, behavioral and attitudinal properties among members of the same social class or occupation are not likely to be totally shared. In sum, regardless of how the issues are debated, these two basic principles remain: (1) groups of people do share important attributes and reactions, and (2) there always remain large individual differences.

Individual variations arise for three main reasons. First, there is great genetic-constitutional diversity in the natural world; second, individuals and groups always have divergent life histories; and third, social stratifications provide some members or categories of members with a head start over others. Social variables partially constrain this individual variability. Thus, there is likely to be more similarity among people of one class or ethnicity than across these social groupings. The analysis of social influences, especially from a developmental perspective, involves comparison of the power of various social system variables to transcend other social and personality factors and compete for influence. Thus, when Kohn (1976) reports that current occupational conditions will prevail over earlier experienced class-based family influences when there is conflict between them, he is comparing the power of certain social variables to shape our behaviors and attitudes. The profound question remains, however, whether there are developmental influences that remain firm even in the face of current social pressures and contingencies, and if so, what they are. Surface behavior may shift in the face of immediate contingencies, yet important personal agendas remain which may have a less obvious but nonetheless powerful influence.

With respect to developmental and social influences, it should be quite evident that the metaphor of *osmosis* for internalization of cultural values is a poor one for understanding how we come to be what we are. We do not passively acquire all the traits, beliefs, values, and patterns of behavior of one or both of our parents. On the contrary, we are quite selective. This is what Freud tried to explain with his sex-typed process of identification, the boy introjecting the father's values, the girl the mother's. But this explanation, while not necessarily wrong, is clearly incomplete. Other principles apply. In their classic research on modeling, for example, Bandura, Ross, and Ross (1963) showed that children model the parental characteristics that imply competence in obtaining the good things of life. The child seems to value the ability to deal with the world effectively. Identification with the competent parent, or with the properties assumed relevant to such competence, is a major principle of internalization.

The important message here is that viewing the individual as firmly embedded within the social system reveals only a part of the picture of stress, coping, and adaptation. It is not enough to say that culture or social structural variables, by themselves, account for how people appraise harm, threat, or challenge and how they cope with the sources of stress in living. Although the adult is partly a product of his or her social history and thinks, feels, and acts in accordance with that history, he or she is also a distinctive individual, with preformed and constantly re-forming belief systems, patterns of commitment, and often obscure agendas. Historical or developmental influences help us explain why people are what they are, but they are distal variables. The more proximal variables, such as the beliefs and commitments that shape cognitive appraisals in every situation, as well as the demands, constraints, and resources of the immediate social environment, are what help us understand and predict a person's sources of stress and ways of coping.

Society as Affected by Persons and Groups

Berger and Luckmann (1966) have pointed out that not only are people born into a social system that affects their thoughts, feelings, and actions throughout their lives, but they also in turn influence this system, thereby producing social change. This perspective on the person and society appears to be given little emphasis in sociological theory and research, but it is very important in stress and coping theory, which is also concerned with how the person affects the environment through coping. The view of humans as both shapers and users of the social structure is mandated by the recognition that coping involves changing the environment as well as oneself (see also Chapter 6).

The two perspectives, people as shapers and people as shaped, have striking political implications. Disease, deviance, and maladaptive outcomes can be viewed as the failure of the individual to cope adequately, because of either genetic defects or the lack of effective adaptational skills. We can, in effect, blame the victim for the failure of adaptation. Alternatively, we can blame the failure on the inadequacies of a society that has not provided suitable adaptational niches for everyone.

The view that coping failure is at the root of maladaptation and disease is compatible with conservative political ideology, which focuses on the inadequacy of the person rather than the environment and is captured by Shakespeare's line from *Julius Caesar*, "The fault, dear Brutus, is not in our stars, but in ourselves. . . ." The style of therapy that follows from this premise calls for abandoning ineffective coping in favor of more serviceable forms. On the other hand, those who see the problem of coping failure as the fault of society regard coping skills training with suspicion and favor concentrating effort on changing the social system (e.g., Albee, 1980). Both stances obviously have merit; regardless of its source, the problem is the faulty relationship between the person and the social structure, and it is this relationship that must be changed. Moreover, it is not possible to produce a perfect social order any more than it is to make human beings into perfect coping machines. Therefore, it makes more sense to us to avoid polarization on the issue and to encourage the use of any approach that seems most suitable for the problem at hand (see also Jahoda, 1981, for a useful discussion of cultural/political values about work and unemployment).

Stress, Coping, and Adaptation in the Individual

Having placed the individual within the social system and considered the interplay of both, how can we use the insights gained to understand stress and coping and their adaptational outcomes? To us the only meaningful form of understanding is a relational one: Since people are shaped by the social system, through multiple forms of influence, and since each individual's experience and biological makeup are to some extent unique, they must act out both their social and individual destinies. This juxtaposition of individual and social identities inevitably creates some degree of mismatch between the individual and portions of the social system, and even within the individual. Stress, then, is the product of conflicts among these relationships, aroused in the course of living. The outcomes of such conflict are expressed in terms of morale or the sense of well-being, social (and work) functioning, and somatic health.

This idea is of course not new in the social and behavioral sciences. In early psychoanalytic thought the emphasis was placed on intrapsychic conflict and struggle; the id representing individual biology, the ego representing the cognitive structure growing out of the struggle to gratify instinct, and the superego as the internalized representation of the culture as manifested largely in the parent. There has been a shift away from this emphasis on intrapsychic struggles and toward transactions between the person and the environment, both social and physical, which was presaged in later psychoanalytic thought (e.g., Freud, *Civilization and Its Discontents*, 1957). The emphasis in stress theory has also shifted to the question of fit between the person and the environment and to events that are demanding, threatening, or harmful. This latter emphasis is an overcorrection to some extent in its militant rejection of internal dynamics and often results in a superficial examination of external social demands (e.g., life events) without an equal concern for psychological dynamics that give them personal meaning.

In sociology, the earliest stress concepts followed this tradition of conflict or person–environment mismatch and were expressed in the concept of alienation. In a thoughtful and rich analysis of the concept, Kanungo (1979) notes that Rousseau was the first to offer a sociological treatment of alienation, and its modern treatment is founded on the writings of Marx (1936), Weber (as cited in Gerth & Mills, 1946), and Durkheim (1893). Marx focused on the estrangement from one's own humanity that is caused by work in industrial society. In his view, work becomes only a means of satisfying other needs rather than an intrinsic basis of satisfaction. Weber viewed alienation similarly; he regarded it as reflecting a larger and increasing division between the purpose of work and the personal satisfaction derived from it. Durkheim described this state as anomie, that is, the perception that the social norms regulating behavior and value had broken down for the individual, resulting in a pervasive sense of normlessness and isolation.

There are numerous sources of confusion in the concept of alienation and its variants (see Kanungo, 1979). One is that writers sometimes seem to be referring to the reaction of a particular individual and sometimes to collectivities, as when a group of workers is said to be alienated. The latter refers to a collective or common experience that is reflected, for example, in widespread absentee-ism or lowered production. On the other hand, alienation often refers to an individual's idiosyncratic views. This is another ex-ample of slippage between the social and psychological levels of anlaysis (see Chapter 10).

A second source of confusion is that the term alienation some-times refers to certain *objective* social conditions, for example, the alienating properties of mechanization or dangerous working condi-tions, and sometimes to *subjective* psychological states experienced by an individual or a group. This difficulty is the result of failure to make a clear conceptual distinction between antecedent or "objec-tive" conditions and the consequent subjective state of alienation arising therefrom. We have seen the same problem again and again in our review and analysis of the meanings of psychological stress, which sometimes refer to stimulus conditions or stressors and some-times to the reaction or the stress response. Although other sources of confusion are cited by Kanungo, these two are especially note-worthy and pernicious in research on alienation, just as they are in research on the stress concept in general.

The contradictory meanings of alienation notwithstanding, three of its characteristics have significance for the psychology of stress and coping. First, regardless of the conceptualization, alienation is viewed as a product of the mismatch between culturally prescribed aspira-tions and the avenues available in the social structure for persons to realize these aspirations, to paraphrase Merton (1957). Second, again following Merton, aberrant behavior, including criminality, psycho-pathology, terrorism, and revolutionary activity, can be regarded as symptoms of this mismatch, either in the individual or in the collec-tivity. Such a position clearly embeds the individual or group within a social structure and treats maladaptation as a product of a troubled relationship between them. The above approach is similar to our own analysis of stress and coping as a disturbed relationship between a person and a particular environment.

Third, whenever alienation is defined as a response as opposed to an antecedent condition, what is described behaviorally and sub-jectively are states psychologists frequently treat as aspects of hu-man emotional distress, as stress reactions, or as the social conse-quences of stress reactions such as absenteesim or socially deviant patterns of behavior (e.g., Manderscheid, Silbergeld, & Dager, 1975).

One can readily see that the sociological concern with anomie and alienation overlaps heavily with our concern with psychological stress as a disturbance of the person–environment relationship which is mediated cognitively through appraisal and generates adaptational efforts, or coping. However, there are also certain problems in drawing a parallel between the concepts of alienation and psychological stress.

The first problem was touched on earlier, namely, that the relationship between the social system and the individual is overly simplified. When, for example, Merton speaks of a mismatch between aspirations that are culturally prescribed and the avenues for achieving them, one must remember that people vary in what they assimilate from a culture that is often contradictory and far too complex for any human existence to reflect completely. People also show tremendous variability in the ways they manage (or cope with) the mismatch.

Many sociological analyses of this problem assume too much uniformity in the movement from the social system (macro level) to the individual personality (micro level). As a result, a mismatch between the person and the environment tends to be seen as an aberration rather than common, and deviancy is seen as akin to pathology when, in reality, within acceptable limits it is the rule. Society works not because people all have the same beliefs and commitments, but because they can respond to social demands while simultaneously managing their private thoughts and feelings. Not only can individual variabilities be tolerated and even transcended to meet social goals, but the very diversity and innovation they contain contribute to the public and individual good (see also Benedict on synergy, as discussed in Maslow, 1964).

A second problem, perhaps more serious, is that the concept of mismatch is structural and static whereas stress and coping must be seen as a dynamic process. The fit or match between the person and the environment is constantly changing from moment to moment, from occasion to occasion (see Chapter 9). It is this very struggle, which includes the presence of tension, the steps to modify the tension and the problems causing it, and the immediate and long-range outcomes, in which we should be interested. Neither is the fit ever perfect, since the social structure is not static, and neither is the way it is experienced psychologically and dealt with.

It will be useful now to return to House's (1981) and Jessor's (1979) concern with proximal social variables within the context of stress and coping. We can do this by recognizing that the social system operates on the individual by creating demands and by providing resources which the individual can and must use to survive and flourish. Any analysis of these proximal variables must also include the constraints against thinking, feeling, and acting that are indigenous to the culture and the ways these operate in every social setting. We have examined constraints in some depth in the context of coping in Chapter 6. In the following discussions we shall take up social demands and social resources.

Social Demands

Aside from the many demands of our physical environment, including those that are by-products of society such as crowding, crime, noise, and pollution, there are a host of demands that stem directly from society itself. The more complicated and intricate the web of social patterns, the more such demands there are and the more difficult is the process of recognizing them and reconciling them with each other.

We must again distinguish between demands created by the immediate social environment at any given moment and those internal demands founded in the socialization process that reflect the person's developmental history and that are manifested in belief systems, patterns of commitment, and styles of coping.

Social demands refer to normative patterns of expectation about behavior. Society places many shifting and complex expectations on its members through the roles they are required to play. People may dissociate themselves psychologically from these demands through processes such as distancing or intellectualizing (cf. Moss, 1973), but when the sense of identification or commitment is lost through these self-protective processes, the person must often pay a price in low morale, impaired social functioning, and even damage to health. Furthermore, when social expectations are violated or demands not met, we are punished with expressions of disapproval that not only threaten our need to belong but also endanger the prospect of gaining the material and social advantages we require to meet central and sustaining life goals. When the violation is severe and concerns an important social value, the punishment may be comparably severe ("an eye for an eye") and lead to imprisonment, ostracism, banishment, or even death.

A social demand can be important in shaping a person's thoughts, feelings, and actions while not necessarily being a source of stress. The critical factors in creating stress are *conflict, ambiguity,* and *overload*. With respect to *conflict*, an otherwise benign social demand can cause stress if satisfying it violates a strongly held value. For example, an engineer who holds antinuclear views is likely to find an assignment that is related to nuclear arms very stressful, even if the assignment is inherently interesting and challenging. Conflict can also arise when, in order to satisfy the demands of one role, the requirements of another role must suffer. This conflict is commonly experienced by mothers of preschool children who also work outside the home. Role *ambiguity* is stressful because the person is unclear as to what is expected. Without such clarity he or she is unable to plan effectively or to behave in a directed manner (see Chapter 4 for discussion of ambiguity as a factor in threat). Finally, social demands can be stressful when their requirements *overload* the person's resources. A woman might not have any psychological conflict between her parenting and working roles, but she is likely to find that the energy and stamina required by working a full day and then returning to an evening of housework and child care is fatiguing and therefore stressful.

Although there are many other social contexts in which stress is experienced, by far the greatest attention in research has been given to conflict and ambiguity within and between the family and work roles. Fine analytic reviews have been offered, one by Croog (1970) on the family as a source of stress and another by Gross (1970) on work stress.

Croog (1970) identifies six areas of inquiry about family stress, including family forms and structures, broken families, value conflicts among family members, changes connected with the life cycle, role conflict within the family, and destructive interactional patterns. This allows him to review a wide variety of research familiar to social scientists, including some on divorce, and on the pathogenic parental patterns described by Lidz, Cornelison, Fleck and Terry (1957) and Bateson, Jackson, Haley, and Weakland (1956) (which others might regard as effects rather than causes of illness). Since Croog's review in 1970, there has been new interest in the effects of divorce especially on children (e.g., Hetherington, Cox, & Cox, 1978; Wallerstein, 1977; Wallerstein & Kelly, 1980), and in abuse, including wife abuse, husband abuse, and child abuse.

Gross identifies three main types of work stress, those connected with the propagation of a career, those involving performance- or task-induced stress, and those connected with organizational structures that affect interperonsal relations. What is new since Gross's review is behavioral medicine's emphasis on the impact of work-related stresses on health (see, for example, Caplan, Cobb, & French, 1975, 1979; Cobb & Rose, 1973; Frankenhaeuser,

1979; House, McMichael, Wells, Kaplan, & Landerman, 1979; Kasl, 1978; Rose et al., 1978, to list some prominent examples). New questions are also being asked about disaffection from work even among high-level professionals, particularly physicians (Sarason, 1977), and about the impact of life cycle factors on morale (Estes & Wilensky, 1978).

Rather than reviewing research on family- and work-related stress, it is more fruitful to stay with a major theme of this chapter and cite research that clearly demonstrates how culture and social structure influence what is stressful for persons and how this manifests itself in emotional life. In this respect we can recall the work of Kardiner, Linton, Dubois, and West (1945), Whiting and Child (1953), Kluckhohn (1968), Opler (1959), and Singer and Opler (1956) on behavioral patterns of schizophrenics who are from Italian- or Irish-American backgrounds. From our point of view, the challenge is to show how the culture and social structure work their way downward to shape individuals' values, commitments, and beliefs. Ultimately these latter factors play a part in determining sources of stress, coping processes, and adaptational outcomes.

It is equally challenging to understand *individual* patterns of stress and coping in the context of the social structure and specific social encounters. Relevant to this point, Pearlin and Lieberman (1979) write:

> Characteristics such as sex, race, marital status, and socioeconomic class indicate where people are positioned in the society. Such information is of paramount importance, for the ways that people's experience becomes organized and structured depend significantly on who they are and where they are located in the broader social order. The important conditions of life and the wide variety of experiences that unfold in life are typically associated with the social statuses of people. (p. 218)

Here we would remind the reader that, as distal variables, social class and other sociodemographic variables operate in terms of the (proximal) meanings they have for an individual with a special history and personality.

Croog (1970) points out that it is difficult to distinguish between factors in the family group that are stressful and those in the personalities of the individual family members that make particular kinds of family events stressful for them. For example, marital stress can be ascribed *both* to difficulties in the marital relationship and to personality characteristics of the partners that antedate the marriage and set the stage for trouble. Marital problems can also be caused or exacerbated by conditions outside the home such as the work situation or relationships with in-laws. Moreover, cultural practices may affect the likelihood and form of such problems. For example, in the Japanese culture it is the custom for newlyweds to live with the husband's parents, which forces the wife into a subordinate role that she must accept, no matter how unpleasant it is.

Let us consider some examples of family and work stress that highlight the ordering of causal variables from those in the social structure, through the mediation of individual factors, to the individual's reaction. A fine illustration which includes both the family and work context comes from the research of Pearlin and his associates (Pearlin, 1975a; Pearlin & Johnson, 1975; Pearlin & Lieberman, 1979).

Pearlin has adopted a stance with respect to the concept of social stress very similar to our own, namely, that (1) stress is incompletely defined by reference to major events in our lives, and (2) it must also be assessed in terms of continuing troubled relationships—what we call daily hassles—which may actually be more important as sources of stress in the long run than major life events. Pearlin and Lieberman (1979) write:

> We begin by distinguishing two major types of events. One is represented in the gains and losses of major alterations of roles that predictably occur in the course of the unfolding life-cycle. We refer to these as *normative events* in order to underscore the expectedness and regularity of their occurrence. The second type of event we refer to as *non-normative*; these are often crises that, although they commonly occur, are not easily predictable by people because they are not built into their movement across the span of life. Some of these relatively eruptive events may lead to loss, such as being fired from one's job or being divorced. Other non-normative events, such as illness, are disruptive without necessarily entailing role loss. In addition to the normative and non-normative events of life we shall examine *persistent role problems*. These are not events having a discrete onset in time but, on the contrary, acquire their presence insidiously and become relatively fixed and ongoing in daily role experiences. Problems of this order are often chronic, low-keyed frustrations and hardships that people have to contend with in their occupations, their economic life and in their family relations. The normative and non-normative events and the more persistent role problems collectively constitute what we occasionally call life-strains. (pp. 220)

A large probability sample was obtained by Pearlin and his associates in the Chicago area which was made up of persons who ranged in age from 18 to 64. Extensive survey data were obtained from this sample on life stress, distress, and symptoms, as well as on patterns of family interaction. The reader may recall our earlier discussion of Pearlin's work on ascribed status inequality in married couples as a source of stress. Using the above data set, Pearlin (1975a) has also reported on conflict between work and family roles as a source of stress among women and a factor in depressive affect (see also Brown & Harris, 1978).

Analysis of these data shows that social stress arises from the confluence of many social and psychological factors. For example, self-reports of depression are more likely to occur among women who had become disenchanted with homemaking. The degree of disenchantment increases with age, or perhaps more correctly, with one's position in the life cycle. Disaffection with the homemaking role and depression are more likely when the duties of homemaking are onerous and no husband is in the home, or when the homemaker is isolated from people outside the immediate family. With respect to women who are employed outside the home, Pearlin also observes that there is greater risk that work will come into conflict with maternal and homemaking roles when the woman places high value on her work outside the home and is absorbed by it. Many women, however, cope successfully with this conflict by dissociating the two roles, when circumstances allow it and when they are clearly motivated to do so; when they leave the office, they put work out of their minds and, conversely, when they leave the house they put family problems out of their minds.

Here we see that two central roles indigenous to the social system, work and family, are capable of creating conflict and stress, but as in the case of the earlier illustration of status inequality, the stress depends on how these roles are valued and how the conflict is coped with; the stress is less or nonexistent when certain other factors are also present. In the instance cited, disaffection from homemaking and depression are dependent on age or stage of life, the severity of task demands, the availability of social contacts, and the presence of a helping husband. With respect to work outside the home, the strength of competing values and the extent to which the woman can keep the roles separate in thought and action—a form of coping—are also crucial in managing role conflicts. Such findings suggest that for role stress to occur, variables of the social structure must interact with individual personality characteristics.

Social Resources and Supports

The social environment is not just a major source of stress; it also provides vital resources which the individual can and must draw upon to survive and flourish. That people gain sustenance and support from social relationships has been known intuitively for a long time, and should be, in a sense, obvious. What is less obvious is how this works. The empirical case for the importance of social relationships as a mediator of health outcomes still lacks definition of process and specification of the conditions under which health is affected. As Schaefer, Coyne, and Lazarus (1982) have noted, current interest and research on this problem were stimulated by several theoretical pieces that interpreted the effects of social disconnection (losing social ties due to death or separation, being unmarried, and being geographically and socially mobile) in light of the idea that social relationships sustain health (Cassel, 1976; Cobb, 1976; Dean & Lin, 1977; Kaplan et al., 1977). There now exist a number of empirical studies in which low social support is implicated in negative health outcomes ranging from neurosis (Henderson et al., 1978) and complications of pregnancy (Nuckolls et al., 1972) to mortality from all causes (Berkman & Syme, 1979). (For reviews, see Thoits, 1982; Turner, 1981.)

The key dilemma of this expansive area of theory and research is the extent to which the problem has been oversimplified. The modern history of what is an old idea has been characterized by a great deal of enthusiasm, oversimplified research, and finally the gradual appearance of more thoughtful and sophisticated treatments of the issues.

A pamphlet distributed to health professionals and the public by the State of California, entitled "Friends Can Be Good Medicine" (1981), provides a good example of simplistic fervor. The introduction states that "This book is designed to help you see the vital role that friendship plays in your life and to help you find out when, how and why loving, caring relationships with others can enhance your physical and mental health" (p. 3).

Fischer (1982) commented on the "friendship cure-all" advanced in this pamphlet. "Early last year," he states:

> . . . Californians heard the message that friends can be good medicine on the radio, saw it on television, read it on bumper stickers and shopping bags, and discussed it in 2,000 workshops and special meetings . . . in California, close to six million people probably got the message. . . . (p. 74)

Fischer attacks the reasoning and cause-effect assumptions of this pamphlet and the tendency to ignore sociodemographic factors in the connections between social relationships and health. Further, he notes that the costs involved in obtaining and maintaining a helpful social network are not mentioned in the pamphlet, nor is any information given about how to build a network of good friends (cf. Lazarus, in press-b). If one feels disappointed in social ties or lonely and isolated, one is apt to feel even more so after reading how important positive relationships are for health. For these and other reasons, it can be argued not only that the pamphlet trivializes social relationships and supports but that it may even have harmful effects on its lay readers.

On the other hand, there is a growing body of thoughtful review articles analyzing social support in a more sophisticated fashion and calling for better research and measurement. Most of these articles have a strong psychological flavor in which the person is seen as actively engaged in cultivating and using social supports, and in possibly having to pay a price for doing so. Also, efforts are being made to differentiate the well-intentioned offer of social support from how it is perceived by the intended recipient. Significant examples of these more sophisticated treatments can be seen in G. Caplan (1974) and R. Caplan (1979), Dean and Lin (1977), DiMatteo and Hays (1981), Dunkel-Schetter and Wortman (1981, 1982), Kaplan et al. (1977), Rundall and Evashwick (1982), Suls (1982), and Thoits (1982). Suls, for example, differentiates between the positive and negative effects of social support in prevention, coping, and recovery from illness; these are summarized in Table 8.1. Murawski, Penman, and Schmitt (1978) offer similar qualifications about emphasizing solely positive effects of social support.

Many of the most sophisticated treatments of social support concern the physically ill, perhaps because of the accessibility of patients and the straightforwardness with which the patients' struggles can be examined. Wortman and Dunkel-Schetter (1979), for example, reviewed a number of studies and found that a large proportion of the problems most often reported by cancer patients are interpersonal and include difficulty communicating with friends about the cancer, speaking with their family about the future, and relating to people whose behavior changes after they learn the diagnosis (see also Dunkel-Schetter & Wortman, 1982). The authors identify patient concerns for which social support could be important, such as the need for clarification and reassurance about what is happening to them, evidence that others care, and help in dealing with the awkward behavior of others. The latter issue has also been

Table 8.1
Possible Positive and Negative Effects of Social Support

	Positive Effects	Negative Effects
Prevention	Reduce uncertainty and worry Set good example Share problems Calm model Distract	Create uncertainty and worry Set bad example Create new problems Calm model Distract Germs
Coping	Label beneficial Provide sympathy Give helpful information	Label negative Subject to irritation and resentment Give misleading information
Recovery	Maintain regimen Contrast with health (incentive) Create desire to stop being a nuisance	Discourage regimen Contrast with health (depressant) Create power/dependence need

Reprinted with permission from J. Suls. Social support, interpersonal relations, and health: Benefits and liabilities. In G. Sanders & J. Suls (Eds.), *Social Psychology of health and illness*. Hillsdale, NJ: Erlbaum, 1982, p. 264. Copyright 1982 by Lawrence Erlbaum Associates, Inc.

addressed substantially by Wright, Wright, and Dembo (1948) with respect to handicapped persons.

Below we take up some of the issues that are raised in the more sophisticated treatments of social supports and address them in a way that is compatible with our conceptualization of stress, coping, and adaptation.

Some of the current confusion about social support arises because there are at least two very different ways social support might be relevant to adaptation. First, it is usually assumed that being embedded in a social network is essential for people to feel good about themselves and their lives. The classic work of Bowlby (1969, 1973, 1980) on attachment emphasizes that even infrahuman species such as monkeys form close attachments to other members of the species and are distressed by separation and loss, partly on the basis of biological makeup and partly because of their inevitable dependence on maternal care. Alfred Adler's (see Ansbacher & Ansbacher, 1956) views originally emphasized the learning of social interest through infant dependency, although he later argued that wanting to relate to others was also an inborn need. Separation from others to whom attachments have been formed is nearly always traumatic, as is inadvertent isolation. Without ongoing social relationships, much of the meaningfulness of human existence is lacking or impaired. Viable social relationships make possible identification and involvement, which can be viewed as the polar opposite of alienation and anomie (Kanungo, 1979; Kaplan, 1980).

Second, perhaps the most common theme in the social epidemiological literature on social support and health is that support acts as an immediate buffer to stress and its destructive somatic consequences. It can help to prevent stress by making harmful or threatening experiences seem less consequential, or provide valuable resources for coping when stress does occur. The case for this stress-buffering role is still being debated because evidence of an interaction between social support and stress is difficult to produce methodologically. Some evidence does exist (e.g., LaRocco, House, & French, 1980; Nuckolls et al., 1972; Turner, 1981); however, a number of studies have been unable to demonstrate this effect (e.g., Andrews, Tennant, Hewson, & Schonell, 1978; Aneshensel & Stone, 1982; Lin, Simeone, Ensel, & Kuo, 1979).

Another reason for the confusion about the role of social supports in health is that studies in this area have conceptualized and measured social support variables in very different ways. House (1981), for example, reviewed a considerable number of different though overlapping taxonomies of social support and offers one of his own; our research group has done similarly (Schaefer et al., 1982), as have numerous other writers on the subject. There is every reason to believe that some of these distinctions will prove fruitful in explaining emotional and health-related outcomes. Furthermore, necessary distinctions among the variables have been overlooked. For example, lack of social support may stem from losing social ties through separation, divorce, or death. But such loss is highly stressful over and above the reduction of social support that it entails. To show that low social support that arises out of loss impairs health is not the same as showing that social support is a positive force in health maintenance; the stressful consequences of loss must be separated from the measure of support, yet most studies confound these variables.

Equally important, the fundamental distinction between the number of types of relationships a person has—a relatively distal variable—and the perception of the value of social interactions—a proximal variable—has often been ignored. The former concept refers to social *networks*, the latter to social *support* as it is sensed and appraised by the person. In the former, the benefits of social relationships are assumed, not measured or enumerated, whereas in the latter the supportive quality of the relationships is part of the measure itself, either in general or in specific contexts. The most frequently cited studies treat social networks, psychosocial assets, and perceived social support as interchangeable concepts, which perpetuates the conceptual and empirical confusion. Let us examine the two concepts briefly.

The social network. Mitchell (1969) defines the social network as the "specific set of linkages among a defined set of persons" or for a given individual. The network can be described by reference to composition and structure, that is, the number of people involved and the number who know one another well, as well as their relational content, for example, friends versus kinspersons (see also Barnes, 1972). Having many social ties is the polar opposite of being isolated, the latter being a risk factor for many physical and psychological problems (Cassel, 1976). If one treats humans as inherently social, then a reasonably good-sized network means the potential for having one's basic social needs met. In turn, being embedded in a social network could motivate the person who is, say, a parent to protect his or her health in order to be able to care for the children effectively.   .

When used to indicate level of social support, social network measures make the key assumption that having a relationship is equivalent to getting support from it. No attention is paid to the social demands and hence the stressful aspects of that relationship. A second assumption is that larger and broader networks are better than small ones. Berkman and Syme (1979), for example, used as a measure a composite index of marital status, numbers of close friends and relatives, frequency of contact with friends and relatives, and membership in clubs and community organizations. In a nine-year follow-up study of a large sample of nearly 7,000 persons, their social network index modestly but significantly predicted all-cause mortality while controlling for health status and risk factors such as smoking, drinking, and socioeconomic status. For both sexes and all ages between 30 and 69, people with the fewest social ties had the highest mortality rate. These and other studies support the idea that having a large social network is valuable in protecting health, although they provide little insight about how this works and the limitations of the generalization. Perhaps people with large networks are able to get the benefits of support without as much psychological cost as people with small networks. Alternatively, perhaps the key lies in the possibility that people with large networks have other things in their favor, too, such as being socially competent and skillful copers and thus better able than others to extract the valuable social ore from the available resource material. It is also possible that the relationships between social relations and health obtained by Berkman and Syme are artifacts of extreme cases of social isolation and that this explanation of health does not apply as strongly at the middle portion of the distribution.

When we think about the value of social networks, therefore, we must bear in mind that social relationships create problems which comprise a significant share, probably the lion's share, of the sources of stress in life. The balance between costs and benefits probably differs among persons, social roles, and stressful encounters. Marriage, for example, does not confer the same degree of protection from morbidity or mortality on women as it does on men (e.g., Ernster, Sachs, Selvin, & Petrakis, 1979; Ortmeyer, 1974). There is also a large research literature, noted above, which identifies the family as a source of stress (Croog, 1970) as well as a factor in psychopathology (Liem & Liem, 1978). Finally, we can learn from Mechanic's (1962) classic study of students under stress that the quality of support varies widely even within the same type of social relationship such as marriage, and that well-meaning but inept efforts to reassure others and to reduce their stress may actually increase it.

We now know too that the benefits of marriage clearly depend on many factors, such as the nature of the stressful demands with which the person must contend. For example, Pearlin and Johnson (1977) have observed that there is a greater disposition of unmarried people to depression and other psychological disturbances, but these researchers believe that this is a reflection of the greater exposure of unmarrieds to hardship and stress. They expected to find that when marrieds and unmarrieds had to contend with the same life conditions, they would be similar in regard to depression. This turned out to be only partly correct, since even when the married and the single in their sample were equated with respect to stress in their lives, the unmarried subjects still showed more depression. Only when married and unmarried people enjoyed circumstances that were relatively problem-free was the comparative risk of depression also similar. When conditions were favorable, people without spouses were found not particularly vulnerable to depression;

however, when both groups were confronted by social and economic sources of stress, the single group was more prone to depression. Pearlin and Johnson sum up by saying that "The combination most productive of psychological distress is to be simultaneously single, poor, isolated, and exposed to burdensome parental obligations." Concluding their findings, they write:

> What we have learned suggests that marriage can function as a protective barrier against the distressful consequences of external threats. Marriage does not prevent economic and social problems from invading life [we would add here that it can add to these and other problems] but it can apparently help people fend off the psychological assaults that such problems otherwise create. Even in an era when marriage is an increasingly fragile arrangement, this protective function may contribute to its viability, at least in the absence of alternative relations providing similar functions. (p. 714)

Perceived social support. In contrast with the social network, social support refers to the nature of the interactions occurring in social relationships, especially how these are evaluated by the person as to their supportiveness (e.g., Sarason, Levine, Basham, & Sarason, 1983). In Jessor's (1979) analysis, perceived social support is the most proximal feature of a range of interpersonal variables. Its use as a research tool may be illustrated by Gore's (1978) study of 100 men who lost their jobs when a factory closed. Gore employed a number of questionnaire items about perceived supportiveness of wife, friends, and relatives. The men who were not immediately reemployed and who felt unsupported had higher levels of serum cholesterol and illness symptoms than the men who felt supported; moreover, lack of support was associated with more depression regardless of employment status. In a similar vein, Andrews et al. (1978) found that psychological impairment in a crisis was associated with low expectations of help from friends, relatives, or neighbors in a sample of suburban Australians; network-based measures in this study were unrelated to such impairment.

Types of social support. There is now recognition that there are different types of social support, each with different antecedents and consequences. Weiss (1974) lists six functions essential for well-being: attachment, social integration, opportunity for nurturance, reassurance of one's worth, a sense of reliable alliance, and obtaining guidance. Conspicuous by their absence from this list are material aid and services, and information support. Dean and Lin (1977) identify only two functions or types, expressive and instrumental, but regard the former as more important, as do other writers such as Kaplan et al. (1977); perhaps this reflects the current concern with emotion in behavioral medicine. Other writers have made similar distinctions but have not applied them in research (e.g., Bloom, 1978; Gore, 1978). Most studies have emphasized attachment and affiliative (emotional) functions over the instrumental, material, or social integrative (Brown, Bhrolchain, & Harris, 1975; Cobb, 1976; Dean & Lin, 1977; Henderson et al., 1978).

Schaefer et al. (1982) distinguished three types of functions of social support. These consist of *emotional support* (including attachment, reassurance, being able to rely on and confide in a person), which contributes to the feeling that one is loved or cared about; *tangible support* (involving direct aid such as loans or gifts, and services such as taking care of someone who is ill, doing a job or chore, etc.); and *informational support* (providing information or advice, and giving feedback about how a person is doing). Cassel (1976) has suggested that feedback helps the person maintain social identity and a sense of integration in society. We note too that tangible support, when proferred freely and voluntarily, may signal that the other person cares and that the recipient is valued, and in this way it can overlap with emotional support. The basic assumption underlying the current interest in social support is that, other things being equal, people will have better morale and health, and function better, if they receive or believe that they will receive social support when it is needed. This assumption is to some extent justified by a growing body of evidence, although little is known about what constitutes productive or counterproductive support.

Those who speak of social support tend, in the main, to view it as a feature of the social environment. We have treated it here as a *resource*, available in the social environment, but which the person must cultivate and use. Elsewhere we have spoken about coping competence as including a set of social skills a person learns and draws upon in stressful encounters with the environment. Thus, we are inclined to see social support as falling under the heading of coping. Too little is known about the processes involved in the use of social resources under stress, or about how their use might prevent stress. Our knowledge is still too rudimentary in the ways social support operates to choose firmly among the theoretical options concerning its effects and modes of operation.

Our research includes a naturalistic experiment (Folkman & Lazarus, in press), cited elsewhere in this volume in connection with emotion and coping from a process perspective, in which students facing a college examination were asked about who they sought help from and who was helpful at three stages of the stressful encounter: before the exam, shortly after the exam but before grades were announced, and after grades were announced. This experiment produced solid evidence that the type of support changed from one stage to another. For example, information support seeking was highest during the anticipatory stage, when logically students had the need to clarify what would be expected of them, but it dropped dramatically after the exam was over. On the other hand, emotional support seeking was low during the anticipatory stage but rose dramatically after the exam and remained high after grades were announced.

These two perspectives, the classic epidemiological one in which social networks and supports are viewed as a feature of the social environment and the psychological, process-centered one in which seeking or using social support is viewed as a function of the source of stress or the stage of a stressful encounter, are quite different but complementary. It is in the latter sense of social support as a process that we begin to be concerned with social relationships as sources of stress as well as being valuable personal resources in the social environment. This perspective brings us back from the society or its substructures, which is the focus of sociology, to the individual as an active agent, influenced by society and in turn influencing it, which is the focus of psychology.

From our point of view, social support is the opposite side of the coin of social demands. To live well, people must recognize and manage social demands constantly, as well as recognize and use available social resources. On both sides of the coin, what happens is partly a matter of luck, since the demands vary in their severity and intractability, as do social resources. On the other hand, variations also exist in the capability or skills with which people manage social demands and draw upon existing resources. As was implicit in our discussion of coping in Chapter 6, the optimal management of social demands and the optimal use of social resources also depend on managing within the social constraints which are found in every social setting.

Social Change

Just as the physical environment is constantly changing, so the social environment is also in a state of flux, thereby creating stress. The sociological question of how society is changed represents in a sense the collective version of the psychological question of how the individual influences the immediate social environment, whether that environment is merely a specific context of a stressful encounter such as the family or a larger social unit or social institution such as a labor union.

Although biological evolution is a very slow process, social evolution or social change has become very rapid (cf. Toffler, 1970), as suggested in the following somewhat whimsical passage by Aldous Huxley (1965):

> Anatomically and physiologically, man has changed very little during the last twenty or thirty thousand years. The nature of genetic capacities of today's bright child are essentially the same as those of a child born into a family of Upper Paleolithic cave-dwellers. But whereas the contemporary bright baby may grow up to become almost anything—a Presbyterian engineer, for example, a piano-playing Marxist, a professor of biochemistry who is a mystical agnostic and likes to paint in watercolours—the [Paleolithic] baby could not possibly have grown into anything except a hunter or foodgatherer, using the crudest of stone tools and thinking about his narrow world of trees and swamps in terms of some hazy system of magic. Ancient and modern, the two babies are indistinguishable. Each of them contains all the potentialities of the particular breed of human being to which he or she happens to belong. But the adults into whom the babies will grow are profoundly dissimilar; and they are dissimilar because in one of them very few, and in the other a good many, of the baby's inborn potentialities have been actualized. (p. 32)

Attention to today's rapid social change leads to the question, Do people experience more stress now than they did in the past? There is no way of adequately answering this question, of course, since we lack the necessary observations with which to compare past and present. Analyses such as Toffler's imply that the answer is yes. Our own analysis, uncomplicated by evidence, is that this is probably untrue, that what has changed is the *kind* of stress people must deal with and the resources available to do so, not the degree. For example, in the past people died early of infectious diseases; today they live longer but are increasingly likely to suffer the debilitating diseases and incapacities of old age. Gruenberg (1977), for instance, notes that now old people seldom die of pneumonia. Deprived of "the old man's friend," they live on with growing incapacity even though their lives are no longer attractive and fruitful. Instead of trying to help people live longer, says Gruenberg, medicine should be seeking to increase their functional capacities. Thus, it seems that it is not so much that the degree of stress is greater or less, but rather that its roots and nature are different in different eras. The question of survival, for example, has always been a source of major concern in stress. In primitive times it might have been attached to keeping the fire alive, today to avoiding nuclear holocaust.

That stress is a constant in human history, although its sources are continuously shifting, might be illustrated through the analogy of military competition. New weapons were discovered which for a time greatly shifted the balance of power. Armored ships and tanks seemed impregnable until counterarmor and more powerful cannon were developed. Guided missiles were overwhelming until they could be brought down by opposing missiles of the same type.

Wellard (1965) provides an amusing example of the principle:

> Elephants wandered happily all through North Africa till well into the Christian era, the Atlas Mountains being their favourite habitat. But first the Carthaginians captured them for military purposes, using up thousands of them in their three long wars with the Romans . . . : protected by flank armour and carrying a bell under their neck to excite them, they were at first successful in panicking men and horses, destroying ramparts and trampling down the heavy-armoured infantry. But the Romans quickly devised anti-elephant weapons: fire and trumpets. The Carthaginian elephant "cavalry" was thus easily stampeded and was liable to end up by trampling to death more friends than foes. This classical military miscalculation necessitated an "anti-anti-missile" device . . . consist[ing] of a spike and mallet with which the mahout aboard his elephant could destroy his "secret weapon" when it went out of control. Thereafter, the elephant became, like the battleship, more of a status symbol in warfare than a useful weapon. . . . (pp. 26–27)

Thus, stress can be viewed as a struggle between opposing forces, that is, as demands that are always in some measure countered by coping resources and processes. The stress created by infectious disease, difficulties in obtaining food, limitations on travel and transportation, communications, and so on were ultimately countered by social change. In turn, the new changes created new imbalances and greater stress until countered by further change.

What are some of the ways social change might be stressful for individuals and groups? One is that it may make new demands on people, as when technological developments force industrial workers, managers, and professionals to learn new concepts and procedures, a process that is apt to be at least temporarily threatening and disruptive. Another way is that it makes certain functions and jobs obsolete and confronts people with unemployment or with the label of "deadwood." Social change can produce a loss of the anchors on which people have long depended, thereby creating a sense of foundering in a world that no longer seems predictable or even familiar. Changes in institutionalized patterns of work, observed among physicians, for example, by Sarason (1977) and by Thomas (1983), can also result in deep dissatisfaction with one's professional role in middle life.

Mead's (1970) discussions of generational conflict and the isolation of the modern family reflect this theme, as did Reisman's (1950) earlier concepts of the tradition-directed versus other-directed person. Changing social conditions can create threats that did not exist before—economic depression, the danger of violence, crowding, and so on. During periods in which role patterns are changing, as in the case of the roles of men and women today (see Veroff, 1981), there are options that present people with new and difficult existential and practical choices. Riley (in press) has made a careful examination of the impact of social change on people who are aging, noting the many ways in which age stratification intersects social change and creates psychological stress in individuals. She writes:

> These two dynamics of individual aging and social change, though interdependent, tend to be poorly synchronized with one another. Though particularly pronounced in modern societies, this potential for asynchrony is inherent in the age stratification system, imposing strains upon both individual and society. Thus people start their lives in one historical period, when all the age strata and people's cognitive maps of these strata are organized in one particular way; but as these people age, the full set of age strata is continually being reorganized from one period to the next. For example, people who were young earlier in this century learned societal age patterns and norms of that period; most went to school for no more than 6 or 7 years—adequate education for the jobs then held by their fathers or older siblings. They developed images of old age from the characteristics at that time of their few surviving grandparents. Similarly, people who are young today see the entire occupational ladder before it is transformed by micro-technology; they see retirement as currently institutionalized as an entitlement. But none of these young people will themselves be old in the same society in which they began. They must move through a society that is changing. Hence there is an intrinsic pressure for readjustments between their lifelong expectations and needs and the changing exigencies of society. . . .

The nature of the social changes that have taken place in our own society since World War II, and its psychological impact, is the subject of one of the nation's foremost survey researchers, Daniel Yankelovich (1981). According to Yankelovich, not only have many social rules and institutions that define how we should live and relate to others changed, but cherished cultural values which give meaning and define commitments in living have also changed within just one generation. He uses the phrases "new rules" and "a world turned upside down" to point up the extent to which the American public feels the pressure of this social change.

For example, the ethic of self-denial has given way to a sense of freedom to indulge oneself. The work ethic has lost its primacy, and there is a widespread commitment to self-fulfillment. There is less investment in child-rearing and willingness to sacrifice for children. Marriage is no longer considered the permanent or the only way of life, and there is a growing investment on the part of women in work, powered partly by economic considerations and partly by career aspirations. Many of the values and standards of conduct that were supported just a generation ago are no longer important to most people, and new ones have taken their place. Yet there are conflicts and contradictions, too, a certain nostalgia for some of the old rules and values, and a widespread impression that old workable values have been lost and that the new values may be counterproductive and not capable of being sustained by economic realities. With respect to our earlier distinction between the social system components of culture and social structure, changes in both have occurred, that is, in the beliefs and values that are passed from one generation to the next, and in the operative demands, constraints, and resources carried by social institutions and the immediate contexts of social relations.

A related theme is found in Baumrind's (1978) discussion of social reality from the perspective of dialectical materialism. Although she does not cast her analysis in terms of the psychological stresses created by social change, these effects are implicit when she writes:

> . . . different human environments necessarily produce different forms of human consciousness and self-realization and therefore different developmental progressions. For example, the Horatio Alger ideal of success based on effort reflects the expanded range of possibilities available to many Americans during the period of free enterprise capitalism, just as the ascetic ideal of voluntary simplicity with its theme of "small

is beautiful" reflects the constricted range of possibilities brought about by the postindustrial restrictions on economic expansion. The change in consciousness expressed in these contradictory ideals is grounded in changes in the respective objective social structural realities. There is objective reason today to doubt an earlier belief that humans' life on earth can be rationally and steadily perfected by means of science and technology. The depletion of the earth's resources poses a threat to the future. If the future promises less than the present, then the axiomatic ethical values epitomized in the Protestant Ethic are outmoded and the meaning of a realized individual must be defined anew. For instance, deferral of gratification and overweening respect for rationality, rather than universal characteristics of maturity, may be appropriate definers only in a society where such characteristics have clear survival value. (p. 64)

Patterns of child-rearing have also changed, creating profound effects on children. Based on a survey of public media materials, Stendler (1950) has noted that attitudes toward child-rearing have oscillated in cycles over the 60-year period from 1890 to 1950. From 1890 to 1900 a tender-minded view prevailed. The growing child was seen as a delicate flower that needed cultivation with love and gentleness. An editor of a magazine of the day devoted to child-rearing wrote, "Love, petting and indulgence will not hurt a child if at the same time he is taught to be unselfish and obedient. Love is the mighty solvent." Another editor outlined a plan for dealing with a boy who was labeled as lazy, careless, and good-for-nothing. He wrote in exhortation, "I thought I would try to win him with love alone, and never strike him. . . . Mothers who have trouble with their children, bring them up the Christian way . . . with a loving and tender heart, and you will surely succeed . . ." (p. 122). From this perspective the child must be led, not driven, persuaded, not commanded. Consistency and firmness must be tempered with understanding and justice. Corporal punishment is undesirable.

From 1910 to 1930, however, the mood shifted toward the tough-minded. If a child refused to obey a parental command, the parent was to demand complete obedience lest the child be spoiled. The demand for obedience was a contest of wills that the child must be made to lose, much as one tames or breaks a horse. A child had to be raised on a rigid schedule with times fixed for eating and toileting. Mothers were exhorted in child-rearing magazines that only such tight discipline would produce a sound adult, and no deviation from the set pattern was to be countenanced.

One could speculate that during this period in our history of increasing migration from farm to city and the need for a strong, vital labor force, it was useful for society to swing the pendulum from indulgence to tough-mindedness. Its children were being trained through stringent methods of child-rearing to cope with their roles as workers in factories and offices. In the motion picture documentary *Rosie the Riveter*, one of the factory workers during World War II points out how the emphasis in many "women's magazines" shifted, when the war was over and the men were returning to the work force, from recipes that called for a short time in the kitchen to those that took a whole day to prepare. There was a concurrent backward shift to the "feminine" role of women as wives and mothers, along with a flurry of articles urging women to give up their jobs and stay at home or their children would go morally astray. This is another example of the interplay between the goals of society at a given time and how those goals are reflected in the changing values of the individual and the family.

Aries (1962) has documented the evolution of the place of the child in European society through the Middle Ages to the present, and others, including Bell (1962), Gans (1967), Reich (1970), Reisman (1950), and Whyte (1956) have written about the changing values in American society from the 1800s to the present. All these writers, and others dealing with utopian thought through history (e.g., Manuel, 1965), deal in one way or another with social change and its impact.

Is change in society necessarily stressful? It is difficult to say, because of our lack of relevant evidence. Social change brings with it the potential for stressful and distressing conflicts between parents from the "old school" and children growing up under new conditions, as well as among people of the same generation whose development and functioning occur during periods in which such change is taking place. One presumes that the more rapid the change, the more it is likely to be a source of stress, and that the effects of such change depend greatly on the individual or social group as a function of expectations, beliefs, commitments, coping resources, and ways of living. It should be noted that lack of change can be stressful, too, as when one is bored or fails to gain a promotion or increase in pay. The notion that people like "difference-in-sameness" suggests that a degree of change or variety is essential to positive morale. Change is both stressful and exhilarating, depending on its character, on the person's nature and location in society, and on his or her expectations. Even stressful change, as in the case of bereavement or divorce at the individual level or changes in cultural values at the social level, may produce growth and ultimately a more effective way of life. This view is consistent with our own that it is not change per se that constitutes stress, but rather the way it is appraised and dealt with by the individual. The interplay between the person and the social system is exceedingly complex and changing.

Although people's emotional lives are shaped by society, they also influence the social environment. Moreover, not only is the social environment a major source of stress, but it also provides the resources a person can use to achieve his or her ends and to gain support.

At every turn we are speaking not of a simple, one-way relationship from social structure to individual, but of a two-way relationship. Both the social system and the person are constantly interacting to produce both common and unique outcomes, depending on the characteristics of each. The best model ultimately conceives of the two systems, individual and social, as interwoven (cf. Moos, 1973) and creating a new field (cf. Lewin, 1935; Murphy, 1966). To deal with this effectively requires that we move from a strictly interactional viewpoint toward a transactional and systems theory perspective, as we will discuss in Chapters 9 and 10.

Summary

This chapter began with a discussion of three different perspectives on the individual and society. First, society was viewed as a way of serving people's basic survival-related adaptational needs. Second, it was viewed as a shaper of persons and groups; social rules and institutions regulate relationships and shape emotions and behavior. The culture, for example, helps define what is important, desirable, damaging, or ignoble, and how emotions should be expressed and managed. These factors can also be examined from the perspective of the immediate social structure rather than the culture. To understand the way the distal social environment, which is without personal significance for the individual, affects the person requires understanding its proximal psychological meaning, which is determined through cognitive appraisal. Despite the unifying influence of the social context, there are always individual differences in thoughts, feelings, and behaviors. The third perspective has to do with the ways people and groups influence the social system. This view highlights the idea that the relationship between the individual and society is bidirectional, each influencing the other.

Stress, coping, and their adaptational outcomes must be viewed in the context of the individual's relationship to society. Stress is created by mismatches between individual and social identities. This theme is evident in the sociological concepts of alienation and anomie. The concept of mismatch is limited, however, because it tends to assume too much uniformity in what people assimilate from their culture and how these cultural values and beliefs are translated at the individual level, and because the concept is structural and static.

The social system creates demands and resources for the individual. Social demands, or normative expectations about behavior, can influence a person's thoughts, feelings, and actions, but are not necessarily sources of stress. Stress results when these demands create conflict, are ambiguous, or lead to overload. These factors have been studied most often in relation to family and work roles. Ultimately, stress depends on how these roles are valued, and how conflict, ambiguity, and overload are coped with.

The social environment also creates social relationships, which are necessary if the individual is to survive and flourish. Whether social resources directly affect health outcomes or instead act as buffers of stress is unclear, as are the mechanisms through which the effects of social resources are transmitted. A number of researchers have examined *social networks*, which are a relatively static component of the person's social environment. The underlying assumption is that having social relationships is equivalent to getting support from them, and attention is usually not given to the demands these potential resources can create or to fluctuations in the quality of support provided by members of the network. *Perceived social support* refers to the nature of the interactions occurring in social relationships, especially as they are subjectively evaluated as to supportiveness. A number of types of social support have been recognized, including attachment and affiliative functions, and instrumental, material, or integrative functions, all of which overlap with emotional, tangible, and informational support. It is also useful to view social support as a resource that the person must cultivate and use, and as falling under the rubric of coping. The basic assumption is that people will have better adaptational outcomes if they receive or believe that they will receive social support when it is needed.

The final section of the chapter dealt with social change. Social change can lead to stress by making new demands on people, producing the loss of what seems predictable or familiar, creating a

sense of isolation, or posing new threats. New social rules and institutions emerge within a single generation, creating constant demands for change at the individual level. Social change does not
have to be harmful, however; it can produce growth and lead to a
more satisfying way of life. Whether or not change creates stress,
and either positive or negative connsequences, depends on how the
change is appraised and coped with.

9

Cognitive Theories of Emotion

In the 1940s and 1950s emotion was treated as drive or unidimensional arousal and viewed either as the causal antecedent or as the variable that intervenes between the stimulating environment and the behavioral and cognitive response (cf. Duffy, 1962; Lindsley, 1951). A newer conceptualization—in some ways also older because it has roots anteceding behaviorism—is that emotion flows from cognition, that is, one first evaluates the personal significance of what is happening, and this evaluation becomes the cognitive basis for the emotional reaction. Our own thinking has been consistently cognitive (cf. Lazarus, 1966), but in effect, we have gone from a cognitive theory of stress and coping to a theory broad enough to encompass emotion.

We begin this chapter with a short overview of the history and present status of cognitively oriented theories of emotion. We have three objectives: first, to show where we have been in the recent past; second, to examine the conceptual and research tasks of cognitive approaches to emotion; and third, to note some ongoing efforts to accomplish these tasks. We then extend our line of argument to the complex relationship between cognition and emotion and conclude with a discussion of the problem of reductionism.

Early Cognitive Formulations

Dissatisfaction with the principles of tension reduction as the basis of human and animal adaptation became evident in the 1950s and 1960s. McClelland (1951; McClelland, Atkinson, Clark, & Lowell, 1953), Harlow (1953), and others were providing insurmountable evidence that tissue deficits leading to hunger and thirst, for example, could not account for learning and adaptation. Monkeys and rats showed more curiosity and exploratory behavior when sated physiologically than when highly aroused by the tissue tensions of hunger and thirst. Even Freudian drive theory came into question. Perhaps the most dramatic and influential attack on the tension-reduction concept was White's (1960) closely reasoned analysis of the defects of traditional drive theory in which he rejected the idea that children were driven solely by hunger or oral sexuality in wanting to explore, manipulate, or control the environment. One of his memorable passages about how a child eats a meal includes the new, cognitively based drive of "effectance motivation." White wrote:

> For one thing, there are clear signals that additional entertainment is desired during a meal. The utensils are investigated, the behavior of spilled food is explored, toys are played with throughout the feeding. . . . Around one year there is likely to occur what Levy (1955) calls "the battle of the spoon," . . . the moment "when the baby grabs the spoon from the mother's hand and tries to feed itself." From Gesell's painstaking description of the spoon's "hazardous journey" from dish to mouth we can be sure that the child is not motivated at this point by increased oral gratification. He gets more food by letting mother do it, but by doing it himself he gets more of another kind of satisfaction—a feeling of efficacy, and perhaps already a growth in the sense of competence. (p. 10)

In another version of this theme, Klein (1958) states that drive cannot adequately be defined without reference to cognitive processes:

> It seems more economical to . . . think of drive as a construct which refers, on the one hand, to the "relating" process—the meanings—around which selective behavior and memories are organized; and in terms of which goalsets, anticipations and expectations develop, and, on the other hand, to those processes which accommodate this relational activity to reality. In this way drive is defined solely in terms of behavior and thought products. . . . (pp. 8–9)

The above stirrings of a cognitive theory of motivation and emotion are also part of the history of ego psychology, an outgrowth of Freudian thought that moved from energy concepts and the seething cauldron as the force behind learning and adaptation and toward the primacy of thought as a key feature of the human neural endowment. The drive concept was not abandoned, however, only modified by the addition of new instinctual drives such as thought, reasoning, and curiosity. The so-called cognitive revolution, in which cognition replaced drive as the mainspring of behavior, took longer to evolve, even though it had as its forebears Kurt Lewin, Fritz Heider, and George Kelly, who were thoroughgoing cognitivists.

What is perhaps most interesting about the early cognitive approaches to emotion is that they were exemplified by two-factor theories in which the concept of drive—expressed in terms of arousal—was retained and to which cognition was added, much as White and Klein added cognition to the drive concept in their discussions of motivation. The prime examples of this type of cognitive formulation of emotion are provided by Schachter (1966) and Mandler (1975). The basic idea underlying their theories is that the perception of autonomic nervous system arousal, a diffuse, generalized increase in end-organ activity (e.g., heart rate, blood pressure), interacts with cognitive activity to create the experience of a particular emotion. Schachter's and Mandler's versions of this William Jamesian idea overlap considerably, but with important differences.

According to Schachter, emotion is a perception of arousal that is labeled according to available cognitive and environmental information. The experiment most commonly cited to demonstrate this process (Schachter & Singer, 1962) appeared to show that an injection of epinephrine, which generated diffuse autonomic arousal, led some subjects to report and display happiness when they were in a social context in which confederates role-played a happy mood, and led other subjects to report and display anger when confederates behaved in an insulting manner. In other words, emotion qualities such as happiness and anger were merely handy explanations given to arousal. This social induction of different emotions was especially effective when subjects were given no explanation about the way epinephrine would affect their bodily sensations, meaning that their reactions required some kind of cognitive interpretation. The main findings semed to fit Schachter's definition of emotion as a process through which sensations of diffuse physiological arousal are cognitively labeled.

For Mandler, too, autonomic arousal is a nonspecific, diffuse bodily reaction and, as in the case of Schachter, it is said to set the stage for an emotional reaction whose quality depends on the meaning given to what is happening. Mandler (1975) writes, "Thus arousal provides the emotional tone for a particular cognition, and cognition provides the quality to the emotional state" (p. 68). This view seems to differ little from Schachter's, but Mandler does two additional things. First, he expands the treatment of cognitive activity, extending it far beyond mere labeling to an analysis of the meaning of the situation that is more in accord with cognitive appraisal. Second, he allows for the possibility that the arousal itself could be brought about by a "meaning analysis that transforms an otherwise innocuous stimulus into a functional releaser of the autonomic nervous system" (p. 68). Thus, autonomic arousal and the cognitive process of creating meaning are for Mandler the essential conditions of emotion. Moreover, Mandler allows for continuous feedback from the reaction and for new evaluations that modify the original appraisal.

Mandler's interactive concept of arousal and cognitive interpretation, which acknowledges that arousal can be generated by a cognitive appraisal of a relationship with the environment, addresses one of the major limitations of Schachter's cognitive view of emotion. Schachter begs the issue of what it is that induces the arousal in the first place. In most emotional encounters, there is a fairly clear experience of a situation as anger-inducing, happiness-inducing, and so on, and there is then no problem of deciding what the reaction is all about. Schachter's explanation applies primarily to those situations in which people *don't know* why they are upset, in short, to highly ambiguous contexts. The limitations of the Schachter theory have been discussed in critiques and in reports of unsuccessful attempts to replicate the Schachter and Singer (1962) experiment (e.g., Kemper, 1978; Marshall & Zimbardo, 1979; Maslach, 1979; Plutchik & Ax, 1967). Some studies on the other hand, are more supportive (e.g., Erdmann & Janke, 1978).

Our own approach is more purely cognitive than Mandler's, and certainly more so than Schachter's. We say that the person arrives on the scene of a transaction with values, beliefs, commitments, and goals which set the stage for an emotion by making the person responsive to certain facets of the situation. These properties do not automatically mean emotion, however; they must first be engaged in that transaction. Emotion, and therefore arousal, thus depends on how the person construes the situation. Furthermore, Schachter and Mandler speak of the arousal involved in emotion as generalized and diffuse, whereas we argue in favor of specific patterns of arousal according to the eliciting cognitive appraisal, as the reader will remember from our discussion of generality versus specificity in Chapter 7.

The debate over the role of autonomic feedback has a long history. William James, for example, argued that it is the core of emotion; Walter Cannon argued otherwise. One of the best treatments of this elaborate and complex literature is provided by Frijda (unpublished). Whatever the case may be, we emphasize that cognitive processes are heavily involved and even necessary in the generation of an emotional state, and that progress toward further understanding will come from the search for further details and principles about how this might work.

The Fundamental Tasks of a Cognitive Theory of Emotion

The conceptual issues that must be addressed by a full-fledged cognitive theory of emotion overlap substantially with those appropriate to a cognitive theory of stress, coping, and adaptation. These include two major tasks. The first is to specify the intervening cognitive and coping activities that make it possible to translate an encounter with the environment into short-term emotional reactions and long-term outcomes and to cast these in process terms in order to incorporate change during an encounter and across types of encounters. The second major task is to move from description to cause and consequence by specifying the variables or conditions under which each type of appraisal—with its emotional consequences—occurs, as well as how the person and situation causal antecedents, processes, and outcomes are functionally related. Any cognitive theory of emotion that leaves out any of these major tasks of theory building is incomplete. A further task is to consider how the person properties so important for individual differences in reaction come into being, develop, and change over the life course.

Appraisal and Coping

Principles about the role of cognitive processes in particular emotions have long existed, although they have often been more implicit than explicit. For example, aggression, or more properly, anger, has been presumed to depend on frustration and, in a more cognitive version, on the perceived intention of another to hurt or to give one less than one's due (see, for example, Pastore, 1949). Similarly, anxiety is often characterized as an emotion that results from the perception of future danger under ambiguous and symbolic conditions (see Lazarus & Averill, 1972). Depression too has long been interpreted in several ways: as an emotional state following loss and characterized by a sense of hopelessness, or as anger toward another that is turned inward in order to ward off its painful intrapsychic or social consequences. Thus, we must be wary of seeming to argue that cognitive approaches to emotion are something new in psychology; on the contrary, ideas such as these have constituted philosophical-psychological treatments of emotion for centuries. What has been lacking is a combination of systematic efforts, built on theory, to specify cognitive precursors or accompaniments of emotion, as well as research efforts to test such propositions empirically.

There are limited conceptual treatments along the above lines currently available. Some are directed at a particular emotion such as anger (e.g., Averill, 1982), grief (Parkes, 1973), and envy and jealousy (Hupka, 1981). Heider (as described by Benesch & Weiner, 1982) speculated along these lines about a wider range of emotions, and Kemper (1978) has proposed a set of principles about social interactions, which are intepreted or appraised according to certain social values that involve status and power relationships. Weiner, Russell, and Lerman (1978, 1979; see also Weiner & Graham, in press) have formulated some of the attributions underlying diverse achievement-relevant emotions and view emotions systematically from the standpoint of such attributions. (We shall point out later how attribution and appraisal processes differ.) Finally, Beck (1971) has identified specific cognitions that elicit a number of emotions, thus meeting the first requirement of a cognitive theory of emotions.

Cognitive appraisal theory by itself, however, is incomplete as an approach to emotion. Remember that as an emotional encounter transpires, rapid changes occur in the relationship with the environment. Appraisal theory covers those changes that come about as a result of the person having time in which to reflect on what is happening and his or her own emotional reactions. Reference must also be made to coping, however, which affects the physical and social environment on which an emotional relationship depends. Each process of coping has different implications for emotion, not only with respect to how well the encounter is being dealt with from a problem-focused standpoint, but also with respect to the direct regulation of emotion through attentional diversions or cognitive coping such as denial, distancing, and redefinition of the situation. Many of these cognitive coping strategies alter or distort the initial appraisal in such a way as to change the emotion being experienced. Thus, if putting on a cheerful, hypomanic demeanor is an individual's way of managing depressive affect, then the cognitive appraisals for depression will not alone explain the manifest emotion; the decision, whether conscious or not, to battle the depression with a different demeanor and behavior pattern must also be taken into account.

The example of depression and hypomania also suggests that a person can simultaneously hold more than one set of cognitive appraisals, producing a pattern of ambivalence or rapid fluctuation or leading to the suppression of one in favor of the other. We think it is rare, in fact, for stressful appraisals to be totally consistent or unconflicted, and this adds to the difficulty of predicting emotional reactions without regard to coping.

The task of specifying appraisals for each emotion also requires a temporal perspective. For example, we wish or anticipate certain outcomes and experience emotions accordingly; then, as those outcomes eventuate, we may find they are not what we wished or anticipated, and experience yet other emotions. Cognitions about the past, present, and future are involved in emotions such as anxiety, disappointment, satisfaction, relief, and even anger and must be considered if we are to understand emotional flux as involving a shifting person–environment relationship.

Several writers have struggled with this problem with interesting theoretical results. Ortony and Clore (1981), for example, have incorporated what they call low-level and high-level goals into their cognitive analysis of emotions. Low-level goals are short-range and in the service of higher-level goals, which involve maintaining general well-being. For example, consider the long-range goal of becoming a physician with high income, prestige, and satisfying and humane work. Such a long-range, or high-level, goal involves numerous subordinate goals that could be thought of as necessary steps, or low-level goals, such as getting good grades in pre-med courses, being accepted into medical school, doing an internship and obtaining board certification, setting up a practice, learning how to practice one's specialty, and so on. Threats to these subordinate goals have an emotional potential because to be thwarted in any one endangers the high-level goal, which would have to be abandoned or changed in the interests of general well-being.

In the well-established tradition of social learning theory in which human behavior is viewed in terms of the interaction of value and expectation, Ortony and Clore (1981) use expectations and goals (values) to predict emotion. Thus, they state that a positive expectation that is not realized will result in disappointment; if the outcome is not clear, there will be hope; if it is positive, there will be satisfaction. Similarly, a negative expectation followed by a negative outcome will result in fears that are confirmed (although Ortony and Clore are vague about what the resulting emotion will be); if the outcome is positive, relief will be experienced. Ortony and Clore's formulation thus incorporates two key ideas: cognitive appraisals that are based on expectations, values, and realized outcomes; and a temporal progression that moves from anticipation to outcome.

Frijda (unpublished) has also made ambitious efforts along these lines, introducing cognitive processes by means of the Lewinian emphasis on the psychological environment, which Frijda calls "situational meaning structure." For Frijda, the situation is what is happening from the point of view of the person and therefore includes all the person and environment features of that particular relationship. Each emotional experience stems from a different situational meaning structure, a theme that except for language usage is precisely what we intend by a cognitive theory of emotion. He discusses three types of components of situational meaning structure: "core components" that make the situation emotional, such as relevance (cf. our concept of stakes and Ortony and Clore's concept of goal expectations) and clarity; "content components" that shape the quality of the emotion, such as controllability, degree of uncertainty, and valence; and "object components" such as self-referents versus other referents.

Still another emerging cognitive theory of emotion has been proposed by Scherer (1982, in press). Scherer's analysis has the interesting feature of a stepwise series of what he calls "stimulus evaluation checks," a minimum number of which are necessary for an emotion. Information about several situational facets is evaluated in these checks, including time, expectation, probability, and predictability for the *event itself;* pleasantness, goal relevance, and the justice of what happens for *evaluations of outcome;* causal agent, its motivation, and legitimacy for *attributions of causation;* the person's power to influence the event and to cope with the consequences for *coping;* and conformity of the event to cultural norms and its consistency with a real or ideal self-image for the facet involving *comparison of the event with external or internal standards.* This information is evaluated in a sequence of stimulus evaluation checks that are assumed to create the total cognitive basis for an emotion of a particular quality and intensity.

Leventhal (1980; Leventhal & Nerenz, 1983), who concentrates on emotions generated by illness, also offers a cognitive, stage model of emotion that has much in common with our own and other versions. The main processes include perceptual representations, interpretation, or appraisal, and coping. Emotion enters at the appraisal or interpretive stage, although it is also capable of modification through feedback from coping and its effects.

Finally, Epstein (1983a) presents what might be called a cognitively oriented self-theory of emotions built around the theme that people develop a self-theory, a world theory, and concepts relating the two on the basis of which they interpret events in their lives and experience emotions. Epstein's treatment of appraisal is more restricted than ours; appraisal is omitted as part of the emotional experience itself, yet it is critical in determining what the emotional reaction will be. Thus, a process may instigate an emotion such as anger, but, on the basis of how the person construes the appropriate or desired response options to be available, the emotion might change to something else, such as sadness or fear. This seems to us to be another way of speaking of secondary appraisal and coping as found in our own cognitive theory.

The cognitive theories of emotion now emerging and illustrated by the above examples all share very similar assumptions about the role of cognitive processes, especially evaluative ones such as cognitive appraisal, in the generation of an emotional reaction in an encounter with the environment. They are all meaning-centered, relational, process-centered, and recursive, that is, responsive at every stage to feedback and change. The theories also call for ipsative as well as normative research designs, especially in the case of Epstein (1983), who explicitly argues that the study of emotions should compare the same person with himself or herself as well as with others, and consider both the stabilities of reaction tendencies and their responsiveness to diverse environmental requirements.

This latter issue turns us toward the second major task of a cognitive theory of emotion, namely, anchoring the subjective experience and cognitive activity of the person in the context of an environment and in personality antecedents.

Causal Antecedents

The above systems of thought tend to confound the objective environment with the subjective in the way they analyze antecedent factors, and hence they move from tautology only in varying degrees. When Epstein (1983) looks to antecedent situation variables, for example, he is concerned with the situation as subjectively defined, and it includes such social variables as rejection, being given love and affection, being attacked, and so on. With respect to personality antecedents he emphasizes self-esteem, which is a subjective concept. Similarly, Scherer refers to information such as expectations, attributions of causation, conformity to social norms, and so on. These tend to be defined subjectively. These variables are not true antecedents in the sense of being capable of predicting the appraisal process itself, since they are already perceptions and appraisals.

Whether this is a serious handicap to a cognitive theory of emotion might be seriously debated. One might even debate whether the objective environment can ever be entered into an equation that is used to predict how the environment is experienced by the person. We admit to some ambivalence about this issue. On the one hand, we cling to the idea that it will ultimately be necessary to separate factors of the environment into those that are mediated subjectively and those that are independent of subjective experience, perhaps to compare the two. On the other hand, from a practical standpoint we are quite firm in our view that the emotional response of the person can be best known from how he or she appraises (and reappraises) what is happening, which is a subjective frame.

The antecedents of emotion also involve important ontogenetic considerations. The view that how one thinks about situations shapes emotion quality and intensity means that the individual's capacity to experience particular emotions depends on the level of his or her understanding of social relationships and their significance for well-being. This view makes it mandatory to direct attention to what infants and growing children know about their social world. Anger and fear probably emerge earlier in development than complex and more symbolically based emotions such as indignation, guilt, and embarrassment (although anger and fear can also express highly complicated and symbolic social and psychological meanings). A number of developmental psychologists have begun to address this question. Other scholars who have been exploring this problem include Campos, Ciochetti, Cowan, Hesse, Hoffman, Kagan, Lewis, Sroufe, and Weiner. Although information on cognitive determinants of emotion in young children is generally still meager, the growth of interest in this area is leading to serious research efforts and an increase in our understanding.

Attribution Theory

We must now take one further step and consider attribution theory, which has itself begun to offer an approach to emotion exemplified by the work of Weiner and his colleagues (Weiner, in press; Weiner et al., 1978, 1979, 1982; see also Heckhausen, 1982, and Russell, 1982).

Building on the work of Heider (1958), who proposed that the concepts people have about causality affect their social behavior, attribution theory has grown into an important area of social psychological thought, research, and controversy. Weiner has extended attribution theory to emotion, reasoning that how people explain their successes and failures affects, not only their behavioral commitment to achievement, but the feelings they experience in the wake of their efforts. One can, for example, attribute success to external factors such as luck or the nature of the task, or to internal factors such as one's own effort or ability; these diverse attributions then influence the emotional reaction. Substantial milage has been gained from these and other attribution-related categories (e.g., controllable vs. uncontrollable and stable vs. unstable causes) in the interpretation of emotional response.

Attributions of causality are cold perceptions or cognitions; they are simply statements about how things work. They are relevant to emotions, but not equivalent to cognitive appraisal, which adds the dimension of the *significance of the attribution for the person's well-being*. Thus, when we say to ourselves that a success is due to luck, as an attribution this is just a fact of life, but as an appraisal it may be threatening because it connotes *dependence* on luck, which is unpredictable, or because it denigrates our own contribution to the outcome. An attribution that effort or persistence rather than ability explains our success, or its absence our failure, may have a depressing impact as an appraisal if we have doubts about being able to sustain our efforts long enough to succeed. In the same vein, the attribution that superior ability is involved in success may be threatening if we have doubts about our ability.

Our approach to meaning as significant for one's well-being is parallel with Kreitler and Kreitler's (1976). They state:

> . . . meaning generation is regulated by two focal questions: "What does it mean?" and "What does it mean to me and for me?" . . . For the sake of clarifying this question it seems advisable to present it also in some rephrased forms, such as, "Does it affect me at all?", "In what

way does it affect me?", "Am I concerned in any way?", "Should I be
concerned?", "Am I involved personally?", "Should I be involved?",
"Is any action required on my part?", "Am I to act or not?" . . . "In
which sense(s) does it or may it affect (or concern) my goals, my
norms, my beliefs about myself, and my beliefs about the environment
or any of its aspects?" Evidently, the formulation "What does it mean
to me or for me?" is merely a label summarizing these different variants of the question. (pp. 77–78)

The reader should note that this treatment of personal meaning
is the exact counterpart of primary and secondary appraisal. We have
said that primary appraisal concerns whether one is involved in an
event personally, whether one has stakes in it. Personal values, goals,
and commitments, as well as beliefs about oneself and the world, are
two of the prime antecedents of such involvement, which is essential
to the experience of emotion. Secondary appraisal, on the other hand,
goes beyond the mere recognition of involvement to the question of
the actions required or the possibilities for action. Once one is involved, this process is not merely a matter of cold analysis or attribution but of sensing that one's well-being is at stake. This personal
involvement is no doubt why Sweeney, Shaeffer, and Golin (1982)
found that depressed subjects made different attributions for negative outcomes when these occurred to others than when they themselves were the target of negative outcomes. One can go beyond mere
attributions about causation and investigate the person's recognition
of assaults on personal pride, violations of wishes and expectations,
personal losses, and the like, all of which represent appraisals of the
personal significance of a social interchange.

A study by Dion and Earn (1975) illustrates how attribution
theory stops short of appraisal. Subjects in this study were presented with a performance task that involved an opponent, who
was actually the experimenter. Subjects in the "prejudice" group
were asked to submit to their opponent personal data identifying,
among other things, their ethnic status (Jewish). In return, they
received information from the opponent that was similarly detailed,
except that the opponent was identified as Christian. Subjects in the
"no-prejudice" group exchanged vague information that did not reveal their ethnic status or the ethnic status of their opponent. All
subjects were made to fail in their performance task. Dion and Earn
found that subjects in the prejudice group experienced stronger
negative affect and greater stress. The authors write:

> Presumably, the stressfulness of an event depends not on its intrinsic qualities but on an individual's interpretation of it as harmful or not. Such a process certainly operated in the present study. Subjects in the prejudice and non-prejudice conditions objectively confronted the identical situation of experiencing severe failure compared with their opponents. The prejudice manipulation, however, influenced their appraisal of this failure. By raising the spector of deliberate, religious discrimination by the alleged opponents, an attribution of prejudice quite likely made the experience of failure subjectively more threatening. (p. 949)

As in other attribution-type studies, Dion and Earn do not assess the appraisal process itself, but only infer the process from the particular pattern of antecedent-consequent relationships, in this case, the greater distress of the subjects when they saw the significance of the event for their well-being, which is the crucial step in appraisal.

Attributions must themselves be interpreted by individuals as to their personal significance in accordance with individual values and commitments. This added interpretation is what we mean by appraisal and is what generates emotions. Without this second step, attribution theory cannot provide the basis for a cognitive theory of emotion, although it does deal with important sources of information about person–environment encounters on which a cognitive appraisal is clearly predicated.

The Relationship Between Cognition and Emotion

A long tradition that reaches back through the Middle Ages and the Church to Classical Greece holds that emotion (passion) is separated from cognition (reason) and motivation (will or volition). Emotion was generally treated as primitive, with the implication that thought and rationality were Godlike. As Averill (1974) points out, not only does this view create a split between thought and feeling, but it also perpetuates the tendency to study emotions as a phenomenon of lower brain centers.

Although the place of emotion has been elevated in cognitive theories of emotion, in that it is seen as the product of highly complex cognitive activity, the impression remains that, as in older times, cognition and emotion, and motivation too, are separate and distinct entities that affect each other. The distinctions among the concepts are drawn too sharply, and the person described by such a conceptualization is fragmented and incomplete. (See Arnheim, 1958, for related discussion; Murphy, 1966, for a field-theoretical view; and Cowan, 1982, for a Piagetian-centered developmental discussion.) We are left with a shattered Humpty-Dumpty of a person that hardly approximates an integrated psychological system (see Lazarus et al., 1982). Although viewing thought as an antecedent of feeling is a step forward in the understanding of stress and emotion, because it provides a perspective on emotion that is meaning-centered, we still run the risk of making the same conceptual errors of the past in that emotion and cognition continue to be treated as separate entities.

Although we regard cognition (of meaning) as a necessary condition of emotion, one conceptual error is postulating that emotions precede thoughts or, conversely, that thoughts precede emotions; this forces us into either–or terms and pins us down to linear, unidirectional schemes that are at variance with what we have said about transaction (assuming, of course, that transaction applies within the person as well as between the person and the environment). Rather, causality is bidirectional. There is, for example, a long history of extensive and solid research showing that emotions often have major disruptive effects on cognitive activity (for reviews and analyses see, for example, Basowitz et al., 1955; Child & Waterhouse, 1953; Lazarus, 1966; Lazarus et al., 1952; Sarason, 1972; Sarason, Mandler, & Craighill, 1952). A later trend has been to view emotions not merely as disrupting cognitive activity, but as affecting it in many different ways, as in research on positive emotional states (e.g., Isen, 1970; Isen & Levin, 1972; Isen, Shalker, Clark, & Karp, 1978; Isen, Wehner, Livsey, & Jennings, 1965; Nasby & Yando, 1982; Wright & Mischel, 1982). Therefore, we cannot legitimately disregard emotion as an antecedent variable in the cognition–emotion relationship. There is also a large body of evidence (e.g., Lazarus, 1966, 1980; Lazarus et al., 1970; Weiner & Graham, in press) showing that emotions are shaped by thought processes. Therefore, neither can we legitimately disregard emotion as an outcome variable in the cognition–emotion relationship. Our own position, in fact, emphasizes this latter pattern.

Clearly, the error is to treat the relationship as a one-way street. As we noted earlier, the direction observed depends on one's point of entry into the ongoing process. Thus, if the sequence seems to begin with (1) thought, followed by (2) emotion, followed again by

(3) thought, and if we begin at point (1) in the above sequence, we must discover that cognition antecedes and in a sense probably determines emotion; however, if we start at point (2) in the sequence, we must discover that emotion determines thought. Both principles, of course, are correct.

Another conceptual error is to fail to remember that although emotion and cognition are theoretically separable, in nature they are almost always conjoined or fused. Anger, for example, not only refers to a particular psychological reaction, and to action impulses whether expressed or inhibited, but to hostile thoughts about an environmental agent. It does not make good sense to suggest, as Epstein (1983a) does, that a cognitive appraisal ends when the emotion proper begins; quite clearly the cognitive activity continues and is an essential part of the emotional response. In fact, when anger-related cognitions end or change, the emotion of anger disappears or changes to another emotion. The physiological reaction may live on a while longer but by itself it cannot be said to be anger; it is only a somatic residual that will disappear when the emotion of anger ends.

Cognitive coping processes such as isolation and intellectualization or distancing, which are aimed at regulating feeling, can create a dissociation between thoughts and feelings; avoidance and denial too help the person evade the emotional implications of an event. Moreover, attack can occur without anger, and avoidance without fear, which are instances in which the usual link between cognition and emotion has been broken. Yet such separations are less the rule of living and more often a matter of coping under special circumstances. In sum, the full experience of emotion includes three fused components—thought, action impulses, and somatic disturbances—which, when separated, leave us with something other than what we mean by an emotional state. Our theories should reflect the natural integrity of Humpty-Dumpty when he was whole. The idea that emotion and cognition are conjoined to form a meaningful unit is becoming more widely accepted as a way of thinking about the relations between cognition and emotion (see Fuller, 1982; Lewis, Sullivan, & Michalson, in press; Sarbin, 1982).

Do all emotions require cognitive mediation? One implication of our cognitive approach is that cognitive appraisal is a necessary as well as sufficient condition of emotion. This position has been criticized searchingly by Zajonc (1980). He writes that affect is erroneously regarded in contemporary psychological theory as postcognitive, occurring only after extensive cognitive operations have taken place, whereas in reality affective judgments are fairly independent of, and even precede, the perceptual and cognitive activities on which they are said to depend. Zajonc argues that, not only can affect occur without extensive perceptual and cognitive encoding, but affect and cognition are controlled by separate and partially independent neural systems. Zajonc thus seems to be saying two things contrary to what we have agrued above: first, that cognition does not necessarily determine affect and that the actual direction is from affect to cognition; and second, that cognition and affect should be regarded as relatively independent subsystems (see also Tomkins, 1981, for a similar view) rather than as fused and highly interdependent. Debate about whether cognition is a necessary condition of emotion continues with additional contributions by Zajonc (1984) and Lazarus (1984), who—along with others cited there—take opposing theoretical positions as to the phenomena that fall under the rubric of emotion.

In our view, the most serious mistake in Zajonc's analysis lies in his approach to cognition, which, reflecting a common trend in cognitive psychology today, uses the computer as an analogue of the mind (e.g., Newell & Simon, 1961; Shannon & Weaver, 1962; Weiner, 1960). Within this model emotion is generally viewed as emerging at the final stage of serial processing, the mind (computer) already having received, registered, encoded, stored, and retrieved bits of information that in and of themselves are meaningless. These bits of information are systematically scanned by the computer-mind, and meaning and emotion are created when, as in a binary system, a match is made between a bit of information and an internal schemata (e.g., a belief, value, goal, or commitment) that causes a "light" to go on.

It is not surprising that anyone concerned with emotion might be troubled by this model with its implication that emotion lies at the end of a slow, tortuous cognitive chain of information processing. Some theorists, such as Erdelyi (1974) and Neisser (1967), have suggested that emotion can influence the process at any stage. Zajonc comes to the conclusion that there is another, independent, system that makes possible rapid, nonreflective emotional reactions. In our view, regardless of such amendments, using the computer as a model of the mind leads inevitably to misunderstanding the ways people actually appraise and respond to their environment, at least when transactions are emotionally laden.

One source of misunderstanding has to do with the extent to which people must process information before it takes on meaning. As we have argued, humans are meaning-oriented, meaning-building creatures who are constantly evaluating everything that happens, which is a constructionist rather than positivist position. These evaluations are guided by cognitive structures that orient the person with respect to what is relevant and important for well-being (Folkman, Schaefer, & Lazarus, 1979; Wrubel et al., 1981). The structures arise in part from phylogenetic development and in part from social experience (see Kemper, 1981), and operate in the form of beliefs and commitments that influence appraisals at the outset of any encounter (see Chapter 3). As fully formed beings with these cognitive structures in place, we do not wait until the environmental code is fully unraveled through information processing before we evaluate what is going on; we respond early in the processing sequence to partial cues, sometimes with such speed that meaning and emotion seem to occur simultaneously with perception. The phenomenon of subception—the autonomic discrimination of a threat without conscious awareness (discussed in Chapter 3)—illustrates this process. We are able to use grossly incomplete information from the environmental display to make inferences about its significance for well-being; we do not have to completely process all the information from the display.

A second source of misunderstanding has to do with the concept of information that is processed as *meaningless* (see also Haugeland, 1978). When information is appraised as having significance for our well-being, it becomes what we have called "hot information" (Folkman et al., 1979), or information that is laden with emotion. Subsequent processing takes place with this hot information, which means that the stuff of processing is no longer cold, meaningless bits. Notice that what we are saying here differs from the idea that emotion arises at the end of serial information processing, or that it interrupts information processing, or that emotion operates as an independent system. We are saying that it is not only possible, but in the context of most stressful events highly probable, that emotion and information (and therefore cognition) are conjoined for large portions of the evaluative appraisal process.

Where are we then with respect to the question of whether cognitive mediation is a necessary condition for emotion? Our answer is that by and large cognitive appraisal (of meaning or significance) underlies and is an integral feature of emotional states. Are there any exceptions? We think not, even when the emotional response is instantaneous and nonreflective, as emphasized in Arnold's (1960) use of the term appraisal (see Chapter 2). Where we have any doubts, it is in the area of phylogenetically based triggers or releasers of fear, such as those postulated by Hebb (1946). Perhaps humans are wired to react instinctually with fear to spiders, snakes, or strangeness. Many of these apparently automatic reactions, however, seem to disappear or at least go underground with an ontogenetic shift to higher mental processes, just as phylogenetic accretions of the neocortex only suppress or regulate but do not banish lower functions. For all intents and purposes, however, we argue that cognitive appraisal always mediates emotional reactions to a greater or lesser degree, although emotions once generated can then affect the appraisal process.

Emotion and the Problem of Reductionism

Theory and research about emotion have been plagued by two forms of reductionism. One form is evident in the search for dimensions that underlie the language of emotion. The second form, which has had a greater impact on the field, views emotions within a phylogenetic perspective, entirely from the point of view of the central nervous system.

The Dimensions of Emotion

Because of the human capacity for language and self-observation and introspection, the richest source of information consists of people's reports of their subjective experience (cf. Epstein, 1983a). To tap this source in research, we need to listen to how people characterize their emotional experience.

Dictionaries list hundreds of words that people use to describe their emotions, many with overlapping meanings and subtly divergent nuances. To a certain degree, the meanings of these words are culturally determined, but they are also idiosyncratically determined by the person's own history. A fundamental issue, therefore, is the extent to which subjects have a shared understanding of the meanings of these emotion words. For example, are people who say they are fearful but not angry using the word "fear" in the same way to describe their response state?

Ortony and Clore (1981) make the interesting point that some emotion words are trait/emotion hybrids, rather than words that refer purely to an emotional state. For example, the word *proud* can refer to feeling proud, an emotional state, or to being a proud person. These and other distinctions, such as between sensory feelings and emotions, are important to keep in mind, since it is not always clear whether emotion words refer to actual emotional states as opposed to sentiments, longstanding moods, or highly cognitive states that have little emotional heat.

A major theme in theory and research on emotion has been the search for a limited number of dimensions that underlie the large numbers of emotion words. Efforts to seek irreducible elements of emotion had an early beginning in the work of Wundt (1907). His special brand of introspection produced three dimensions along which all emotion was considered to vary: pleasantness–unpleasantness, tenseness–relaxation, and excitement–calm. Most later efforts to dimensionalize emotions have depended on empirical factor analysis procedures and have produced two broad common dimensions, a pleasantness–unpleasantness factor and an arousal or activation factor, a pattern basically similar to Wundt's. Others such as Russell (1980) and Russell and Mehrabian (1977) add a third factor called dominance–submissiveness or, in the case of Daly, Polivy, and Lancee (1983), a factor called intensity. Watson, Clark, and Tellegen (in press) propose a two-factor solution that differs slightly from the others. Debates occur over whether each factor is bipolar or unidimensional and over how to organize emotion factors in space. Plutchik (1980), for example, proposes a circular pattern, and Daly et al. a conical three-dimensional spatial model.

Efforts to eliminate redundancy among emotion words have led to a smaller set of basic emotion dimensions which reduces lists of even nonredundant words to more manageable proportions. Reduced lists of mood or emotion words have been presented by many researchers. Some of the better known versions include those of Schlosberg (1954), Block (1957), Osgood (1966), Nowlis (1965), Lorr, Daston, and Smith (1967), Davitz (1969), Thayer (1978), Izard (1975), Averill (1975), Plutchik (1980), Daly, Polivy, and Lancee (1983), and Watson et al. (in press). Most of these efforts are atheoretical, although Plutchik and Izard use a phylogenetic theoretical perspective.

It is important to recognize the limitations of lists of emotion words and of dimensional analyses of emotions. Emotion lists have little to say about the factors that elicit emotional experience. They are disembodied descriptions of emotion as a response or experience, rather than a reflection of how a person appraises a changing relationship with the environment. An exception is the work of Davitz (1969), who had subjects describe an experience for each of nine emotions and later more explicitly identify what it was in the relationship that was responsible for each emotion.

The problem of disembodied descriptions of responses is even more severe at the dimensional level. In Russell and Mehrabian's (1977) three-factor theory of emotions, for example, we find the conclusion that almost all of the reliable variance in 42 emotion scales had been accounted for by three dimensions. The implications are that these three dimensions adequately describe people's emotional states, and that little additional personal meaning is gained by referring to emotion words falling within the same dimension. There is no room for subtle distinctions, for example, among righteous indignation or anger suffused with guilt or shame (cf. Ortony & Clore, 1981). Above all, like lists of emotion words, simplifying dimensional analyses ignore the important task of specifying the cognitive content of the changing relationship between the person and the environment in any given encounter. Why are there so many different emotion words except that they reveal different shades of meaning about what is construed to be happening in emotional encounters? The elegant simplification of emotion into a few dimensions seems to be purchased at the expense of understanding the person's emotional experience. Our concerns are also echoed by Frijda (unpublished).

To these arguments we would add one more. When researchers write of the structure of emotion they seem to be saying that a particular arrangement is stable; certain dimensions are negatively correlated, so that, for example, if one is sad about something, one cannot also be happy, and when one is worried, one cannot be confident. However, we know from our research with the stages of examination stress (Folkman & Lazarus, in press), described earlier, that the structure of emotions is not stable. In the anticipatory period before the exam, negative and positive emotions such as the above were uncorrelated; as the stages of the exam proceeded from the highly ambiguous conditions of anticipation through the postexamination stage before grades were announced, and into the final stage after subjects learned how they had done, their positive and negative emotions correlated more strongly, the r being $-.25$ at stage two and $-.50$ at stage three, when all the facts with which to evaluate the significance of the experience had become known. Thus, positive and negative emotions are strongly negatively related only when the situation on which they depend is clear with respect to its implications for well-being. When things are highly uncertain, one does not know whether to be happy or sad, disappointed or relieved, and so positively and negatively toned emotions remain unrelated. Relationships among emotions shift around depending on the nature of the information and meanings, that is, the appraisals on which the emotions depend.

The Phylogenetic Perspective

The work of Cannon (1932) on the hypothalamus and the hormonal outputs of neural activity set the stage for viewing emotion as a function of the central nervous system. By turning inward to neuro-humoral systems, the relationship between the environment and the person or animal as a factor in emotion is ignored. This approach also encourages the use of animals for research, since the need is for electrophysiological and surgical studies of neurohumoral anatomy and physiology. In addition, the focus on infrahuman animals leads to a search for the lowest common denominator of emotion among simpler mammalian species. Although animal research can be of great value in the study of stress in the search for neurohumoral universals, the more theories of emotion involve higher mental processes, the less suitable are nonhuman animals as subjects.

These kinds of reduction are well illustrated in an article on emotion by Panksepp (1982) and in comments on this article by scientists from fields as diverse as philosophy, neurophysiology, psychiatry, anthropology, biology, and psychology that appear in the same issue. The debate is concerned with whether emotions can be meaningfully studied when conceptualized phylogenetically on the sole basis of nervous and glandular systems, or whether such study requires considering the ongoing relationships between a creature and its environment. Nowhere are the diverse and often contradictory assumptions held by scientists about emotions, with their implications for how the subject should be studied, better illustrated than in these comments, within the covers of one journal issue, and nowhere is reductionism more in evidence.

Some of the most vigorous criticism of this form of reductionism has come from the field of drug abuse and centers on the concept of addiction. Peele (1981, 1983), for example, argues persuasively that substance abuse has been incorrectly blamed on some special neuro-chemical vulnerability of particular people which creates a need for the substance and an inability to give it up without severe and debilitating withdrawal symptoms. Not only is there evidence against this idea, but no physiological basis has ever been identified after decades of research. Most abusers ultimately give up their drugs, as evidenced by the history of large numbers of substance abusers from the Vietnam War who relinquished drugs after returning to civilian life. According to Peele, any substance can produce dependency for purely psychological and social reasons; therefore the medical-psychiatric concept that drug abuse and alcoholism are diseases is without foundation. Rather than reducing the processes involved in drug dependency to physiological mechanisms, several writers (e.g., Alexander & Hadaway, 1982) encourage examination of the adaptive psychological functions served by drug use, such as its value in coping with stress and distress.

And then we have a stunning commentary against the reductionism of mind to body by the distinguished psychophysiological progenitor of split brain research, Roger Sperry (1982). Such research has sometimes been cited as evidence for the separation of the functions of emotion and cognition in the brain (e.g., Izard, as cited in Zajonc, 1984), a position that actually appears to contradict neurophysiological evidence (e.g., Davidson & Fox, 1982; Sperry, 1982). Sperry tells us that emotional overtones leak across the undivided brain stem to influence neural processing in the other hemisphere. He argues that the affective component appears to be an underlying conscious property of the mind. Current research is aimed at determining more precisely the shades of emotional content that cross through the brain stem to affect cognitive activity in the other hemisphere. With respect to the implications of this position for the mind–body problem and reductionism, Sperry writes:

> Cognitive introspective physiology and related cognitive science can no longer be ignored experimentally, or written off as "a science of epiphenomena" or as something that must in principle reduce to neurophysiology. The events of inner experience, as emergent properties of brain processes, become themselves explanatory causal constructs in their own right, interacting on their own level with their own laws and dynamics. The whole world of inner experience (the world of the humanities), long respected by 20th century materialism, thus becomes recognized and included within the domain of science.
>
> Basic revisions in concepts of causality are involved, in which the whole, besides being "different from and greater than the sum of its parts," also causally determines the fate of the parts, without interfering with the physical or chemical laws of the subentities at their own level. It follows that physical science no longer perceives the world to be reducible to quantum mechanics or to any other unifying ultra element or field force. The qualitative, holistic properties at all different levels become causally real in their own form and have to be included in the causal account. Quantum theory on these terms no longer replaces or subsumes classical mechanics but rather just supplements or complements. (p. 1226)

When psychologists try to deal with areas of confusion in psychological theory by reduction to anatomy and physiology, they are usually attempting to clarify obscurities at one level of analysis by drawing upon obscurities at another. Rarely if ever does this exercise clarify matters. Moreover, as Haugeland (1978) writes, "A common misconception is that reductions supplant the explanations they reduce—that is, render them superfluous. This is not so . . ." (p. 217). One can only pursue the dream of a unified science if understanding at each level of analysis is valid and complete.

Although there is now less tendency in psychology as a whole to reduce all behavior to a common set of principles (see also Engel, 1977, for a discussion in the context of the medical model; and Schwartz, 1982, in the context of behavior medicine), reductionism—often without it being evident to the researcher or theorist— still can be found, especially among those who define and study stress at the physiological level. For example, Selye (1956, 1976, 1980) explicitly defines stress physiologically as the nonspecific bodily response to any demand or noxious agent. When Selye, then, says that psychological threats are included in the category of noxious environmental agents, many believe that he is dealing adequately with stress at the psychological level. He is not.

Although this point has not been widely appreciated, it is clearly understood by some (for example, see the quotation from Levine et al., 1978, in Chapter 2). It has been trenchantly discussed by Lumsden (1981), who writes:

> It is true that Selye now seems to accord some more significant role to cognition (cf. "appreciation" in Selye, 1980: x, xi) in ·human "stress"; but he still wants to hang onto "nonspecificity" and a "response" definition—features deriving from his original experimentation on rats. Thus, Selye's own current writings must also dissuade us from adopting his position. Let me be specific. When we find that by "stress" he now means only that the human body has "a need to reestablish a normal state" (1979a, pp. 68–69), or a need merely "to adjust" to any demand, or, even more clearly, that "The nonspecific demand for activity as such is the essence of stress" (1979b: II), then it is clear that his homeostatic approach refers but to mere, general "arousal." All he is saying, as Hinkle perceived several years ago (1973: 43), is that the individual exists shorn of the necessary psychosocial context; the systematic nature of our cultural physiology is ignored or downplayed. This is not an approach capable of analyzing, understanding or helping the individual as a person, as a member of a socially constructed world suffused with common or partly shared or overlapping (cf. Needham, 1975) meanings, as an actor set within a particular social structure and coping (an active, not a passive process, contrary to Young, 1980: 143) with its role-demands, constraints and challenges. (pp. 12–13)

The confusion of stress at the psychological and physiological levels arises partly because stress is widely conceived as a bodily response, and partly because those who are far removed from psychological thought do not see that noxious stimuli can be defined only by reference to the psychological processes that give meaning to environmental events. If all that needs to be said about stressors were contained in the term *environmental stress*, that is, in life changes such as death of a loved one or natural disasters, then there would be no problem and Selye's treatment of stress would cover the ground. It is only when we look more closely at what makes an event a source of stress that it becomes obvious that Selye's definition does not address the crucial social and psychological aspects of the problem.

The above difficulty is analogous to one that Selye has never resolved even for the physiology of stress, namely, that of the "first cause," the mechanism whereby the central nervous system signals danger. The central nervous system must somehow "judge" or "appraise" the need to stimulate ACTH secretion, which, in turn, will activate the adrenal cortex and hence the General Adaptation Syndrome. One needs a rule for this signaling process. This problem is central in psychological stress, too. That is, the person must sense threat and distinguish it from nonthreat or else be constantly in a state of psychological stress or crisis. We suggest that *cognitive appraisal* is the mediating process that sets the whole train of psychological events into motion, including coping activity, the emotional reaction, and the somatic changes that are part of any stress state.

Summary

Cognitive approaches to emotion evolved during the 1960s, when there was increasing dissatisfaction with the principles of tension reduction and drive as explanations of learning and adaptation. Early cognitive approaches to emotion retained the concept of general arousal and added cognition. Schachter and Singer (1962), for example, defined emotion as a process through which arousal was cognitively labeled. Our approach is more purely cognitive; we say that those values, commitments, and goals that are engaged in a transaction influence how the person construes a situation, and hence the emotions he or she will experience. Cognitive appraisals lead to specific emotion qualities rather than to general arousal.

A number of cognitive theories of emotion have now been proposed that attempt to specify cognitive antecedents of emotion. These theories are meaning-centered, process-oriented, and bidirectional. A common problem is that the specified variables tend to be subjective and therefore are not true antecedents in the sense of being independent of the appraisal process. Ontogenetic factors also need to be considered as antecedents or determinants of emotions, especially among infants and children.

Attribution theory, which is cognitive at its core, has also been applied to the study of emotions. Attributions of causality are "cold" cognitions in that they do not include an evaluation of the significance of the attribution for the person's well-being. Attributions are thus not equivalent to appraisals, although judgments about causality contribute to appraisals.

Traditionally emotion has been treated separately from cognition. It is an error to postulate that feelings precede cognition or that cognition precedes emotion. Causality is bidirectional. It is also an error to view emotion and cognition as separate; in nature they are conjoined. Cognitive activity is an essential part of an emotional response; it provides the evaluation of meaning on which emotion depends. Computer models of the mind that view emotion as emerging at the final stage of processing perpetuate the separation of emotion from cognition. Cognitive appraisal is a continuous process that is often based on partial cues rather than on full information. Thus, emotions can occur very early in the evaluative process.

Reductionism characterizes much of the thinking about emotion. One example is the search for a limited number of dimensions that underlie the large numbers of emotion words. The assumption is that these dimensions adequately describe people's emotional states. A second form is to view emotions as solely within the central nervous system rather than as an evaluation of the person–environment relationship. A major flaw in this approach concerns the first cause, or mediator, in Selye's terms—the mechanism through which the organism determines that its well-being is in jeopardy. The physiologist must ask what makes the neurochemical defense process go into action to deal with a noxious agent. Appraisal is the process that provides such a cause at the psychological level.

10

Methodological Issues

Conceptual systems, including the one we have developed in the preceding chapters, are usually embedded in a set of general methodological assumptions about how to approach the phenomena of concern. In this chapter we make an effort to clarify these assumptions. We begin by discussing issues that arise from dealing with a phenomenon (i.e., stress) that is commonly investigated at three distinct levels of analysis—physiological, psychological, and social. Next we examine the traditional linear, causal model that is the basis of much research in stress, coping, and adaptation and compare it with the transactional, process-oriented model that underlies our theory of stress. Then we focus on the design of transactional process-oriented research and present an overview of three major research designs. The final sections of the chapter are focused on the measurement of the key concepts of stress, appraisal, and coping, and the perennial problem of method variance.

Levels of Analysis

Stress is an interdisciplinary field covering many areas of inquiry that examine phenomena at multiple levels of abstraction (see Schwartz, 1982). At the highest or macro level are sociology and political science, whose universe is the society, social systems, collectivities, or categories of people differentiated as to social class, age, gender, and so on. Psychology is at an intermediate level, its prime unit of analysis being the individual. Anthropology extends from the highest (social) level, as when it is concerned with cultures and subcultures, to the individual psychological level. Physiology approaches stress phenomena from the tissue and cellular level, its emphasis being changes in the neurohumoral regulation of various organismic functions. Biochemistry deals at the molecular level with hormones, which represent the smallest unit of analysis used in connection with stress theory and research. Areas that are more applied, such as medicine, psychiatry, clinical psychology, social work, and nursing, draw upon all these disciplines and in turn contribute to them.

The convergence of different levels of scientific analysis on the common problems of stress and coping theory brings with it the potential for great confusion. Stress and coping do not have the same meanings at one level of analysis as they do at another, nor can stress at one level of analysis be reduced to stress at another. It is vital that we first sort out the concepts at each level and then begin to identify principles for linking them. Thus, we must approach stress at all three levels—sociological, psychological, and physiological—and independently create principles for each, before we can link them together. For example, as noted in the previous chapter, in order to have a sound psychophysiology, the psychological and the physiological components must each have clearly stated principles and measures.

Before attempting to link the three levels, it is important also to acknowledge that they are partially independent; stress experienced at any one level is often but not necessarily experienced at another. This partial independence can be seen in research by Pearlin (1975b) on the effects of status inconsistency, which we cited in Chapter 8.

This research examined inequality in ascribed status (status derived from that of the parents), a social variable which has long been thought to have causal implications for stress in marriage. By means of interviews, Pearlin obtained information about the social status of both the husband's and wife's parents and about the amount of marital stress experienced. It was found that status inequality, per se, did not produce stress in marriage.

Pearlin also obtained information about the importance of status to the spouses (a psychological variable) and about the ongoing process of interaction between them. When the higher-status partner considered status-striving important, he or she felt cheated in having married a lower-status person, and there was much distress in the marital relationship. This was displayed in the description of four aspects of the couple's ongoing interactions: reciprocity, expressiveness, exchange of affection, and the sharing of values. Among those for whom status was important, the lower-status partner was judged by the spouse as unreciprocating in the relationship, and the higher-status partner felt like a loser in comparison with the spouse who had married up. For these marriages, status inequality created a lack of affection as well as inadequacy both in communication and in the sharing of values. The stress persisted even though the couple may have moved up socially after marriage. In sum, by itself the social variable of status inequality was of little or no consequence without regard to the psychological meaning and value that people attached to it.

The research illustrates both the partial independence of the *social and psychological levels* of analysis and their interdependence too. A potential stressor at the structural level (status inequality) will not create stress at the psychological level (the attitude toward marriage and the feelings and behavior of the partners) unless it is mediated by psychological variables concerned with meanings and values. Still, it would not be possible to understand the stress at the psychological level without reference to the social context in which it occurs, namely, the existence of social inequalities, passed down to the next generation, that may or may not be internalized psychologically. The word *may* is the key. Even if social system variables serve as a kind of template for psychological processes (Kemper, 1978), something further is needed at the individual level to affect and effect psychological characteristics. Some persons internalize certain of these social values and ways of thinking whereas others do not. There can never be an automatic connection between the social and psychological levels, but they are apt to be related because to a certain extent psychological processes are imbued with, shaped by, and reflect social values. If psychological characteristics are not measured along with the social variables, then moving from the higher (macro) to the lower (micro) level and predicting one from the other is hazardous.

Failure to acknowledge the independence among levels of analysis, which is evident when measurements of stress at one level are used as indicators of stress at another, would in the above illustration lead one to take stress at the social level as evidence of stress at the individual level. Similarly, physiological stress and somatic illness are often assumed without justification to indicate the presence of psychological stress, or even stress in the social system.

In other instances, physical and psychological levels are confounded, as when heat, cold, bodily injury, and infection are assumed to result in psychological stress; it is difficult to know whether the physiological stress responses that ensue from these physical assaults are the result of physical or psychological processes, or both. One of the best examples of this confounding between psychological and physiological processes can be found in studies of World War II concentration camp victims. Inmates of the camps were not only constantly threatened with death and exposed to the worst kind of psychological and social degradation, but they were also severely debilitated through physical mistreatment. The interactions between psychological and physical suffering make it difficult to know the extent to which each separately contributed to later illness and premature death (see Dimsdale, 1980).

Since we cannot move automatically from stress at the social level to stress at the psychological and physiological levels, and vice versa, what are the principles that can guide our thinking about the relationships that do exist among these levels? We suggest, not surprisingly, that the links among levels are established through cognitive appraisal.

For example, a family may have severe difficulties at the social level, as seen in disrupted patterns of communication and a failure to function properly with respect, for instance, to providing needed support. Yet individual family members can vary in the degree of stress they experience, or indeed may experience no stress.

Our theory holds that psychological stress is determined by the person's appraisal of a specific encounter with the environment; this appraisal is shaped by person factors including commitments, vulnerabilities, beliefs, and resources and by situation factors including the nature of the threat, its imminence, and so on. Let us say that the parents in the troubled family are engaged in a marital conflict. A son might experience psychological stress because he is afraid that if his parents separate, he will no longer receive the emotional and material support he needs. His sister, on the other hand, might not have the same vulnerability. She might believe that even though her parents don't seem to like each other any more, she will still get the support she needs, or perhaps even more when the favored parent is separated from his or her spouse.

A good example of research that covers both the macrosocial and the individual levels (and implicates stress and coping) is provided by Dooley and Catalano (see, for example, Catalano & Dooley, 1983; Dooley & Catalano, 1980), who study the relationship between economic changes and behavior disorders. The macrosocial antecedent variables are economic changes, which affect people's mental health but in ways that depend on other factors in their lives such as whether they have lost a job, their social and material resources, the presence of alternative social roles, and their ways of appraising and coping with what is happening.

Just as the concept of appraisal is useful in linking the social and psychological levels, appraisal is also useful in moving from the psychological to the physiological level. When a situation is appraised as stressful, there is a high probability of somatic disturbance. We do not think that the type and degree of disturbance can be predicted accurately, however, without knowing the type of primary and secondary appraisal, the emotions the person is experiencing, and their intensity. These emotions reflect the person's cognitive appraisal of the event.

Coping too can be examined at all three levels of analysis: bodily defenses that are used to counter noxious agents (physiological forms of coping), as in Selye's General Adaptation Syndrome; psychological processes used by the individual to cope with threatening or challenging encounters; and institutional (social) forms of coping used to protect either the social unit or the individual. Shinn, Mørch, Robinson, and Neuner (1984) examined coping at the social and psychological levels in a study of the stressful encounters reported by social service workers. Three kinds of coping were delineated: "agency coping" (accepting help from the organization), "co-worker coping" (help from peers), and "individual coping." Problem- and emotion-focused coping were examined within each category. A number of morale- and health-related measures were obtained to assess the relationship between coping and outcome.

All forms of coping appear to have contributed to individual well-being. Problem-focused agency and co-worker coping lessened stress by directly affecting the stressful environment. Emotion-focused coping interacted with stressors in affecting health-related outcomes, resulting in a kind of buffering effect, and also directly affected overall morale independently of stressful encounters. Agency and co-worker coping produced slightly greater benefits overall than individual coping. There was some evidence of specificity of effects: individual coping, for example, explained a significant amount of unique variance in psychological symptoms only; agency coping did so for the outcome variables of alienation and job dissatisfaction, and co-worker coping for psychological symptoms and alienation. Sometimes co-worker emotion-focused coping exacerbated the relationship between stressors and somatic symptoms.

These results, though complicated, suggest that it is worthwhile to examine coping at different levels of analysis in that each may have somewhat different effects on outcomes. These findings are also in tune with what we have said earlier (Chapter 8) about the outcomes of coping depending not only on individual effectiveness but also on the presence of a favorable social context.

Traditional Research and Thought

Research and thought on stress, coping, and adaptation as it has traditionally been practiced are concerned primarily with discovering the antecedents or causal variables of an adaptational outcome. Outcomes have ranged from impaired performance, a temporary emotional disturbance that could serve as a precursor of disease, to the increased risk of a disease itself such as ulcer, cardiovascular ailment, cancer, or hypertension. Research seeks the causes of these outcomes in existing environmental or stable person factors, whether the search is guided by theory, prior empirical observations, or hunch.

This style of research works particularly well—and perhaps only—when dealing with a system in which there is a powerful single causal factor, as in John Snow's pump handle with which he was able to turn off a cholera epidemic (see Chapter 1). It is of course easier to be successful in a unicausal system than in one that involves multiple variables as important mediators of the disease outcome, which is the case in stress-related disorders. Despite the multicausal nature of stress and stress-related illness, however, the hope of finding a pump handle continues to power research in stress, coping, and adaptation, especially in epidemiology.

This antecedent-consequent approach to research takes two main directions. The first, which is the more dominant, is motivated by the stimulus definition of stress reviewed in Chapter 1 and focuses on the environment. The assumption here is that some environmental condition (the stimulus) has an impact on the person and social group that produces stress. Clear examples are studies of stressful occupations (see House et al., 1979), such as air traffic control, which result in hypertension and other harmful somatic, subjective, or behavioral adaptational outcomes (e.g., Rose et al., 1978). Life events research (see Dohrenwend & Dohrenwend, 1974) also illustrates this environmentalist focus. Because of their heavy adaptational demands, a preponderance of certain life events such as loss of a loved one, divorce, or change of job are said to be stressors that increase the risk of illness.

The second main direction that research based on the antecedent-consequent model takes is to identify *personality* variables that *mediate* the stressful or damaging effects of environmental factors. A given environmental condition does not affect all individuals in the same way, because of person characteristics such as constitutional predispositions, values and commitments, beliefs, styles of thinking and coping, and specific skills. This style of research attempts to show that personality characteristics (e.g., typologies such as Type A and Type B) have predictive value for adaptational outcomes such as somatic illness or psychological disturbance (e.g., Kobasa, 1979; Weiner et al., 1962).

At a somewhat more complex level, antecedent-consequent research can also be interactive. That is, more than one environmental variable or more than one personality variable may be used, and even more rarely an environmental and a personality variable may be studied as interactive determinants. In the latter case, the personality variables are often seen as mediators of the environmental influence and are said to work by affecting the appraisal of environmental demands or the coping process.

The interaction between personality and environmental variables in producing adaptational outcomes is nicely illustrated by research on suicidal behavior by Braucht (1979). The author first examines several models for studying suicide, including one that focuses on the environment and another that focuses on individual differences. Braucht then presents a study in which the evidence strongly favors an interactional model: In addition to the type of neighborhood (environment), suicide attempts were predicted by the extent to which those who attempted suicide were generally *un*representative of their neighborhoods and experienced *un*representative types of stress (individual differences). The author concludes that real-life behaviors cannot be understood by recourse either to individual difference variables alone or to environmental variables alone.

A similar line of thought is to be found in French's theory and research on person–environment fit (see Caplan, 1983; French et al., 1974; Van Harrison, 1978). A good fit can result when the person's needs and environmental resources are well matched and when the demands of an environment (e.g., a job situation) are matched by equivalent person capabilities. For the French group, stress is a product of a poor person–environment fit, which results in physiological strains and ultimately illness.

In recent years, a number of writers have expressed serious

reservations about the traditional antecedent-consequent model, not about the basic idea that person and environment variables interact in affecting stress and adaptational outcomes—this is a truism—but that this model is used as the major framework for understanding and prediction. We see two important bases for such criticism.

First, the traditional model tends to treat variables as if they are in a linear and unidirectional relationship, as in S-R (stimulus-response) psychology. Even when the conceptual system allows for mediation, as in S-O-R (stimulus-organism-response) psychology, it still presumes that the direction always flows linearly from the environmental stimulus to the response, even when certain properties of the organism modify that response. Little or no attention is paid to the obvious possibility that the person also affects the environment or that environments are often chosen by the person (see Altman, 1976) or are responded to selectively (Nielson & Sarason, 1981).

Second, the traditional model tends to treat the person and the environment as static phenomena, a still photo that captures a moment in time when the person is responding to the environment. If we looked beyond the captured moment, allowing the transaction between the person and the environment to proceed, the response, in turn, may have an impact on the person through feedback and cognitive appraisal, and on the environment, too, as in the case of two people affecting each other during a dispute. In the latter case, we are no longer looking at a still photo, a single act or thought pictured in a discrete time frame, but at a series of stills, joined to form a continuous motion picture that portrays the actual flow of events.

When one shifts from the still photo to the motion picture, one can only *provisionally* designate variables as antecedent or consequent, cause or effect, and so on. In other words, the designation of Variable A as coming first and Variable B as determined by it depends on where one chooses to break the continuity of the process.

Transaction and Process

In contrast to the unidirectional, static, antecedent-consequent model, the *transactional model* views the person and the environment in a dynamic, mutually reciprocal, bidirectional relationship. What is a consequence at Time 1 can become an antecedent at Time 2; and the cause can be either in the person or in the environment. This transactional model forms the metatheoretical foundation on which our cognitive theory of stress rests.

Transactionalism, which is also related to systems theory and dialectics, has a long history that is constantly being rediscovered, as in Bandura's (1978) idea of reciprocal determinism. An extensive philosophical history of this concept can be found in Phillips and Orton (1983).

Another distinguishing feature of transactional thought, the one that gives the term *transaction* a quality missing in the concept of interaction, is that transaction implies a newly created level of abstraction in which the separate person and environment elements are joined together to form a new relational meaning. In interaction, particularly in statistical analyses that fractionate the variances of a cause-and-effect sequence (as in analysis of variance), the interacting variables retain their separate identities. From a transactional perspective, the characteristics of the separate variables are subsumed.

It may be helpful at this point to illustrate the concept with examples from physiology and sociology. The transformation of variables into new, higher-order abstractions is not a new idea and in fact is captured by the analogy of a bodily organ. The separate variables (cells), working together, form a new entity (e.g., a heart) whose function includes but is different from the operation of the individual cells. Sociologically, the distinct characteristics of the separate variables (persons) to one degree or another lose their salience and visibility at a higher level of organization (the group or social system). In other words, the group takes on an identity that is different from the sum of its parts (see, for example, analyses of collective behavior in Smelser, 1963).

Our approach to psychological stress emphasizes cognitive appraisal, which centers on the evaluation of harm, threat, and challenge. An appraisal does not refer to the environment or to the person alone, but to the integration of both in a given transaction. As such, it is a transactional variable. To say that someone is threatened is a judgment limited to a particular encounter in which particular environmental conditions are appraised by a particular person with particular psychological characteristics. Although any given appraisal depends on a unique set of environment and person characteristics, these characteristics are no longer distinct in the new higher-order variable "threat." (See Dewey & Bentley, 1949, for a discussion of these issues.)

In traditional cause-and-effect research, stress is sometimes defined as antecedent environmental conditions, sometimes as intervening states and traits, and sometimes as a response. Most such research makes one or at best a few assessments of situations and persons on the assumption that these sets of variables are stable. Thus, the actual psychological and social processes of importance, namely, how people construe or appraise their ongoing transactions with the environment and how they cope, are never directly examined but only inferred. And so we come to a crucial corollary of the transactional perspective, namely, *process.*

Process is concerned with the unfolding or flow of events. The environment is constantly changing, and so is the person and his or her relationship with it. One's emotional life, for example, is characterized by flux and change. In a stressful encounter, one may feel at first anxious; after a few moments of further interchange, angry; then guilty; then loving and joyful. These feelings express what is happening as the encounter unfolds and as one's own behavior and that of the environment alter the appraised significance of the encounter. Never is an emotional state static. It changes in quality and intensity at rates that can be astonishing.

That emotion shifts as an encounter unfolds is demonstrated in the study of examination stress mentioned earlier (Folkman & Lazarus, in press). We assessed emotions at three stages of the examination. The first was the preparation stage two days before the exam; the second, the waiting period five days after the exam was taken and two days before grades were announced; the third stage was five days after grades were announced. Students were asked at each stage to indicate whether and to what extent they were experiencing each of a number of emotions. The same list of emotions was given at each assessment.

Emotions shifted dramatically across the three occasions. Hopefulness, eagerness, worry, and fear were significantly more intense at the preparation stage than after grades were announced; and emotions such as happiness, relief, disgust, and disappointment were significantly more intense at the outcome than at the preparation stage. The intermediate or waiting stage was characterized by high levels of all the above emotions. We interpreted this to mean that although the exam itself was over, which accounted for the increase in the intensity of outcome emotions such as relief and disappointment, waiting for grades involved stressful anticipation with its concomitant anticipatory emotions such as fear and hope. These shifts in emotions reflect changes in the *meaning* of the person–environment relationship as that relationship shifted throughout the examination process.

Similarly, as we discussed in Chapter 6, the way a person copes changes as an encounter unfolds. For instance, in the above study, students were asked at each stage to indicate on the Ways of Coping checklist how they were coping with respect to the examination. We found that problem-focused forms of coping were at their height during the anticipation stage, presumably in the service of studying for the exam. During the waiting stage, problem-focused forms of coping decreased, and one particular form of emotion-focused coping, distancing, increased. Both changes were dramatic. Distancing included strategies such as "Try to forget the whole thing" and "I'm waiting to see what will happen before doing anything." That strategies for distancing peaked during the second stage makes sense to us; nothing more could be done to change the outcome of the exam, and because grades had not yet been announced, the students did not yet know how they had done. All they could do was wait. Distancing may be a form of emotion-focused coping that is especially suitable for waiting. Other forms of coping such as seeking social support, emphasizing the positive aspects of the event, and wishful thinking also shifted from stage to stage. The important point that is clearly demonstrated by this study is that coping changes as an encounter changes.

Social support can also be viewed as a process that changes with shifts in the person–environment relationship. As we noted in Chapter 8, the kind of social support people sought changed as a function of the stage of the examination. At the preparation stage, the students sought significantly more informational support than emotional support, whereas after the exam they sought significantly more emotional support than informational support.

That emotions, social support, and coping should change as an encounter unfolds is not surprising and, indeed, intuitively makes a great deal of sense. All too often, however, such variables are treated as static, structural, unchanging phenomena. We argue that in order to make progress in understanding stress, coping, and adaptation, the emphasis in theory and research must be given to these phenomena as changing processes. Indeed, the essence of stress, coping, and adaptation is change, since to be effective a person in jeopardy must change something in order to restore a more harmonious relationship with the environment. Life itself consists of continuous adaptations to change or lack of change. Stahl, Grim, Donald, and Neikirk (1975) have expressed this theme in regard to research on hypertension:

> The models used by both disciplines (epidemiology and behavioral science) can be characterized as structural models. In such a model, sociological and psychological variables are directly related to the dis-

ease entity without considering the influence of intervening processes which are directed to some goals and which serve to make the somatic structure a dynamic model. For example, social epidemiologists tend to test the interactive process between the structure (class) and the behavior (hypertension). Using a more psychologically oriented example, the association between hostility (a personality characteristic or structure) and hypertension is postulated without testing directly the conceptual linkage between structure and behavior (p. 32).

Traditional antecedent-consequent research provides no opportunity to observe the ongoing process created by the interplay between causal agents such as a demanding environment and a vulnerable person that over time leads to disease. Again with respect to hypertension, Herd (1977) comments:

We have some knowledge concerning the mechanisms whereby psychological processes may influence cardiovascular function during short periods of time. However, we do not know the mechanisms whereby a susceptibility to transient elevations in blood pressure may convert to sustained arterial hypertension. Finally, we do not know what psychological and physiological characteristics might predispose an individual to develop hypertensive cardiovascular disease when exposed to certain environmental situations over long periods of time.

In the above statement, Herd makes both structural and process-oriented statements. Physiological and psychological predisposing characteristics refer to structure, whereas the mechanisms through which transient elevations in blood pressure become sustained refer to process. It is the latter that most traditional research fails to address satisfactorily.

In Chapter 6 we discussed the idea of process extensively in terms of coping. We pointed out that the coping process has three key features: first, what the person *actually does;* second, a *particular context*, since coping does not occur in a vacuum but is responsive to contextual requirements (cf. Klos & Singer, 1981, and Strack & Coyne, 1983, on how depressive moods are responsive to the behavior of others); and third, how what is done *changes* as the stressful encounter unfolds, or from encounter to encounter when they are united by a common theme (such as bereavement).

Contrast these three features of process with the usual trait approach. (A trait refers to a stable person property that shapes actions and reactions and transcends to some extent the pull of situational pressures.) First, in trait approaches what is *actually* done is not examined, because the person is asked what he or she usually does, which is an abstraction or at best a synthesis of many specific acts, not a description of a particular act or set of acts. Second, there is no specific context, since when the person reports what *usually* happens, particular situations are disregarded. Third, when using a trait approach to measurement, we do not obtain information about change that occurs as an encounter unfolds. In our illustration of bereavement in Chapter 6 we saw that the nature of the difficulty, as appraised by the person, was not the same at the beginning of the period of bereavement as at the end. In order to understand coping, then, we must do *microanalyses* of grieving by giving attention to the daily encounters of living, as well as *macroanalyses* of the total pattern throughout the entire course of bereavement. These types of analyses are done to some extent in clinical studies of grieving but are equally appropriate for the evaluation of any major life event that has significant ramifications for stress, coping, and adaptational outcome.

Before leaving the concept of process, we should comment that our argument is not that structure is irrelevant or unimportant in scientific analysis, but that it has been overemphasized in research on stress, coping, and adaptation at great cost to the understanding of the fundamental phenomena. Structure and process concepts are *both* necessary to understanding.

It is puzzling, therefore, that the dominant methods for studying that which inherently implies change—stress, coping, and adaptational outcomes—focus mainly on structure, when these methods are unable to reveal the ongoing processes on which health/illness, social functioning, and morale all depend. This essentially static outlook seems to set apart much research in the behavioral sciences from research in the physical and biological sciences. The latter have created technology for the study of process that has yet to be fully developed in our own subject matter.

There are signs, however, that research is moving toward a less structural approach. Gortmaker, Eckenrode, and Gore (1982), for example, performed a time series as well as a cross-sectional analysis in a study of stress, health, and health care. They used diaries of daily stress and assessed contacts with health care agencies in the same subjects over time and found that daily rises and falls in stress were associated with parallel rises and falls in seeking health care services and reported symptoms. The research of Epstein (1983a) on emotion and Nygård (1981, 1982) on achievement motivation is also designed to obtain repeated assessments, which are analyzed intraindividually across occasions.

The Design of Transactional, Process-oriented Research

We have made numerous theoretical and metatheoretical statements which, if they are to be translated into research, require a suitable style of research as well as appropriate measurement tools. Although there is undoubtedly more than one research design appropriate to our theory, including use of experimental laboratory research, in our view the most effective at the present stage of our knowledge has two important features: an ipsative–normative design and a naturalistic as opposed to laboratory setting.

The Ipsative–Normative Design

Transaction implies the mutual interplay of person and environment variables. This interplay, in turn, implies process, since the relationship between the person and the environment is constantly changing. In order to capture these changes and the factors that contribute to them, it is necessary to observe the same person again and again. Yet change is not commonly assessed in research (see Shontz, 1976). Dynamic, process-oriented approaches are the exception rather than the rule.

Studying the same person again and again requires comparing the person with himself or herself at different times or under different conditions. This *intraindividual* perspective contrasts with *interindividual* comparisons of that person with other persons under common conditions. When we say that a person copes ineffectively, or is highly vulnerable in some sense, the traditional comparison is interindividual—between that person and others. The person in question falls short of the mark, with respect either to an average or an ideal standard of functioning. This interindividual, or normative, perspective therefore fails to take into account the context in which the observations are made. If, for example, the person must function under severe environmental demands or conditions of deprivation, the use of an interindividual standard of comparison may lead to a distorted evaluation of that person's functioning. By ordinary standards he or she might be judged as having inadequate coping skills or resources or a weak ego, or as lacking resiliency, or the like, when in fact the person is functioning reasonably well in an environment that is posing extraordinary or novel problems. Without information about the social context, we would have only half the story.

The controversy over interindividual versus intraindividual research has a long history, some of which is found in the debates about ideographic and nomothetic research strategies (e.g., Allport, 1962; Holt, 1962). Although the argument is usually cast in either–or terms, an ideal alternative is to observe individuals repeatedly intraindividually *and* do interindividual comparisons. In this regard, Broverman (1962) and Marceil (1977) use the term "ipsative–normative" or "normative–ipsative," ipsative referring to intraindividual observation and comparison, and normative to interindividual comparison. Done properly, ipsative research, which can include observations of many facets of the same person in one context and/or one facet in a variety of contexts, yields intraindividual information which later can be used for interindividual comparisons.

Important issues of stress, coping, and adaptation become accessible to research through the ipsative strategy. Consider the issue of variability and consistency in coping. By repeatedly assessing a person's coping processes in a variety of contexts, it is possible to determine the patterns the person uses and the extent to which those patterns vary across encounters. Being able to describe what is happening in time across encounters also allows processes of interest to be linked firmly to antecedent person and environment variables and to outcome variables such as adaptationally relevant behavior, emotional states, somatic disturbances, health/illness, social functioning, and long-term morale.

Another issue concerns competence. Some people handle most stressful encounters effectively from the point of view of a particular value system; others handle most such encounters ineffectively. Most of us have areas of competence, incompetence, or limited competence which are best revealed by intraindividual profiles of stressful encounters. These profiles can be used to determine the extent to which person and situation factors affect competence through their impact on cognitive appraisal and coping, and suggest foci for treatment, intervention, and education. We have something to say about this in Chapter 11.

A requirement common to these two instances where ipsative research is appropriate or even necessary is that data collection be systematic so that intraindividual data can be compared interindividually or normatively. For example, although we are interested in intraindividual variability and stability in coping, the same metric should be applied across individuals so that we can examine patterns of vulnerability normatively. In order to understand intraindividual variability we might want to know how the person varies around his or her own mean; to look at interindividual differences in variability, we want to know how each person's pattern of variability differs from the group mean. These two approaches yield very different information, yet each is important (see Epstein, 1979, 1980, in press; and the cautionary note by Day, Marshall, Hamilton, & Christy, 1983).

Unfortunately, repeated intraindividual observations are expensive and time-consuming, especially if one wishes to follow recommendations by Monson, Hesley, and Chernick (1982) on using multiple acts to indicate traits. As a consequence, sample sizes for ipsative–normative research tend to be smaller than in designs that call for one-time-only assessments. Research that depends on very large sample sizes to achieve representativeness or statistical power obviously does not lend itself to ipsative research. These sampling goals can, however, sometimes be modified, at least temporarily, in order to gather data that ultimately might provide more powerful explanations of stress and coping phenonema. One-time-only designs may have advantages for addressing some questions, but for the study of transaction and process, and how adaptational outcomes evolve in the short and long run, ipsative–normative research is essential.

Naturalistic Versus Laboratory Research

Laboratory research provides the opportunity to isolate specific variables and test hypotheses about causes and effects. Certainly, to be able to control what one measures is appealing. If what one is measuring bears little resemblance to the phenomena of interest, however, then no amount of precision and control will advance understanding.

The laboratory has certain specific limitations with respect to research in stress, coping, and adaptation. First, the stressors that are commonly used in experimental laboratory studies are at best weak imitations of the stressors people face in their day-to-day lives. Practical and ethical considerations make it difficult if not impossible to expose human subjects to stresses in the laboratory that are as enduring, severe, complex, or meaningful as those in real life. Even minor real-life stressors, or hassles, have more personal meaning than a shock, a loud noise, or a cold pressor. Furthermore, no matter how stressful the aversive laboratory stimulus, the subject knows that he or she can terminate it at any time. The finite nature of the stimulus and/or its ultimate controllability by the subject means that the laboratory stressor will always lack two critical characteristics of many real-life stressors—open-endedness and/or controllability (see also Wortman, Abbey, Holland, Silver, & Janoff-Bulman, 1980).

Second, many adaptational outcomes take time to emerge— days, weeks, months, even years. The few seconds or minutes that comprise most experimental periods are clearly insufficient for observing appraisal and coping processes that eventuate in short-term, let alone long-term outcomes.

Third, laboratory experiments cannot provide much information about variation in sources of stress and patterns of coping with age, or with sociodemographic characteristics such as community, occupation, or socioeconomic status. Increasingly, we are seeing research that could provide baseline data on the incidence of various stress-relevant patterns among diverse occupational groups such as police and air traffic controllers, even though the measurement of stress and stress-related processes in these studies is still inadequate. It will take observational studies in important natural settings with various demographic groups to provide a fuller understanding of social sources of stress and patterns of living.

Finally, and perhaps most important, the belief in laboratory experimentation is based on what is sometimes an illusion that these studies provide precise control over the key variables of human behavior. The stimulus dimensions sampled by the experimenter commonly fail to reflect what is going on psychologically and socially in the experimental context. Moreover, to obtain precision in measurement, the experimenter must severely constrain what the laboratory subject is allowed to do, thus making the response unrepresentative of what it would be in the natural context.

Overview of Our Approach

Let us now pull together what we have been saying about designs for research on stress, coping, and adaptation by visually portraying first the traditional positivist research style described in Chapter 9, then the neobehaviorist version, and finally the ipsative–normative, process-oriented research style.

Figure 10.1 illustrates the traditional research style of studying one or several antecedent variables as possible causes of some long-range adaptational consequence such as illness or impaired social functioning. The research can be experimental or correlational. Its most sophisticated form involves the possibility of interaction between antecedent person and environment variables. The antece-

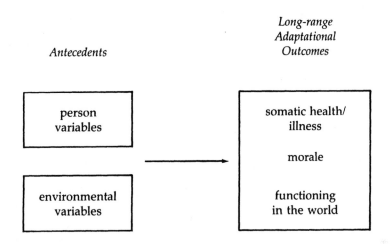

Figure 10.1. Traditional cause-and-effect research—positivism.

dent variable is assessed once, as is the adaptational consequence, and a large *N* is usually preferred.

The reader should note that in this traditional design nothing is directly learned about the processes by which the antecedent variables affect the outcome variables. If these processes are of interest, they are presumed, usually by reference to the concept defining the person or the environment variable. The research may speculate, for example, that the person variable is a particular style of coping, and the environment variable is a demanding or stressful life event such as a job change. If this combination of person and environment variables affects performance on the new job, the coping style (person variable) is taken for the process (cf. Kobasa, 1979). As we noted in Chapter 5, however, coping processes are generally not well predicted by coping style as these styles have been traditionally formulated (see Cohen & Lazarus, 1979).

As neobehaviorist (S-O-R) doctrines became influential, researchers were more willing to think in terms of processes such as appraisal and coping as mediating between antecedent variables and outcomes. These processes were now thought to determine how an environmental demand would be reacted to and how it might affect long-term adaptational outcomes. The neobehaviorist model of research is illustrated in Figure 10.2, which adds mediating variables and short-term consequences (e.g., emotional states) to the antecedent and long-range adaptational outcome variables. We have chosen to include in this figure the main mediating variables of theoretical interest to us; others might substitute or add different mediators.

Notice two features about Figure 10.2. First, the mediators, although labeled as process, are not illustrated as such, since a process implies a specific context and change over time or circumstances. The figure shows how recent writings typically treat mediation, that is, as "moderator variables." Strictly speaking, moderators are used to divide a heterogeneous population into homogeneous subgroups that affect the relationship between a predictor and a criterion. The purpose is to increase the correlation (see Zedeck, 1971). On the other hand, Johnson and Sarason (1979a, b) appear to treat a moderator as any variable that interacts with an environmental condition (e.g., life events) so as to improve its capacity to predict any adaptational outcome. These authors list social support, perceived control over the situation, stimulus seeking, and level of arousability as moderators of the stress-outcome relationship.

Although moderator variables are regarded as mediating processes by Johnson and Sarason, statistically they are treated as merely another antecedent variable that interacts with other antecedent variables such as stressful life events. The only reason such moderator variables belong with the mediating variables in Figure 10.2 is that they are regarded theoretically as mediators, not because they are actually shown to operate as theory requires. Thus, aside from any evidence of their capacity to predict outcomes as interacting variables, moderators do not meet our requirements for mediators or for the study of processes. In effect, the research style in Figure 10.2 fits the traditional cause-and-effect model of the past and not the transactional, process-oriented outlook.

The second feature to notice about Figure 10.2 is the implicit acknowledgment of a process as involving change over time, as suggested by Box 3, which differentiates immediate consequences from long-range adaptational outcomes. By making this distinction, we begin a true process analysis and a search for rules with which to translate a short-term adaptational response, such as an emotion, a coping action, or a somatic disturbance, into an illness or an impaired function. As we noted earlier, for example, rises in blood pressure under stress are a perfectly normal and healthy adapta-

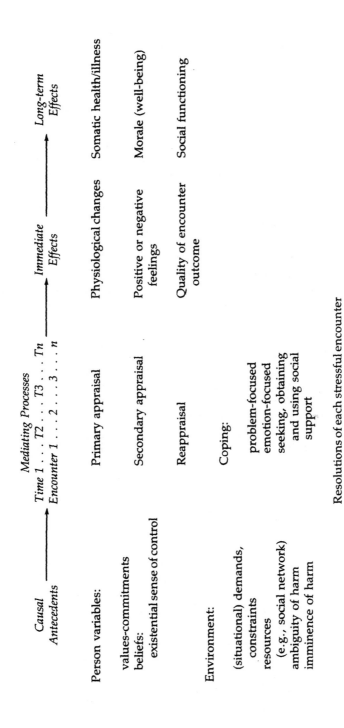

Figure 10.2.   A theoretical schematization of stress, coping, and adaptation.

tional response; what we do not know is how this response is transformed into the disorder known as hypertension.

We move clearly into transactional, process-oriented research in Figure 10.3, which differs from Figure 10.2 only in that it pictures the one box from Figure 10.2 that deals with mediating processes and provides for ipsative comparisons on each variable. For example, coping is assessed in the early and later stages of an encounter or in a different encounter (although with the same theme, say, bereavement). Thus, we are looking at the same persons at different times or under different conditions.

The important addition to Figure 10.3 is that the mediating processes are studied repeatedly and more or less directly (e.g., through self-reports about appraisals and coping, or through behaviors that imply the use of particular forms of coping). That is, opportunities are built into the research to observe or infer what the person is thinking and doing at various points during an encounter or in different encounters. This figure, then, highlights what we mean by ipsative–normative research, through which patterns for given individuals or groups of individuals can be compared. In short, we can look at phenomena within persons as well as across persons within the same research design.

One final step is required in order to integrate what we have said about metatheory and research styles. Figures 10.1, 10.2, and 10.3 all deal with the psychological level of analysis, which is of course our primary concern. Yet we have argued that research and theory in stress, coping, and adaptation is, perforce, interdisciplinary and multileveled, including, in addition to psychological interpretation, the social and physiological. In order to arrange for the crossing of levels according to the principles of transactional, process-centered research, we must twice replicate the basic format of Figure 10.3, once for each level of analysis, and fill in the appropriate variables. This is done in Figure 10.4.

The Measurement of Key Concepts

There are five types of major variables on which our theory and research are predicated: stress, appraisal, coping, person and environment antecedents of stress and coping, and short- and long-term adaptational outcomes. Our contributions to measurement thus far center on the first three—stress, appraisal, and coping.

Mediating Processes

Time 1	Time 2	Time 3	. . . Time N
Encounter 1	Encounter 2	Encounter 3	. . . Encounter N

Appraisal-Reappraisal

Coping:
    problem-focused
    emotion-focused

Social support:
    emotional
    tangible
    informational

Figure 10.3.   A transactional model: ipsative–normative arrangement

Stress

Over the years there has been continued criticism of the stress concept and its utility, based mainly on the fact that it is defined confus-
ingly as a stimulus or response at any of three levels of analysis, or
ambiguously as any or all of these. Criticism is, indeed, warranted
except when sharply focused definitions of stressor or stress response
are used. As we have noted, Lazarus (1966) tried to settle the problem
by regarding stress as a very general concept like emotion, motivation, or cognition, but organized around the meanings of transactions
that tax or exceed the person's resources or the resources of a social
system. From that general standpoint, it is perfectly appropriate to
measure stress as either input, response, or strained relationship, as
long as the one being measured is made explicit.

A striking feature of stress research is the overwhelming concern with major environmental changes, or *life events* as these have
been called. Many life events measures have been developed. Often
the events are weighted according to the amount of adjustment they
require, their desirability, controllability, or some other subjective
dimension. These scales have become the most popular way to measure the effects of stress on somatic and mental health. Beginning

	Causal Antecedents	Mediating Processes	Immediate Effects	Long-term Effects
SOCIAL	SES Cultural templates Institutional systems Group structures (e.g., role patterns) Social networks	Social supports as proffered Available social/institutional means of ameliorating problems	Social disturbances Government responses Sociopolitical pressures Group alienation	Social failure Revolution Social change Structural changes
PSYCHOLOGICAL	Person variables: values-commitments beliefs-assumptions, e.g., personal control cognitive-coping styles Environmental (Situational) variables: situational demands imminence timing ambiguity social and material resources	Vulnerabilities Appraisal–Reappraisal Coping: problem-focused emotion-focused cultivating, seeking & using social support Perceived social support: emotional tangible informational	Positive or negative feelings Quality of outcome of stressful encounters	Morale Functioning in the world
PHYSIOLOGICAL	Genetic or constitutional factors Physiological conditioning—individual response stereotypy (e.g., Lacey) Illness risk factors—e.g., smoking	Immune resources Species vulnerability Temporary vulnerability Acquired defects	Somatic changes (precursors of illness) Acute illness	Chronic illness Impaired physiological functioning Recovery from illness Longevity

Figure 10.4. Three levels of analysis.

with the pioneering work of Holmes and Rahe (1967; see also Dohr-enwend & Dohrenwend, 1974), a complex and extensive research literature evolved that has been reviewed, analyzed, and criticized in many publications (for methodological reviews see Rabkin & Stru-ening, 1976; and Tausig, 1982). Many other reviews—too many to list here—cover life events research on particular health outcomes, such as schizophrenia, depression, cancer, death of the elderly, and cardiovascular disease; or particular life events such as job loss, di-vorce or marital disruption, and bereavement. New research and discussion of life events continues unabated, one of the best over-views being that of Thoits (1983).

There are major defects in the assumptions underlying the life events approach that make it inadequate as the sole metric of stress. The first assumption is that the life events approach to stress mea-surement assumes that change alone is stressful. Change alone does not necessarily generate stress, however, and much stress occurs even in the absence of change. As to the first point, we already know from research on aging (e.g., Neugarten, 1970, 1977; Rosow, 1963) that life events such as menopause, the empty nest, and retire-ment do not necessarily pose serious problems for most people when they occur on schedule and so are expected; and the effects of role losses later in life depend on how they are interpreted and coped with. As to the second point, the absence of change (for example, not getting a promotion at work) and chronic boredom or loneliness can be as stressful as change-induced losses. In sum, it is not change itself, or its absence, that is necessarily stressful, but rather the personal significance of change or no-change, which in turn depends on the person's history, stage of life, and overall pres-ent circumstances (see also Lennon, 1982; Stewart, 1982; Stewart et al., 1982).

A second assumption is that life events must be major, that is, have profound adaptational consequences or produce profound losses, in order to create stress of sufficient magnitude to impair health. Although this thinking seems reasonable (see, for example, Hinkle, 1974), it is incomplete in important ways. Simply knowing that life events have occurred does not permit us to grasp their individual meanings—what they do to the appraised person–envi-ronment relationship—and how they are responded to in the pres-ent on a day-to-day basis. What is major or minor is, in effect, often an individual matter. In this sense, life events measures are psycho-logically distal. What is missing are the more proximal, diverse psy-chological and behavioral activities generated by these events in people who vary in beliefs, commitments, and other personal agendas on which the significance of events is predicated (see DeLongis et al., 1982).

A third assumption is that psychological stress is a major factor in illness; this is the classic psychosomatic hypothesis. Most people in the field accept this assumption as more or less valid, although the quality of the evidence on which it rests can be debated. However, since illness is produced by a large number of factors that do not fall under the rubric of psychological stress, including genetic-constitutional and environmental conditions, it is quite possible that except under extreme conditions of extended psychological harassment the maximum contribution of psychological stress to illness is modest.

The practical problem that flows from the limits and defects in these assumptions is that the relationship between life events indexes and health outcomes is small and accounts for only a small proportion of the variance in health outcomes. The average relationship between scores on life events measures and health outcomes appears to be around .12 (Rabkin & Struening, 1976; Tausig, 1982) and rarely exceeds .30. Thus, life events have little practical significance in the prediction of health outcomes, even though such prediction is the prime reason for using life events indexes.

Despite this practical limitation, the life events approach is popular for three reasons. First, it offers a simple, quantitative, self-report scale of stress defined by environmental changes, the various weightings for which are supported by considerable consensus across group aggregates. Second, a methodologically supportable alternative has not been available until recently. Third, hope continues that the defects of the approach, including limited sampling of stressful events (cf. Goldberg & Comstock, 1980) and absence of concern for individual differences in meaning and resources for coping with the events, could somehow be overcome by modifying the original assessment procedures. To this end, researchers have developed competing measures (e.g., Horowitz, Wilner, & Alvarez, 1979; Pancheri, De Martino, Spiomb, Biondi, & Mosticoni, 1979; Sarason, Johnson, & Siegel, 1978; and a children's version by Coddington, 1972), made changes in procedures of item weighting (Dohrenwend & Dohrenwend, 1974, 1978; Ross & Mirowsky, 1979), or noted that weighting did not matter (Lei & Skinner, 1980; Skinner & Lei, 1980), and have taken into account event desirability (Hough, Fairbank, & Garcia, 1976; Mueller, Edwards, & Yarvis, 1977; Redfield & Stone, 1979; Ross & Mirowsky, 1979; Vinokur & Selzer, 1975; Zilberg,

Weiss, & Horowitz, 1982); in addition, Weiss, Wilner, and Horowitz (in press) have shifted the focus to the *response* to major life events; and finally, moderator variables that might affect the stress–health/illness relationship have been considered (Johnson & Sarason, 1979a, b).

It is not yet clear whether these and other modifications can make the major life events approach a strong enough predictor of health/illness to justify its continued use and popularization as the sole approach to stress measurement. To the extent that these modifications improve the metric, they move the approach from a simplistic, though elegant, measure of stress with an atheoretical input–output rationale to one that is increasingly complex and qualified by mediators. Nevertheless, in our view there remains doubt that this approach, by itself, can ever accomplish what it set out to do. The reasons for these doubts lie in the uncertain and perhaps faulty assumptions we discussed above.

In contrast to the measurement of life events, our research group on the Berkeley Stress and Coping Project developed an approach to stress measurement based on the ordinary daily "hassles" of living (DeLongis et al., 1982; Kanner et al., 1981; Lazarus & DeLongis, 1983). Other researchers too have sensed the value of looking at these types of occurrences. McLean (1976), for example, suggests that these familiar daily stresses are often taken for granted because they seem relatively unimportant compared with major life events, and Pancheri et al. (1979) state that "microevents frequently repeated over long time spans and subconsciously experienced by the person have greater pathogenic potential than episodic dramatic events for which objective control and coping strategies may be more easily developed" (pp. 193–194). We are aware of several other approaches to the measurement of minor events, an early one designed by Cason (1930) to measure what he called "common annoyances," and, more recently, one by Lewinsohn and Talkington (1979) to get at aversive or unpleasant events and another by MacPhillamy and Lewinsohn (1982) to assess positive events. These have not, however, been widely used to study the impact of psychological stress on general health outcomes; the Lewinsohn and Talkington scale has been used to examine the relationship between unpleasant events and depression.

Our research findings have shown, in a regression-based comparison of life events and daily hassles, that hassles are far superior to life events in predicting psychological and somatic symptoms. Hassles accounted for almost all the outcome variance attributable to life events, whereas life events had little or no impact on health outcomes independent of daily hassles (DeLongis et al., 1982; Kanner et al., 1981). This work needs replication.

We also assumed that life events and daily hassles were related because life events—for example, death of a loved one, divorce, job loss—are apt to disrupt social relationships and the habits and patterns of daily living, thereby causing hassles. In checking this assumption, we found a modest relationship (about .20) between hassles and life events, which means that most daily hassles arise independently of life events, from the routine tasks of living. Life events are, therefore, probably one cause of daily hassles, although a relatively minor one compared with disruptions in the daily routine. In the complete measurement of stress in living, it is best to view hassles and life events as supplementing each other. If one had to make a choice, it would seem that the measurement of daily hassles might be sufficient for a repeated metric of stress in living.

A fundamental theoretical issue remains concerning how daily hassles might result in damaged morale, impaired social and work functioning, psychological symptoms, and somatic illness (see Lazarus, in press a). Borrowing from the almost atheoretical life events approach, one alternative is that the process is simply additive, with all the hassles a person experiences summing to a total amount of stress in a given period. This emphasizes mere frequency or intensity of hassles, or some combination of both. Indeed, our findings thus far are consistent with such an interpretation; however, our preferred theoretical alternative has not yet been tested in research. This alternative, predictable from all that we have said throughout this book, centers on the appraised meaning and salience of hassles and the quality of the coping processes inherent in their management. We believe that some hassles are "more equal" than other hassles in their potential to affect adaptational outcomes.

To get at this theme, we must first ask what it means for a person to endorse a hassle. We must not fool ourselves into thinking that an endorsement provides a simple metric of the annoying or troubling occurrences experienced the previous day or during the past week. On the contrary, at least to some extent this endorsement reflects how a person has appraised the encounter. An endorsement may indeed refer to an actual experience, such as being caught in a traffic jam, but its being singled out as a hassle also reflects the personalized meaning that makes it salient, noticeable, and memorable. Some people react to traffic jams philosophically, as expectable and only minimally distressing, whereas others are aroused to deep frustration or fury. One person may be driving to an office where the employer is understanding and considerate or the work is unpressured, whereas another may anticipate criticism or the thwarting of a time-pressured, important work task; still another person may have contributed to the problem by failing to leave any extra time; another may regard the experience as a test of the ability to weave in and out of traffic to gain a small advantage; and yet another may take what is happening as a sign that it is time to move to a less congested community. All these variations in response can occur to a seemingly trivial and not uncommon day's encounter.

The findings from our research strongly suggest that baseline conditions of the person's life affect which of many transactions will be viewed and endorsed as hassles or as *uplifts*, the latter referring to positive or satisfying experiences which we conceived as the counterpart to hassles (DeLongis et al., 1982; Kanner et al., 1981; Lazarus & DeLongis, 1983). For example, in what seems like a paradox, chronically ill people more readily endorse as uplifts getting a good night's sleep or feeling energetic. By the same token, we would expect that people would be more likely to endorse inclement weather as a hassle when they are on vacation than when they are at work. For our purposes, this means simply that in the context of negative life conditions and expectations, positive experiences take on more salience than they do in the context of positive conditions and expectations; similarly, negative experiences become more negative when they occur under positive conditions and expectations (cf. Helson's 1959, adaptation level theory). Thus, hassles are not merely a reflection of what has actually happened but depend on the baseline conditions of life and how experiences are appraised.

The second aspect of how hassles affect health outcomes has to do with the role of coping effectiveness in generating hassles. We suspect that many hassles—perhaps the most important and often recurring in human relationships—reflect not only the events and transactions of living, but also to some extent coping ineptitudes. In effect, whereas daily hassles would be normally considered to fuel the coping process, they are also an outcome of coping. The person who finds it difficult to receive or give criticism is likely to have many more authority-centered hassles at work than is the person who lacks such vulnerability. An untested but promising concept is that hassles that are generated by coping ineptitudes and vulnera-

bilities are far more important in impairing social and work functioning, morale, and health than the ordinary hassles that stem from
adventitious circumstances in the environment. In stress measurement, one can never expect to get away from these person-based
considerations which form the prime basis of individual differences
in stress, coping, and adaptation.

Another possibility about the relationship between hassles and
morale, functioning, and health reverses the direction of causality.
Poor adaptational outcomes such as illness, low morale, and poor
social functioning probably influence the type, frequency, and intensity of daily hassles. For instance, when people feel pessimistic, they
may interpret ordinary irritations as more salient or more negative
than when they feel optimistic.

If hassles are affected by adaptational outcomes, hassles and
uplifts patterns could also serve as diagnostic clues about a person's
well-being. For example, high levels of hassles could indicate not
only that a lot of irritating things are happening in a person's life,
but also that he or she is generally functioning poorly. Some hassles
are also indicative of particular areas of vulnerability (see Chapter 2),
because of strong commitments or inept coping. Most likely the
pattern is recursive, with both directions of causality operating se-
quentially, or perhaps even simultaneously. The same point, incidentally, has been made about the endorsement of life events, especially to the degree that they are subject to interpretation through
cognitive appraisal processes.

This cause-and-effect issue applies to all approaches to the
measurement of stress, whether stress is measured as input, a reaction, or a relationship with the environment. The problem of the
direction of causality, however, does not relieve us of the problem
of seeking ways to measure psychological stress. It only compli-
cates our understanding of stress. This understanding depends on
the development of good measurement techniques that inhere in a
systematic conceptualization.

Cognitive Appraisal

In Chapter 2 we discussed the problem of circularity inherent in the
concept of appraisal. There we noted that the way out of this problem was to make independent measurements of the appraisal process and to seek and measure antecedent variables that predict this
process, such as those person variables identified in Chapter 3 and
environmental variables in Chapter 4. The traditional solution is also

to look for consequent variables, such as coping or short- and long-term adaptational outcomes, which might be predicted from the appraisal process. In this way we can develop rules to describe how appraisal is influenced and in turn influences short- and long-term outcomes, thus eliminating the tautology.

Even when investigators refer to cognitive appraisal explicitly, it is often inferred from relationships between observable antecedent or consequent variables. It is possible, however, to make its measurement more direct. In our research we have been attempting to operationalize the two basic forms of appraisal: primary appraisal (what is at stake for the person) and secondary appraisal (the person's evaluation of coping options).

The degree of stress a person experiences depends on how much of a stake he or she has in the outcome of an encounter. If the encounter seems to have no relevance for the person's well-being, then the primary appraisal will be that it poses no threats, has done no harm, or offers no significant prospects for gain. On the other hand, if the person has something at stake in the outcome, the primary appraisal will be that the encounter does pose a potential threat, harm, or challenge, depending on coping resources and options (secondary appraisal). Therefore, the appropriate entry point for measuring the person's primary appraisal is an assessment of what it is that he or she judges to be at stake in the transaction, and the magnitude of its potential costs and/or benefits.

What is at stake for the individual in a specific encounter is a reflection of his or her commitments. It is not enough to assess degree of commitment in the trait or dispositional sense, however; we must deal with an appraisal in a particular context by asking the person to tell us in some way what is at stake and how much it matters. Many, if not all, stressful encounters probably involve multiple stakes. The outcome of a student examination, for example, may be relevant to overall grade point average and the prospects for being accepted into graduate school, but it may also have relevance to self-esteem, the opinion of faculty, peers, and family, and decisions about academic life.

Our preliminary efforts to assess stakes have involved asking the subject to describe a particular stressful encounter and then to evaluate the extent to which each of a number of stakes is involved in that encounter. The subject tells us, for example, to what extent there could have been harm to a loved one's health, safety, or physical or emotional well-being; to what extent his or her own health, safety, or physical well-being are at stake; to what extent the encounter threatened an important job goal, endangered an important relationship, or damaged the person's self-respect or financial security.

Our initial attempts to measure *secondary appraisal* were reported in an article describing our approach to the measurement of coping (Folkman & Lazarus, 1980). A fundamental feature of secondary appraisal—and the one easiest to assess—is the extent to which the person senses that something can or cannot be done to alter the troubled person–environment relationship. In a later version of the questionnaire, the subject rated the extent to which each of the following statements applied to the specific stressful encounter:

1. You could change or do something about it.
2. You had to accept it.
3. You needed to know more before you could act.
4. You had to hold yourself back from doing what you wanted to do.

With this method, the subject can rate the situation as both changeable and not changeable, which makes sense if one remembers that certain facets of the situation may have been changeable and others not, or that the possibilities for altering the outcome shifted as the encounter unfolded. More precise assessments of secondary appraisals of control need to be developed, including what aspect of the environment and/or self the person is referring to and how the appraisals of control change from one stage of the transaction to another.

These approaches to appraisal do not exhaust the possibilities inherent in its measurement, but they do suggest how it is possible to control primary and secondary appraisal processes directly through self-report procedures and get a partial picture of the state of mind underlying the person's choice of coping. Our findings, across several major studies, show that primary and secondary appraisal variables do indeed help explain coping and emotional response.

Other investigators too have struggled with the measurement of appraisal-like processes. The most similar efforts seem to be the assessments of self-efficacy in Bandura's research about phobic states (see Bandura, 1981, Bandura & Adams, 1977, and Bandura et al., for review). We emphasize that appraisal is a process that occurs in a particular context and, therefore, trait or generalized dispositional concepts such as locus of control, a sense of coherence (Antonovsky, 1979), and generalized beliefs about mastery or self-esteem do not apply. With the exception of the studies cited earlier in the chapters on appraisal, and a recent report by Folkman and Lazarus (in press), there have been few systematic examinations in stress and coping research of the complex thoughts and evaluations people make when they are confronted with a threatening encounter.

Coping

We are among a growing number of researchers who have attempted to assess coping systematically. Our approach, however, sets us apart. We have already explained the differences between our concepts and the psychoanalytic ego psychology approaches, and between process approaches and trait or style approaches (see Chapter 5). We should remind the reader, however, that a process-oriented measurement of coping must (1) refer to specific thoughts, feelings, and acts rather than to what a person reports he or she might or would do; (2) be examined in a *specific* context; and (3) be studied in slices of time so that changes can be observed in what is thought, felt, and done as the requirements and appraisals of the encounter change.

How then can we assess coping? It does not seem fruitful to ask "How did you cope?", because the meaning of the question is apt to be unclear and invite a multitude of interpretations. Consider what would happen if patients were asked "How did you cope with your cancer?" In all likelihood they would respond, but it would not be clear which of the many sources of cancer-induced stress they were referring to. They might have in mind any of the following: the ambiguity about recovery and survival; pain; side effects of surgery or treatment; problems created by the illness in relationships with friends and family; threats to career or family obligations and hopes for the future; loss of dignity; sudden changes in the sense of personal control; and increased awareness of mortality.

In the course of our own deliberations we have become increasingly convinced that we must move away from global assessments toward specifics so that we can learn what it is that is being coped with. We must identify the multiple demands in a stressful transaction and assess coping with respect to those demands and how they shift over time. To do so also means moving further away from the assessment of general styles or traits of coping which extend over time and across situations and which are probably more predictive of long-range outcomes. The challenge for the coping theorist and researcher is to integrate these two approaches—the microanalysis of coping processes and the macroanalysis of styles of coping—in a way that leads to the most satisfactory understanding of short- and long-term outcomes.[1]

It is also questionable whether most people always know what they are doing to cope. Yet restricting measurement to observations of the person's behavior, while useful, requires deep interpretive inference and misses that important aspect we have called cognitive coping. In addition, only rarely do we have an opportunity to observe people coping with real-life encounters, as was done in the Bethesda studies of how parents coped with the imminent death of a child from leukemia (Friedman, Chodoff, Mason, & Hamburg, 1963; Friedman, Mason, & Hamburg, 1963a, b; Wolff et al., 1964).

What can be done to assess coping is to have people reconstruct recent stressful encounters and describe what they thought, felt, and did (see Chapter 6). This is the basic method of assessment we have been trying in our research. We present a "Ways of Coping" checklist that can either be self-administered or, preferably, administered by an interviewer. The most recent version of the Ways of Coping appears on pp. 328–333. The items were suggested by a number of studies (e.g., Sidle, Moos, Adams, & Cady, 1969; Weisman & Worden, 1976–1977), as well as by subjects in our research and members of our research group. In addition to the broad functions of emotion- and problem-focused coping, the items on the checklist involve four basic modes of coping: direct action, inhibition of action, information search, and a complex category referred to as intrapsychic or cognitive coping. Factor analyses of the Ways of Coping (e.g., Folkman & Lazarus, in press) differentiate seemingly problem-focused factors, made up of cognitive and behavioral problem-solving strategies such as trying to come up with several solu-

---

[1]Most coping research up to the present has emphasized global traits or styles using measures such as the Defense Mechanism Inventory of Gleser and Ihilevich (1969), the Coping Operations Preference Inventory (Schutz, 1967), and items from the California Psychological Inventory to measure coping and defense (Joffe & Naditch, 1977). Vickers and Hervig (1981) compared the above three approaches and found them to have little convergence and poor discriminant validity in identifying three styles of coping, namely, denial, isolation, and projection. To these one might add the ubiquitous measures of repression-sensitization or repression-isolation, for which there are three major projective measurement approaches (Gardner et al., 1959; Goldstein, 1959; Levine & Spivack, 1964), which also fail to correlate sufficiently to be regarded as assessing the same concept (Lazarus, Averill, & Opton, 1974). Byrne's (1964) inventory is also clearly trait-centered. Finally, still another inventory approach is the rationally derived Attributes of Psychosocial Competence Scale by Tyler and Pargamet (unpublished). Although the above do not exhaust trait- or style-centered approaches to the measurement of coping, they do reflect the major efforts along these lines (see also Moos, 1974).

tions to the problem, gathering information, and making a plan of action and following it; and a number of emotion-focused factors that include seeking emotional social support, distancing, avoiding, emphasizing the positive aspects of the situation, and self-blame. With further research it will become clearer whether or not there is a relatively stable, invariant set of factors that describe the structure of coping as it is measured by this approach.

We must also be wary about a problem that emerges when we move from our conceptualization of coping to concrete measurement. In Chapter 6 we spoke of the problem-focused and emotion-focused functions of coping rather than types of coping. If we interview a subject and ask what he or she thought or did to cope, we often find it very difficult in practice to determine whether a strategy is problem-focused or emotion-focused. Any thought or act can have multiple coping functions, which defeats a literal attempt to say whether what is being accomplished is the regulation of emotion or the mastery of the troubled relationship through problem solving. We sometimes regulate feeling by solving problems and solve problems by regulating feelings. For example, if a student takes a Valium to control distress that interferes with performance in an exam, that student is problem solving by attempting to manage feeling; if, on the other hand, a student carefully prepared by studying so that he or she could feel a sense of mastery over the danger, the distress of doing badly is being managed by problem-focused coping (see Chapter 6).

Therefore, we are reluctant to rigidly label the factors that emerge from our correlational analysis of coping items as either of the emotion-focused or problem-focused variety, although some of these factors seem to fit better in one or the other category. Making a plan of action, for example, appears to fit our definition of problem-focused coping, and trying to put things in a good light seems to be an instance of emotion-focused coping. From our theoretical perspective, however, it seems better to use these categories of functions as general guides for thought than as pigeonholes into which any particular thought or action must be inevitably placed. The way these thoughts or actions function in any instance can only be known by a careful examination of the context in which they occur, and perhaps through an in-depth examination of their place in the person's overall coping strategy.

At about the time our process measure of coping appeared (Folkman & Lazarus, 1980), a number of other investigators became interested in using the same or similar approaches. Coping processes since then have been studied in diverse contexts and include people coping with loss, threat, and challenge (McCrae, 1982, in press), marriage, parenting, finances, and work (Ilfeld, 1980), juvenile diabetes, work-related stress (Dewe, Guest, & Williams, 1978), stressful life events (Billings & Moos, 1982), and stresses in child care agencies (Shinn, Mørch, Robinson, & Neuner, 1984).

Stone and Neale (1984) have a novel approach, similar conceptually to our own but based on an open-ended procedure. They present their subjects with eight coping categories. After the subjects have become familiar with the categories and their meanings, they are asked whether they did or thought anything that fit these categories with respect to the daily problems that they reported. Thus, emphasis is placed not on particular thoughts and acts which are later grouped empirically, but on more abstract categories defined a priori, such as catharsis, acceptance, seeking social support, relaxation, and religion.

In another variant developed by Wong and Reker (1982), subjects are presented with a list of problems having to do, for example, with family, health, finances, living conditions, and social relationships. The subjects indicate which problems are pertinent and then check on a list of coping strategies those that were used for each problem. Since the problems are apt to be broad and more like a class of encounters than specific stressful events, this approach seems to us to rest midway between an assessment of specific coping acts and thoughts directed at the demands of a specific stressful encounter and an assessment of coping traits or styles.

It is too early to determine whether the approaches developed by Stone and Neale, and Wong and Reker, will be more effective in providing understanding and prediction than the more microanalytic procedure we have developed. The important point is that diverse approaches to the measurement of the coping process are being developed and applied, which increases the likelihood of our finding out how coping is related to short- and long-term adaptational outcomes.

We are well aware of the methodological problems inherent in the style of assessment that we advocate, including inadequate memory, retrospective falsification—which is itself a process of coping—and difficulties of precisely identifying the coping thought or act that is connected with different phases of the encounter. Aside from method variance, however, which we address below, none of these problems is totally refractory to systematic study, and all are shared by just about every other assessment alternative.

The Problem of Method Variance

One cannot obtain observations on stress, coping, and adaptation without having to face the ubiquitous and vexing problem of method variance. Strictly speaking, method variance refers to the dilemma that how one measures a phenomenon affects the content of the observed variance and the findings of research. One consequence is that, as often as not, the findings, and the inferences drawn from them about relationships and processes, do not extend to other methods of measuring the same concepts or relationships (e.g., Nicholls, Licht, & Pearl, 1982, as applied to personality research). This commonly produces a tight system of deduction and induction that works only as long as one uses that one method. Thus, self-report measures may not correlate with projective measures, or with the variables that projective measures are correlated with; experimental models fail to accord with correlational ones (cf. Cronbach, 1957), or they yield different conclusions. Interindividual analyses of a phenomenon produce a different set of relationships than intraindividual analyses of the same phenomenon (which also invites the interpretation that these two perspectives address different questions [cf. Averill, Olbrich, & Lazarus, 1972; Broverman, 1962; Opton & Lazarus, 1967]). Often, too, method variance is overlooked because of the absence of research that replicates important findings.

Because subjective reports are the primary source of data about appraisal, stress and emotion, and coping, this method of measurement with all its virtues and faults carries the brunt of the issue of method variance. Most researchers in the life sciences have long been aware of the limitations and disadvantages of self-report data, which we alluded to above: the problems of memory, the desire of subjects to present themselves in a positive light, language ambiguity, and the use of verbal reports as an ego defense. This is a familiar litany. The controls and checks that have been generated to cope with these problems, including measures of subjects' tendencies to engage in favorable self-presentations (e.g., Crowne & Marlow, 1964), and the use of physiological and behavioral measures to verify self-report-based inferences, do not seem to help much. Rather than reviewing all these procedures, we would like to point up two frequently ignored considerations, namely, the benefits of using self-report, and the costs of using other sources of data.

First, let us consider what would happen to the psychology of emotion if we were unwilling to use subjective reports of how people felt. Since we know little about the physiological patterns associated with different emotional qualities such as fear, anger, guilt, jealousy, love, or exhilaration, and since the behavioral concomitants of these emotion states are equally obscure and easily transformed or disguised, qualitatively different emotions would have to be virtually ruled out as a subject of investigation without the elaboration of self-reports. Indeed, this is what almost happened during the height of behaviorism (cf. Brown & Farber, 1951), when emotion was relegated to a undimensional concept of arousal or drive. But as we noted in Chapter 2, the arousal concept did not fare well, because there was no uniform pattern of arousal among divergent physiological indexes, and because the valence of behavior and experience, that is, whether positively or negatively toned, is just as important as intensity. When all is said and done, in studying emotion we are dependent on what people tell us about their feelings and about how they construe what is happening to them; we cannot abandon this source of information.

Rather than putting this negatively, however, should we not also realize that people are extraordinarily capable of revealing rich patterns of thought and feeling through language? To shut off this source of information is to decorticate the human as an object of investigation and relegate people to infrahuman status. This view is consistent with the current zeitgeist, as evidenced by Lieberman's (1979) call for a return to introspection, and Shrauger and Osberg's (1981) report that self-assessments were at least as predictive as other methods against which they were pitted. Subjective reports allow us to learn more about stress and emotion, and about coping and its adaptational outcomes, than any other single source, despite the difficulties in validation.

Second, all other sources of data have most of the same drawbacks as self-report regarding the validity of inferences about psychological processes. For example, though seemingly more objective, the movements of polygraph pens on lined paper are just as difficult to interpret, if not more so, than what people tell about their experience. Unresolved issues in electrophysiological measurement that make interpretation difficult include knowing what is a proper baseline for assessing change, that is, how to get at the homeostatic steady state from which to interpret arousal as a deviation; what other events—some even nonphysiological—are factors in heart rate, skin conductance, blood pressure, and so on; and which patterns of response, if any, correspond to diverse feeling states.

Even if it eventually becomes clear that a particular pattern of hormonal response or facial expression (see Ekman, 1972; Ekman & Friesen, 1975; Tomkins, 1962, 1963, 1981) goes with a particular emotion state, there will still be no satisfactory way to verify such conclusions without recourse to what the person tells us about his or her feelings. Useful but insufficient information could be gleaned from the expressive and instrumental behavior of the person in a social context, but without confirming subjective reports, there is still the possibility of a discrepancy between the person's behavior and what he or she is experiencing. Thus, we are in a sense entrapped by the need to verify one unknown, the experienced emotion, by reference to other unknowns such as the meaning of the person's actions in a particular environmental context.

The common solution to this problem is, of course, to analyze physiological, behavioral, and subjective data simultaneously in order to make the fullest sense out of what is happening in stressful or emotionally relevant encounters. This is a sound solution in the long run, but often financially and technically impractical. In addition, the methodological and financial problems connected with giving proper attention to all three measurement levels in a naturalistic or experimental study soon become overwhelming. Finally, when studies are done across measurement levels, what is commonly produced from one method is largely uncorrelated with findings from another method and, in effect, method variance overwhelms everything else.

Our preferred solution to the problem of method variance is to persist with a single method, in this case self-report, until the findings or the lack of them are clear. This requires using self-report with care and tenacity in order to identify meaningful relationships and rules about the conditions under which they occur. If we can predict stress levels and adaptational outcomes from self-reports about appraisal and coping, and show that these predictions are consistent with our theoretical model, then we are justified in going beyond self-report to do check experiments using behavioral and physiological data.

Thus, the steps we favor are, first, to use purely self-report data to generate what appear to be stable findings leading to empirically based principles, and then to check out these principles with other methods. We believe that at this stage of our knowledge this is a more economical and practical solution than combining methods catch-as-catch-can before having established findings. Impressive findings from well-constructed self-report data, when replicated and extended, are bound to encourage other investigators to test them with other controlled, multimethod, laboratory or quasi-laboratory methods.

Check studies could combine self-report, behavioral, and physiological measurements to test whether and in what ways self-report data on appraisal and emotion are associated with behavioral and physiological changes consistent with the researcher's interpretations. A study by Weinberger, Schwartz, and Davidson (1979) illustrates this multimethod approach. They used a measure of defensiveness to differentiate subjects who were low in anxiety and repressive from those who were merely low in anxiety. These subgroupings were then used successfully to predict different levels of arousal measured electrophysiologically.

Crucial to the success of check studies of this kind are a set of clearly stated hypotheses about the patterns of relationships implied by our theoretical formulation. The contrast we made between threat and challenge is a case in point. Challenge implies certain emotions such as optimism and/or hope, joy, or eagerness and certain cognitive and behavioral correlates such as expansiveness and realistic and coordinated efforts. Threat, on the other hand, implies anxiety and distress, cognitive and behavioral constriction, and preservative rather than expansive efforts. It might be possible to juxtapose self-reported portrayals of threat and challenge with ratings by observers based on such behavioral correlates. A similar effort could be made, separately or simultaneously, using physiological response patterns. For example, based on Frankenhaeuser's (1975, 1976) research on adrenalin-noradrenalin patterns under stress, we might anticipate that threat would tilt the balance toward adrenalin, and challenge—which we say involves positive striving and a sense of control—should be associated with greater secretion of noradrenalin. Similar hypotheses have been offered for cortisol.

Strictly speaking, what is being proposed here is not a direct test of the validity of inferences about threat and challenge from self-report data. It is, rather, a test of postulated, substantive relationships between threat, challenge, and behavioral and physiological response patterns. This strategy could be seen as using one set of response patterns whose significance is yet unclear to evaluate another set of response patterns whose significance is equally unclear. Nevertheless, findings of agreement or disagreement among the response systems could throw light on the validity of the inferences involved and might have heuristic value in the search for understanding.

There is no shortage of research on stress and coping that

crosses levels of analysis and so relates to the problem of method variance. What is central to our recommendations is simply that it is all right, even wise, to defer such research until there is a network of findings based on one method and tied to a particular theory. This is not to argue against multilevel measurement, but to recognize the hazards of adopting an overly critical stance about method variance problems and ruling out approaches before they have been given a full opportunity to produce results.

Self-report measurement, although the predominant method in the social sciences and even in the life sciences, tends to be the *bête noire* of methodological pursuits. Given the centrality of internal events and processes in our theoretical system, however, it should not be surprising that we are in favor of this method despite its scientific defects. The ultimate proof of our perspective lies in its ability to specify the relationships among the system variables.

Summary

Stress is investigated at the physiological, psychological, and sociological levels of analysis. Stress experienced at one analytic level does not mean that it will be experienced at another, or in the same way; a person who experiences physiological stress does not necessarily experience psychological stress. And stress at the social level does not mean that it will also be experienced at the psychological or physiological levels, or in the same way. Cognitive appraisal is the critical psychological link among the levels when concerning the individual.

Traditional research on stress has been based largely on antecedent-consequent or stimulus-response models. Usually, the antecedent or stimulus is defined as an environmental factor. Personality factors are sometimes introduced as variables that mediate the damaging effects of environmental factors, and in more complex variations, interactive designs are employed that consider multiple environmental or personality variables. The traditional antecedent-consequent model is limited because it tends to treat variables as if they are in a linear and unidirectional relationship, and as static phenomena.

In contrast, the transactional model that underlies our cognitive theory of stress views the person and the environment in a mutually reciprocal, bidirectional relationship, so that an effect at Time 1 can become a cause at Time 2. Further, in traditional models variables retain their separate identities. In a transactional model separate person and environment elements join together to form new meanings via appraisal; threat, for example, does not refer to separate person and environment factors, but to the integration of both in a given transaction. The transactional model is concerned with process and change in contrast to traditional models, which are static and structural. The study of process involves attending to what is actually happening in a specific context, not what usually happens in contexts in general.

The research design that is most appropriate to our theory is ipsative–normative, and naturalistic rather than experimental. Ipsative–normative research allows for both *intra*- and *inter*individual comparisons. Intraindividual analysis enables the investigation of issues such as person and situation antecedents of appraisal and coping, variability and stability in coping, and coping effectiveness and ineffectiveness. Data gathered from intraindividual analysis can also be used for interindividual comparisons. Experimental laboratory research offers an incomplete tool in the study of stress and coping as related to emotion, because stressors in the laboratory do not reflect well those that people experience in real life; they are less complex, meaningful, and enduring. The laboratory setting does not allow enough time for adaptational outcomes to emerge, and it constrains responses.

Traditional research designs call for studying one or several antecedent variables as causes of some long-range outcome. Nothing is learned about the processes through which the antecedent variables affect the outcome. Neobehaviorist models introduced mediators of the antecedent-outcome relationship. Statistically, these variables are treated as merely another antecedent variable that interacts with other antecedents; processes are inferred, not observed. The neobehaviorist models are thus closer to the traditional cause-and-effect model than to a transactional, process-oriented model. Transactional, process-oriented research examines mediating processes *repeatedly* and more or less directly, using an ipsative–normative approach. This format can also be applied to the physiological and sociological levels of analysis.

Our main contribution to the measurement of key concepts has centered on the measurement of stress, appraisal, and coping. The approach that has dominated the measurement of stress has been to assess major environmental changes or life events. This approach has defects in its major assumptions, which are that change alone is stressful and that life events must be major in order to create stress of sufficient magnitude to impair health. Life events have little practical significance in the prediction of health outcomes, but this approach is pursued because it is simple to administer, and there is hope that modifications will prove fruitful. An alternative that supplements the life events approach is to measure the ordinary daily hassles of living. Hassles appear to be better predictors of health outcomes than life events. Evidence suggests that hassles and life events are partly independent. A major issue is how hassles might affect adaptational outcomes. They may be additive, or the mechanisms might be more complex, involving, for example, the meaning of endorsing a hassle on a questionnaire, baseline conditions, and coping ineptitudes. Hassles can also be viewed as an outcome of poor health, morale, and functioning, thus reversing the direction of causality.

Our measurement of appraisal has focused on the concepts of primary and secondary appraisal. We have made preliminary attempts to assess primary appraisal by asking the subject what is at stake in a specific encounter; the stakes include concerns about a loved one as well as about one's physical and emotional well-being. Secondary appraisal is assessed by asking the subject to evaluate his or her coping options in a specific encounter, including the extent to which the troubled person–environment relationship can be changed and/or has to be accepted.

To measure coping we ask the subject to indicate on a coping checklist what he or she thought, felt, and did to cope with the various demands of a specific encounter. These coping responses can be rationally or empirically classified according to function (e.g., problem- or emotion-focused) or type (e.g., avoidance, information seeking, seeking emotional support). Other investigators are developing similar process-oriented approaches.

Method variance is a perennial problem in the measurement of stress phenomena. Subjective self-report is the primary source of data about stress, appraisal, emotion, and coping and carries the brunt of the task of assessing the relevant variables. The advantages to self-report outweigh the disadvantages. In the long run, convergent techniques, such as physiological and behavioral observations, will be needed to validate and amplify findings based on self-reports, though their present use may be premature.

Ways of Coping (Revised)

Please read each item below and indicate, by circling the appropriate category, to what extent you used it *in the situation you have just described.*

		Not used	Used some-what	Used quite a bit	Used a great deal
1.	Just concentrated on what I had to do next—the next step.	0	1	2	3
2.	I tried to analyze the problem in order to understand it better.	0	1	2	3
3.	Turned to work or substitute activity to take my mind off things.	0	1	2	3
4.	I felt that time would make a difference—the only thing to do was to wait.	0	1	2	3
5.	Bargained or compromised to get something positive from the situation.	0	1	2	3
6.	I did something which I didn't think would work, but at least I was doing something.	0	1	2	3
7.	Tried to get the person responsible to change his or her mind.	0	1	2	3
8.	Talked to someone to find out more about the situation.	0	1	2	3

(continued)

Ways of Coping (continued)

		Not used	Used some- what	Used quite a bit	Used a great deal
9.	Criticized or lectured myself.	0	1	2	3
10.	Tried not to burn my bridges, but leave things open somewhat.	0	1	2	3
11.	Hoped a miracle would happen.	0	1	2	3
12.	Went along with fate; sometimes I just have bad luck.	0	1	2	3
13.	Went on as if nothing had happened.	0	1	2	3
14.	I tried to keep my feelings to myself.	0	1	2	3
15.	Looked for the silver lining, so to speak; tried to look on the bright side of things.	0	1	2	3
16.	Slept more than usual.	0	1	2	3
17.	I expressed anger to the person(s) who caused the problem.	0	1	2	3
18.	Accepted sympathy and understanding from someone.	0	1	2	3
19.	I told myself things that helped me to feel better.	0	1	2	3
20.	I was inspired to do something creative.	0	1	2	3
21.	Tried to forget the whole thing.	0	1	2	3

(continued)

Ways of Coping (continued)		Not used	Used some-what	Used quite a bit	Used a great deal
22.	I got professional help.	0	1	2	3
23.	Changed or grew as a person in a good way.	0	1	2	3
24.	I waited to see what would happen before doing anything.	0	1	2	3
25.	I apologized or did some-thing to make up.	0	1	2	3
26.	I made a plan of action and followed it.	0	1	2	3
27.	I accepted the next best thing to what I wanted.	0	1	2	3
28.	I let my feelings out somehow.	0	1	2	3
29.	Realized I brought the prob-lem on myself.	0	1	2	3
30.	I came out of the experience better than when I went in.	0	1	2	3
31.	Talked to someone who could do something concrete about the problem.	0	1	2	3
32.	Got away from it for a while; tried to rest or take a vacation.	0	1	2	3
33.	Tried to make myself feel bet-ter by eating, drinking, smok-ing, using drugs or medica-tion, etc.	0	1	2	3

(continued)

Ways of Coping (continued)

		Not used	Used some-what	Used quite a bit	Used a great deal
34.	Took a big chance or did something very risky.	0	1	2	3
35.	I tried not to act too hastily or follow my first hunch.	0	1	2	3
36.	Found new faith.	0	1	2	3
37.	Maintained my pride and kept a stiff upper lip.	0	1	2	3
38.	Rediscovered what is important in life.	0	1	2	3
39.	Changed something so things would turn out all right.	0	1	2	3
40.	Avoided being with people in general.	0	1	2	3
41.	Didn't let it get to me; refused to think too much about it.	0	1	2	3
42.	I asked a relative or friend I respected for advice.	0	1	2	3
43.	Kept others from knowing how bad things were.	0	1	2	3
44.	Made light of the situation; refused to get too serious about it.	0	1	2	3
45.	Talked to someone about how I was feeling.	0	1	2	3
46.	Stood my ground and fought for what I wanted.	0	1	2	3

(continued)

Ways of Coping (continued)	Not used	Used some-what	Used quite a bit	Used a great deal
47. Took it out on other people.	0	1	2	3
48. Drew on my past experiences; I was in a similar situation before.	0	1	2	3
49. I knew what had to be done, so I doubled my efforts to make things work.	0	1	2	3
50. Refused to believe that it had happened.	0	1	2	3
51. I made a promise to myself that things would be different next time.	0	1	2	3
52. Came up with a couple of different solutions to the problem.	0	1	2	3
53. Accepted it, since nothing could be done.	0	1	2	3
54. I tried to keep my feeling from interfering with other things too much.	0	1	2	3
55. Wished that I could change what had happened or how I felt.	0	1	2	3
56. I changed something about myself.	0	1	2	3
57. I daydreamed or imagined a better time or place than the one I was in.	0	1	2	3

(continued)

Ways of Coping (continued)

		Not used	Used some-what	Used quite a bit	Used a great deal
58.	Wished that the situation would go away or somehow be over with.	0	1	2	3
59.	Had fantasies or wishes about how things might turn out.	0	1	2	3
60.	I prayed.	0	1	2	3
61.	I prepared myself for the worst.	0	1	2	3
62.	I went over in my mind what I would say or do.	0	1	2	3
63.	I thought about how a person I admire would handle this situation and used that as a model.	0	1	2	3
64.	I tried to see things from the other person's point of view.	0	1	2	3
65.	I reminded myself how much worse things could be.	0	1	2	3
66.	I jogged or exercised.	0	1	2	3
67.	I tried something entirely different from any of the above. (Please describe).	0	1	2	3

11

Treatment and Stress Management

In this chapter we turn our attention to the implications of our thinking for treatment and stress management, by which we mean anything that is done professionally to prevent or ameliorate debilitating stress and coping inadequacies. Indeed, all clinical interventions that deal with psychopathology and distress are concerned with stress in one way or another, including approaches that do not use the term explicitly.

Our chapter title refers to "treatment" and "stress management." Treatment or therapy is the word preferred by those who work one-on-one with individual clients, families, or small groups; stress management refers to formal programs for people in general, less often for special groups characterized by some shared problem. The primary purpose of this chapter is to link our theoretical formulation, particularly the concepts of cognitive appraisal and coping, to both kinds of intervention. Our analysis requires a brief overview of the existing approaches.

Approaches to Treatment

Numerous books have appeared, especially with the advent of the behavior therapies and their cognitively oriented variants, that outline divergent therapeutic approaches. There is no simple organizing principle with which to categorize these approaches. Some center on particular syndromes of stress and distress such as phobias and depression, others on adaptational problems of impulse control such as smoking or excessive eating, and still others on inadequacies in coping skills such as unassertiveness. Since a general approach to treatment usually transcends a specific symptom or problem area, it is more fruitful to look for broad guiding principles than to categorize therapies along problem- or symptom-centered lines.

We will not include here the question of treatment efficacy, that is, whether treatment helps people, in what ways, and how well. Accounts of theory and research on the efficacy of interventions can be found in sources such as Mahoney and Arnkoff (1978), Bergin and Strupp (1972), and the annual reviews of behavior therapy by Franks and Wilson beginning in 1973.

The progenitors and adherents of diverse therapeutic approaches identify their systems with descriptive terms—sometimes broad, sometimes narrow—such as psychoanalysis, dynamic therapy, behavior therapy, rational-emotive therapy (Ellis, 1962, 1975; Ellis & Grieger, 1977), stress-inoculation (Meichenbaum, 1977; Meichenbaum & Novaco, 1978; Novaco, 1976, 1977a, b), or reciprocal inhibition (Wolpe, 1958, 1978, also called systematic desensitization). Although these approaches often differ in theoretical rationale, they frequently have common procedures. Hollon and Beck (1979) have used three categories—theoretical rationale, strategies of treatment, and specific tactics or procedures employed to produce changes—to compare various therapies (see Table 11.1).

As must be evident throughout this book, we do not emphasize physiological approaches (referred to as biological by Hollon and Beck), not because of any closed-minded judgment about their potential value, but because our emphasis is on psychological concerns. Were this category to include somatophysiological strategies, however, such as biofeedback, relaxation, meditation, and physical conditioning (dieting and exercise), interesting questions would arise as to whether these tactics work by affecting physiological response patterns, psychological response patterns, or both. For example, biofeedback for tension headache, rather than directly affecting the frontalis muscle, may help by giving people a greater sense of control over their reactions and by setting in motion new ways of relating to the environment; and relaxation, meditation, and exercise, in addition to providing a greater sense of well-being, may break an ongoing cycle of rumination by changing what the person attends to (Pennebaker & Lightner, 1980). The same question of differentiating psychological and physiological processes is evident in the placebo effect in medicine.

Table 11.1 Therapy

Approach	Theory	Process	Procedure
Biological:	Biochemical imbalance	Restoration of normal physiological processes	Pharmacotherapy and/or somatic therapies
Dynamic:	Anger directed against the self following real or symbolic loss	Insight into unconscious conflict and cathartic discharge of affect	1. Supportive: Amelioration of aggravating unconscious conflicts 2. Depth: Resolution of unconscious conflicts
Behavioral: Affective	Anxiety inhibits potentially gratifying behaviors	Reduction of conditioned anxiety	Systematic desensitization or alternative counter-conditioning procedures
Operant	Deficit in reinforcement or excess in punishment	Increase occurrence of reinforcement (decrease punishment)	1. Direct contingency management by therapist 2. Skills training
Self-control	Deficit in self-reinforcement or excess self-punishment	Increase administration of self-reinforcement (decrease self-punishment	Skills training in (a) self-monitoring; (b) self-evaluation; and (c) self-reinforcement
Cognitive:	Maladaptive beliefs and distorted information processing	Change beliefs and alter information-processing distortions	1. Cognitive therapy: Inductive reasoning, empirical examination of beliefs, training in (a) self-monitoring; (b) cognitive hypothesis testing; and (c) cognitive restructuring 2. RET: Deductive reasoning and persuasion

Reprinted with permission from Hollon, S. D., & Beck, A. T. Cognitive therapy of depression. In P. C. Kendall & S. D. Hollon (Eds.), *Cognitive behavioral interventions: Theory, research, and procedures.* New York: Academic Press, 1979, p. 153.

The *dynamic therapies* in Hollon and Beck's (1979) scheme refer to approaches originating in Freudian psychoanalysis. In later, neo-Freudian approaches (such as Horney's), the emphasis shifted from uncovering encapsulated childhood wishes and fears that operate unconsciously yet peremptorily in adult life to an increasing emphasis on understanding how the childhood conflicts and defenses function in adult transactions and are maintained in the present despite their heavy cost.

There is debate as to whether psychoanalytic and behavior therapies can be reconciled. Some writers (e.g., Messer & Winokur, 1980) express skepticism, whereas others (e.g., Goldfried, 1982a, b; Marmor & Woods, 1980; Wachtel, 1977) are more optimistic. In his attempt to integrate psychoanalytic and behavior therapy, Wachtel has helped to demystify the process whereby early developmental difficulties interfere with later adaptation. He writes:

> From this perspective, adult personality and life style appear to be the inevitable results of something that happened years ago and are of interest, if at all, only as signs of what must have happened at the time things *really* mattered. To alter the patient's difficulties in any lasting and extensive way would seem to require an uncovering of the residue of the past. To attempt to intervene at the level of current functioning and current influences would appear futile. (p. 22)

Wachtel goes on to ask, ". . . can the presence of these inclinations in the patient be accounted for by the way he or she is currently living, and might these manifestations change if the way of living changed?" (p. 41). Wachtel says yes, and his elaboration provides the major theme in his efforts to integrate the two perspectives. Dysfunctional behavior patterns, which have their roots in childhood, become self-perpetuating rather than merely recapitulating the past. In other words, these patterns are sustained by styles of behaving which, in turn, elicit and maintain maladaptive reactions on the part of significant others. Wachtel illustrates this process with a client who goes out of his way to appear independent. This client unconsciously wishes to be cared for and nurtured yet at the same time fears such passive desires. The conscious attitudes and actions of independence, however, should be regarded, not simply as a defense against desires of the past, but also as a compulsive pattern that creates the dependent needs in the present. Such a person takes on excessive responsibilities and thereby denies and thwarts opportunities to enjoy normal dependence, and so is kept continually yearning for dependence while pursuing the excessive pattern of independence. The desires and conflicts that dominate the person's life flow from as well as cause the troubled style of life.

What distinguishes the Freudian theme of repressed wishes and fears from what cognitive behavior therapists speak of as personal, sometimes hidden, agendas (Goldfried, 1980) is the emphasis on understanding how such agendas operate in interpersonal relationships, in both the past and the present. These agendas do not have to be pathogenic, as can be seen in another illustration by Wachtel (1977):

> For example, the two-year-old who has developed an engaging and playful manner is far more likely to evoke friendly interest and attention on the part of adults than is the child who is rather quiet and withdrawn. The latter will typically encounter a less rich interpersonal environment, which will further decrease the likelihood that he will drastically change. Similarly, the former is likely to continue to learn that other people are fun and eager to interact with him; and his pattern, too, is likely to be more firmly fixed as he grows. Further, not only will the two children tend to evoke different behavior from others, they will also interpret differently the same reaction from another person. Thus, the playful child may experience a silent or grumpy response from another as a kind of game and may continue to interact until perhaps he does elicit an appreciative response. The quieter child, not used to much attention, will readily accept the initial response as a signal to back off.
>
> If we look at the two children as adults, we may perhaps find the difference between them still evident: one outgoing, cheerful, and expecting the best of people; the other rather shy, and unsure that anyone is interested. A childhood pattern has persisted into adulthood. Yet we really don't understand the developmental process unless we see how, successively, teachers, playmates, girlfriends, and colleagues have been drawn in as "accomplices" in maintaining the persistent pattern. And, I would suggest, we don't understand the possibilities for change unless we realize that even now there are such "accomplices," and that if they stopped playing their role in the process, it would be likely eventually to alter. (p. 52)

Thus, the *dynamic approaches* that have evolved from the Freudian position have turned from an exclusive concern with infantile wishes and the fears they generate to a concern with how counterproductive coping solutions originating earlier in life continue to operate in the present. Strategy and tactics aside, treatment is an attempt to help the client discover the origins of poor coping and how it is perpetuated and/or to acquire more effective coping strategies. Attention has thus shifted, even in the dynamic systems of therapy, from a concentration on purely intrapsychic processes to the way in which people's agendas interact with the demands and opportunities of their current social environment.

How new forms of coping are acquired is a topic of controversy between the *behavioral* and *cognitive-behavioral* approaches noted in Table 11.1. All three of the behavioral subcategories of Hollon and Beck's analysis emphasize some form of conditioning or deconditioning process. Those in the *affective* group adhere to the principles of "classical" (Pavlovian) conditioning of pathogenic habits. Through such conditioning, neutral cues in the environment generate anxiety, and avoidant coping responses are "stamped in" as habitual reactions because they reduce the anxiety. These avoidant responses prevent the person from learning to confront the cues with alternative ways of acting and reacting. From the Freudian point of view, the problem is not merely accidental fear conditioning to neutral cues or a hostile environment (although this too is relevant); there must be some pre-existing characterological vulnerability that makes routine situations capable of generating disabling emotional distress and inept forms of coping.

In both the conditioned anxiety-avoidance model and the psychodynamic approach, the sources of anxiety must be exposed and "deconditioned" in treatment so that new, more adaptive modes of coping can be learned in the presence of the cues that originally evoked anxiety and its conditioned (habitual) avoidance. The tactics for doing this vary, even among therapists who subscribe to the anxiety-avoidance model. One tactic is systematic desensitization, which originated with Wolpe (1958, 1978; Wolpe & Lazarus, 1966). In his procedure, called reciprocal inhibition, the anxiety-producing stimuli are made to occur during an incompatible positive reinforcement by some pleasurable activity; the latter presumably inhibits the former, thus resulting in deconditioning. In practice, the tactic is to expose the client to a hierarchy of stimuli scaled from non-anxiety-inducing to highly anxiety-inducing. The exposure proceeds gradually up the scale of intensity as the client becomes habituated to the anxiety-producing cues. Frequently relaxation training is used simultaneously in order to facilitate the deconditioning process.

Operant conditioning systems, based on B. F. Skinner's (1938, 1953) work, are designed to positively reinforce desirable behavior or negatively reinforce undesirable behavior (see, for example, Lewinsohn, 1973, 1975, with depression). The former category includes assertiveness training for people who have difficulty expressing their wishes out of fear of hostility or rejection. The aim is twofold: for the clients to discover that acting assertively achieves their ends and generates respect from others rather than hostility. Success serves as positive reinforcement that presumably helps these people acquire the desired new modes of social functioning. Aversive conditioning strategies fall in the latter category of negative reinforcement. Antabuse, which is designed to eliminate the unwanted drinking habits that had been acquired through positive reinforcement, is a powerful negative reinforcement because it creates nausea when combined with alcohol. Other conditioning approaches emphasize the learning of self-control through comparable deconditioning strategies whereby the client monitors his or her own behavior and uses reinforcement to shape behavior patterns in the desired direction. Rosenbaum and Merbaum (in press) distinguish between self-control or self-regulatory processes that arise from within and are generalized across situational contexts, and those that are shaped by manipulating external demands or constraints. (For accounts of strategies used to achieve self-control, see Doerfler & Richards, 1981; Mahoney & Arnkoff, 1978; Perri & Richards, 1977.) This therapeutic approach illustrates operantly focused programs of behavior change that center on attempts to control one's own unwanted behavior.

In recent years there has been a proliferation of *cognitive-behavioral* therapeutic programs that emphasize the mediating role of cognitive processes in sustaining or eliminating maladaptive patterns. (For an analysis of the diverse meanings given to the terms cognitive and behavioral by protagonists of this school, see Schwartz, 1982.) These programs, with their emphasis on cognitive processes and their role in determining emotion and behavior, are the most compatible with our theoretical formulation.

One of the earliest cognitive-behavioral approaches is Ellis's (1962, 1975) rational-emotive therapy, which holds that the person's conception of a situation is more important in determining his or her reactions than is the objective situation. According to Ellis, a person makes a faulty and counterproductive interpretation of the significance of an event because of certain characteristics, irrational beliefs, or assumptions, for example, that it is essential to be liked or approved of by everyone, or that to fail at a job means the person is worthless. The therapeutic strategy is to help the client give up such irrational beliefs and to think more logically. Goldfried (1980) refers to a similar strategy as "cognitive restructuring," and others have used the term "situational redefinition" (see also Beck, in press a). Whatever the language, the basic theme is that faulty reasoning underlies maladaptation. A goal of therapy is to teach the specific failures of logic that are responsible for the distress or poor functioning for which help is sought and to help the person think more constructively.

Another variant of this line of thought is Beck's (1976) cognitive-behavior therapy. According to Beck (in press b) depressive clients share certain negative and distorted beliefs about themselves, the world, and the future. These cognitive distortions take the form of *selective abstraction,* in which the person ignores contradictory and more salient evidence and forms a conclusion about an event on the basis of an isolated negative detail; *arbitrary inference,* in which a negative appraisal is made in the absence of evidence; *overgeneralization,* whereby a general, negative conclusion is drawn from a single event and applied in an unjustified way to dissimilar situations; *magnification* (sometimes called "catastrofication"), in which the significance of a negative event is overestimated or magnified; and *all-or-none thinking,* the tendency to think in absolutes (everything is either good or bad, mostly the latter). As with Ellis's approach, the task of therapy is to get the client to give up the maladaptive modes of thought on which emotional distress or depression is based in favor of more accurate ones.

Ellis's and Beck's work raises an interesting question that has long been debated in psychology: Do maladative modes of thought arise from a faulty premise on which an appraisal or conclusion is built, or from faulty reasoning perhaps due to emotional interference? Henle's (1962, 1971) examination of syllogistic thinking in college students suggests the former, namely, that thinking follows logical steps and that faulty conclusions are accounted for more often by hidden or omitted premises. Henle suggests that the premises on which conclusions are based are sustained by selective attention, based in turn on personal agendas. Beck and (especially) Ellis also adopt this perspective.

Other forms of cognitive-behavior therapy are advocated by Meichenbaum (1977; Meichenbaum & Jaremko, 1983) and Goldfried (1979, 1980; Goldfried & Davison, 1976; Goldfried & Goldfried, 1975). Meichenbaum, like Goldfried, Beck, and others, emphasizes cognitive restructuring, on the premise that the person's distress stems from faulty ways of construing troubling events and relationships. Although it draws also on Ellis, Meichenbaum's therapeutic approach is closer to that of Beck; the client is helped to increase his or her awareness of negative self-statements and images and to learn the specific new problem-solving and coping skills. There is less emphasis on Ellis's formal analysis of irrational beliefs and more emphasis on positive self-statements and self-instruction.

A particularly interesting programmatic feature of Meichenbaum's approach is *stress-inoculation training* (see also Novaco, 1979). Stress-inoculation means acquiring sufficient knowledge, self-understanding, and coping skills to facilitate better ways of handling expected stressful confrontations. The program has three phases. In the educational phase, information is provided about the way distressing emotions are generated, with an emphasis on the cognitive factors or self-statements that are involved. In the rehearsal phase, alternative self-statements are provided for use under conditions of emotional distress. The strategies help the client assess the situation, control unwanted thoughts and emotions, motivate behavior, and ultimately evaluate his or her performance. In the application phase, the client tries out what has been learned and practices it.

Novaco's (1979) version of stress-inoculation, which follows the same three phases, is used with groups of people, such as police officers, who share a common source of stress. Police officers face the problem of controlling their anger in confrontations with lawbreakers. Here the education phase is concerned with teaching the ways of thinking that underlie anger. A group format is used to discuss the experiences of anger each police officer has had. This group discussion helps the officers discover their own particular, perhaps hidden, vulnerabilities to anger, including the threat to their self-esteem. Novaco's work with stress-inoculation training closely parallels that of Meichenbaum and reflects a common theoretical model in which emotion is seen as controlled through better understanding, positive self-statements, and self-instruction.

The cognitive-behavioral approaches to treatment that we have selected are relatively elaborated systems of theory, strategy, and tactics. Other approaches include *modeling*, emphasized by Bandura (1969, 1971) and others (e.g., Cautela, 1971; Kazdin, 1975) and widely used in the treatment of fears and phobias; *role-taking*, in which the client is asked to imagine an encounter and to reverse roles by playing the part of another (cf. Kelly's [1955] *fixed-role therapy*, and Moreno's [1947] *psychodrama*); and *imaginal processes* (see Anderson, 1980; Bandura, 1977b, 1977; Klinger, 1971; Singer, 1974), which are used to identify important emotional themes, generate positive and negative emotional states, and help in learning new modes of coping.

Evidence of the close conceptual tie between the cognitive-behavioral therapists' analyses of stress and coping and our own cognitive formulation can be seen in the previously cited writings of Goldfried, Meichenbaum, Novaco, and Rosenbaum (in press). Goldfried (1980), for example, characterizes therapy as coping skills training, and Rosenbaum (in press) has reviewed the relationship between our transactional approach to stress and coping and his own concept of learned resourcefulness.

Most commonly the practice of psychotherapy is not tied to any narrow, rigid pattern of tactics. Therapists usually address not one modality in the client, but several, including behavior, affect, and cognition. For example, the approaches which emphasize cognition, such as those of Beck and Ellis, extend to the emotional life, too, and are typically as much concerned with behavior as they are with reasoning and thinking. This many-sided approach is what Arnold Lazarus (1981) calls "multimodal therapy," in which a systematic effort is made to construct an individual profile of the client and to address the many facets of his or her specific personality and problems. In characterizing different therapeutic systems, it is wise not to take too literally what their adherents say about strategy, tactics, and modality, since in practice most clinicians are flexible in approach.

How Treatment Works

We have seen that there are a number of different models of treatment, each with its own theory about maladaptation, its causes, and how it can be ameliorated, prevented, or overcome. The range of treatment choices gives rise to debates about how treatment should be designed and how it might work. Although we cannot resolve these issues here, we should give attention to key issues that are related to our own thinking about stress and coping.

We begin with our suspicion—shared by others—that often a given tactic produces change in ways other than is postulated. An interesting illustration comes from research by Andrasik and Holroyd (1980) with subjects suffering from tension headaches. Biofeedback treatment calls for presenting an electrophysiological display of the tension in the frontalis (forehead) muscle. Headache sufferers can then view the physiological results of their efforts to reduce the muscle tension which is thought either to underlie or to be a correlate of their headache symptoms.

In the Andrasik and Holroyd research, four subject groups were given different treatments. Three groups received biofeedback. One of these groups was instructed in the normal procedure for decreasing frontalis muscle tension; subjects in the second group were led to believe they were decreasing tension when in fact they were maintaining stable levels; the third group of subjects were led to believe they were decreasing tension when they were actually increasing it. The fourth group was a no-treatment control.

Summarizing their results, Andrasik and Holroyd write that "irrespective of whether subjects learned to increase, decrease, or maintain constant levels of frontal muscle tension, subjects showed similar reductions in headache symptoms" (p. 583); this improvement was found in both frequency and severity. Moreover, the differences between the treatment and the no-treatment control group were maintained in a follow-up evaluation long after the treatment ended (see also Holroyd & Andrasik, 1982). Thus, although the usual assumption about biofeedback is that it reduces the peripheral cause of headache, specifically muscle tension, learned reduction of muscle tension actually played little if any role in successful treatment.

What, then, could account for the positive effects of biofeedback in this study? The answer is not clear. Holroyd (1979) and Andrasik and Holroyd (1980) have argued that the effects of biofeedback may be indirect. One possibility is that effects are produced by alterations in cognition and behavior. When asked to indicate the strategies they used to control muscle tension, however, subjects cited a wide variety of activities including behavioral changes, controlled breathing, focusing attention on monotonous mental tasks or on bodily sensations, imagery or fantasy, muscle relaxation, thinking of nothing, praying, problem solving, rational reevaluation, and self-instructions. Another possible explanation for the success of the treatment is that headache sufferers learn to monitor the onset of headache symptoms, which Andrasik and Holroyd (1980) suggest may be more crucial than learning to directly modify EMG (electromyographic or muscle tension) activity.

Biofeedback treatment was originally based on a purely biophysical concept centered on the conditioned control of peripheral neuromuscular or neurochemical processes (see Anchor, Beck, Sieveking, & Adkins, 1982, for a more detailed history). That autonomic nervous system reactions, traditionally viewed as outside voluntary control, were at least partly under voluntary control (Miller, 1969, 1978, 1980; Miller & Dworkin, 1977) had been a surprising discovery.

The emphasis, however, had been on peripheral rather than central systems. The explanation rested on the control of local muscle activity, which was considered to be a cause of the tension headache symptom, not on higher nervous system activity such as that involved in cognitive appraisal and coping.

Andrasik and Holroyd's (1980) findings, however, suggest that central neural processes are of primary importance in the positive effects of the biofeedback treatment. This view closely parallels those of Schwartz (1973) and Lazarus (1975a), who have argued that the important factors in the therapeutic relationship are how the person construes what is happening and coping, all of which involve higher forms of brain activity. The biofeedback procedure, then, can be regarded as merely the occasion that sets in motion certain adaptationally important processes involving appraisal and coping which alter the likelihood and/or potency of the stress symptoms.

Indeed, it is quite possible to view all therapy as a procedure that could generate new ways of evaluating the sources of stress and ways of coping that characterize the person's life outside the therapeutic context. Viewed in this light, it is not merely what the therapist or the client does in the treatment setting that matters, but that therapy facilitates the complex natural process of finding new and more serviceable ways of appraising and coping. These processes of change can and do occur without treatment in the normal course of living.

Now to approach the question of how treatment works, we can draw partly on the analysis of Hollon and Beck (1979) and discern four superordinate themes about the process of therapeutic change, each with subvariants: (1) feelings shape thought and action; (2) actions shape thought and feeling; (3) the environment shapes thought, feeling, and action; and (4) thoughts shape feeling and action. We caution the reader that these seemingly simple, clear-cut formulations are merely heuristic aids for thinking, and not adequate descriptions of the therapeutic process. We have already gone on record in Chapter 9 as believing that the distinctions among thought, feeling, and action in emotion theory are far from clear, and further, that these facets of emotion are interdependent and have mutually reciprocal effects. Thus, in saying that feelings shape thought and action, we must recognize too that a feeling when it occurs is also immediately cognized, which changes subsequent thought, action, and the emotional state itself. The formulations below are therefore merely idealized analytic guides for examining the interrelationships among the key psychological processes.

Feelings Shape Thought and Action

We pointed out in earlier chapters that before psychology shifted toward a more cognitive emphasis, emotions were believed to be powerful determinants of thought and action. There were two major conceptualizations of this process. In the first, emotions were seen as drives or motivators in the acquisition (learning) of behavior. This view was central to drive-reinforcement learning theory and was allied also to Freud's tension-reduction model for learning. The conceptualization of emotions as drives or motivators is still to be found among writers such as Tomkins (1962, 1963, 1981, 1982), who views affect as the basis for psychological development in that we seek to preserve and enhance positive and reduce negative feelings. In the second conceptualization, emotions were seen as sources of interference or disruption of ongoing activities (see Easterbrook, 1959; Mandler, 1975). This view is illustrated in the literature on test anxiety (e.g., Krohne & Laux, 1982; Wine, 1971), and in more recent information-processing formulations (e.g., Erdelyi, 1974). From both these standpoints, emotions are primary forces in shaping thought and action.

How emotion as drive might work in behavioral therapy can be illustrated by Dollard and Miller's (1950) translation of Freud into a Hullian (Hull, 1937, 1943) orientation. In effect, if one assumes that anxiety motivates avoidant activity, and also disrupts thinking, then treatment must reverse the process whereby anxiety shapes thought and action in maladaptive directions. Whatever the method of de-conditioning and reconditioning—for example, systematic desensitization, which we described earlier, or implosive therapy or flooding, in which strong anxiety is created under benign conditions to decouple anxiety from the cues that generate it (Hogan, 1967; Levis & Carrera, 1967; Stampfl, 1970)—the person must learn to experience previously disrupting cues without disorganizing anxiety. As Epstein (1983a) puts it:

> The requirement of therapy is to arrange conditions in which a client can experience a feared stimulus without defenses, and thereby perceive it for what it is and not for what it is feared to be. While this is easily said, it is not so easily done. (p. 60)

Furthermore, maladaptive behavior patterns that spring from pathogenic modes of managing anxiety now have to be unlearned. In this formulation, emotions (anxiety) are primary because they motivate thoughts and actions.

The adjuncts to many deconditioning therapies such as biofeedback, relaxation, meditation, and physical fitness are directed at symptoms, including tension or anxiety, and can help break the conditioned link between anxiety and destructive habits of coping with it. If the client's trouble is disabling tension or anxiety, lowering the level of disturbance can itself be viewed as therapeutic. Moreover, a supportive relationship with the therapist can be an agent of psychological and physiological comfort (as well as insight, in Freudian terms), providing rewards to the client during the struggle to come to grips with the problem. This type of reinforcement could also be an end in itself during therapy for a short-term emotional crisis.

Whether the conceptualization is that of emotions as drive, the lowering of which reinforces the acquisition of unwanted behavior, or as an interference with cognitive and behavioral activites, the usual intervention task is to lower its level so that its harmful effects can be eliminated. An exception is implosive therapy, in which intense anxiety is created so that the client will discover that the worst threats do not materialize, again with a view to disconnecting the learned cues for anxiety from the anticipated negative reinforcement. If feelings shape thought and action in the above ways, then by implication one must attack such feelings in whatever way is possible.

Actions Shape Thought and Feeling

A second theme is that the key to treatment is to get the client to behave differently so that new, more effective coping patterns can be acquired, whether through reinforcement of an operant kind or through insight or cognitive restructuring gained from attempting to avoid previous behavior. This type of conceptualization has had considerable influence in social psychology in the theory of attitude formation and change, illustrated by the work of Bem (1972), Bem and Funder (1978), Festinger and Carlsmith (1959), Funder (1982), Rosenberg (1969), and others. After the person behaves in a certain way, his or her cognitive-affective structure may change because of what is learned, and the dissonance among behavior, thought, and feeling may be reduced. In effect, thoughts and feelings are brought into accord with actions. Social learning theorists (e.g., Bandura, 1971, 1977b; Rotter, 1966), as well as developmentalists such as Piaget (1952), assume that cognitive structures are created and modified through the process of acting on and experiencing the environment and obtaining feedback from it.

Behavior therapists who totally eschew cognitive mediators of action or who think these mediators are secondary to behavior try to change how clients *act* in problem situations rather than the way they *think* about them. These therapists believe that the best way to change how a person feels about or construes a situation is first to change the behavior patterns on which new discoveries about the self and the world can be predicated. Moreover, if one accepts the premise that how people act and react shapes the behavior of others toward them and how they feel, then by changing their behavior, people can also change the environment and thereby create an entirely new relationship to the world.

The Environment Shapes Thought, Feeling, and Action

Less common as a therapeutic model is the effort to change the person by changing the social and/or physical environment. Here the emphasis shifts somewhat from the internal dynamics of the person to the actions and reactions of others that lock the person into a damaging circle of relationships. This approach, which is our third theme, is emphasized in Coyne's (1976) analysis of depression. The depressive's behavior does, indeed, produce annoyance, withdrawal, and distant or hostile behavior in others, thus confirming depressives' dim view of themselves and their interpersonal relationships (see also Blumberg & Hokanson, 1983; Gotlib & Robinson, 1982; Strack & Coyne, 1983; Weakland, Fisch, Watzlawick, & Bodin, 1974). This of course does not explain the cause of depression but only helps us understand the social factors that maintain it.

One therapeutic solution is to advise these clients' family and friends on how to act and react toward them. This technique appears to have originated in clinical work with children. The awareness that young children cannot do much about their social environments, since they are so dependent on their parents or parent substitutes, led to therapeutic approaches in which the child was seen clinically in the company of the family. Family therapy helped the participants to view the problem child differently, which led to important changes in their behavior toward the child; these changes in turn elicited more adaptive responses from the child.

Additional examples are found in efforts to train others to provide useful support for a person in crisis and to distinguish between behaviors that are helpful and those that are harmful. This approach has been particularly useful for families of the alcoholic. Efforts to sensitize medical and nursing personnel to the special needs and vulnerabilities of helpless, senile, or dying patients are also relevant. Field experiements by Rodin and Langer (1977), Langer and Rodin (1976), and others in which inmates of custodial homes for the elderly were given greater control over their activities also illustrate this theme.

A provocative example of treatment along these lines has been presented by Watzlawick and Coyne (1980) with an aging client who had suffered a stroke and whose behavior had been steadily deteriorating. After talking with the family, a provisional assessment was made that by being overprotective, the family had inadvertently deprived the client of responsibility for caring for himself and doing things around the house, thus infantilizing him and allowing his damaged condition to further deteriorate behaviorally. The lack of responsibility seemed to increase his mental confusion. The family was enjoined to make more demands on the client, with the result that he began to function better. The transactional features of this situation were graphically described by Watzlawick and Coyne (1980):

> Much of the interaction involved either the wife or sons making a hopeful prognostic statement or indicating that he had functioned better shortly after the stroke than he did currently, followed by a terse denial by the patient. When he attempted to speak, they often finished sentences for him and occasionally answered for him. But the most remarkable, recurrent pattern of interaction consisted of their combined efforts to encourage Mr. B to pull himself together, try harder, and to see his situation more optimistically—whereupon he invariably responded with increased helplessness, pointing out to them how little they understood the severity of his physical handicaps and of his dejection, to which they then responded with increased, obviously well-meant optimism and encouragement. The family thus seems to be caught in a typical Game without End—an interactional impasse in which more of a problem-perpetuating "solution" by one party is countered by more of the same reaction by the other. (p. 14)

This case report is a stunning example of a therapeutic intervention that changed the client's coping process and its adaptational consequences by changing the family environment so as to make more demands on him, a strategy clearly consistent with our transactional formulation of stress, coping, and adaptation.

In Chapter 8 we noted that maladaptation can be interpreted as a failure of the individual or as a failure of society. From the latter perspective, holding the individual responsible is sometimes described as "blaming the victim." There are political overtones inherent in deciding whether to help people learn to cope with existing realities, as in most treatment programs, or in trying to change social structures in ways that facilitate adaptation. Indeed, as we also pointed out in Chapter 8, some difficulties can be dealt with only at the group or organizational level.

Although the emphasis in this chapter is on individual coping, the formulation that the environment shapes thoughts, feelings, and actions invites us to think briefly about the other side of the coin, namely, how better adaptation might come about through changing the social or organizational structure. Much of organizational psychology, for example, gives attention to how the work setting might facilitate or impair adaptation (cf. Levinson, 1973; Schein, 1980), although there is only negligible concern with *how* to produce change. There is great interest in this general topic in Sweden, as reflected in several works about how to modify work environments in the interest of preserving health (see, for example, Frankenhaeuser, 1981; Gardell, 1976; Levi, 1980). More directly related to treatment, Albee (1980) has pressed for change in the delivery of mental health care and for social changes that would facilitate health (see, for example, the Vermont series on the primary prevention of psychopathology, Albee & Joffe, 1977). The issue as to whether to focus on the individual or on social structures need not be treated in an either–or fashion; both directions of intervention lie open to those who want to ameliorate suffering and improve competence and well-being.

Thoughts Shape Feeling and Action

The view that how we act and feel depends on the way we think, specifically how we appraise the significance of encounters for our well-being, is a major premise of our formulation of stress and coping which has been spelled out in detail in previous chapters and is the assumption underlying the cognitive-behavioral therapies of Beck, Ellis, Goldfried, Meichenbaum, and Novaco, which we cited earlier in this chapter.

The idea that thoughts shape feeling and action is also expressed in the psychoanalytic approach in the concept of *insight*. According to this view, which we touched on earlier, early childhood wishes and fears become encapsulated and thus inaccessible to the neurotic person's understanding of current life problems, and these wishes and fears continue to operate silently. Initially, this thinking led to the belief that treatment required reliving early traumas so that they could be released through abreaction or catharsis. However, the idea that the release of dammed-up energy was the fundamental agent of change eventually lost favor. The central task of psychoanalytic therapy then shifted to the discovery of these traumas in order to gain insight into the private agendas that interfered with effective functioning in adulthood. Insight, whether representing truth or a new set of more serviceable myths about oneself, is thus the psychoanalytic version of the cognitive processes we have been emphasizing as factors in appraisal.

It soon became obvious, however, that insight was not enough, and attention turned to "working through" or reeducation (Shaffer & Lazarus, 1952), in which the client lived out numerous experiences of anxiety and distress. Insight was still viewed as the prime agent of change, but an active process of experiencing stressful encounters and engaging in coping thoughts and actions with their attendant emotions was also considered necessary. It is thus erroneous for behaviorally oriented writers to castigate psychodynamic therapies as purely intrapsychic and unconcerned with actions, for without a struggle outside the therapy setting, the insights won in treatment would remain intellectual rather than emotional.

Wachtel (1977) writes, for example, that "intellectual versus emotional insight appears as a distinction whose importance derives from whether, or how thoroughly, the patient is exposed to those cues that really make him anxious" (p. 94). Understanding without feeling is intellectual insight. Exposure to the cues generating anxiety is essential if the client is to unlearn pathological and pathogenic modes of coping which help him or her avoid the distressing anxiety. Without this working through or reeducation (deconditioning) process, the discovery and verbalization of hidden agendas underlying the person's difficulty is apt to be therapeutically fruitless. Put differently, in addition to insight or understanding, therapeutic change requires that the client experience troubling feelings in the life contexts that naturally generate them, as well as changes in behavior; these experiences allow the client to learn the wishes and fears obstructing effective functioning. Nevertheless, the basic theme is that thought (cognitive appraisal) shapes feeling and action. If one wishes to change feeling and action, one must get the client to change how he or she thinks about what is happening.

The Choice of Therapeutic Strategy

In intervention, must we choose among the four themes concerning causal directions in the relationships among thought, feeling, and action? We think not. Although we have forcefully and consistently argued that cognition is a necessary condition of emotion—specifically, that cognitive appraisal shapes emotion and coping—our view is transactional, which means that regardless of our theoretical predilection for a cognitive interpretation, we do not take a general stand on how best to intervene. Earlier we acknowledged that the relations among cognition, emotion, and motivation are bidirectional rather than unidirectional. The same reasoning applies to the relationships among cognition, emotion, and behavior. Given their functional interdependence, it should be impossible to influence one factor in this complex without inducing changes in the others. If one succeeds in changing thought, one of the powerful conditions of change in feeling and action has been created; if feelings are changed, action and thought will probably change too; and if actions change, thought and feeling will follow; it seems unwise to set these alternatives against each other.

Nevertheless, our conceptualization states unequivocally that to produce therapeutic changes in the way people manage their lives, one must in one way or another produce changes in cognitive appraisal and coping. If a person is anxious, fearful, angry, depressed, or whatever, these feelings will go away only if that person ceases to appraise encounters in the old way and comes to appraise them differently. When one is in danger or feels a sense of loss, it is appropriate to feel fear or sadness or even depression. What is counterproductive is to feel this way when it is not appropriate or functional to do so. Even when there is a realistic basis for an appraisal and its attendant emotional distress, the failure to cope effectively must ultimately be overcome, preferably at the earliest possible juncture. We are in no way equivocating here on the necessary role of cognition and coping in emotion and adaptational consequences. Our neutrality with respect to therapeutic strategy is not an expression of uncertainty or ambivalence about the causal role of appraisal and coping in emotion and long-term adaptational outcomes, but rather it reflects the conviction that there is currently no basis for saying that the change is better brought about by directly influencing appraisal and coping as opposed to indirectly influencing feelings, actions, or social settings.

Findings that compare one treatment with another seldom permit us to rule out alternative interpretations about how change comes about. For example, when deconditioning procedures are used, how the person construes what is happening in and out of the therapeutic context is not assessed. Thus, the arrangement of variables in a conditioning paradigm does not clearly represent the process that is actually taking place, nor does it eliminate cognitive or other processes involved in the therapeutic relationship as possible explanations. Sollod and Wachtel (1980) have put it this way:

> In general, we regard this work [therapies devoted to analysis of mediating cognitions] as highly promising, but we see a danger that in its "rediscovery" of cognition, some of the virtues of the *behavioral* perspective from which it began will be lost. Of particular concern is the necessity to retain the emphasis on *action* that has characterized the behavioral approach to clinical problems. We suspect, for example, that future research will reveal that far more of the success of Ellis's (1962) rational-emotive therapy—which has been so attractive to cognitively oriented behavior therapists—is due to its emphasis on structured real-life tasks and to the therapist's vigorous urging that the patient do things differently than to the rationalistic analysis of the patient's "irrational" ideas. (p. 4)

It is interesting that the therapies that seem to have the most influence and lasting power are those that are both flexible and multifaceted or multimodal, to use Arnold Lazarus's term. It should not seem surprising that when treatment involves more than one modality—that is, cognition, behavior, and/or feeling—it should have a greater prospect of setting corrective processes in motion.

Therapy from the Perspective of Our Stress and Coping Theory

If one accepts the premise that stress and coping are important features of maladaptive functioning, and that therapy is concerned with reducing levels of stress and improving coping, then our conceptualization might provide a useful perspective within which to view treatment. Below we examine the implications for treatment of our metatheoretical emphasis on transaction and process, as well as our substantive concerns with cognitive appraisal and coping. In addition, we give some attention to the classic problem of motivation for treatment.

Transaction and Process

Dissatisfaction with the Freudian approach has much to do with its overemphasis on intrapsychic processes and issues of character and its failure to give enough attention to the environment. When things go wrong, the tendency of psychodynamicists is to assume that the person's weaknesses, ineptitudes, or early traumas are to blame, which is, as we have said, often part of the story, but not the whole. The psychodynamic perspective has always reflected the conservative value of helping people accommodate to the world rather than doing something to change it to meet their requirements. Likewise, the behavior therapist's preoccupation with the environmental stimulus that produces disturbed reactions overemphasizes outer conditions and underemphasizes the characteristics of the person that generate misfit between the person and the environment.

A *transactional model*, as we discussed it in Chapter 9, says that stress is neither in the environment nor in the person but a product of their interplay. People are not passive recipients of environmental demands; they actively select and shape the environments of their lives to a greater or lesser extent. In choosing their work environment, for example, young adults assess their competencies and interests, as well as the opportunities that are available. These same young adults also make choices about their love relationships and social environments that match their concepts about themselves. Thus, their social and work environments are to some extent given, but in other ways they are selected according to personal values, preferences, abilities, and so on. Through this selectivity, and through cognitive processes such as appraisal, an organization of person and environment variables emerges, as illustrated by the psychological stress states of harm, threat, and challenge.

Translated into the task of treatment, this means that we cannot focus solely on what is wrong with individuals, which is the most widespread bias of treatment, but must consider the characteristics of their environments and how they were selected. Treatment that is centered on changing these environments when possible is just as appropriate as treatment designed to change the person. In a discussion of psychotherapy, Weimer (1980) suggests that "if therapy is ever to be effective it must constitute procedures capable of tapping the abstract rules which literally are the client's mind, and redirecting their activity so that a better attunement between the client and his environment results" (p. 383). This "attunement between the client and his environment" clearly states the key theme of transaction.

Weimer also discussed how the social organization within which the person functions contains many regulations and prohibitions about human conduct that create important sources of stress in living. This view melds nicely with our own concern with the relationship between the individual and the social system, which we discussed in Chapter 8, and particularly the social demands, constraints, and resources with which the well-functioning person must deal. Weimer continues with the therapeutically oriented comment:

> . . . it should now be apparent that social and cultural phenomena, which represent those factors that separate man from the other animals, cannot be either disregarded or reduced to explicit factors subject to conscious control and change. Insofar as a client's problems are even considered for treatment, they are inevitably social rather than individual, and thus fit into a complex system that has originated in human action but not human design. We have as yet done virtually nothing to study the social and cultural nature of the attunement of man to his environment. . . . (p. 391)

A clear and concrete manifestation of a transactional perspective may be found in the concept of *vulnerability* to stress (see Chapter 2), which is a joint function of both the person and the environment. A person is vulnerable to stress under environmental conditions that evoke values and goals to which the person has strong commitments, and to harm or threat, especially, in situations that potentiate negative beliefs about his or her prospects.

Vulnerability, defined in this way, is a transactional variable because it is not relevant under all environmental conditions but only under those that interact functionally with relevant person factors. Although some people can be said to be generally vulnerable compared with others in that many conditions make them feel harmed or threatened, vulnerability is never a result of person or environment variables alone.

The above discussion also leads us toward the metatheoretical perspective of *process*, since transaction and process are in some respects interwoven. As we have said, process refers to two properties of encounters: (1) that psychological stress reactions and coping (including thoughts, feelings, and actions) are contextual, that is, they change from one type of encounter to another; and (2) that psychological stress and coping change as the encounter unfolds. Thus, when we noted above that even vulnerable people are not threatened under all conditions but only certain kinds, or that relatively invulnerable people will still experience threat under certain conditions, we were speaking of process as well as transaction. Similarly, during the course of a stressful encounter anger may give way to fear or relief, or a feeling of mastery or security may give way to threat, with its attendant emotional pattern.

What makes the awareness of process especially important in therapy is its relevance to the assessment of what has gone wrong in the person's life and the kinds of encounters and coping processes that must be examined. Therapy must be built around the client's particular areas of vulnerability and coping ineptitudes, as well as strengths. One of the great advantages of the clinical method is that it studies a single person carefully, and often longitudinally, reconstructing what has happened and is happening as the person struggles in situational contexts such as the marital relationship, difficulties with people at work, situations generating fear, anger, or helplessness, and those generating positive feelings and a sense of security and self-worth. Because therapists study the person's functioning and feelings over diverse contexts, they are less likely to mistake a single distressing experience for the warp and woof of the person's entire pattern of adaptation. Our own ipsative style of research, discussed in Chapter 10, is designed to do the same thing.

Considered in broad perspective, vulnerability is simultaneously an intraindividual and interindividual concept (cf. Epstein, 1983b). It is intraindividual when the focus is on the pattern of psychological stress *within* an individual, which means learning which situations generate stress and which do not. It is interindividual when the person is compared with other people. To compare people when they face overwhelming environmental pressures, however, is not productive, since most people will experience stress in those situations. The concept of vulnerability achieves special utility when a person's pattern of vulnerability is compared with others', and we can say that this person reacts with stress even in situations where others do not.

Cognitive Appraisal, Emotion, and Coping

The theoretical outlook presented in this book began as an attempt to understand psychological stress through an analysis of how people appraise the significance of encounters for their well-being (Lazarus, 1966). It also became a theory of *emotion*, a somewhat broader subject, because it seemed that emotions, like psychological stress, are products of how people interpret the changing, moment-to-moment fates of their most cherished values and commitments.

There is an implication in this way of thinking about emotion that applies particularly to therapy. If emotions are products of how we appraise what is happening, then by paying attention to a person's emotions and their flux, we also learn about that person's most important values, goals, and commitments and how he or she thinks these are faring. Thus, to paraphrase Freud's statement that dreams are the royal road to the unconscious, emotions can be said to be the royal road to understanding the person's most important agendas and how well the person believes these agendas are being realized in day-to-day living. When all is said and done, treatment always centers on the emotional life of the person, and so there must not only be a theory of change but a theory of emotion as the basis for therapy.

People do not generally seek help for single or occasional episodes of stress, even though an episode may produce distress and impaired functioning on those occasions. What motivates people to seek treatment is frequent overwhelming or disruptive stress that operates in an area that is central to the person. Although stress theory often focuses on single stressful encounters, as is also done in therapy when a client recounts a particular incident, the troubles that send the person into therapy usually represent a general and extended pattern of living rather than an adventitious happening.

Cognitive appraisal and coping are multifaceted processes, and they can go wrong in many different ways (see Chapter 7). The client may tend to appraise threat where it is inappropriate and so experience counterproductive emotions and engage in unsuitable coping activity, or there may be a failure to appraise threat when it is appropriate. In these instances, the defect centers on primary appraisal and its determinants. The problem can also inhere in secondary appraisal, as when a client appraises his or her coping resources unrealistically. For many clients the problem centers on coping, for example, being unable to relinquish problem-focused coping or being ineffective in emotion-focused coping such as gaining distance from a problem or seeking adequate emotional support.

One cannot frame a strategy of treatment or direct it properly without pinpointing, even if only tentatively, where the problem lies. This principle holds true even in strictly behavioral therapy. In Wolpe's (1978) systematic desensitization procedure, for example, the therapist must first learn what is phobic for the patient and what is not in order to create a hierarchy of stimuli from nonthreatening to extremely threatening. A person's thoughts, emotions, and actions are not disembodied entities that are easily changed by comforting words; they have an organic connection to everything in that person's life. Even therapists who emphasize the use of coping self-statements recognize this principle. Meichenbaum and Cameron (1983), for example, write:

> . . . it is important to understand that they [cognitive self-statements] are not offered as catch-phrases or as verbal palliatives to be repeated mindlessly. There is a difference between encouraging the use of a formula or psychological litany that tends to lead to rote repetition and emotionless patter *versus* problem-solving thinking that is the object of stress inoculation training. Formula-oriented thoughts that are excessively general tend to prove ineffective. (p. 141)

The task of understanding the client, and his or her appraisal and coping processes and their determinants, cannot be discarded in treatment without risk. In the same vein, information by itself is inadequate for regulating stress. Averill (1979), discussing research on this issue, identifies several kinds of information, including information about the potential harm in an encounter, physiological or emotional reactions about to be experienced or being experienced, overt or instrumental behavior that is called for or possible, and possible cognitive coping or emotion-focused coping. Averill gives attention to the use of these kinds of information in interventions and in the practical regulation of stress. Particularly interesting to us is the following comment:

> . . . a phobic may realize perfectly well that the object of his fear (e.g., a small spider, or open spaces) cannot cause any harm, yet he is still afraid; the person who knows that smoking is dangerous to his health, and who sincerely wants to stop smoking, may still continue to inhale carcinogenic agents; and the depressed individual may know that things are not all *that* bad, but still feel sad and helpless. Simply providing further information in such cases is likely to be of little value. It is not enough for the depressed, addicted, or phobic individual to "know" better, he must also "be" better; and being better may require the development of cognitive structures in which the desired attitudes and behavior become part of the individual's own self- and object-world. (p. 384)

Recognition that the entry point for cognitive therapy varies from person to person is evident in Wessler's (1982a, b) system of cognitive appraisal therapy, which is closely related to Ellis's (1962) rational-emotive therapy. Wessler proposes eight steps in any cognitive-emotive-behavioral episode, each of which can be the target of interventions: (1) the stimulus, internal or external, such as another person's action, a phobic object, or emotion; (2) the individual's selection of what to attend to, which sometimes reflects the operation of perceptual defense; (3) the perception and symbolic representation of the stimulus; (4) nonevaluative interpretations, which may involve forecasts and expectations about what will happen, attributions, and other cold cognitions; (5) evaluative interpretations (appraisals) of more fully processed information, in effect, potentially hot cognitions; (6) the emotional response to the processed information; (7) the behavioral response, for example, approach, avoidance, or attack behavior (as distinguished from tendencies to act that may be inhibited or controlled by decisional processes); and (8) cognitive feedback from the reaction and the reinforcing consequences of the patient's behavior.

Without quibbling about the strictly linear quality of these steps—for example, cold cognitions being followed by hot cognitions—this analysis is useful because it recognizes that one can intervene at any of the steps to change the process. Wessler (1982a) gives an analysis of public speaking anxiety to illustrate the use of the model. From the perspective of cognitive appraisal therapy, what is crucial is not the speech (step 1) or the person's knowledge that the speech will be given at a scheduled time (steps 2 and 3). Most likely the person will anticipate a poor performance or a poor audience reaction (step 4) and so the anticipated outcome will be appraised as very negative (step 5). The anxiety that flows from this appraisal (step 6) may be reduced, however, by procrastinating (step 7), which brings some immediate relief (step 8) but is a counterproductive (neurotic) choice from the standpoint of the goal of making the speech. The focus of CAT (cognitive appraisal therapy) is on steps 4 and 5, namely, to help the person make more favorable appraisals about performance, the audience reaction, or both, and to reappraise the outcome in more positive ways.

Beck (in press a, b) too seems to take a stepwise approach in encouraging change in the client, beginning with the application of his principles of faulty cognitive processes to understand the particular case. The client is encouraged to examine internal factors such as thoughts, impulses, and feelings in contrast to behavior; then encouragement is given to examine what is happening more objectively, almost as a disinterested observer might, to gain perspective by expanding the frame of reference by which the client judges events, himself or herself, and others, and to change the inappropriate cognitive set that has characterized previous stressful encounters, thereby forcing a change in relationships. These steps are designed to provide what the psychodynamic therapist has traditionally called insight, as well as the behavioral working through of the problem by having the client act out the insights in troubling encounters. Cognitive-behavior therapists such as Beck use the term *cognitive restructuring* instead of the psychoanalytic, past-oriented concept of insight, and they concentrate on what is happening now, along with emphasizing changes in behavior with the goal of altering the damaging pattern of person–environment relationships.

Primary appraisal processes, secondary appraisal, emotions, and coping are often intertwined and difficult to disentangle. Yet there is utility in making an assessment or diagnosis, so to speak, of how the variables of the cognitive-affective-coping system are working in the client's problematic and distressing experiences. The occurrence of strong emotions in the client offers important clues as to what is happening. When these clues indicate that actions run contrary to the stakes in an encounter or to the client's resources, or when feelings and actions are disjointed, we must look at the mix of cognitive appraisal and coping processes, and to their personal and situational causes, to understand what is happening and to design a suitable systematic program of intervention. What a cognitive theory of stress, emotion, and coping offers is a set of antecedent variables and processes along with some principles concerning their interplay. From these the therapist and client can extract the crucial understandings and behavioral antidotes.

The Problem of Motivation

The shift in psychological thought toward cognition has forced motivation, once a central theme in psychological theory, to take a back seat. Little is now being written about the role of motivation in treatment. Earlier accounts took the view, which is still relevant, that the most important decision of a patient precedes treatment, and that is to seek professional help. It has long been assumed that only a person willing to undergo the struggle to change will begin treatment and stay with it. From this standpoint, commitment, in the sense that a deliberate decision is made, grows out of the recognition that things are going badly and that treatment might help. The therapist attempts to generate and sustain motivation. Psychoanalysts point to the transference relationship, the reduction of distress (through catharsis or abreaction), and the patient's hope that things will improve by following the treatment regimen as motivating features of therapy.

For relatively minor problems such as smoking—minor not in the sense of health consequences but in how it is usually perceived—one gets the decided impression that self-initiated (i.e., self-motivated) quitting is statistically more common than quitting that is brought about in formal treatment (see Pechacek & Danaher, 1979). People who do a certain amount of externalizing of responsibility for the decision to quit may need a therapeutic regimen with its social support in order to sustain the struggle; these people may have a poorer prognosis than those who see clearly that successful quitting depends largely on their own level of commitment. Yet so far has the "cognitive revolution" gone that in Pechacek and Danaher's analysis of successful quitting, they never once mention motivation or commitment (see also Prochaska & DiClemente, 1983, for a similar pattern). Instead, many of the conclusions they draw about successful quitting suggest that feedback from quitting—that is, positive changes, increased self-efficacy, credibility of the treatment, and gaining new skills—helps sustain the person in the difficult task of self-control.

From this standpoint, Pechacek and Danaher's cognitively based conclusion that successful quitting is produced when "the treatment produces rapid enhancement of self-efficacy by performance accomplishments, vicarious learning, and/or by persuasive communications" (p. 411) seems wrong to us, at least for many clients. A sharp increase in self-efficacy could actually weaken commitment by producing a false sense of security about their ability to sustain the initial success (e.g., "I can handle a puff or two without having to smoke the whole pack").

Therapists cannot depend solely on the commitment the client brings to therapy. An initial commitment is apt to wax and wane during treatment. It is crucial at each stage for the client to *decide* to do what the therapist is asking in the therapy setting and to further decide to use what is learned outside that setting. It is motivation that leads to these decisions.

Stress Management Versus One-on-One Therapy

The problem with stress management programs is that, in contrast to most one-on-one clinical treatments, they are not tailored to the particular dynamics of the individual but are usually created for people in general. No attempt is made to pin down the special vulnerabilities and coping deficiencies that have gotten the individual into trouble (see, for example, Turk, Sobel, Follick, & Youkilis, 1980). These programs will be ineffective for people whose troubles stem from conflicts or personal agendas that lurk below the surface, because they leave the underlying difficulty untouched.

To appreciate this criticism one need only consider the well-documented principle that a particular approach will be effective only with certain kinds of people. People self-select with respect to the programs they try, sometimes after much trial and error. One of the tasks of research on interventions to help people manage stress, and of personality research in general, is to locate the personality characteristics that mediate the outcome. (For reviews see Cohen & Lazarus, 1979, 1983.)

In an attempt to bridge the gap between the ways social and clinical psychologists approach the issue of how to help people cope, Brickman and colleagues (1982) describe four different models of helping based on attributions of responsibility for creation of the problem and responsibility for a solution. The *moral model* holds that people are responsible for both creating their problems, and finding solutions; the *compensatory model* is that people are not responsible for their problems but are responsible for solutions; the *medical model* assumes that people are not responsible for either their problems or solutions; and the *enlightenment model* is that people are not responsible for solutions but are responsible for their problems. These models are held by care-givers as well as the recipients of help.

Brickman et al. go on to show that the particular pattern of attribution of responsibility affects the way help is given and received. The authors hypothesize, for example, that:

> . . . models in which people are held responsible for solutions (the compensatory and moral models) are more likely to increase people's competence than models in which they are not held responsible for solutions (the medical and enlightenment models). It may also be beneficial not to hold people responsible for problems, though the evidence for this is less clear. (p. 375)

This thesis is interesting and provocative; it is also transactional in that it takes into account the fit between the assumptions of client and therapist and considers the cognitive-behavioral consequences of those assumptions. To the extent that there is a mismatch between the client's model and the therapist's, general programs of stress management will fail until the underlying assumptions of both are clarified. The same principle, of course, applies in one-on-one therapy. In addition, Brickman et al. raise important questions about whether some models are uniformly better or better for different clients; whether care-givers lose their motivation more readily if they use some models rather than others; and the role of organizational structures and professional role socialization in the choice of model.

There are signs of restiveness with the proliferation of programs for stress management and social skills training that are directed to large segments of the population. Timnick (1982) has likened such programs to the Charles Atlas Dynamic Tension Body-building Program of a few generations ago that used the advertisement of a "97-pound weakling" who could stand up to a bully after he took the course and acquired a super-body. Timnick reviews a number of social skills training programs and raises the serious question of whether they accomplish all or even part of what they claim. She suggests that many are trivial and little more than "a pastiche of gimmicks and pat statements" (p. 49), with an underlying assumption that there is only one right, successful, or acceptable way of interacting with others:

> The proliferation of social-skills training projects and courses could make for a more civilized society in which more people actually connect. It could also lead to a world of robots—flashing smiles and wishing one another a nice day. It's too soon to tell. But regardless of the merits or shortcomings of the movement, it is growing. No one knows exactly how many psychologists are now teaching social skills or doing research in the area, but the American Psychological Association estimates there may be as many as several thousand. More will no doubt join them soon. (p. 49)

Providing Information and Skills Training

Group programs may be useful when coping failure is due to an uncomplicated lack of knowledge, skill, or experience; the therapeutic task is then appropriately defined as filling in these gaps. An excellent example is a book by Yates (1976) entitled *Coping: A Survival Manual for Women Alone*, in which women who have experienced marital separation, divorce, or widowhood or who are simply alone and feeling inadequate about managing their lives are encouraged to believe that they are capable of handling things. The manual provides useful information and advice on money, credit, traveling, car problems, and children in a single-parent family, as well as information about more diffuse issues such as sexuality and loneliness. Similarly, training in assertiveness is often viewed as providing skills that are needed in identifying and speaking up for one's rights.

More sophisticated approaches are appearing to the problem-solving skills involved in coping. D'Zurilla and Nezu (1982), for example, have developed a model called Social Problem Solving that is based on social learning theory and aimed at improving social competence. The authors consider five general, stage-related skills: (1) problem orientation or a problem-solving set; (2) problem definition and formulation; (3) generation of alternatives, including both strategy-level solutions and specific step-by-step means; (4) decision making; and (5) solution implementation and verification. Another version of social skills training for children has been offered by Ladd and Mize (1983). This type of model has value as a more detailed, in-depth examination of what is involved in problem solving, or, in our language, problem-focused coping. What is missing, however, are concerns with the emotional factors that may underlie maladaptation and impair rational problem-solving processes, as well as the regulation of the distressing emotions that arise when an encounter involves hot as opposed to cold cognitions. Social Problem Solving thus seems more oriented to the cold laboratory context than to the troubling and highly emotional experiences that bring people to treatment.

The intervention approach geared to providing information and skills training can also be illustrated with research on procedures for preparing for painful and distressing medical procedures. These programs operate on the implicit assumption that successful preparation involves little more than increasing knowledge about what is going to happen. Research on this type of intervention gained impetus from early work by Janis (1958) with patients facing surgery (see also Janis, 1967) and has been discussed in the context of behavioral medicine by Anderson and Masur (1983), Kendall et al. (1979), and Cohen and Lazarus (1979, 1983). There are many studies on this type of intervention. A now classic series of experiments by Leventhal and his colleagues (see review by Leventhal & Nerenz, 1983) offers a particularly representative illustration.

In one study, for example, Leventhal, Brown, Shacham, and Engquist (1979) compared the level of distress reported during a cold pressor test among subjects given three types of preparatory information. This study is interesting in that the authors were concerned with the mechanisms through which information influences appraisal. Subjects in this study were given three types of preparatory information: *sensation information*, which provides the individual with a set of objective features of the stimulus, namely, the tactile, thermal, and visual changes likely to be experienced during stressor impact; *arousal information*, which involves descriptions of emotional behaviors and the objective and subjective signs of arousal such as heart-beating, hand-sweating, tenseness, and so forth; *procedural information* describing experimental procedures; and *intensity information*, that is, warning of high pain or no pain. Subjects were placed in one of three groups: sensation, arousal, and procedural information. The last group served as a control. These groups were subdivided into high- and no-pain warning groups so that there were, in all, six conditions, three with pain warning and three without. Distress ratings were calculated over a six-minute period, the length of time the subject had a hand submerged in the cold pressor. In the pain-warning condition, sensory information significantly reduced distress during the final judgments (last four minutes of immersion) in relation to both procedural and arousal information, whereas arousal information had no substantial effect on distress reduction. When there was no warning of pain, there was an even more marked decline in distress for the sensory-information group. Overall, the results supported past findings (e.g., see Leventhal & Nerenz, 1983, for review) that indicate sensation information reduces distress during contact with a noxious stressor.

The authors suggest that different kinds of preparatory information alter the way the noxious stimuli information is processed to change the subject's experience of the stressor. Sensory information leads to an *objective*, nonaffective experience of the stimulus, whereas magnitude information of a pain warning leads to an *emotional* experience of the stimulus. Leventhal and his colleagues hypothesize that objective information is coded or categorized in terms of specific sensory features, such as coldness, numbness, pins and needles, and so forth, and emotional distress reactions habituate. Information that is emotionally processed, such as magnitude-of-pain information, on the other hand, is encoded or integrated in an emotional schema or pain memory (Leventhal & Everhart, 1979), and the stimulus and coding continue to stimulate distress.

Leventhal et al. (1979) raise an interesting alternative hypothesis, namely, that the reduced distress reaction was more a function of avoidance than of how the information was coded. They conducted two follow-up experiments and concluded that the mechanism underlying the reduction of emotional distress is the formation of a schema of the objective or informational features of the stimulus which facilitates the habituation process. They point to other studies that offer similar evidence. For example, Morgan and Pollock (1977) studied world-class runners. They found that elite runners carefully monitor leg and muscular sensations while performing (sensory features), whereas outstanding but nonelite runners distract from these sensations, which they regard as threat cues or signs of an anticipated wall or limit to their endurance. "Thus, monitoring per se is not the critical factor in the runner's control of distress; it is the schematization of cues that is central" (p. 710). Similarly, they note that in hospital settings, where there is a threatening situation making pain and emotional schematization highly likely, distress reduction is achieved by combinations of monitoring strategies (sensation information) and reassurance that the procedures will help (e.g., Johnson & Leventhal, 1974).

Most naturalistic investigations of the effects of information have been concerned primarily with the relationship between information and outcome in health settings. As we pointed out earlier, most such studies are concerned with intervention. After reviewing a number of such studies, Cohen and Lazarus (1979) identified four types of information frequently used:

> (1) information about the nature of the disease or about the medical reasons for initiating particular treatments; (2) information describing in detail the medical procedures to be carried out; (3) information about particular sensations or side effects to be expected; and (4) information about coping strategies the person can use in adjusting to the upcoming threat. (p. 247)

The results of these studies are unclear. Usually any information is given in the context of support, encouragement, attention, and often implicit challenge. Thus, it is difficult to determine whether informational or supportive elements are more important in aiding patients' adjustment. Furthermore, these studies are concerned with the effects of information on outcome and do not address questions concerning how various types of information differentially influence appraisal, nor the mechanisms through which such influence occurs.

When experiments that examine the mechanisms through which information affects stressful appraisals are carried out in natural settings, it is necessary to carefully distinguish among types of information, as, for example, was done in the Leventhal et al. study, and to separate the content of information from the context of support and encouragement in which it is offered, as Cohen and Lazarus (1979) point out.

For those persons who have responsibility for advising people of impending dangers of any sort, the question always arises as to how to represent the danger in a manner that will promote effective preparation and minimize the destructive or impeding aspects of threat. In general, it seems advantageous to create an atmosphere that is more challenging than threatening. The way such an atmosphere or appraisal is created differs from setting to setting, and from group to group. Anecdotal accounts from medical settings, natural disasters, and even educational settings, however, suggest that one strategy seems relatively universal—focusing on the possibilities of success rather than failure.

The effect of this strategy is evident in a series of experimental studies by Tversky and Kahneman (1981), who were able to reverse preferences dramatically in hypothetical decision problems by casting problems in terms of gains or losses. The effect is illustrated in the following problems. The percentage of respondents who chose each option is indicated in brackets.

> Problem 1: Imagine that the U.S. is preparing for the outbreak of an unusual Asian disease, which is expected to kill 600 people. Two alternative programs to combat the disease have been proposed. Assume that the exact scientific estimate of the consequences of the programs are as follows:
> If Program A is adopted, 200 people will be saved. [72%]
> If Program B is adopted, there is a 1/3 probability that 600 people will be saved, and 2/3 probability that no people will be saved. [28%] Which of the two programs would you favor? (p. 453)

A second group of respondents was given the same cover story with the alternative programs described as follows:

> If Program C is adopted 400 people will die. [22%]
> If Program D is adopted there is a 1/3 probability that nobody will die, and 2/3 probability that 600 people will die. [78%] (p. 453)

Tversky and Kahnemann demonstrate these reversals of preferences in a number of conditions. The effect appears robust. Success versus failure represents only one of several dimensions on which information can vary. As we noted at the outset of this section, information can also vary according to its specificity and it can vary according to its emphasis on sensation, arousal, or procedure (cf. Leventhal et al., 1979).

Finally, there is some evidence that a person factor, namely, defense style, interacts with type of information in affecting outcome in medical settings. A series of studies reported by Goldstein (1973) indicates that people who do not typically avoid information show better recovery if they receive specific information and worse recovery if they receive general information. "Avoiders," on the other hand, do better with general than specific information. The interaction between repression-sensitization and information has also been examined. There is some indication that sensitizers should be prepared extensively for medical procedures, but that repressors should be left alone (Shipley et al., 1978, 1979). However, Cohen and Lazarus (1973) found no interaction effect.

When Information and Skills Training Fail

The dominant form of help presently offered to those who face serious illness and loss is problem-focused, directly mainly at teaching ways to manage the side effects of chemotherapy, swallow a stomach tube, or relax during a sigmoidoscopy. These interventions are worthwhile, but they tend to ignore other kinds of existential distress that are part of the plight of people whose illnesses have profound implications for the quality of their lives and well-being. The lack of attention given to distress of this sort in interventions that are problem-focused is compounded by the societal and professional tendency to downplay negative and encourage positive thoughts and feelings. Lazarus (in press b) has referred to this as the trivialization of distress. It is as if the victims of tragedy are told that they have no right to feel bad about their plight; people who react with distress are described as having failed to cope adequately. In a sense, these people are victims, not only of illness, but also of the judgments of those who set themselves up as wanting to help.

Furthermore, skills training can also fail because of longstanding personal difficulties involving conflicts, hidden agendas, and fears originating early in life that have been continually reinforced and maintained by later patterns of living, or from pervasive beliefs in one's inadequacy. The presence of these complicating factors may, indeed, have obstructed the learning of necessary social and coping skills. The burden of intervention then shifts from simple training or education to a more traditional therapeutic goal, defined variously as deconditioning and relearning, changing unserviceable beliefs that underlie faulty coping, and/or acquiring new modes of understanding and coping.

Typically, then, what starts out to be a simple training or educational program emerges as an exploration of personal dynamics in order to gain and use the understanding about what went wrong. A study by McFall and Twentyman (1973) highlights the point that in assertiveness training the clients need to learn more than merely saying the right things to assert themselves. Clients often learn to behave more assertively, but without conveying any real sense of assertiveness; one can see through their words and acts to the non-assertiveness beneath.

Thus, we must be wary of the assumption that when coping has failed even in contexts in which something could have been done to improve the troubled person–environment relationship, all we need to do is to teach the necessary skills. Sometimes the very obstacle that has led to the coping deficiency in the first place will now obstruct the coping skills training. This is one of the reasons why dynamic therapists have long been dubious about the value of advice to the client when the problem is ringed with conflicts; advice under these circumstances is likely to be followed, if at all, with merely superficial compliance (cf. Kelman, 1961).

Many training programs, versions of which have been known as long as there have been people in trouble, appear thoughtful, sensible, even insightful, and appeal to whatever current formulation about the human condition is widely respected at a particular time. Cognitive behavior therapists are fond of citing the ancient Greek Stoic Epictetus, who, as we mentioned in Chapter 2, wrote that "Man is disturbed not by things but the views he takes of them." The solution to life stress and distress offered by the Stoics was to abjure all honors, rewards, and material possessions that generate the emotional attachments, both positive and negative, that create human misery, and learn to live in a calm and detached manner.

More modern versions of those ancient prescriptions are found in the doctrines "A sound mind in a sound body" and "The body is the temple of the soul" and foreshadowed programs that urge people to engage in exercise and diet programs and to avoid alcohol, drugs, and tobacco. The usual assumption is that if one feels well physically, the stresses of living and working will be less debilitating. Meditation, another ancient theme now often loosely translated into relaxation training, is commonly taught in programs whose goal is to lower tension and hence control stress.

Another tactic is to provide training in what we think and do when confronted with stressful encounters (e.g., Bramson, 1981; Burns, 1980). Because it is built on cognitive-behavior therapy reasoning and is the most ambitious and complex, this approach deserves special attention. Bramson offers programmatic advice for those who are having trouble handling difficult people, a common source of stress in the work setting. He suggests six general steps: assessing the situation; avoiding wishing (unrealistically) that such people would change or simply go away; distancing oneself from the troubling behavior in order to understand it and even empathize with it; formulating a coping strategy that could change the unproductive pattern of interaction; implementing the plan by first practicing how to act or role-playing with a friend and then choosing an appropriate time for confrontation; and monitoring what is done to assess why it might not be working and perhaps ultimately to evaluate the possibilities for avoiding that person.

Bramson also offers a catalogue of seven kinds of people whose behavior patterns are especially difficult to deal with: those who are indecisive, hostile-aggressive, negativistic, know-it-all, complaining, unresponsive, and overagreeable. For indecisive people, a suggested strategy is to help them express their concerns or conflicts, to provide them with support, and to limit the alternatives offered to them; for hostile-aggressive persons the suggestion is to stand up to them without fighting, and to expect to feel anger but not allow it to get out of control; for know-it-alls the advice is to make factual rather than dogmatic statements, and even to accept a subordinate role to accomplish what needs to be done.

The doctrine in Burns's (1980) book *Feeling Good*, which is based on Beck's (1976) work with depression, begins with a simple theoretical analysis followed by inspirational enjoinders to build self-esteem. It offers self-statements to practice in a variety of emotional encounters that generate anger or depression, and an analysis of the faulty premises which guide the person's thoughts and actions, such as an addiction to be approved, to be loved, to be perfect, and to deprecate one's work or performance. The basic effort is directed at substituting rational premises for the faulty ones that provoke emotional distress.

Some programs combine several of the tactics identified above. For example, sources of psychological stress and coping deficiencies are addressed with positive self-statements and new behaviors, and simultaneously the person is instructed to engage in systematic relaxation, meditation, and/or physical fitness through exercise and diet. A program offered by Smith (Smith & Ascough, in press), referred to as cognitive-affective stress management training, illustrates this eclectic type of approach. It begins with a group lecture-discussion about stress from a cognitive-behavioral perspective, recommends sensible eating and exercise, and provides training in meditation and relaxation. One aim is to sensitize participants to stress-inducing beliefs and self-statements and to replace them with positive ones, thus following somewhat the line of thought described by Meichenbaum (1977) and others. At each group session, participants are encouraged to talk about how things are going and how they are managing in relaxation and in the control of stress. They are encouraged to keep a log about their progress, which is a procedure used in many programs. As the program proceeds, participants are sensitized to the tendency to evade stressful confrontations and encouraged to experiment with the desensitization of anxiety, anger, or fear through properly regulated confrontations in which actions that have been previously avoided are tried out. It is quite possible that one of the most constructive features of such a program is the sensitization of its participants to the sources of stress in their lives and to the counterproductive things they do when confronted with stress. To succeed, however, the process must go beyond mere sensitization to the acquisition of new ways of functioning that can be used when needed and sustained over time.

These group programs constitute a movement away from those devised for people in general and toward more personalized intervention. A kind of group therapy situation allows participants to talk about what is happening, to hear reaction from others including the leader, and to apply the techniques to their individual problems. Programs that involve people who share a common source of stress, as, for example, Novaco's (1979) stress inoculation training for anger control among police officers, go even further toward an individualized approach.

The analysis in generalized formal programs such as those of Bramson (1981) and Burns (1980) are impressive, and we have little doubt that if the programs were practiced as proposed, they could be useful. Norman Vincent Peale's conviction about the power of positive thinking or the Stoics' about detachment from passions also offer meaningful if perhaps limited solutions to life's problems. Unfortunately, those people who have the most to gain from these precepts are commonly blocked from following them because of other agendas and vulnerabilities.

We have little doubt too that physical conditioning, relaxation, and meditation can have favorable effects on people (e.g., Benson, 1976; Blumenthal, Williams, Needels, & Wallace, 1982; Boswell & Murray, 1979; Carrington, 1977; Davidson, Goleman, & Schwartz, 1976; DeGood & Redgate, 1982; Goldman, Domitor, & Murray, 1979; Goleman & Schwartz, 1976; Lyles, Burish, Korzely, & Oldham, 1982; Sinyor, Schwartz, Peronnet, Brisson, & Seraganian, 1983). It is a sound premise that we are helped to cope with difficulties by feeling physically well, and that feeling well is facilitated by exercise, diet, and other good health habits. Similarly, being able to relax and shift attention away from one's troubles offers a potential advantage in daily living. On the other hand, Heide and Borkovec (1983) have shown that for some clients relaxation procedures can increase rather than reduce anxiety, pointing again to ubiquitous individual differences. The bottom line of stress management, however, is that these programs must stimulate new ways of appraising the conditions that produce distress and of coping with them in ways that are more effective. Anything that sets such processes in motion could be helpful in principle, but it will succeed only if the cognitive and behavioral work necessary for change takes place.

The Outlook for Stress Management Programs

It is premature to come to any conclusion about generalized, formal programs of stress management and their less generalized, quasi-group therapy versions. What is presently most disconcerting is the tendency of their proponents to overstate the help they can give, and the lack of concern with evaluating their consequences. The current atmosphere of interest and need, and the enthusiasm with which new programs are developed, do not seem conducive to proper evaluation. The fact that there is a widespread consensus about need obscures whether such programs add much to the inspirational approaches and philosophies of living that have characterized past eras. Psychologists have long known that personal validation of their results is notoriously unreliable because of the ubiquitous placebo effect; if people believe something will help, they commonly find it helpful, at least for a time. Evaluation of one-on-one therapies is difficult because of the multiple factors that must be considered, such as the type of presenting problem, the type of person, the type of therapist, and the therapist's approach. Anyone who claims to have found a panacea for human distress, whether cast in the language of stress management or as a philosophy of life, fails to recognize the long history of attempts to do this and fails to take into account individual differences and the actual life circumstances of people in trouble.

A review of four major books on stress management by Roskies (1983) nicely and somewhat sardonically addresses some of the doubts we have been describing above. Roskies writes:

> In recent years our traditional understanding of the causes of disease has been transformed by a powerful new concept: stress. From its humble origins as a laboratory term in the 1950's, stress has now become a shorthand symbol for explaining much of what ails us in the contemporary world, invoked to explain conditions as diverse as nail biting, smoking, homicide, suicide, cancer, and heart disease. From an anthropological perspective, stress serves the same purpose in modern society as ghosts and evil spirits did in former times, making sense of various misfortunates and illnesses that otherwise might remain simply random games of chance. . . .
>
> It would be un-American to accept a new cause for disease without seeking to cure or control it. Thus, it is not surprising that the ranks of self-help manuals have recently been joined by books devoted to teaching us how to manage stress. Among the array of do-it-yourself guides to increasing sexual pleasure, building the body beautiful, and unlocking hidden mental and emotional capacities is a new crop of manuals devoted to taming the killer stress. The stress management guides under review here have all been published within the past year or so, and although the sales pitch varies from threats of dropping dead to promises of maximum well-being, all are dedicated to the premise that the individual can avert or diminish the potential harm of stress by using new, improved coping strategies.
>
> Unfortunately, these stress management guides share one other important characteristic: Judged by the criteria established by *Contemporary Psychology* to evaluate self-help books . . . , all are woefully inadequate. Explanations of why and how stress is harmful are simplistic and often inaccurate. Techniques for self-diagnosis are vague, inappropriate, and in some cases may even be harmful to individuals who should probably seek other types of help. Claims for the efficacy of the proposed "cures" are exaggerated and supported mainly by anecdotes and irrelevant statistics. Finally, even though all these manuals are clearly labeled as do-it-yourself treatment programs, not one has been tested in this format. (p. 542)

Our own bias is that stress management programs represent a current fad that will, in all likelihood, be replaced by new fads and ways of thinking. There can never be a simple procedure for generating the cognitive, behavioral, and emotional processes that can propel the person toward better morale, social and work function-ing, and physical health. Nothing we say, however, is likely to convince professional workers and faddists alike to stop searching for intervention procedures that will work for all or most people or to stop swearing by one or another procedure. With luck, we will learn something important and useful about what goes wrong—and what goes right—in human adaptation.

Summary

In this chapter we employed our theoretical formulation to examine one-on-one therapies and stress management programs. One-on-one approaches to treatment can be broadly classified as biological or physiological; dynamic, which originated in Freudian psycho-analysis; behavioral, which emphasizes some form of conditioning or deconditioning process; and cognitive-behavioral, which empha-sizes cognitive processes and their role in shaping emotions and behavior. The cognitive-behavioral formulations, such as those of Ellis (1962, 1975), Beck (1976), Goldfried (1980), and Meichenbaum (1977; Meichenbaum & Jaremko, 1983), seem to be highly compatible with our cognitive theory of stress and coping.

Treatment can bring about change in four somewhat oversimpli-fied ways: feelings can shape thought and action; actions can shape thought and feeling; and thoughts can shape feeling and action. Feelings, thoughts, and actions are interdependent: if thought is changed, feelings and actions will probably change too. Similarly, if actions change, thoughts and feelings will too. Therefore, it is an empirical question which strategy works best, and in all likelihood multiple strategies increase the odds of producing the necessary changes for better functioning. One way or another, however, if there is to be therapeutic change, there must be changes in cognitive appraisal and coping.

Applying our theoretical approach to intervention means that a given problem of adaptation must be viewed transactionally; it must be seen as a product of the interplay between the person and his or her environment. For example, rather than being solely a person problem, vulnerability arises from being in certain environmental contexts that interact with relevant person factors. Interventions must also be process-oriented; what has happened and is happening for the person must be studied across diverse incidents and/or contexts.

Emotions reveal the person's most important agendas and how

well the person thinks he or she is faring in relation to these agendas; they can help pinpoint what is taking place that is creating malfunctioning or distress. The person may tend to appraise threat inappropriately or not appraise threat when it is appropriate, or the deficit may have to do primarily with coping. The entry point (feelings, thought, action) and the target of therapy (appraisal, coping) will vary from person to person. Whether or not the person enters therapy and stays with it will depend on his or her motivation.

Stress management programs, in contrast to one-on-one therapies, are usually created for people in general. Although these programs may be helpful, their effectiveness is limited for people whose troubles stem from individual conflicts or personal agendas that these programs do not address. Problem-focused stress management programs are also inadequate for people who suffer distress because of existential concerns that may be realistically related to their troubles. For example, providing information to people facing difficult medical procedures will not help them with their concerns about the implications of their illness for their well-being. Some group programs provide more personalized intervention and attempt to address individual concerns. To be effective, any stress management program must stimulate the person to appraise situations and/or cope with their demands in new ways. Until reliable evaluation studies become available, it is difficult to know which stress management programs, if any, succeed in these goals.

The task of dealing effectively with stress-related human misery and malfunction remains one of the main incentives for continuing research and thought about stress, appraisal, and coping.

References

Abramson, L., Garber, G., & Seligman, M. E. P. (1980). Learned helplessness in humans: An attributional analysis. In J. Garber & M. E. P. Seligman (Eds.), *Human helplessness: Theory and applications*. New York: Academic Press.

Abramson, L. Y., Seligman, M. E. P., & Teasdale, J. P. (1978). Learned helplessness in humans: Critique and reformulation. *Journal of Abnormal Psychology, 87*, 49–74.

Ader, R. (1980). Psychosomatic and psychoimmunological research. Presidential Address. *Psychosomatic Medicine, 42*, 307–321.

Ader, R. (1981). Animal models in the study of brain, behavior and bodily disease. In H. Weiner, M. A. Hofer, & A. J. Stunkard (Eds.), *Brain, behavior, and bodily disease*. New York: Raven.

Adler, A. (1930). Individual psychology. In C. Murchison (Ed.), *Psychologies of 1930*. Worcester, MA: Clark University Press.

Ainsworth, M., Salter, D., & Wittig, B. A. (1967). Attachment and exploratory behavior of one-year-olds in a strange situation. In B. M. Foss (Ed.), *Determinants of infant behavior* (Vol. 4). London: Wiley.

Ainsworth, M., & Wittig, B. A. (1970). Attachment and exploratory behavior of one-year-olds in a strange situation. *Child Development, 41*, 49–67.

Albee, G. W. (1980). A competency model must replace the defect model. In L. A. Bond & J. C. Rosen (Eds.), *Competency and coping during adulthood*. Hanover, NH: University Press of New England.

Albee, G. W., & Joffe, J. M. (Eds.). (1977). *Primary prevention of psychopathology. Vol. 1: The issues*. Hanover, NH: University Press of New England.

Aldrich, C. K., & Mendkoff, E. (1963). Relocation of the aged and disabled: A mortality study. In B. L. Neugarten (Ed.), *Middle age and aging: A reader in social psychology*. Chicago: University of Chicago Press.

Aldwin, C., Folkman, S., Schaefer, C., Coyne, J. C., & Lazarus, R. S. (1980, September). *Ways of coping: A process measure*. Paper presented at meetings of American Psychological Association, Montreal.

Alexander, B. K., & Hadaway, P. F. (1982). Opiate addiction: An adaptive orientation. *Psychological Bulletin, 92,* 367–381.

Alexander, F. (1950). *Psychosomatic medicine.* New York: Norton.

Alexander, F., French, T., & Pollack, G. H. (1968). *Psychosomatic medicine.* Chicago: University of Chicago Press.

Allen, B. P., & Potkay, C. R. (1981). On the arbitrary distinction between states and traits. *Journal of Personality and Social Psychology, 41,* 916–928.

Allport, F. H. (1955). *Theories of perception and the concept of structure.* New York: Wiley.

Allport, G. W. (1962). The general and the unique in psychological science. *Journal of Personality, 30,* 405–422.

Altman, I. (1976). Environmental psychology and social psychology. *Personality and Social Psychology Bulletin, 2,* 96–113.

Altman, I., & Wohlwill, J. G. (Eds.). (1977). *Human behavior and environment: Advances in theory and research.* New York: Plenum.

Anchor, K. N., Beck, S. E., Sieveking, N., & Adkins, J. (1982). A history of clinical biofeedback. *American Journal of Clinical Biofeedback, 5,* 3–16.

Anderson, C. R. (1977). Locus of control, coping behaviors, and performance in a stress setting: A longitudinal study. *Journal of Applied Psychology, 62,* 446–451.

Anderson, K. O., & Masur, F. T., III. (1983). Psychological preparation for invasive medical and dental procedures. *Journal of Behavioral Medicine, 6,* 1–40.

Anderson, M. P. (1980). Imaginal processes: Therapeutic applications and theoretical models. In M. J. Mahoney (Ed.), *Psychotherapy process: Current issues and future directions.* New York: Plenum.

Andrasik, F., & Holroyd, K. A. (1980). A test of specific and nonspecific effects in the biofeedback treatment of tension headache. *Journal of Consulting and Clinical Psychology, 48,* 575–586.

Andreasen, N. J. C., Noyes, R., Jr., & Hartford, C. E. (1972). Factors influencing adjustment of burn patients during hospitalization. *Psychosomatic Medicine, 34,* 517–525.

Andrew, J. M. (1970). Recovery from surgery with and without preparatory instruction for three coping styles. *Journal of Personality and Social Psychology, 151,* 223–226.

Andrews, G., Tennant, C., Hewson, D., & Schonell, M. (1978). The relation of social factors to physical and psychiatric illness. *American Journal of Epidemilogy, 108,* 27–35.

Aneshensel, C. S., & Huba, G. J. (1983). Depression, alcohol use, and smoking over one year: A four-wave longitudinal causal model. *Journal of Abnormal Psychology, 92,* 134–150.

Aneshensel, C. S., & Stone, J. D. (1982). Stress and depression. *Archives of General Psychiatry, 3,* 1392–1396.

Ansbacher, H. L., & Ansbacher, R. R. (Eds). (1956). *The individual psychology of Alfred Adler.* New York: Basic Books.

Antonovsky, A. (1972). Breakdown: A needed fourth step in the conceptual armamentarium of modern medicine. *Social Science and Medicine, 6,* 537–544.

Antonovsky, A. (1979). *Health, Stress and coping.* San Francisco: Jossey-Bass.

Appley, M. H., & Trumbull, R. (1967). *Psychological stress: Issues in research. New York: Appleton-Century-Crofts.*

Archer, R. P. (1979). Relationships between locus of control, trait anxiety, and state anxiety: An interactionist perspective. *Journal of Personality, 47,* 305–316.

Aries, P. (1962). *Centuries of childhood: A social history of family life.* (trans. from the French by R. Baldich.). New York: Vintage.

Arnheim, R. (1958). Emotion and feeling in psychology and art. *Confinia Psychiatrica, 1,* 69–88.

Arnold, M. B. (1960). *Emotion and Personality* (2 vols.). New York: Colombia University Press.

Arnold, M. B. (Ed.). (1970). *Feelings and emotion.* New York: Academic Press.

Asch, S. E. (1952). *Social psychology.* Englewood Cliffs, NJ: Prentice-Hall.

Atkinson, J. W. (1964). *An introduction to motivation.* Princeton, NJ: Van Nostrand.

Atkinson, J. W., & Birch, D. (1978). *Introduction to motivation* (2nd ed.). New York: Van Nostrand.

Auerbach, S. M. (1973). Trait-state anxiety and adjustment to surgery. *Journal of Consulting and Clinical Psychology, 40,* 264–271.

Austin, S. H. (1975). Coping and psychological stress in pregnancy, labor and delivery with "natural childbirth" and "medicated patients." *Dissertation Abstracts International, 35*(11), 5631-B.

Averill, J. R. (1968). Grief: Its nature and significance. *Psychological Bulletin, 70,* 721–748.

Averill, J. R. (1973). Personal control over aversive stimuli and its relationship to stress. *Psychological Bulletin, 80,* 286–303.

Averill, J. R. (1974). An analysis of psychophysiological symbolism and its influence on theories of emotion. *Journal for the Theory of Social Behavior, 4,* 147–190.

Averill, J. R. (1975). A semantic atlas of emotional concepts. *JSAS Catalogue of Selected Documents in Psychology, 5,* 330 (Ms. No. 421).

Averill, J. R. (1979). A selective review of cognitive and behavioral factors involved in the regulation of stress. In R. A. Depue (Ed.), *The psychobiology of the depressive disorders: Implications for the effects of stress.* New York: Academic Press.

Averill, J. R. (1982). *Anger and aggression: An essay on emotion.* New York: Springer-Verlag.

Averill, J. R., O'Brien, L., & DeWitt, G. W. (1977). The influence of response effectiveness on the preference for warning and on psychophysiological stress reactions. *Journal of Personality, 45,* 395–418.

Averill, J. R., Olbrich, E., & Lazarus, R. S. (1972). Personality correlates of differential responsiveness to direct and vicarious threat. *Journal of Personality and Social Psychology, 21,* 25–29.

Averill, J. R., & Opton, E. M., Jr. (1968). Psychophysiological assessment: Rationale and problems. In P. McReynolds (Ed.), *Advances in psychological assessment* (Vol. 1). Palo Alto, CA: Science and Behavior Books.

Badia, P., & Culbertson, S. (1970). Behavioral effects of signalled vs. unsignalled shock during escape training in the rat. *Journal of Comparative and Physiological Psychology, 72*(216).

Badia, P., Culbertson, S., & Harsh, J. (1973). Choice of longer or stronger signalled shock over shorter or weaker unsignalled shock. *Journal of Experimental Animal Behavior, 19*(25).

Badia, P., Harsh, J., & Abbott, B. (1979). Choosing between predictable and unpredictable shock conditions: Data and theory. *Psychological Bulletin, 86,* 1107–1131.

Badia, P., McBane, B., Suter, S., & Lewis, P. (1966). Preference behavior in an immediate versus variably delayed shock situation with and without warning signal. *Journal of Experimental Psychology, 72,* 847–852.

Badia, P., Suter, S., & Lewis, P. (1967). Preference for warned shock: Information and/or preparation, *Psychological Reports, 1967, 20,* 271–274.

Bakan, D. (1968). *Disease, pain and sacrifice: Toward a psychology of suffering.* Chicago: University of Chicago Press.

Baker, G. W., & Chapman, D. W. (Eds.). (1962). *Man and society in disaster.* New York: Basic Books.

Bandura, A. (1969). *Principles of behavior modification.* New York: Holt, Rinehart & Winston.

Bandura, A. (1971). Psychotherapy based upon modeling principles. In A. Bergin & S. Garfield (Eds.), *Handbook of psychotherapy and behavior change.* (New York: Wiley.

Bandura, A. (1977a). Self-efficacy: Toward a unifying theory of behavioral change. *Psychological Review, 84,* 191–215.

Bandura, A. (1977b). *Social learning theory.* Englewood Cliffs, NJ: Prentice-Hall.

Bandura, A. (1978). The self-system in reciprocal determinism. *American Psychologist, 33,* 344–358.

Bandura, A. (1981). Self-referent thought: A developmental analysis of self-efficacy. In J. H. Flavell & L. D. Ross (Eds.), *Cognitive social development: Frontiers and possible futures.* New York: Cambridge University Press.

Bandura, A. (1982). Self-efficacy mechanism in human agency. *American Psychologist, 37,* 122–147.

Bandura, A., & Adams, N. E. (1977). Analysis of self-efficacy theory of behavioral change. *Cognitive Therapy and Research, 1,* 287–310.

Bandura, A., Adams, N. E., & Byer, J. (1977). Cognitive processes mediating behavioral change. *Journal of Personality and Social Psychology, 35,* 125–139.

Bandura, A., Adams, N. E., Hardy, A. B., & Howells, G. N. (1980). Tests of the generality of self-efficacy theory. *Cognitive Therapy and Research, 4,* 39–66.

Bandura, A., Ross, D., & Ross, S. A. (1963). A comparative test of the status envy, social power, and the secondary reinforcement theories of indentification learning. *Journal of Abnormal and Social Psychology, 67,* 527–534.

Barber, T. X., & Coules, J. (1959). Electrical skin conductance and galvanic skin response during hypnosis. *International Journal of Experimental Hypnosis, 7,* 79–92.

Barefoot, J. C., Dahlstrom, W. G., & Williams, R. B. (1983). Hostility, CHD incidence, and total mortality: A 25-year follow-up study of 255 physicians. *Psychosomatic Medicine, 45,* 59–63.

Barker, R. G., Dembo, T., & Lewin, K. (1941). Frustration and regression: A study of young children. *University of Iowa Studies in Child Welfare, 18*(1).

Barnes, J. A. (1972). *Social networks.* New York: Addison-Wesley Reprints.

Barrabee, P., Barrabee, E. L., & Finesinger, J. E. (1955). A normative social adjustment scale. *American Journal of Psychiatry, 112,* 252–259.

Basowitz, H., Persky, H., Korchin, S. J., & Grinker, R. R. (1955). *Anxiety and stress.* New York: McGraw-Hill.

Bateson, G., Jackson, D. D., Haley, J., & Weakland, J. (1956). Toward a theory of schizophrenia. *Behavioral Science, 1,* 251–264.

Baum, A., Singer, J. E., & Baum, C. S. (1981). Stress and the environment. *Journal of Social Issues, 37,* 4–35.

Baumrind, D. (1975). Early socialization and the discipline controversy. In *University programs modular studies.* Morristown, NJ: General Learning Press.

Baumrind, D. (1978). A dialectic materialist's perspective on knowing social reality. *New Directions for Child Development, 2,* 61–82.

Bayer, L. M., Whissel-Buechy, D., & Honzik, M. P. (1980). Adolescent health and personality. *Journal of Adolescent Health Care, 1,* 101–107.

Bean, G., Cooper, S., Alpert, R., & Kipnis, D. (1980). Coping mechanisms of cancer patients: A study of 33 patients receiving chemotherapy. *Cancer Journal for Clinicians, 30,* 257–259.

Beck, A. T. (1967). *Depression: Clinical, experimental and theoretical aspects.* New York: Harper & Row.

Beck, A. T. (1971). Cognition, affect, and psychopathology. *Archives of General Psychiatry, 24,* 495–500.

Beck, A. T. (1976). *Cognitive therapy and the emotional disorders.* New York: International Universities Press.

Beck, A. T. (in press–a). Cognitive approaches to stress. In C. Lehrer & R. L. Woolfolk (Eds.), *Clinical guide to stress management.* New York: Guilford.

Beck, A. T. (in press–b). Cognitive therapy of depression: New perspectives. In P. Clayton (Ed.), *Depression.* New York: Raven.

Beisser, A. R. (1979). Denial and affirmation in illness and health. *American Journal of Psychiatry, 136,* 1026–1030.

Bell, D. (1962). *The end of ideology.* New York: Pantheon.

Belloc, N. G. (1973). Relationship of health practices and mortality. *Preventive Medicine, 2,* 67–81.

Belloc, N. B., & Breslow, L. (1972). Relationship of physical health status and health practices. *Preventive Medicine, 1,* 409–421.

Belloc, N. B., Breslow, N., & Hochstim, J. (1971). Measurement of physical health in a general population survey. *American Journal of Epidemiology, 93,* 328–336.

Bem, D. J. (1970). *Beliefs, attitudes and human affairs.* Belmont, CA: Brooks/Cole.

Bem, D. J. (1972). Self-perception theory. In L. Berkowitz (Ed.), *Advances in experimental social psychology* (Vol. 6). New York: Academic Press.

Bem, D. J., & Funder, D. C. (1978). Predicting more of the people more of the time: Assessing the personality of situations. *Psychological Review, 85,* 485–509.

Benesh, M., & Weiner, B. (1982). On emotion and motivation: From the notebooks of Fritz Heider. *American Psychologist, 37,* 887–895.

Benner, P. (1982). *A phenomenological study of mid-career men: Relationships between work meaning, work involvement, and stress and coping at work.* Unpublished doctoral dissertation, University of California, Berkeley.

Benner, P., Roskies, E., & Lazarus, R. S. (1980). Stress and coping under extreme conditions. In J. E. Dimsdale (Ed.), *Survivors victims, and perpetrators: Essays on the Nazi Holocaust.* Washington, DC: Hemisphere.

Bennett, D. H., & Holmes, D. S. (1975). Influence of denial (situational redefinition) and projection on anxiety associated with threat to self-esteem. *Journal of Personality and Social Psychology, 32,* 915–921.

Benson, H. (1976). *The relaxation response.* New York: Avon.

Berger, P. L., & Luckmann, T. (1966). *The social construction of reality.* New York: Doubleday.

Bergin, A. E., & Strupp, H. H. (1972). *Changing frontiers in the science of psychotherapy.* Chicago: Aldine-Atherton.

Bergman, L. R., & Magnusson, D. (1979). Overachievement and catecholamine excretion in an achievement-demanding situation. *Psychosomatic Medicine, 41,* 181–188.

Berkman, L., & Syme, S. L. (1979). Social networks, host resistance, and mortality: A nine-year follow-up study of Alameda County residents. *American Journal of Epidemiology, 109,* 186–204.

Berlyne, D. E. (1960). *Conflict, arousal and curiosity.* New York: McGraw-Hill.

Bettelheim, B. (1960). *The informed heart.* New York: The Free Press.

Bibring, E. (1953). The mechanism of depression. In P. Greenacre (Ed.), *Affective disorders.* New York: International Universities Press.

Biderman, A. D., & Zimmer, H. (Eds.). (1961). *The manipulation of human behavior.* New York: Wiley.

Billing, E., Lindell, B., Sederholm, M., & Theorell, T. (1980). Denial, anxiety and depression following myocardial infarction. *Psychosomatics, 21,* 639–645.

Billings, A. G., & Moos, R. H. (1982). Stressful life events and symptoms: A longitudinal model. *Health Psychology, 1,* 99–118.

Blau, Z. S. (1973). *Old age in a changing society.* New York: Franklin Watts.

Block, J. (1957). Studies in the phenomenology of emotions. *Journal of Abnormal and Social Psychology, 54,* 358–363.

Block, J. (1982). Assimilation, accommodation, and the dynamics of personality development. *Child Development, 53,* 281–295.

Block, J. H., & Block, J. (1980). The role of ego-control and ego-resiliency in the organization of behavior. In W. A. Collins (Ed.), *Development of Cognition, affect, and social relations. The Minnesota Symposia on Child Psychology* (Vol. 13). Hillsdale, NJ: Erlbaum.

Bloom, J. R. (1978, October). *Social support, coping and adjustment to mastectomy.* Paper presented at the International Congress on Cancer, Buenos Aires, Argentina.

Bloom, L. J., Houston, B. K., Holmes, D. S., & Burish, T. G. (1977). The effectiveness of attentional diversion and situational redefinition for reducing stress due to a nonambiguous threat. *Journal of Research in Personality, 11,* 83–94.

Blumberg, S. R.; & Hokanson, J. E. (1983). The effects of another person's response style on interpersonal behavior in depression. *Journal of Abnormal Psychology, 92,* 196–209.

Blumenthal, J. A., Williams, R. S., Needels, T. L., & Wallace, A. G. (1982). Psychological changes accompany aerobic exercize in healthy middle-aged adults. *Psychosomatic Medicine, 44,* 529–536.

Bolles, R. C. (1974). Cognition and motivation: Some historical trends. In B. Weiner (Ed.), *Cognitive views of human motivation.* New York: Academic Press.

Bond, L. A., & Rosen, J. C. (Eds.). (1980). *Competence and coping during adulthood.* Hanover, NH: University Press of New England.

Boswell, P. C., & Murray, E. J. (1979). Effects of meditation on psychological and physiological measures of anxiety. *Journal of Consulting and Clinical Psychology, 47,* 606–607.

Bourne, P. G. (Ed.). (1969). *The psychology and physiology of stress: With reference to special studies of the Vietnam war.* New York: Academic Press.

Bourque, L. B., & Back, K. W. (1977). Life graphs and life events. *Journal of Gerontology, 32,* 669–674.

Bowers, K. (1973). Situationism in psychology: An analysis and critique. *Psychological Review, 80,* 307–336.

Bowlby, J. (1961). Processes of mourning. *International Journal of Psychoanalysis, 42,* 317–340.

Bowlby, J. (1969). *Attachment and loss: Attachment* (Vol. 1). New York: Basic Books.

Bowlby, J. (1973). *Attachment and loss* (Vols. 1 & 2). New York: Basic Books.

Bowlby, J. (1980). *Attachment and loss: Loss, sadness and depression* (Vol. 3). New York: Basic Books.

Bradburn, N. (1969). *The structure of well-being.* Chicago: Aldine.

Bramson, R. M. (1981). *Coping with difficult people.* New York: Doubleday.

Braucht, G. N. (1979). Interactional analysis of suicidal behavior. *Journal of Consulting and Clinical Psychology, 47,* 653–669.

Brehm, J. W. (1966). *A theory of psychological reactance.* New York: Academic Press.

Breznitz, S. (1967). Incubation of threat: Duration of anticipation and false alarm as determinants of the fear reaction to an unavoidable frightening event. *Journal of Experimental Research in Personality, 2,* 173–179.

Breznitz, S. (1971). A study of worrying. *British Journal of Social and Clinical Psychology, 10,* 271–279.

Breznitz, S. (1976). False alarms: Their effects on fear and adjustment. In I. G. Sarason & C. D. Spielberger (Eds.), *Stress and anxiety* (Vol. 3). New York: Halsted.

Breznitz, S. (1983a). The seven kinds of denial. In S. Breznitz (Ed.), *The denial of stress.* New York: International Universities Press.

Breznitz, S. (Ed.). (1983b). *The denial of stress.* New York: International Universities Press.

Brickman, P., Rabinowitz, V. C., Karuza, J., Jr., Coates, D., Cohen, E., & Kidder, L. (1982). Models of helping and coping. *American Psychologist, 37,* 368–384.

Brim, O. G., Jr., & Ryff, C. D. (1980). On the properties of life events. In P. B. Baltes & O. G. Brim (Eds.), *Life-span development and behavior* (Vol. 3). New York: Academic Press.

Broverman, D. M. (1962). Normative and ipsative measurement in psychology. *Psychological Review, 4,* 295–305.

Brown, G. W., Bhrolchain, M. N., & Harris, T. (1975). Social class and psychiatric disturbance among women in an urban population. *Sociology, 9,* 225–254.

Brown, G. W., & Harris, T. (1978). *Social origins of depression: A study of psychiatric disorder in women.* New York: The Free Press.

Brown, J., & Farber, I. E. (1951). Emotions conceptualized as intervening variables—with suggestions toward a theory of frustration. *Psychological Bulletin, 48,* 465–495.

Bryant, F. B., & Veroff, J. (1982). The structure of psychological well-being: A sociohistorical analysis. *Journal of Personality and Social Psychology, 43,* 653–673.

Buchwald, A. M., Coyne, J. C., & Cole, C. S. (1978). A critical evaluation of the learned helplessness model of depression. *Journal of Abnormal Psychology, 87,* 180–193.

Bulman, R. J., & Wortman, C. B. (1977). Attributions of blame and coping in the "Real World": Severe accident victims react to their lot. *Journal of Personality and Social Psychology, 35,* 351–363.

Burke, R. J., & Weir, T. (1979). Patterns in husbands' and wives' coping behavior. *Psychological Reports, 44,* 951–956.

Burns, D. D. (1980). *Feeling good.* New York: William Morrow.

Byrne, D. (1964). Repression-sensitization as a dimension of personality. In B. A. Maher (Ed.), *Progress in experimental personality research* (Vol. 1). New York: Academic Press.

Caine, L. D. (1964). Life course and social structure. In R. E. L. Faris (Ed.), *Handbook of modern sociology.* Chicago: Rand McNally.

Campbell, A. (1976). Subjective measures of well-being. *American Psychologist, 31,* 117–124.

Campbell, A., Converse, P. E., & Rodgers, W. L. (1976). *The quality of American life.* New York: Russell Sage Foundation.

Cannon, W. B. (1932). *The wisdom of the body.* New York: Norton (2nd ed., 1939).

Caplan, G. (1974). *Support systems and community mental health.* New York: Behavioral Publications.

Caplan, R. (1979). Patient, provider, and organization: Hypothesized determinants of adherence. In S. J. Cohen (Ed.). *New directions in patient compliance.* Lexington, MA: Heath.

Caplan, R. D. (1983). Person-environment fit: Past, present, and future. In C. L. Cooper (Ed.), *Stress research.* New York: Wiley.

Caplan, R. D., Cobb, S., & French, J. R. P., Jr. (1975). Relationships of cessation of smoking with job stress, personality, and social support. *Journal of Applied Psychology, 60,* 211–219.

Caplan, R. D., Cobb, S., & French, J. R. P., Jr. (1979). White collar work load and cortisol: Disruption of a circadian rhythm by job stress? *Journal of Psychosomatic Research, 23,* 181–192.

Carlson, J. G. (1982). Some concepts of perceived control and their relationship to bodily self-control. *Biofeedback and self-regulation, 7,* 341–375.

Carrington, P. (1977). *Freedom in meditation.* Garden City, NY: Anchor/ Doubleday.

Cason, H. (1930). Common annoyances: A psychological study of every-day aversions and irritations. *Psychological Monographs, 40* (Whole No. 182).

Cassel, J. (1976). The contribution of the social environment to host resistance. *American Journal of Epidemiology, 104,* 107–123.

Catalano, R., & Dooley, D. (1983). Health effects of economic instability: A test of economic stress hypothesis. *Journal of Health and Social Behavior, 24,* 46–60.

Cautela, J. R. (1971). Covert extinction. *Behavior Therapy, 2,* 192–200.

Child, I. L., & Waterhouse, I. K. (1953). Frustration and the quality of performance: II. A theoretical statement. *Psychological Review, 60,* 127–139.

Clark, J. G. (1979). Cults. *Journal of the American Medical Association, 242*(3), 279–281.

Cobb, S. (1976). Social support as a moderator of life stress. *Psychosomatic Medicine, 38,* 300–314.

Cobb, S., & Rose, R. M. (1973). Hypertension, peptic ulcer, and diabetes in air traffic controllers. *Journal of the American Medical Association, 224,* 489–492.

Coddington, R. D. (1972). The significance of life events as etiologic factors in the diseases of children: I. A survey of professional workers. *Journal of Psychosomatic Research, 16,* 7–18.

Coelho, G. V., Hamburg, D. A., & Adams, J. E. (Eds.). (1974). *Coping and adaptation.* New York: Basic Books.

Cofer, C. N., & Appley, M. H. (1964). *Motivation: Theory and research.* New York: Wiley.

Cohen, E. A. (1953). *Human behavior in the concentration camp.* New York: Norton.

Cohen, F., Lazarus, R. S., Moos, R. H., Robins, L. N., Rose, R. M., & Rutter, M. (1982). Panel report on psychosocial assets and modifiers of stress. In G. R. Elliot & C. Eisdorfer (Eds.), *Stress and human health.* New York: Springer.

Cohen, F., & Lazarus, R. S. (1973). Active coping processes, coping dispositions, and recovery from surgery. *Psychosomatic Medicine, 35,* 375–389.

Cohen, F., & Lazarus, R. S. (1979). Coping with the stresses of illness. In G. C. Stone, F. Cohen, & N. E. Adler (Eds.), *Health psychology: A handbook.* San Francisco: Jossey-Bass.

Cohen, F., & Lazarus, R. S. (1983). Coping and adaptation and health and illness. In D. Mechanic (Ed.), *Handbook of health, health care, and the health professions.* New York: The Free Press.

Conte, H. R., Weiner, M. B., & Plutchik, R. (1982). Measuring death anxiety: Conceptual, psychometric, and factor-analytic aspects. *Journal of Personality and Social Psychology, 43,* 775–785.

Conway, F., & Siegelman, J. (1978). *Snapping.* New York: Lippincott.

Coover, G. D., Ursin, H., & Levine, S. (1973). Plasma-corticosterone levels during active-avoidance learning in rats. *Journal of Comparative and Physiological Psychology, 82*(170).

Costa, P. T., & McCrea, R. R. (1980). Somatic complaints in males as a function of age and neuroticism: A longitudinal analysis. *Journal of Behavioral Medicine, 3,* 245–258.

Costello, C. G. (1978). A critical review of Seligman's laboratory experiments on learned helplessness and depression in humans. *Journal of Abnormal Psychology, 87,* 21–31.

Cowan, E. L. (1980). The Primary Mental Health Project: Yesterday, today, and tomorrow. *Journal of Special Education, 14,* 133–154.

Cowan, P. A. (1982). The relationship between emotional and cognitive development. In D. Cicchetti & P. Hesse (Eds.), *Emotional development.* San Francisco: Jossey-Bass.

Coyne, J. C. (1976). Toward an interactional description of depression. *Psychiatry, 39,* 28–40.

Coyne, J. C. (1982). A critique of cognitions as causal entities with particular reference to depression. *Cognitive Therapy and Research, 6,* 3–13.

Coyne, J. C., Aldwin, C., & Lazarus, R. S. (1981). Depression and coping in stressful episodes. *Journal of Abnormal Psychology, 90,* 439–447.

Coyne, J. C., & Gotlib, I. H. (1983). The role of cognition in depression: A critical appraisal. *Psychological Bulletin, 94,* 472–505.

Crandall, V. C., Katkovsky, W., & Crandall, V. J. (1965). Children's beliefs in their control of reinforcement in intellectual academic achievement. *Child Development, 36,* 91–109.

Cronbach, L. J. (1957). The two disciplines of scientific psychology. *American Psychologist, 12,* 671–684.

Croog, S. (1970). The family as a source of stress. In S. Levine & N. A. Scotch (Eds.). *Social Stress.* Chicago: Aldine.

Crowne, D., & Marlowe, D. (1964). *The approval motive.* New York: Wiley.

Cutrona, C. E. (1983). Causal attributions and perinatal depression. *Journal of Abnormal Psychology, 92,* 161–172.

Daley, E. M., Polivy, J., & Lancee, W. J. (1983). A conical model for the taxonomy of emotional experience. *Journal of Personality and Social Psychology, 45,* 443–457.

Dansak, D. A., & Cordes, R. S. (1978–1979). Cancer: denial or suppression. *International Journal of Psychiatry in Medicine, 9,* 257–262.

Darwin, C. (1872). *The expression of the emotions in man and animals.* New York: Appleton.

Davidson, R. J., & Fox, N. A. (1982). Asymmetrical brain activity discriminates between positive and negative affective stimuli in human infants. *Science, 218,* 1235–1237.

Davidson, R. J., Goleman, D. J., & Schwartz, G. E. (1976). Attentional and affective concomitants of meditation: A cross-sectional study. *Journal of Abnormal Psychology, 85,* 235–238.

Davitz, J. R. (1969). *The language of emotion.* New York: Academic Press.

Day, H. D., Marshall, D., Hamilton, B., & Christy, J. (1983). Some cautionary notes regarding the use of aggregated scores as a measure of behavioral stability. *Journal of Research in Personality, 17,* 97–109.

Dean, A., & Lin, N. (1977). The stress-buffering role of social support. *Journal of Nervous and Mental Disease, 169,* 403–417.

Deane, G. E. (1969). Cardiac activity during experimentally induced anxiety. *Psychophysiology, 6,* 17–30.

deCharmes, R. (1968). *Personal causation: The internal affective determinants of behavior.* New York: Academic Press.

DeGood, D. E., & Redgate, E. S. (1982). Interrelationship of plasma cortisol and other activation indices during EMG biofeedback training. *Journal of Behavioral Medicine, 5,* 213–223.

Delgado, R. (1977). Religious totalism: Gentle and ungentle persuasion under the first amendment. *Southern California Law Review, 51*(1).

Delong, D. R. (1970). *Individual differences in patterns of anxiety arousal, stress-*

relevant information and recovery from surgery. Unpublished doctoral dissertation, University of California, Los Angeles.

DeLongis, A., Coyne, J. C., Dakof, G., Folkman, S., & Lazarus, R. S. (1982). Relationship of daily hassles, uplifts, and major life events to health status. *Health Psychology, 1,* 119–136.

Dember, W. N. (1974). Motivation and the cognitive revolution. *American Psychologist, 29,* 161–168.

Depue, R. A., Monroe, S. M., & Shachman, S. L. (1979). The psychology of human disease: Implications for conceptualizing the depressive disorders. In R. A. Depue (Ed.), *The psychobiology of the depressive disorders: Implications for the effects of stress.* New York: Academic Press.

Derogatis, L. R., Abeloff, M. D., & Melisaratos, N. (1979). Psychological coping mechanisms and survival time in metastatic breast cancer. *Journal of the American Medical Association, 242,* 1504–1508.

Dewe, P., Guest, D., & Williams, R. (1978, September). *Methods of coping with work-related stress.* Paper presented at Conference of Ergonomics society on Psychophysiological Response to Occupational Stress, University of Nottingham.

Dewey, J., & Bentley, A. F. (1949). *Knowing and the known.* Boston: Beacon.

Diamond, E. L. (1982). The role of anger and hostility in essential hypertension and coronary heart disease. *Psychological Bulletin, 92,* 410–433.

Diener, E. (in press). Subjective well-being. *Psychological Bulletin.*

Diggory, J. C., & Rothman, D. Z. (1961). Values destroyed by death. *Journal of Abnormal and Social Psychology, 63,* 205–209.

Dill, D., Feld, E., Martin, J., Beukema, S., & Belle, D. (1980). The impact of the environment on the coping efforts of low-income mothers. *Family Relations, 29*(4), 503–509.

DiMatteo, M. R., & Hays, R. (1981). Social support in the face of serious illness. In B. H. Gottlieb (Ed.), *Social networks and social support in community mental health.* Beverly Hills, CA: Sage.

Dimsdale, J. E. (1974). The coping behavior of Nazi concentration camp survivors. *American Journal of Psychiatry, 131,* 792–797.

Dimsdale, J. E. (Ed.). (1980). *Survivors, victims, and perpetrators: Essays on the Nazi Holocaust.* Washington, DC: Hemisphere.

Dion, K. L., & Earn, B. M. (1975). The phenomenology of being a target of prejudice. *Journal of Personality and Social Psychology, 32,* 944–950.

Ditto, W. B. (1982). Daily activities of college students and the construct validity of the Jenkins Activity Survey. *Psychosomatic Medicine, 44,* 537–543.

Dobson, K. S., & Neufeld, R. W. J. (1979). Stress-related appraisals: A regression analysis. *Canadian Journal of Behavioral Science, 11,* 274–285.

Dobson, K. S., & Shaw, B. F. (1981). The effects of self-correction on cognitive distortions in depression. *Cognitive Therapy and Research, 5,* 391–403.

Doerfler, L. A., & Richards, C. S. (1981). Self-initiated attempts to cope with depression. *Cognitive Therapy and Research, 5,* 367–371.

Dohrenwend, B. S., & Dohrenwend, B. P. (Eds.). (1974). *Stressful life events: Their nature and effects.* New York: Wiley.

Dohrenwend, B. S., & Dohrenwend, B. P. (1978). Some issues in research on stressful life events. *Journal of Nervous and Mental Disease, 166,* 7–15.

Donald, C. A., & Ware, J. E., Jr. (1982). The quantification of social contacts and resources. Rand Health Insurance Experiment Series, R-2937-HHS, Santa Monica, CA: Rand Corporation.

Dollard, J., & Miller, N. E. (1950). *Personality and psychotherapy.* New York: McGraw-Hill.

Dooley, D., & Catalano, R. (1980). Economic changes as a cause of behavioral disorder. *Psychological Bulletin, 87,* 450–468.

Dooley, D., Catalano, R., Jackson, R., & Brownell, A. (1981). Economic life, and symptom changes in a nonmetropolitan community. *Journal of Health and Social Behavior, 22,* 144–154.

Dubos, R. (1959). *Mirage of health: Utopias, progress, and biological change.* New York: Harper & Row (Perennial Library).

Duffy, E. (1962). *Activation and behavior.* New York: Wiley.

Dunkel-Schetter, C., & Wortman, C. B. (1981). Dilemmas of social support: Parallels between victimization and aging. In S. Kiesler & J. N. Morgan (Eds.), *Aging: Social change.* New York: Academic Press.

Dunkel-Schetter, C., & Wortman, C. B. (1982). The interpersonal dynamics of cancer: Problems in social relationships and their impact on the patient. In H. S. Friedman & M. R. DiMatteo (Eds.), *Interpersonal issues in health care.* New York: Academic Press.

Durkheim, E. (1893). *De la division du travail social.* Paris: F. Alcan. (cited in Kanungo, 1979).

Dweck, C. S., & Wortman, C. B. (1982). Learned helplessness, anxiety, and achievement motivations. In H. W. Krohne & L. Laux (Eds.), *Achievement, stress, and anxiety.* Washington, DC: Hemisphere.

D'Zurilla, T. J., & Nezu, A. (1982). Social problem solving in adults. In P. C. Kendall (Ed.), *Advances in cognitive-behavioral research and therapy* (Vol. 1). New York: Academic Press.

Easterbrook, J. A. (1959). The effect of emotion on cue utilization and the organization of behavior. *Psychological Review, 66,* 183–201.

Edwards, C. (1979). *Crazy for God.* Englewood Cliffs, NH: Prentice-Hall.

Eitinger, L. (1964). *Concentration camp survivors in Norway and Israel.* London: Allen & Unwin.

Ekehammar, B. (1974). Interactionism in personality from a historical perspective. *Psychological Bulletin, 81,* 1026–1048.

Ekman, P. (1972). Universals and cultural differences in facial expressions of emotion. In J. K. Cole (Ed.), *Nebraska Symposium on Motivation.* Lincoln: University of Nebraska Press.

Ekman, P., & Friesen, W. (1975). *Unmasking the face.* Englewood Cliffs, NJ: Prentice-Hall.

Ekman, P., Levenson, R. W., & Friesen, W. V. (1983). Autonomic nervous system activity distinguishes among emotions. *Science, 221,* 1208–1210.

Ekman, P., & Scherer, K. (Eds.) (in press). *Approaches to emotion*. Hillsdale, NJ: Erlbaum.

Elder, G. H., Jr. (1974). *Children of the Great Depression*. Chicago: University of Chicago Press.

Elder, G. H., Jr. (1980). History and the life course. In D. Bertaux (Ed.), *Biography and society*. New York: Sage.

Elliott, G. R., & Eisdorfer, C. (1982). *Stress and human health*. New York: Springer.

Elliott, R. (1966). Effects of uncertainty about the nature and advent of a noxious stimulus (shock) upon heart rate. *Journal of Personality and Social Psychology, 3*, 353–356.

Ellis, A. (1962). *Reason and emotion in psychotherapy*. New York: Lyle Stuart.

Ellis, A., (1975). *How to live with a "neurotic" at home and at work*. New York: Crowne.

Ellis, A., & Grieger, R. (Eds.). (1977). *Handbook of rational-emotive therapy*. New York: Springer.

Endler, N. S., & Magnusson, D. (Eds.). (1976). *Interactional Psychology and personality*. New York: Wiley.

Engel, B. T. (1960). Stimulus-response and individual response specificity. *Archives of General Psychiatry, 2*, 305–313.

Engel, B. T., & Bickford, A. F. (1961). Response specificity. *Archives of General Psychiatry, 3*, 478–489.

Engel, G. L. (1968). A life setting conducive to illness: The giving up–given up complex. *Bulletin of the Menninger Clinic, 32*, 355–365.

Engel, G. L. (1974). Memorial lecture: The psychosomatic approach to individual susceptibility to disease. *Gastroenterology, 67*, 1085–1093.

Engel, G. L. (1977). The need for a new medical model: A challenge for biomedicine. *Science, 196*, 129–136.

Epstein, S. (1962). The measurement of drive and conflict in humans: Theory and experiment. In M. R. Jones (Ed.), *Nebraska Symposium on Motivation*. Lincoln: University of Nebraska Press.

Epstein, S. (1976). Anxiety, arousal and the self-concept. In I. G. Sarason & C. D. Spielberger (Eds.), *Stress and anxiety* (Vol. 3). Washington, D.C.: Hemisphere.

Epstein, S. (1977). Traits are alive and well. In D. Magnusson & N. W. Endler (Eds.), *Personality at the crossroads*. Hillsdale, NJ: Erlbaum.

Epstein, S. (1979). The stability of behavior: I. On predicting most of the people much of the time. *Journal of Personality and Social Psychology, 37*, 1097–1126.

Epstein, S. (1980). The stability of behavior: II. Implications for psychological research. *American Psychologist, 35*, 790–806.

Epstein, S. (1983a). A research paradigm for the study of personality and emotions. In M. M. Page (Ed.), *Personality: Current theory and research. Nebraska Symposium on Motivation, 1982*. Lincoln: University of Nebraska Press.

Epstein, S. (1983b). Natural healing processes of the mind: Graded stress inoculation as an inherent coping mechanism. In D. Meichenbaum & M. E. Jaremko (Eds.), *Stress reduction and prevention.* New York: Plenum.

Epstein, S. (in press). Aggregation and beyond: Some basic issues on the prediction of behavior. *Journal of Personality.*

Epstein, S., & Clarke, S. (1970). Heart rate and skin conductance during experimentally induced anxiety: The effects of anticipated intensity of noxious stimulation and experience. *Journal of Experimental Psychology, 84,* 105–112.

Epstein, S., & Roupenian, A. (1970). Heart rate and skin conductance during experimentally induced anxiety: The effect of uncertainty about receiving a noxious stimulus. *Journal of Personality and Social Psychology, 16,* 20–28.

Erdelyi, M. H. (1974). A new look at the new look: Perceptual defence and vigilance. *Psychological Review, 81,* 1–25.

Erdmann, G., & Janke, W. (1978). Interactions between physiological and cognitive determinants of emotions: Experimental studies on Schachter's theory of emotions. *Biological Psychology, 6,* 61–74.

Eriksen, C. W. (1962a). *Behavior and awareness: A symposium of research and interpretation.* Durham, NC: Duke University Press.

Eriksen, C. W. (1962b). Figments, fantasies, and follies: A search for the subconscious mind. In C. W. Erikson (Ed.), *Behavior and awarness: A symposium of research and interpretation.* Durham, NC: Duke University Press.

Erikson, E. H. (1963). *Childhood and society* (2nd ed.). New York: Norton.

Ernster, V. L., Sachs, S. T., Selvin, S., & Petrakis, N. L. (1979). Cancer incidence by marital status: U.S. Third National Cancer Survey. *Journal of the National Cancer Institute, 63,* 567–585.

Estes, R. J., & Wilensky, H. L. (1978). Life cycle squeeze and the morale curve. *Social Problems, 25,* 277–292.

Farberow, N. L. (1980). Indirect self-destructive behavior in diabetics and Buerger's Disease patients. In N. L. Farberow (Ed.), *The many faces of suicide: Indirect self-destructive behavior.* New York: McGraw-Hill.

Feather, N. T. (1975). *Values in education and society.* New York: The Free Press.

Fenichel, O. (1945). *The psychoanalytic theory of neurosis.* New York: Norton.

Ferster, C. B. (1973). A functional analysis of depression. *American Psychologist, 28,* 857–870.

Festinger, L., & Carlsmith, J. M. (1959). Cognitive consequences of forced compliance. *Journal of Abnormal and Social Psychology, 58,* 203–210.

Fiore, N. (1979). Fighting cancer: One patient's perspective. *New England Journal of Medicine, 300,* 284–289.

Fischer, C. (1982, January). The friendship cure-all. *Psychology Today,* pp. 74–78.

Fish, T. A. (1983). *The relationships among cognitive appraisals and performance in a naturalistic, public speaking situation.* Unpublished dissertation, University of Calgary, Alberta, Canada.

Fiske, D. W., & Maddi, S. R. (1961). Conceptual framework. In D. W. Fiske & S. R. Maddi (Eds.), *Functions of varied experience.* Homewood, IL: Dorsey.

Folkins, C. H. (1970). Temporal factors and the cognitive mediators of stress reaction. *Journal of Personality and Social Psychology, 14,* 173–184.

Folkins, C. H., Lawson, K. D., Opton, E. M., Jr., & Lazarus, R. S. (1968). Desensitization and the experimental reduction of threat. *Journal of Abnormal Psychology, 73,* 100–113.

Folkman, S. (1984). Personal control and stress and coping processes: A theoretical analysis. *Journal of Personality and Social Psychology, 46,* pp. 839–852.

Folkman, S., Aldwin, C., & Lazarus, R. S. (1981, August). *The relationship between locus of control, cognitive appraisal and coping.* Paper presented at meetings of the American Psychological Association, Los Angeles.

Folkman, S., & Lazarus, R. S. (1980). An analysis of coping in a middle-aged community sample. *Journal of Health and Social Behavior, 21,* 219–239.

Folkman, S., & Lazarus, R. S. (in press). If it changes it must be a process: A study of emotion and coping during three stages of a college examination. *Journal of Personality and Social Psychology.*

Folkman, S., Schaefer, C., & Lazarus, R. S. (1979). Cognitive processes as mediators of stress and coping. In V. Hamilton & D. M. Warburton (Eds.), *Human stress and cognition: An information-processing approach.* London: Wiley.

Fontana, A. F., Hughes, L. A., Marcus, J. L., & Dowds, B. N. (1979). Subjective evaluation of life events. *Journal of Consulting and Clinical Psychology, 47,* 906–911.

Frankenhaeuser, M. (1975). Experimental approaches to the study of catecholamines and emotion. In L. Levi (Ed.), *Emotions: Their parameters and measurement.* New York: Raven.

Frankenhaeuser, M. (1976). The role of peripheral catecholamines in adaptation to understimulation. In G. Serban (Ed.), *Psychopathology of human adaptation.* New York: Plenum.

Frankenhaeuser, M. (1979). Psychoneuroendocrine approaches to the study of emotion as related to stress and coping. In H. E. Howe & R. A. Dienstbier (Eds.), *Nebraska Symposium on Motivation, 1978.* Lincoln: University of Nebraska Press.

Frankenhaeuser, M. (1980). Psychobiological aspects of life stress. In S. Levine & H. Ursin (Eds.), *Coping and health.* New York: Plenum.

Frankenhaeuser, M. (1981). Coping with stress and work. *International Journal of Health Services, 2,* 491–510.

Frankenhaeuser, M. (1982). Challenge-control interaction as reflected in sympathetic-adrenal and pituitary-adrenal activity: Comparison between the sexes. *Scandinavian Journal of Psychology,* (Suppl. 1), 158–164.

Frankenhaeuser, M. (1983). The sympathetic-adrenal and pituitary-adrenal response to challenge: Comparison between the sexes. In T. M. Dembroski, T. H. Schmidt, & G. Blümchen (Eds.), *Biobehavioral bases of coronary heart disease*. New York: Karger.

Frankenhaeuser, M., Von Wright, M. R., Collins, A., Von Wright, J., Sedvall, G., & Swahn, C. G. (1978). Sex differences in psychoendocrine reactions to examination stress. *Psychosomatic Medicine, 40,* 334–343.

Frankl, V. (1959). *Man's search for meaning*. Boston: Beacon.

Franks, C. M., & Wilson, G. T. (Eds.) (1973–). *Annual Review of Behavior Therapy Theory and Practice*. New York: Brunner/Mazel.

French, J. R. P., Jr., Rodgers, W., & Cobb, S. (1974). Adjustment and person–environment fit. In G. V. Coelho, D. A. Hamburg, & J. E. Adams (Eds.), *Coping and adaptation*. New York: Basic Books.

Frenkel-Brunswik, E. (1949). Intolerance of ambiguity as an emotional and perceptual personality variable. *Journal of Personality, 18,* 108–143.

Freud, A., & Burlingham, D. (1943). *War and children*. New York: Medical War Books.

Freud, S. (1920). *A general introduction to psychoanalysis*. New York: Boni & Liveright.

Freud, S. (1953). *Three essays on sexuality. Standard edition* (Vol. 8). London: Hogarth (first German edition, 1905).

Freud, S. (1955). *Beyond the pleasure principle. Standard edition* (Vol. 18). London: Hogarth (first German edition, 1920).

Freud, S. (1957). *Civilization and its discontents* (Joan Riviere, Trans.). London: Hogarth. (first German edition, 1930).

Friedman, M., & Rosenman, R. H. (1974). *Type A behavior and your heart*. New York: Knopf.

Friedman, S. B., Chodoff, P., Mason, J. W., & Hamburg, D. A. (1963). Behavioral observations on parents anticipating the death of a child. *Pediatrics, 32,* 610–625.

Friedman, S. B., Mason, J. W., & Hamburg, D. A. (1963). Urinary 17-hydroxycorticosteroid levels in parents of children with neoplastic diseases: A study of chronic psychological stress. *Psychosomatic Medicine, 25,* 364–376.

Friends can be good medicine (1981). California Department of Mental Health. San Francisco: Pacificon Productions.

Frijda, N. H. *The emotions*. Manuscript being prepared for publication by Cambridge University Press.

Fritz, C. E., & Mathewson, J. H. (1957). Convergence behavior in disasters: A problem in social control. Washington, DC: National Academy of Sciences, National Research Council, Disaster Study No. 9.

Fromm, E. (1955). *The sane society*. New York: Rinehart.

Fuller, R. (1982). The story as the engram: Is it fundamental to thinking? *Journal of Mind and Behavior, 3,* 127–142.

Funder, D. C. (1982). On assessing social psychological theories through the study of individual differences: Template matching and forced compliance. *Journal of Personality and Social Psychology, 43,* 100–110.

Funkenstein, D. H., King, S. H., & Drolette, M. E. (1957). *Mastery of stress.* Cambridge, MA: Harvard University Press.

Gaines, L. L., Smith, B. D., & Skolnick, B. E. (1977). Psychological differentiation, event uncertainty, and heart rate. *Journal of Human Stress, 3,* 11–25.

Galbrecht, C. R., Dykman, R. A., Reese, W. G., & Suzuki, T. (1965). Intrasession adaptation and intersession extinction of the components of the orienting response. *Journal of Experimental Psychology, 70,* 585–597.

Gans, H. (1967). *Levittowners.* New York: Pantheon.

Garber, J., & Hollon, S. D. (1980). Universal versus personal helplessness in depression: Belief in uncontrollability or incompetence? *Journal of Abnormal Psychology, 89,* 56–66.

Garber, J., Miller, S. M., & Abramson, L. Y. (1980). On the distinction between anxiety and depression: Perceived control, certainty, and the probability of goal attainment. In J. Garber & M. E. P. Seligman (Eds.), *Human helplessness: Theory and applications.* New York: Academic Press.

Garber, J., & Seligman, M. E. P. (1980). *Human helplessness: Theory and applications.* New York: Academic Press.

Gardell, B. (1976). Technology, alienation and mental health. Summary of a social and psychological research programme on technology and the worker. *Acta Sociologica, 19,* 83–94.

Gardner, R. W. (1962). Cognitive controls of attention and inhibition: A study of individual consistencies. *British Journal of Psychology, 53,* 381–388.

Gardner, R. W., Holzman, P. S., Klein, G. S., Linton, H. B., & Spence, D. P. (1959). Cognitive control: A study of individual consistencies in cognitive behavior. *Psychological Issues, 1*(4).

Garmezy, N. (1976). Vulnerable and invulnerable children: Theory, research, and intervention. *JSAS Catalogue of Selected Documents in Psychology, 6,* 96, Ms. No. 1337.

Gastorf, J. W., Suls, J., & Sanders, G. S. (1980). Type A coronary-prone behavior pattern and social facilitation. *Journal of Personality and Social Psychology, 38,* 773–780.

Gastorf, J. W., & Teevan, R. C. (1980). Type A coronary-prone behavior and fear of failure. *Motivation and Emotion, 4,* 71–76.

Geen, R. G., Stonner, D., & Kelley, D. R. (1974). Aggression anxiety and cognitive appraisal of aggresion-threat stimuli. *Journal of Personality and Social Psychology, 29,* 196–200.

George, A. L. (1974). Adaptation to stress in political decision making: The individual, small group, and organizational contexts. In G. V. Coelho, D. A. Hamburg, & J. E. Adams (Eds.), *Coping and adaptation.* New York: Basic Books.

George, J. M., Scott, D. S., Turner, S. P., & Gregg, J. M. (1980). The effects of psychological factors on physical trauma on recovery from oral surgery. *Journal of Behavioral Medicine, 3,* 291–310.

Gerth, H. H., & Mills, C. W. (1946). *From Max Weber: Essays in sociology.* New York: Oxford University Press.

Gerth, H. H., & Mills, C. W. (1953). *Character and the social structure.* New York: Harcourt, Brace.

Gibbons, F. X., & Wright, R. A. (1981). Motivational biases in causal attributions of arousal. *Journal of Personality and Social Psychology, 40,* 588–600.

Gilmore, T. M. (1978). Locus of control as a mediator of adaptive behavior in children and adolescents. *Canadian Psychological Review, 19,* 1–26.

Glass, D. C. (1977a). *Behavior patterns, stress and coronary disease.* Hillsdale, NJ: Erlbaum.

Glass, D. C. (1977b). Stress, behavior patterns, and coronary disease. *American Scientist, 65,* 177–187.

Glass, D. C., Krakoff, L. R., Contrada, R., Hilton, W. F., Kehoe, K., Manucci, E. G., Collins, C., Snow, G., & Elting, E. (1980). Effect of harassment and competition upon cardiovascular and plasma catecholamine responses in Type A and Type B individuals. *Psychophysiology, 17,* 453–463.

Gleser, G. C., & Ihilevich, D. (1969). An objective instrument for measuring defense mechanisms. *Journal of Consulting and Clinical Psychology, 33,* 51–60.

Goffman, E. (1971). *Relations in public.* New York: Basic Books.

Goffman, E. (1974). *Frame analysis.* New York: Harper & Row.

Goldberg, E. G., & Comstock, G. W. (1980). Epidemiology of life events: Frequency in general populations. *American Journal of Epidemiology, 111,* 736–752.

Goldfried, M. R. (1979). Anxiety reduction through cognitive-behavioral intervention. In P. C. Kendall & S. D. Hollon (Eds.), *Cognitive-behavioral interventions: Theory, research, and procedures.* New York: Academic Press.

Goldfried, M. R. (1980). Psychotherapy as coping skills training. In M. J. Mahoney (ed.), *Psychotherapy process: Current issues and future directions.* New York: Plenum.

Goldfried, M. R. (1982a). A behavior therapist looks at rapprochement. In M. R. Goldfried (Ed.), *Converging trends in the practice of psychotherapy.* New York: Springer.

Goldfried, M. (1982b). On the history of therapeutic integration. *Behavior Therapy, 13,* 572–593.

Goldfried, M. R., & Davison, G. C. (1976). *Clinical behavior therapy.* New York: Holt, Rinehart & Winston.

Goldfried, M. R., & Goldfried, A. P. (1975). Cognitive change methods. In F. H. Kanfer & A. P. Goldstein (Eds.), *Helping people change.* New York: Pergamon.

Goldman, B. L., Domitor, P. J., & Murray, E. J. (1979). Effects of Zen meditation on anxiety reduction and perceptual functioning. *Journal of Consulting and Clinical Psychology, 47,* 531–536.

Goleman, D. J., & Schwartz, G. E. (1976). Meditation as an intervention in stress reactivity. *Journal of Consulting and Clinical Psychology, 44,* 456–466.

Goldschmidt, W. (1974). Ethology, ecology, and ethological realities. In G. V. Coelho, D. A. Hamburg, & J. E. Adams (Eds.), *Coping and adaptation.* New York: Basic Books.

Goldstein, A. M. (1980). The "uncooperative" patient: Self-destructive behavior in hemodialysis patients. In N. L. Farberow (Ed.), *The many faces of suicide: Indirect self-destructive behavior.* New York: McGraw-Hill.

Goldstein, M. J. (1959). The relationship between coping and avoiding behavior and response to fear-arousing propaganda. *Journal of Abnormal and Social Psychology, 58,* 247–252.

Goldstein, M. J. (1973). Individual differences in response to stress. *American Journal of Community Psychology, 1,* 113–137.

Gong-Guy, E., & Hammen, C. L. (1980). Causal perception of stressful events in depressed and nondepressed outpatients. *Journal of Abnormal Psychology, 89,* 662–669.

Gordon, S. L. (1981). The sociology of sentiments and emotion. In M. Rosenberg & R. H. Turner (Eds.), *Social psychology: Sociological perspectives.* New York: Basic Books.

Gore, S. (1978). The effect of social support in moderating the health consequences of unemployment. *Journal of Health and Social Behavior, 19,* 157–165.

Gortmaker, S. L., Eckenrode, J., & Gore, S. (1982). Stress and the utilization of health services: A time series and cross-sectional analysis. *Journal of Health and Social Behavior, 23,* 25–38.

Gorzynski, J. G., Holland, J., Katz, J. L., Weiner, H., Zumoff, B., Fukushima, D., & Levin, J. (1980). Stability of ego defenses and endocrine responses in women prior to breast biopsy and ten years later. *Psychosomatic Medicine, 42,* 323–328.

Gosney, D. (1977, February). Inside the camp: Mental anguish. *Redwood City Tribune,* pp. 1ff.

Gotlib, I. H., & Asarnow, R. F. (1979). Interpersonal and impersonal problem-solving skills in mildly and clinically depressed university students. *Journal of Consulting and Clinical Psychology, 47,* 86–95.

Gotlib, I. H., & Robinson, L. A. (1982). Responses to depressed individuals: Discrepancies between self-report and observer-rated behavior. *Journal of Abnormal Psychology, 91,* 231–240.

Gove, W. R. (1973). Sex, marital status and mortality. *American Journal of Sociology, 79,* 45–67.

Grinker, R. R., & Spiegel, J. P. (1945). *Men under stress.* New York: McGraw-Hill.

Gross, E. (1970). Work, organization, and stress. In S. Levine & N. A. Scotch (Eds.), *Social Stress.* Chicago: Aldine.

Gross, N. A., Mason, W. S., & McEachern, A. W. (1958). *Explorations in role analysis.* New York: Wiley.

Grosser, G. H., Wechsler, H., & Greenblatt, M. (Eds.) (1964). *The threat of impending disaster.* Cambridge, MA: The MIT Press.

Gruenberg, E. (1977). The failure of success. *Milbank Memorial Fund Quarterly, 55*(1), 3–24.

Gurin, G., & Gurin, P. (1970). Expectancy theory in the study of poverty. *Journal of Social Issues, 26,* 83–104.

Gurland, B. J., Yorkston, N. J., Stone, H. R., & Frank, J. D. (1974). *Structured and scaled interview to assess maladjustment.* New York: Springer.

Gutmann, D. L. (1974). The country of old men: Cross-cultural studies in the psychology of later life. In R. L. Levine (Ed.), *Culture and personality: Contemporary readings.* Chicago: Aldine.

Haan, N. (1969). A tripartite model of ego functioning: Values and clinical research applications. *Journal of Nervous and Mental Disease, 148,* 14–30.

Haan, N. (1977). *Coping and defending: Processes of self–environment organization.* New York: Academic Press.

Hackett, T. P., & Cassem, N. H. (1974). Development of a quantitative rating scale to assess denial. *Journal of Psychosomatic Research, 18,* 93–100.

Hackett, T. P., & Cassem, N. H. (1975). Psychological management of the myocardia infarction patient. *Journal of Human Stress, 1,* 25–38.

Hackett, T. P., Cassem, N. H., & Wishnie, H. A. (1968). The coronary-care unit: An appraisal of its psychologic hazards. *New England Journal of Medicine, 279,* 1365–1370.

Hacket, T. P., & Weisman, A. D. (1964). Reactions to the imminence of death. In G. H. Grosser, H. Wechsler, & M. Greenblatt (Eds.), *The threat of impending disaster.* Cambridge, MA: The MIT Press.

Haggard, E. A. (1943). Experimental studies in affective processes: Some effects of cognitive structure and active participation on certain autonomic reactions during experimentally induced stress. *Journal of Experimental Psychology, 33,* 257–284.

Hamburg, D. A., & Adams, J. E. (1967). A perspective on coping behavior: Seeking and utilizing information in major transitions. *Archives of General Psychiatry, 17,* 277–284.

Hamburg, D. A., Hamburg, B., & deGoza, S. (1953). Adaptive problems and mechanisms in severely burned patients. *Psychiatry, 16,* 1–20.

Hamilton, V. (1975). Socialization anxiety and information processing: A capacity model of anxiety-induced performance deficits. In I. G. Sarason & C. D. Spielberger (Eds.), *Stress and anxiety (Vol. 2). Washington, DC: Hemisphere.*

Hammen, C. L., & Cochran, S. D. (1981). Cognitive correlates of life stress and depression in college students. *Journal of Abnormal Psychology, 90,* 23–27.

Hammen, C., & deMayo, R. (1982). Cognitive correlates of teacher stress and depressive symptoms: Implications for attributional models of depression. *Journal of Abnormal Psychology, 91,* 96–101.

Hammen, C. L., Krantz, S., & Cochran, S. (1981). Relationships between depression and causal attributions about stressful life events. *Cognitive Therapy and Research, 5*, 351–358.

Hansell, S. (1982). Student, parent, and school effects on the stress of college applications. *Journal of Health and Social Behavior, 23*, 38–51.

Harburg, E., Blakelock, E. H., & Roeper, P. J. (1979). Resentful and reflective coping with arbitrary authority and blood pressure: Detroit. *Psychosomatic Medicine, 41*, 189–202.

Harlow, H. F. (1953). Mice, monkeys, men and motives. *Psychological Review, 60*, 23–32.

Harris, J. D. (1943). Habituatory response decrement in the intact organism. *Psychological Bulletin, 40*, 385–422.

Hartke, R. J., & Kunce, J. T. (1982). Multidimensionality of health-related locus-of-control scale items. *Journal of Consulting and Clinical Psychology, 50*, 594–595.

Hartshorne, H., & May, M. A. (1928). *Studies in the nature of character: Studies in deceit* (Vol. 1). New York: Macmillan.

Hartshorne, H., May, M. A., & Maller, J. B. (1929). *Studies in the nature of character: Studies in service and self-control* (Vol. 2). New York: Macmillan.

Hartshorne, H., May, M. A., Maller, J. B., & Shuttleworh, F. K. (1930). *Studies in the nature of character: Studies in the organization of character* (Vol. 3). New York: Macmillan.

Haugeland, J. (1978). The nature and plausibility of cognitivism. *The Behavioral and Brain Sciences, 2*, 215–260.

Hay, D. & Oken, S. (1972). The psychological stresses of intensive care unit nursing. *Psychosomatic Medicine, 34*, 109–118.

Haynes, S. G., Feinleib, M., & Kannel, W. B. (1980). The relationship of psychosocial factors to coronary heart disease in the Framingham Study: III. Eight-year incidence of coronary heart disease. *American Journal of Epidemiology, 1980, 3*, 37–58.

Hebb, D. O., (1946). On the nature of fear. *Psychological Review, 53*, 259–276.

Heckhausen, H. (1977). Achievement motivation and its constructs: A cognitive model. *Motivation and Emotion, 1*, 283–329.

Heckhausen, H. (1982). Task-irrelevant cognitions during an exam: Incidence and effects. In H. W. Krohne & L. Laux (Eds.), *Achievement, stress, and anxiety*. Washington, DC: Hemisphere.

Heide, F. J., & Borkovec, T. D. (1983). Relaxation-induced anxiety: Paradoxical anxiety enhancement due to relaxation training. *Journal of Consulting and Clinical Psychology, 51*, 171–182.

Heider, F. (1958). *The psychology of interpersonal relations*. New York: Wiley.

Heimler, E. (1963). Children of Auschwitz. In G. Mikes (Ed.), *Prison*. London: Routledge & Kegan Paul.

Heinicke, C., & Westheimer, J. (1965). *Brief separations*. New York: International Universities Press.

Helson, H. (1959). Adaptation level theory. In S. Koch (Ed.), *Psychology: A study of a science* (Vol. 1). New York: McGraw-Hill.

Henderson, S. K., Byrne, D. G., Duncan-Jones, P., Adcock, S., Scott, R., & Steele, G. P. (1978). Social bounds in the epidemiology of neurosis: A preliminary communication. *British Journal of Psychiatry, 132,* 463–466.

Hendrick, I. (1943). The discussion of the "Instinct to Master." *Psychoanalytic Quarterly, 12,* 561–565.

Henle, M. (1962). On the relation between logic and thinking. *Psychological Review, 69,* 366–378.

Henle, M. (1971). Of the Scholler of nature. *Social Research, 38,* 93–107.

Hennessy, J. W., & Levine, S. (1979). Stress, arousal, and the pituitary-adrenal system: A psychoendocrine hypothesis. In J. Sprague & A. Epstein (Eds.), *Progress in psychobiology and physiological psychology.* New York: Academic Press.

Herd, J. A. (1977, October). *Cardiovascular correlates of psychological stress.* Paper presented at conference on The Crisis in Stress Research: A Critical Reappraisal of the Role of Stress in Hypertension, Gastrointestinal Illness, Female Reproductive Dysfunction. Boston University School of Medicine, Department of Psychosomatic Medicine.

Hetherington, E. M., Cox, M., & Cox, R. (1978, May). *Family interaction and the social, emotional, and cognitive development of children following divorce.* Paper presented at the Johnson Conference on the Family, Washington, DC.

Hilgard, E. R. (1949). Human motives and the concept of the self. *American Psychologist, 4,* 374–382.

Hinkle, L. E., Jr. (1973). The concept of "stress" in the biological and social sciences. *Science, Medicine & Man, 1,* 31–48.

Hinkle, L. E., Jr. (1974). The effects of exposure to culture change, social change and changes in interpersonal relationships to health. In B. S. Dohrenwend & B. P. Dohrenwend (Eds.), *Stressful life events: Their nature and effects.* New York: Wiley.

Hinkle, L. E., Jr. (1977). The concept of "stress" in the biological and social sciences. In Z. J. Lipowski, D. R. Lipsitt, & P. C. Whybrow (Eds.), *Psychosomatic medicine: Current trends and clinical implications.* New York: Oxford University Press.

Hitchcock, L. S. (1982). *Improving recovery from surgery: The interaction of preoperative interventions, coping processes, and personality variables.* Unpublished doctoral dissertation, University of California, Berkeley.

Hochschild, A. R. (1979). Emotion work, feeling rules and social structure. *American Journal of Sociology, 85,* 551–575.

Hochschild, A. R. (1983). *The managed heart.* Berkeley, CA: The University of California Press.

Hofer, M. A., Wolff, E. T., Friedman, S. B., & Mason, J. W. (1972). A psychoendocrine study of berevement, Parts I and II. *Psychosomatic Medicine, 34,* 481–504.

Hogan, R. A. (1967). Preliminary report of the extinction of learned fears via short-term implosive therapy. *Journal of Abnormal Psychology, 72,* 106–109.

Hollon, S. D., & Beck, A. T. (1979). Cognitive therapy of depression. In P. C. Kendall & S. D. Hollon (Eds.), *Cognitive behavioral interventions: Theory, research and procedures.* New York: Academic Press.

Hollon, S. D., & Garber, J. (1980). A cognitive-expectancy theory of therapy for helplessness and depression. In J. Garber & M. E. P. Seligman (Eds.), *Human helplessness.* New York: Academic Press.

Holmes, D. S., & Houston, B. K. (1974). Effectiveness of situational redefinition and affective isolation in coping with stress. *Journal of Personality and Social Psychology, 29,* 212–218.

Holmes, T. H., & Masuda, M. (1974). Life changes and illness susceptibility. In B. S. Dohrenwend & B. P. Dohrenwend (Eds.), *Stressful life events: Their nature and effects.* New York: Wiley.

Holmes, T. H., & Rahe, R. H. (1967). The social readjustment rating scale. *Journal of Psychosomatic Research, 11,* 213–218.

Holroyd, K. A. (1979). Stress, coping, and the treatment of stress-related illness. In J. R. McNamara (Ed.), *Behavioral approaches to medicine: Application and analysis.* New York: Plenum.

Holroyd, K. A., & Andrasik, F. (1982). Do the effects of cognitive therapy endure? A two year follow-up of tension headache sufferers treated with cognitive therapy or biofeedback. *Cognitive Therapy and Research, 6,* 325–33.

Holroyd, K. A., & Lazarus, R. S. (1982). Stress, coping, and somatic adaptation. In L. Goldberger & S. Breznitz (Eds.), *Handbook of stress: Theoretical and clinical aspects.* New York: The Free Press.

Holt, R. R. (1962). Individuality and generalization in the psychology of personality. *Journal of Personality, 30,* 377–404.

Horner, M. S. (1972). Toward an understanding of achievement-related conflicts in women. *Journal of Social Issues, 28,* 157–175.

Horowitz, M. J. (1974). Stress response syndromes. *Archives of General Psychiatry, 31,* 768–781.

Horowitz, M. J. (1976). *Stress response syndromes.* New York: Jason Aronson.

Horowitz, M. J. (1982). Psychological processes induced by illness, injury, and loss. In T. Millon, C. Green, & R. Meagher (Eds.), *Handbook of clinical health psychology.* New York: Plenum.

Horowitz, M. J., Hulley, S., Alvarez, W., Reynolds, A. M., Benfari, R., Blair, S., Borhani, N., & Simon, N. (1979). Life events, risk factors, and coronary disease. *Psychosomatics, 20,* 586–592.

Horowitz, M. J., Wilner, N., & Alvarez, W. (1979). Impact of event scales: A measure of subjective stress. *Psychosomatic Medicine, 41,* 209–218.

Hough, R. L., Fairbank, D. T., & Garcia, A. M. (1976). Problems in the ratio measurement of life stress. *Journal of Health and Social Behavior, 17,* 70–82.

House, J. S. (1979). Occupational stress and coronary heart disease: A review and theoretical integration. *Journal of Health and Social Behavior, 15,* 12–27.

House, J. S. (1981). Social structure and personality. In M. Rosenberg & R. H. Turner (Eds.), *Social psychology: Sociological perspectives.* New York: Basic Books.

House, J. S., McMichael, A. J., Wells, J. A., Kaplan, B. H., & Landerman, L. R. (1979). Occupational stress and health among factor workers. *Journal of Health and Social Behavior, 20,* 139–160.

Houston, B. K. (1972). Control over stress, locus of control, and response to stress. *Journal of Personality and Social Psychology, 21,* 249–255.

Hull, C. L. (1937). Mind, mechanism, and adaptive behavior. *Psychological Review, 44,* 1–32.

Hull, C. L. (1943). *Principles of behavior.* New York: Appleton-Century-Crofts.

Hultsch, D. F., & Plemons, J. K. (1979). Life events and life-span development. In P. Baltes & O. G. Brim (Eds.), *Life-span development and behavior* (Vol. 2). New York: Academic Press.

Hunter, E. J. (1979, May). *Combat casualities who remain at home.* Paper presented at Western Regional Conference of the Inter University Seminar, "Technology in Combat." Naval Postgraduate School, Monterey, CA.

Hupka, R. B. (1981). Cultural determinants of jealousy. *Alternative Lifestyles, 4,* 310–356.

Huxley, A. (1965). Human potentialities. In R. E. Parson (Ed.), *Science and human affairs.* Palo Alto, CA: Science and Behavior Books.

Ilfeld, F. W. (1980). Coping styles of Chicago adults: Description. *Journal of Human Stress,* June, 2–10.

Isen, A. M. (1970). Success, failure, attention, and reaction to others: The warm glow of success. *Journal of Personality and Social Psychology, 15,* 294–301.

Isen, A. M., & Levin, P. F. (1972). Effect of feeling good on helping: Cookies and kindness. *Journal of Personality and Social Psychology, 21,* 384–388.

Isen, A. M., Shalker, T. E., Clark, M., & Karp, L. (1978). Affect, accessibility of material in memory and behavior: A cognitive loop? *Journal of Personality and Social Psychology, 36*(1), 1–12.

Isen, A. M., Wehner, G. M., Livsey, W. J., & Jennings, J. R. (1965). Affect, awareness, and performance. In S. S. Tomkins & C. E. Izard (Eds.), *Affect, cognition and personality.* New York: Springer.

Izard, C. E. (1975). Patterns of emotion and emotion communication in hostility and aggression. In P. Pliner, L. Kramer, & T. Alloway (Eds.), *Nonverbal communication of aggression.* New York: Plenum.

Izard, C. E. (in press). The primacy of emotions in human development and in emotion-cognition relationships. In C. E. Izard, J. Kagan, & R. B. Zajonc (Eds.), *Emotions, cognition, and behavior.* New York: Cambridge University Press.

Izard, C. E., Kagan, J., & Zajonc. R. (Eds.). (in press). *Emotions, cognition and behavior.* New York: Cambridge University Press.

Jahoda, M. (1981). Work, employment, and unemployment: Values, theories and approaches in social research. *American Psychologist, 36,* 84–191.

James, W. H., Woodruff, A. B., & Werner, W. (1965). Effect of internal and external control upon changes in smoking behavior. *Journal of Consulting Psychology, 29,* 184–186.

Janis, I. L. (1951). *Air war and emotional stress.* New York: McGraw-Hill.

Janis, I. L. (1958). *Psychological Stress: Psychoanalytic and behavioral studies of surgical patients.* New York: Wiley.

Janis, I. L. (1967). Effects of fear arousal on attitude change: Recent Developments in theory and experimental research. In L. Berkowitz (Ed.), *Advances in Experimental Social Psychology.* New York: Academic Press.

Janis, I. L. (1972). *Victims of groupthink.* Boston: Houghton-Mifflin.

Janis, I. L. (1974). Vigilance and decision-making in personal crises. In G. V. Coelho, D. A. Hamburg, & J. E. Adams (Eds.), *Coping and adaptation.* New York: Basic Books.

Janis, I. L., & Mann, L. (1977). *Decision making.* New York: The Free Press.

Janoff-Bulman, R., & Brickman, P. (1982). Expectations and what people learn from failure. In N. T. Feather (Ed.), *Expectancy, incentive and action.* Hillsdale, NJ: Erlbaum.

Janoff-Bulman, R., & Marshall, G. (1982). Mortality, well-being, and control: A study of a population of institutionalized aged. *Personality and Social Psychology Bulletin, 8,* 691–698.

Jemmott, J. B., III, & Locke, S. E. (1984). Psychosocial factors, immunologic mediation, and human susceptibility to infectious diseases: How much do we know? *Psychological Bulletin, 95,* 78–108.

Jenkins, C. D., Zyzanski, S. J., Ryan, T. J., Flessas, A., & Tannenbaum, S. I. (1977). Social insecurity and coronary-prone Type A responses as identifiers of severe atherosclerosis. *Journal of Consulting and Clinical Psychology, 45,* 1060–1067.

Jennings, J. R., & Choi, S. (1981). Type A components and psychophysiological responses to an attention-demanding performance task. *Psychosomatic Medicine, 43,* 475–487.

Jessor, R. (1981). *The perceived environment in psychological theory and research.* In D. Magnusson (Ed.), *Toward a psychology of situations: An interactional perspective.* Hillsdale, NJ: Erlbaum.

Joffe, P. E., & Naditch, M. P. (1977). Paper and pencil measures of coping and defense processes. In N. Haan (Ed.), *Coping and defending: Processes of self-environment organization.* New York: Academic Press.

Johnson, J., & Leventhal, H. (1974). Effects of accurate expectations and behavioral instructions on reactions during a noxious medical examination. *Journal of Personality and Social Psychology, 29,* 710–718.

Johnson, J. E. (1973). Effects of accurate expectations about sensations on the sensory and distress components of pain. *Journal of Personality and Social Psychology, 27,* 261–275.

Johnson, J. H., & Sarason, I. G. (1979a). Moderator variables in life stress research. In I. G. Sarason & C. D. Spielberger (Eds.), *Stress and anxiety* (Vol. 6). Washington, DC: Hemisphere.

Johnson, J. H., & Sarason, I. G. (1979b). Recent developments in research on life stress. In V. Hamilton & D. M. Warburton (Eds.), *Human stress and cognition: An information processing approach.* London: Wiley.

Jung, C. G. (1933). *Modern man in search of a soul.* New York: Harcourt, Brace & World.

Jung, C. G. (1953). *Collected works. Vol. 7: Two essays on analytical psychology.* New York: Pantheon.

Kahn, J. P., Kornfeld, D. S., Blood, D. K., Lynn, R. B., Heller, S. S., & Frank, K. A. (1982). Type A behavior and the thallium stress test. *Psychosomatic Medicine, 44,* 431–436.

Kahn, J. P., Kornfeld, D. S., Frank, K. A., Heller, S. S., & Hoar, P. F. (1980). Type A behavior and blood pressure during coronary artery bypass surgery. *Psychosomatic Medicine, 42,* 407–413.

Kahn, R. L., Wolfe, D. M., Quinn, R. P., Snoek, J. D., & Rosenthal, R. A. (1964). *Organizational stress: Studies in role conflict and ambiguity.* New York: Wiley.

Kahneman, D., & Tversky, A. (1971). Subjective probability: A judgment of representativeness. *Cognitive Psychology, 3,* 430–454.

Kahneman, D., & Tversky, A. (1973). On the psychology of prediction. *Psychological Review, 80,* 237–251.

Kanner, A. D., Coyne, J. C., Schaefer, C., & Lazarus, R. S. (1981). Comparisons of two modes of stress measurement: Daily hassles and uplifts versus major life events. *Journal of Behavioral Medicine, 4,* 1–39.

Kanter, R. M. (1977). *Work and family in the United States: A critical review and agenda for research and policy.* New York: Russell Sage Foundation.

Kanungo, R. N. (1979). The concepts of alienation and involvement revisited. *Psychological Bulletin, 86,* 119–138.

Kaplan, B. H., Cassel, J. C., & Gore, S. (1977). Social support and health. *Medical Care, 15*(5), 47–58.

Kaplan, H. B. (1976). Antecedents of negative self-attitudes: Membership group devaluation and defensiveness. *Social Psychiatry, 11,* 15–25.

Kaplan, H. B. (1980). *Deviant behavior in defense of self.* New York: Academic Press.

Kardiner, A., Linton, R., Dubois, C., & West, J. (1945). *The psychological frontiers of society.* New York: Colombia University Press.

Kasl, S. V. (1978). In C. L. Cooper & R. Payne (Eds.), *Stress at work.* New York: Wiley.

Kasl, S. V., & Cobb, S. (1970). Blood pressure changes in men undergoing job loss: A preliminary report. *Psychosomatic Medicine, 32,* 19–38.

Kasl, S. V., Evans, A. S., & Niederman, J. C. (1979). Psychosocial risk factors in the development of infectious mononucleosis. *Psychosomatic Medicine, 41,* 445–466.

Katz, J. J., Weiner, H., Gallagher, T. G., & Hellman, L. (1970). Stress, distress, and ego defenses. *Archives of General Psychiatry, 23,* 131–142.

Kazdin, A. E. (1975). Covert modeling, imagery assessment, and assertive behavior. *Journal of Consulting and Clinical Psychology, 43,* 716–724.

Kelly, G. A. (1955). *The psychology of personal constructs* (Vol. 1). New York: Norton.

Kelman, H. C. (1961). Processes of opinion change. *Public Opinion Quarterly, 25,* 57–58.

Kemper, T. D. (1978). *A social interaction theory of emotions.* New York: Wiley.

Kemper, T. D. (1981). Social constructionist and positivist approaches to the sociology of emotions. *American Journal of Sociology, 87,* 337–362.

Kendall, P. C., & Hollon, S. D. (Eds.) (1979). *Cognitive behavioral interventions: Theory, research, and procedures.* New York: Academic Press.

Kendall, P. C., Williams, L., Pechacek, T. F., Graham, L. E., Shisslak, C., & Herzoff, N. (1979). Cognitive-behavioral and patient education interventions in cardiac catheterization procedures: The Palo Alto Medical Psychology Project. *Journal of Consulting and Clinical Psychology, 47,* 49–58.

Kent, M. W., & Rolf, J. E. (Eds.). (1979). *Primary prevention of psychopathology. Vol. 3: Social competence in children.* Hanover, NH: University Press of New England.

King, G. A., & Sorrentino, R. M. (1983). Psychological dimensions of goal-oriented interpersonal situations. *Journal of Personality and Social Psychology, 44,* 140–162.

Kinsman, R. A., Dirks, J. F., Jones, N. F., & Dahlem, N. W. (1980). Anxiety reduction in asthma: Four catches to general application. *Psychosomatic Medicine, 42,* 397–405.

Klass, E. T. (1981). A cognitive analysis of guilt over assertion. *Cognitive Therapy and Research, 5,* 283–297.

Klausner, S. Z. (Ed.) (1968). *Why man takes chances: Studies in stress seeking.* New York: Doubleday.

Klausner, S. Z. (1971). *On man and his environment.* San Francisco: Jossey-Bass.

Klein, D. C., & Seligman, M. E. P. (1976). Reversal of performance deficits and perceptual deficits in learned helplessness and depression. *Journal of Abnormal Psychology, 85,* 11–26.

Klein, G. S. (1958). Cognitive control and motivation. In G. Lindzey (Ed.), *Assessment of human motives.* New York: Holt, Rinehart & Winston.

Klinger, E. (1971). *The structure and functions of fantasy.* New York: Wiley.

Klinger, E. (1975). Consequences of commitment to and disengagement from incentives. *Psychological Review, 82,* 1–25.

Klinger, E. (1977). *Meaning and void.* Minneapolis: University of Minnesota Press.

Klos, D. S., & Singer, J. L. (1981). Determinants of the adolescent's ongoing thought following simulated parental confrontations. *Journal of Personality and Social Psychology, 41,* 975–987.

Kluckhohn, F. R. (1968). Variations in the basic values of family systems. In N. W. Bell & E. F. Vogel (Eds.), *A modern introduction to the family* (rev. ed.). New York: The Free Press.

Knapp, R. K., Kause, R. H., & Perkins, C. C., Jr. (1959). Immediate vs. delayed shock in T-maze performance. *Journal of Experimental Psychology, 58,* 357–362.

Knight, R. B., Atkins, A., Eagle, C. J., Evans, N., Finkelstein, J. W., Fukushima, D., Katz, J., & Weiner, H. (1979). Psychological stress, ego defenses, and cortisol productions in children hospitalized for elective surgery. *Psychosomatic Medicine, 41,* 40–49.

Kobasa, S. C. (1979). Stressful life events, personality, and health: An inquiry into hardiness. *Journal of Personality and Social Psychology, 37,* 1–11.

Kobasa, S. C., Maddi, S. R., & Courington, S. (1981). Personality and constitution as mediators in the stress-illness relationship. *Journal of Health and Social Behavior, 22,* 368–378.

Kobasa, S. C., Maddi, S. R., & Kahn, S. (1982). Hardiness and health: A prospective study. *Journal of Personality and Social Psychology, 42,* 168–177.

Kobasa, S. C., & Puccetti, M. C. (1983). Personality and social resources in stress resistance. *Journal of Personality and Social Psychology, 45,* 839–850.

Koenig, R. (1973). Dying versus well-being. *Omega, 4,* 181–194.

Kohn, M. L. (1969). *Class and conformity.* Homewood, IL: Dorsey.

Kohn, M. L. (1976). Social class and parental values: Another confirmation of the relationship. *American Sociological Review, 41,* 538–545.

Kohn, M. L., & Schooler, C. (1973). Occupational experience and psychological functioning: An assessment of reciprocal effects. *American Sociological Review, 38,* 97–118.

Kohn, M. L., & Schooler, C. (1978). The reciprocal effects of the substantive complexity of work and intellectual flexibility: A longitudinal assessment. *American Journal of Sociology, 84,* 24–52.

Koocher, G. P., O'Malley, J. E., Gogan, J. L., & Foster, D. J. (1980). Psychological adjustment among pediatric cancer survivors. *Journal of Child Psychology and Psychiatry, 21,* 163–173.

Korchin, S. J. (1964). Anxiety and cognition. In C. Scheerer (Ed.), *Cognition: Theory, research, promise.* New York: Harper & Row.

Koriat, A., Melkman, R., Averill, J. R., & Lazarus, R. S. (1972). The self-control of emotional reactions to a stressful film. *Journal of Personality, 40,* 601–619.

Krantz, D. S., Arabian, J. M., Davia, J. E., & Parker, J. S. (1982). Type A behavior and coronary artery bypass surgery: Intraoperative blood pressure and perioperative complications. *Psychosomatic Medicine, 44,* 273–284.

Krantz, D. S., & Schulz, R. (1980). A model of life crisis, control, and health outcomes: Cardiac rehabilitation and relocation of the elderly. In A. Baum & J. E. Singer (Eds.), *Advances in environmental psychology* (Vol. 2). Hillsdale, NJ: Erlbaum.

Krantz, S. E. (1983). Cognitive appraisals and problem-directed coping: A prospective study of stress. *Journal of Personality and Social Psychology, 44*, 638–643.

Kreitler, H., & Kreitler, S. (1976). *Cognitive orientation and behavior.* New York: Springer.

Krohne, H. W., & Laux, L. (Eds.) (1982). *Achievement, stress, and anxiety.* New York: Hemisphere.

Krohne, H. W., & Rogner, J. (1982). Repression-sensitization as a central construct in coping research. In H. W. Krohne & L. Laux (Eds.), *Achievement, stress, and anxiety.* Washington, DC: Hemisphere.

Kübler-Ross, E. (1969). *On death and dying.* New York: Macmillan.

Lacey, J. I. (1967). Somatic response patterning and stress: Some revisions of activation theory in psychological stress. In M. H. Apley and R. Trumbul (Eds.), *Psychological Stress.* New York: Appleton-Century-Crofts.

Ladd, G. W., & Mize, J. (1983). A cognitive-social learning model of social-skill training. *Psychological Review, 90*, 127–157.

Langer, E. J. (1975). The illusion of control. *Journal of Personality and Social Psychology, 32*, 311–328.

Langer, E. J., & Rodin, J. (1976). The effects of choice and enhanced personal responsibility for the aged: A field experiment in an institutional setting. *Journal of Personality and Social Psychology, 34*, 191–198.

LaRocco, J. M., House, J. S., & French, J. R. P., Jr. (1980). Social support, occupational stress, and health, *Journal of Health and Social Behavior, 21*, 202–218.

Lau, R. R. (1982). Origins of health locus of control beliefs. *Journal of Personality and Social Psychology, 42*, 322–334.

Lau, R. R., & Ware, J. F., Jr. (1982). Refinements in the measurement of health-specific locus-of-control beliefs. *Medical Care, 29*, 1147–1158.

Lawler, K. A., Allen, M. T., Critcher, E. C., & Standard, B. A. (1981). The relationship of physiological responses to the coronary-prone behavior pattern in children. *Journal of Behavioral Medicine, 4*, 203–216.

Lawton, M. P. (1977). The impact of the environment on aging and behavior. In J. E. Birren & K. W. Schaie (Eds.), *Handbook of the psychology of aging.* New York: Van Nostrand Reinhold.

Lawton, M. P. (1980). *Environment and aging.* Monterey, CA: Brooks/Cole.

Lazarus, A. A. (1971). *Behavior therapy and beyond.* New York: McGraw-Hill.

Lazarus, A. A. (1981). *The practice of multimodal therapy.* New York: McGraw-Hill.

Lazarus, R. S. (1961). A substitute-defensive conception of apperceptive fantasy. In J. Kagan & G. Lessor (Eds.), *Contemporary issues in apperceptive methods.* Springfield, IL: Thomas.

Lazarus, R. S. (1966). *Psychological stress and the coping process.* New York: McGraw-Hill.

Lazarus, R. S. (1968). Emotions and adaptation: Conceptual and empirical relations. In W. J. Arnold (Ed.), *Nebraska symposium on motivation.* Lincoln: University of Nebraska Press.

Lazarus, R. S. (1975a). A cognitively oriented psychologist looks at biofeedback. *American Psychologist, 30,* 553–561.

Lazarus, R. S. (1975b). The self-regulation of emotion. In L. Levi (Ed.), *Emotions: Their parameters and measurement.* New York: Raven.

Lazarus, R. S. (1976). Discussion. In G. Serban (Ed.), *Psychopathology of human adaptation.* New York: Plenum.

Lazarus, R. S. (1980). Cognitive behavior therapy as psychodynamics revisited. In J. Mahoney (Ed.), *Psychotherapy process: Current issues and future directions.* New York: Plenum.

Lazarus, R. S. (1982). Thoughts on the relations between emotion and cognition. *American Psychologist, 37,* 1019–1024.

Lazarus, R. S. (1984). On the primacy of cognition. *American Psychologist, 39,* 124–129.

Lazarus, R. S. (in press-a). Puzzles in the study of daily hassles. *Journal of Behavioral Medicine.*

Lazarus, R. S. (in press–b). The trivialization of distress. In J. C. Rosen & L. J. Solomon (Eds.), *Preventing health risk behaviors and promoting coping with illness. Vol. 8. Vermont Conference on the Primary Prevention of Psychopathology.* Hanover, NH: University Press of New England.

Lazarus, R. S., & Alfert, E. (1964). The short-circuiting of threat. *Journal of Abnormal and Social Psychology, 69,* 195–205.

Lazarus, R. S., & Averill, J. R. (1972). Emotion and cognition: With special reference to anxiety. In C. D. Spielberger (Ed.), *Anxiety: Current trends in theory and research* (Vol. 2). New York: Academic Press.

Lazarus, R. S., Averill, J. R., & Opton, E. M., Jr. (1970). Toward a cognitive theory of emotions. In M. Arnold (Ed.), *Feelings and emotions.* New York: Academic Press.

Lazarus, R. S., Averill, J. R., & Opton, E. M., Jr. (1974). The psychology of coping: Issues of research and assessment. In G. V. Coelho, D. A. Hamburg, & J. E. Adams (Eds.), *Coping and adaptation.* New York: Basic Books.

Lazarus, R. S., & Cohen, J. B. (1977). Environmental stress. In I. Altman and J. F. Wohlwill (Eds.), *Human behavior and the environment: Current theory and research.* New York: Plenum.

Lazarus, R. S., Coyne, J. C., & Folkman, S. (1982). Cognition, emotion, and motivation: The doctoring of Humpty-Dumpty. In R. W. J. Neufeld (Ed.), *Psychological stress and psychopathology.* New York: McGraw-Hill.

Lazarus, R. S., Deese, J., & Osler, S. F. (1952). The effects of psychological stress upon performance. *Psychological Bulletin, 49,* 293–317.

Lazarus, R. S., & DeLongis, A. (1983). Psychological stress and coping in aging. *American Psychologist, 38,* 245–254.

Lazarus, R. S., & Erikson, C. W. (1952). Effects of failure stress upon skilled performance. *Journal of Experimental Psychology, 43,* 100–105.

Lazarus, R. S., Eriksen, C. W., & Fonda, C. P. (1951). Personality dynamics and auditory perceptual recognition. *Journal of Personality, 19,* 471–482.

Lazarus, R. S., & Folkman, S. (1984). Coping and adaptation. In W. D. Gentry (Ed.), *The handbook of behavioral medicine.* New York: Guilford, 282–325.

Lazarus, R. S., Kanner, A. D., & Folkman, S. (1980). Emotions: A cognitive-phenomenological analysis. In R. Plutchik & H. Kellerman (Eds.), *Theories of Emotion. Vol. 1. Emotion: Theory, Research, and Experience.* New York: Academic Press.

Lazarus, R. S., & Launier, R. (1978). Stress-related transactions between person and environment. In L.A. Pervin & M. Lewis (Eds.), *Perspectives in interactional psychology.* New York: Plenum.

Lazarus, R. S., Opton, E. M., Jr., Nomikos, M. S., & Rankin, N. O. (1965). The principle of short-circuiting of threat: Further evidence. *Journal of Personality,* 1965, *33,* 622–635.

Lazarus, R. S., Speisman, J. C., Mordkof, A. M., & Davison, L. A. (1962). A laboratory study of psychological stress produced by a motion picture film. *Psychological Monographs, 76* (34, Whole No. 553).

Lefcourt, H. M. (1973). The function of the illusions of control and freedom. *American Psychologist, 28,* 417–425.

Lefcourt, H. M. (1976). *Locus of control: Current trends in theory and research.* New York: Halstead.

Lefcourt, H. M. (1981). *Research with the locus of control construct. Vol. 1: Assessment methods.* New York: Academic Press.

Lefcourt, H. M., Miller, R. S., Ware, E. E., & Schenk, D. (1981). Locus of control as a modifier of the relationship between stressors and moods. *Journal of Personality and Social Psychology, 41,* 357–369.

Lehrman, D. S. (1964). The reproductive behavior of ring doves. *Scientific American, 211,* 48–54.

Lei, H., & Skinner, H. A. (1980). A psychometric study of life events and social readjustment. *Journal of Psychosomatic Research, 24,* 57–65.

Lennon, M. D. (1982). The psychological consequences of menopause: The importance of timing of a life stage event. *Journal of Health and Social Behavior, 23,* 353–366.

Levenson, R. W., Sher, K. J., Grossman, L. M., Newman, J., & Newlin, D. B. (1980). Alcohol and stress response dampening: Pharmacological effects, expectancy, and tension reduction. *Journal of Abnormal Psychology, 89,* 528–538.

Leventhal, H. (1980). Toward a comprehensive theory of emotion. In L. Berkowitz (Ed.), *Advances in experimental social psychology.* New York: Academic Press.

Leventhal, H., Brown, D., Shacham, S., & Engquist, G. (1979). Effect of preparatory information about sensations, threat of pain and attention on cold pressor distress. *Journal of Personality and Social Psychology, 37,* 688–714.

Leventhal, H., & Everhart, D. (1979). Emotion, pain, and physical illness. In C. Izard (Ed.), *Emotions and psychopathology.* New York: Plenum.

Leventhal, H., & Nerenz, D. R. (1983). A model for stress research with some implications for the control of stress disorders. In D. Meichenbaum & M. Jaremko (Eds.), *Stress prevention and management: A cognitive behavioral approach.* New York: Plenum.

Levi, L. (1980). *Preventing work stress.* New York: Addison-Wesley.

Levine, M., & Spivack, G. (1964). *The Rorschach index of repressive style.* Springfield, IL: Charles C. Thomas.

Levine, J., & Zigler, E. (1975). Denial and self-image in stroke, lung cancer, and heart disease victims. *Journal of Consulting and Clinical Psychology, 43,* 751–757.

Levine, S., Goldman, L., & Coover, G. D. (1972). Expectancy and the pituitry-adrenal system. *Physiology, emotion, and psychosomatic illness.* CIBA symposium.

Levine, S., & Scotch, N. A. (1970). *Social stress.* Chicago: Aldine.

Levine, S., Weinberg, J., & Ursin, H. (1978). Definition of the coping process and statement of the problem. In H. Ursin, E. Baade, & S. Levine (Eds.), *Psychobiology of stress: A study of coping men.* New York: Academic Press.

Levinger, G. (1966). Sources of marital dissatisfaction among applicants for divorce. *American Journal of Orthopsychiatry, 36,* 803–807.

Levinson, D. J., Darrow, C. N., Klein, E. B., Levinson, M. H., & McKee, B. (1978). *The seasons of a man's life.* New York: Knopf.

Levinson, H. (1973). *The great jackass fallacy.* Boston: Harvard University Division of Research, Graduate School of Business Administration.

Levis, D. J., & Carrera, R. N. (1967). Effects of ten hours of implosive therapy in the treatment of outpatients: A preliminary report. *Journal of Abnormal Psychology, 72,* 504–508.

Levy, D. M. (1943). *Maternal over-protection.* New York: Colombia University Press.

Levy, D. M. (1955). Oppositional syndromes and oppositional behavior. In P. H. Hoch & I. Zubin (Eds.), *Psychopathology of childhood.* New York: Grune & Stratton.

Levy, D. M. (1966). *Maternal overprotection* (2nd ed.). New York: Norton.

Lewin, K. A. (1935). *A dynamic theory of personality* (Trans., K. E. Zener & D. K. Adams). New York: McGraw-Hill.

Lewin, K. A. (1936). *Principles of topological psychology* (Trans., F. Heider & G. Heider). New York: McGraw-Hill.

Lewinsohn, P. M. (1973). Clinical and theoretical aspects of depression. In K. S. Calhoun, H. E. Adams, & K. M. Mitchell (Eds.), *Innovative treatment methods in psychotherapy.* New York: Wiley.

Lewinsohn, P. M. (1975). The behavioral study and treatment of depression. In M. Herson, R. Eisler, & P. Miller (Eds.), *Progress in behavior modification*. New York: Academic Press.

Lewinsohn, P. M., Mischel, W., Chaplin, W., & Barton, R. (1980). Social competence and depression: The role of illusory self-perceptions. *Journal of Abnormal Psychology, 89*, 203–212.

Lewinsohn, P. M., & Talkington, J. (1979). Studies of the measurement of unpleasant events and relations with depression. *Applied Psychological Measurement, 3*, 83–101.

Lewis, M., Sullivan, M. W., & Michalson, L. (in press). The cognitive-emotional fugue. In C. E. Izard, J. Kagan, & R. Zajonc (Eds.), *Emotions, cognition and behavior*. New York: Cambridge University Press.

Lidell, H. S. (1964). The role of vigilance in the development of animal neurosis. In P. H. Hoch & J. Zubin (Eds.), *Anxiety*. New York: Hafner.

Lidz, T., Cornelison, A. R., Fleck, S., & Terry, D. (1957). The intrafamilial environment of schizophrenic patients: II. Marital schism and marital skew. *American Journal of Psychiatry, 114*, 241–248.

Lieberman, M. A. (1975). Adaptive processes in late life. In N. Datan & L. H. Ginsberg (Ed.), *Life-span development psychology*. New York: Academic Press.

Lieberman, D. A. (1979). Behaviorism and the mind: A (limited) call for a return to introspection. *American Psychologist, 34*, 319–333.

Lieberman, M. A., & Tobin, S. S. (1983). *The experience of old age: Stress, coping, and survival*. New York: Basic Books.

Liem, R., & Liem, J. (1978). Social class and mental illness reconsidered: The role of economic stress and social support. *Journal of Health and Social Behavior, 19*, 139–156.

Lin, R., Simeone, R. S., Ensel, W. M., & Kuo, W. (1979). Social support, stressful life events and illness: A model and empirical test. *Journal of Health and Social Behavior, 20*, 108–119.

Lindemann, E. (1944). Symptomatology and management of acute grief. *American Journal of Psychiatry, 101*, 141–148.

Linden, W., & Feurstein, M. (1981). Essential hypertension and social coping behavior. *Journal of Human Stress, 7*, 28–34.

Lindsley, D. B. (1951). Emotion. In S. S. Stevens (Ed.), *Handbook of experimental psychology*. New York: Wiley.

Linsenmeier, J. A. W., & Brickman, P. (1980). *Expectations, performance, and satisfaction*. Unpublished manuscript, University of Illinois, Evanston.

Lipowski, Z. J. (1970–1971). Physical illness, the individual and the coping process. *International Journal of Psychiatry in Medicine, 1*, 91–102.

Lipowski, Z. J. (1977). Psychosomatic medicine in the seventies: An overview. *American Journal of Psychiatry, 134*, 233–244.

Locke, D., & Pennington, D. (1982). Reasons and other causes: Their role in attribution processes. *Journal of Personality and Social Psychology, 42*, 212–223.

Locke, E., Bryan, J., & Kendall, L. (1968). Goals and intentions as mediators of the effects of monetary incentives on behavior. *Journal of Applied Psychology, 52,* 104–121.

Loevinger, J. (1976). *Ego development.* San Francisco: Jossey-Bass.

Long, J. M., Lynch, J. J., Machiran, N. M., Thomas, S. A., & Malinow, K. L. (1982). The effect of status of blood pressure during verbal communication. *Journal of Behavioral Medicine, 5,* 165–172.

Lorr, M., Daston, P., & Smith, I. R. (1967). An analysis of mood states. *Educational and Psychological Measurement, 27,* 89–96.

Lovallo, W. R., & Pishkin, V. (1980). Performance of Type A (coronary prone) men during and after exposure to uncontrollable noise and task failure. *Journal of Personality and Social Psychology, 38,* 963–961.

Lowenthal, M. F. (1977). Toward a sociopsychological theory of change in adulthood and old age. In J. E. Birren & K. W. Schaie (Eds.), *Handbook of the psychology of aging.* New York: Van Nostrand Reinhold.

Lowenthal, M. F., Thurnher, M., & Chiriboga, D. (1975). *Four stages of life.* San Francisco: Jossey-Bass.

Lucas, R. A. (1969). *Men in crisis.* New York: Basic Books.

Lumsden, D. P. (1981). Is the concept of "stress" of any use, anymore? In D. Randall (Ed.), *Contributions to primary prevention in mental health: Working papers.* Toronto: Toronto National Office of the Canadian Mental Health Association.

Lundberg, U. (1982). Type A behavior and its relation to personality variables in Swedish male and female university students. *Scandinavian Journal of Psychology, 21,* 133–138.

Lyles, J. N., Burish, T. G., Korzely, M. G., & Oldham, R. K. (1982). Efficacy of relaxation training and guided imagery in reducing the aversiveness of cancer chemotherapy. *Journal of Consulting and Clinical Psychology, 50,* 509–524.

Lyons, T. F. (1971). Role clarity, need for clarity, classification, tension, and withdrawal. *Organizational Behavior and Human Performance, 6,* 99–110. (cited in Kasl, 1978)

MacDonald, A. P. (1970). Internal-external locus of control and the practice of birth control. *Psychological Reports, 27,* 206.

Macoby, M. (1976). *The gamesman.* New York: Simon & Schuster.

MacPhillamy, D. J., & Lewinson, P. M. (1982). The pleasant events schedule: Studies on reliability, validity, and scale intercorrelation. *Journal of Consulting and Clinical Psychology, 50,* 363–380.

Mages, N. L., & Mendelsohn, G. A. (1979). Effects of cancer on patients' lives: A personological approach. In G. C. Stone, F. Cohen, & N. E. Adler (Eds.), *Health psychology: A handbook.* San Francisco: Jossey-Bass.

Magnusson, D., & Endler, N. S. (Eds.) (1977). *Personality at the crossroads.* Hillsdale, NJ: Erlbaum.

Mahl, G. F. (1949). Anxiety, HCL secretion, and peptic ulcer etiology. *Psychosomatic Medicine, 11,* 30–44.

Mahl, G. F. (1952). Relationship between acute and chronic fear and the gastric acidity and blood sugar levels in *Macca mulatta* monkeys. *Psychosomatic Medicine, 14,* 182–210.

Mahl, G. F. (1953). Physiological changes during chronic fear. *Annals of the New York Academy of Sciences, 56,* 240–249.

Mahoney, M. J. (Ed.). (1980). *Psychotherapy process: Current issues and future directions.* New York: Plenum.

Mahoney, M. J., & Arnkoff, D. B. (1978). Cognitive and self-control therapies. In S. L. Garfield & A. E. Bergin (Eds.), *Handbook of psychotherapy and behavior change: An empirical analysis.* New York: Wiley.

Main, M. (1977). Analysis of a peculiar form of reunion behavior seen in some day-care children: Its history and sequelae in children who are home-reared. In R. Webb (Ed.), *Social development in childhood: Daycare programs and research.* Baltimore: Johns Hopkins University Press.

Main, M., & Weston, D. R. (1982). Avoidance of the attachment figures in infancy: Description and interpretations. In C. M. Parkes & J. Stevenson-Hinde (Eds.), *Place of attachment in human behavior.* New York: Basic Books.

Malmo, R. B. (1959). Activation: A neuropsychological dimension. *Psychological Review, 66,* 367–386.

Manderscheid, R. W., Silbergeld, S., & Dager, E. Z. (1975). Alienation: A response to stress. *Journal of Cybernetics, 5,* 91–105.

Mandler, G. (1975), *Mind and emotion.* New York: Wiley.

Manuel, F. (1965). Toward a psychological history of utopias. *Daedalus, 94,* 293–322.

Marceil, J. C. (1977). Implicit dimensions of idiography and nomothesis: A reformulation. *American Psychologist, 32,* 1046–1055.

Marx, K. *Capital.* New York: Modern Library.

Marmor, J., & Woods, S. (Eds.). (1980). *The interface between psychodynamic and behavioral therapies.* New York: Plenum.

Marshall, G. D., & Zimbardo, P. G. (1979). Affective consequences of inadequately explained physiological arousal. *Journal of Personality and Social Psychology, 37,* 970–985.

Maslach, C. (1979). Negative emotional biasing of unexplained arousal. *Journal of Personality and Social Psychology, 37,* 953–969.

Maslow, A. H. (1964). Synergy in the society and the individual. *Journal of Individual Psychology, 20,* 153–164.

Mason, J. W. (1971). A re-evaluation of the concept of "non-specificity" in stress theory. *Journal of Psychiatric Research, 8,* 323–333.

Mason, J. W. (1974). Specificity in the organization of neuroendocrine response profiles. In P. Seeman & G. Brown (Eds.), *Frontiers in neurology and neuroscience research.* Toronto: University of Toronto.

Mason, J. W. (1975a). Emotion as reflected in patterns of endocrine integration. In L. Levi (Ed.), *Emotions: Their parameters and measurement.* New York: Raven.

Mason, J. W. (1975b). A historical view of the stress field: Part I. *Journal of Human Stress, 1,* 6–12.

Mason, J. W. (1975c). A historical view of the stress field: Part II. *Journal of Human Stress, 1,* 22–36.

Mason, J. W., Maher, J. T., Hartley, L. H. Mougey, E., Perlow, M. J., & Jones, L. G. (1976). Selectivity of corticosteroid and catecholamine response to various natural stimuli. In G. Serban (Ed.), *Psychopathology of human adaptation.* New York: Plenum.

Masserman, J. H. (1943). *Behavior and neurosis.* Chicago: University of Chicago Press.

Matthews, K. A. (1982). Psychological perspectives on the Type A behavior pattern. *Psychological Bulletin, 91,* 293–323.

Matthews, K. A., & Siegel, J. M. (1983). Type A behaviors by children, social comparison, and standards for self-evaluation, *Developmental Psychology, 19,* 135–140.

May, R. (1950). *The meaning of anxiety.* New York: Ronald Press.

May, R. (1958). Contributions of existential psychotherapy. In R. May, E. Angel, & H. F. Ellenberger (Eds.), *Existence: A new dimension in psychiatry and psychology.* New York: Basic Books.

McClelland, D. C. (1951). *Personality.* New York: Sloane.

McClelland, D. C., Atkinson, J. W., Clark, R. A., & Lowell, E. L. (1953). *The achievement motive.* New York: Appleton-Century-Crofts.

McClosky, H., & Schaar, J. H. (1965). Psychological dimensions of anomie. *American Sociological Review, 30,* 14–40. *Psychosomatic Medicine, 11,* 30–44.

McCrae, R. R. (1982). Age differences in the use of coping mechanisms. *Journal of Gerontology, 37,* 454–560.

McCrae, R. R. (1984). Situational determinants of coping responses: Loss, threat, and challenge. *Journal of Personality and Social Psychology, 46,* 919–928.

McCranie, E. W., Simpson, M. E., & Stevens, J. S. (1981). Type A behavior, field dependence, and serum lipids. *Psychosomatic Medicine, 43,* 107–116.

McDowell, I., & Praught, E. (1982). On the measurement of happiness: An examination of the Bradburn scale in the Canada Health Survey. *American Journal of Epidemiology, 116,* 949–958.

McFall, R. M. (1982). A review and reformulation of the concept of social skills. *Behavioral Assessment, 4,* 1–33.

McFall, R. M., & Twentyman, C. T. (1973). Four experiments on the relative contribution of rehearsal, modeling and coaching to assertion training. *Journal of Abnormal Psychology, 81,* 199–218.

McGrath, J. E. (1970). *Social and psychological factors in stress.* New York: Holt, Rinehart & Winston.

McLean, P. (1976). Depression as a specific response to stress. In I. G. Sarason & C. D. Spielberger (Eds.), *Stress and anxiety* (Vol. 3). Washington, DC: Hemisphere.

Mead, M. (1970). *Culture and commitment: A study of the generation gap.* Garden City, NY: Natural History Press/Doubleday.

Mechanic, D. (1962). *Students under stress: A study in the social psychology of adaptation.* New York: The Free Press. Reprinted in 1978 by the University of Wisconsin Press.

Mechanic, D. (1966a). *Medical sociology: A selective view.* New York: The Free Press.

Mechanic, D. (1966b). Response factors in illness: The study of illness behavior. *Social Psychiatry, 1,* 11–20.

Mechanic, D. (1974). Social structure and personal adaptation: Some neglected dimensions. In G. V. Coelho, D. A. Hamburg, & J. E. Adams (Eds.), *Coping and adaptation.* New York: Basic Books.

Mechanic, D. (1978). *Medical sociology* (2nd ed.). New York: The Free Press.

Meichenbaum, D. (1975). A self-instructional approach to stress management: A proposal for stress inoculation training. In C. D. Spielberger & I. G. Sarason (Eds.), *Stress and anxiety* (Vol. 2). New York: Wiley.

Meichenbaum, D. (1977). *Cognitive-behavior modification: An integrative approach.* New York: Plenum.

Meichenbaum, D., & Cameron, R. (1983). Stress inoculation training: Toward a general paradigm for training coping skills. In D. Meichenbaum & M. E. Jaremko (Eds.), *Stress reduction and prevention.* New York: Plenum.

Meichenbaum, D., & Jaremko, M. E. (Eds.). (1983). *Stress reduction and prevention.* New York: Plenum.

Meichenbaum, D., & Novaco, R. (1978). Stress inoculation: A preventative approach. In C. D. Spielberger & I. G. Sarason (Eds.), *Stress and anxiety* (Vol. 5). New York: Halstead.

Melges, F. T., & Bowlby, J. (1969). Types of hopelessness in psychopathological process. *Archives of General Psychiatry, 20,* 690–699.

Meltzer, J., & Hochstim, J. (1970). Reliability and vitality of survey data on physical health. *Public Health Reports, 85,* 1075–1086.

Mendelsohn, G. A. (1979). The psychological consequences of cancer: A study of adaptation to somatic illness. *Cahiers d'Anthropologie, 2,* 53–92.

Menninger, K. (1954). Regulatory devices of the ego under major stress. *International Journal of Psychoanalysis, 35,* 412–420.

Menninger, K. (1963). *The vital balance: The life process in mental health and illness.* New York: Viking.

Merton, R. K. (1957). *Social structure.* Glencoe, IL: The Free Press.

Messer, S. B., & Winokur, M. (1980). Some limits to the integration of psychoanalytic and behavior therapy. *American Psychologist, 35,* 818–827.

Miller, I. W., III, Klee, S. H., & Norman, W. H. (1982). Depressed and nondepressed inpatients' cognitions of hypothetical events, experimental tasks, and stressful life events. *Journal of Abnormal Psychology, 91,* 94–97.

Miller, J. G. (1953). *The development of experimental stress-sensitive tests for predicting performance in military tasks.* PRB Tech. Report 1079. Washington, DC: Psychological Research Associates.

Miller, N. E. (1948). Studies of fear as an acquirable drive: I. Fear as motivation and fear-reduction as reinforcement in learning of new responses. *Jounal of Experimental Psychology, 38,* 89–101.

Miller, N. E. (1959). Liberalization of basic S-R concepts: Extensions to conflict behavior, motivation and social learning. In S. Koch (Ed.), *Psychology: A study of a science* (Study 1, Vol. 2). New York: McGraw-Hill.

Miller, N. E. (1969). Learning of visceral and glandular responses. *Science, 163,* 434–445.

Miller, N. E. (1978). Biofeedback and visceral learning. *Annual Review of Psychology, 29,* 373–404.

Miller, N. E. (1980). A perspective on the effects of stress and coping on disease and health. In S. Levine & H. Ursin (Eds.), *Coping and health* (NATO Conference Series III: Human Factors). New York: Plenum.

Miller, N. E., & Dworkin, B. R. (1977). Effects of learning on visceral functions. *New England Journal of Medicine, 296,* 1274–1278.

Miller, S. M. (1980). When is a little information a dangerous thing? Coping with stressful events by monitoring vs. blunting. In S. Levine & H. Ursin (Eds.), *Coping and health.* New York: Plenum.

Miller, W. R., & Seligman, M. E. P. (1975). Depression and learned helplessness in man. *Journal of Abnormal Psychology, 84,* 228–238.

Mills, R. T., & Krantz, D. S. (1979). Information, choice, and reactions to stress: A field experiment in a blood bank with laboratory analogue. *Journal of Personality and Social Psychology, 37,* 608–620.

Mirsky, I. A. (1964). Discussion in the Timberline conference on psychophysiologic aspects of cardiovascular disease. *Psychosomatic Medicine, 26,* (Part II), 533–534.

Mischel, W. (1973). Toward a cogntive social learning reconceptuatlization of personality. *Psychological Review, 80,* 252–283.

Mitchell, J. C. (Ed.). (1969). *Social networks in urban situations.* Manchester, England: Manchester University Press.

Mlott, S. R., & Mlott, Y. D. (1975). Dogmatism and locus of control in individuals who smoke, stopped smoking, and never smoked. *Journal of Community Psychology, 3,* 53–57.

Monat, A. (1976). Temporal uncertainty, anticipation time, and cognitive coping under threat. *Journal of Human Stress, 2,* 32–43.

Monat, A., Averill, J. R., & Lazarus, R. S. (1972). Anticipatory stress and coping reactions under various conditions of uncertainty. *Journal of Personality and Social Psychology, 24,* 237–253.

Monat, A., & Lazarus, R. S. (1977). *Stress and coping: An anthology.* New York: Colombia University Press.

Monson, T. C., Hesley, J. W., & Chernick, L. (1982). Specifying when personality traits can and cannot predict behavior: An alternative to abandoning the attempt to predict single-act criteria. *Journal of Personality and Social Psychology, 43,* 385–399.

Moos, R. H. (1973). Conceptualizations of human environments. *American Psychologist, 28,* 652–665.

Moos, R. H. (1974). Psychological techniques in the assessment of adaptive behavior. In G. V. Coelho, D. A. Hamburg, & J. E. Adams (Eds.), *Coping and adaptation.* New York: Basic Books.

Moos, R. H. (1975). Assessment and impact of social climate. In P. McReynolds (Ed.), *Advances in psychological assessment* (Vol. 3). San Francisco: Jossey-Bass.

Moos, R. H. (Ed.) (1977). *Coping with physical illness.* New York: Plenum.

Moos, R. H., & Tsu, V. D. (1977). The crisis of physical illness: An overview. In R. H. Moos (Ed.), *Coping with physical illness.* New York: Plenum.

Moreno, J. L. (1947). *The theatre of spontaneity: An introduction to psychodrama.* New York: Beacon House.

Morgan, W. P., & Pollock, M. L. (1977). Psychological characterization of the elite distance runner. *Annals of the New York Academy of Sciences, 301,* 382–403.

Moskowitz, D. S. (1982). Coherence and cross-situational generality in personality: A new analysis of old problems. *Journal of Personality and Social Psychology, 43,* 754–768.

Moss, G. E. (1973). *Illness, immunity, and social interaction: The dynamics of biosocial resonation.* New York: Wiley.

Mueller, D. P., Edwards, D. W., & Yarvis, R. M. (1977). Stressful life events and psychiatric symptomatology: Change or undesirability? *Journal of Health and Social Behavior, 18,* 307–317.

Murawski, B. J., Penman, D., & Schmitt, M. (1978, October). Social support in health and illness: The concept and its measurement. *Cancer Nursing,* 365–371.

Murphy, G. (1966). *Personality.* New York: Basic Books.

Murphy, L. B., & associates (1962). *The widening world of childhood: Paths toward mastery.* New York: Basic Books.

Murphy, L. B. (1974). Coping, vulnerability and resilience in childhood. In G. V. Coelho, D. A. Hamburg, & J. E. Adams (Eds.), *Coping and adaptation.* New York: Basic Books.

Murphy, L. B., & Moriarty, A. E. (1976). *Vulnerability, coping, and growth: From infancy to adolescence.* New Haven: Yale University Press.

Murray, H. A. (1938). *Explorations in personality.* New York: Oxford University Press.

Nasby, W., & Yando, R. (1982). Selective encoding and retrieval of affectively valent information: Two cognitive consequences of children's mood states. *Journal of Personality and Social Psychology, 43,* 1244–1253.

Natelson, B. H., Krasnegor, N., & Holaday, J. W. (1976). Relations between behavioral arousal and plasma cortisol levels in monkeys performing repeated free-operant avoidance sessions. *Journal of Comparative and Physiological Psychology, 90,* 958–969.

Needham, R. (1975). Polythetic classification: Convergence and consequences. *Man, 10,* 349–369.

Neisser, U. (1967). *Cognitive psychology.* New York: Appleton-Century-Crofts.

Neufeld, R. W. J. (1975). Effect of cognitive appraisal on *d'* and response bias to experimental stress. *Journal of Personality and Social Psychology, 31,* 735–743.

Neufeld, R. W. J. (1976). Evidence of stress as a function of experimentally altered appraisal of stimulus aversiveness and coping adequacy. *Journal of Personality and Social Psychology, 33,* 632–646.

Neugarten, B. L. (1968a). Adult personality: Toward a psychology of the life cycle. In B. L. Neugarten (Ed.), *Middle age and aging: A reader in social psychology.* Chicago: University of Chicago Press.

Neugarten, B. L. (1968b). *Middle age and aging: A reader in social psychology.* Chicago: University of Chicago Press.

Neugarten, B. L. (1970). Dynamics of transition of middle age to old age: Adaptation and the life cycle. *Journal of Geriatric Psychiatry, 4,* 71–87.

Neugarten, B. L. (1977). Personality and aging. In J. L. Birren & K. W. Schaie (Eds.), *Handbook of the psychology of aging.* New York: Van Nostrand Reinhold.

Neugarten, B. L. (1979). Time, age, and the life cycle. *American Journal of Psychiatry, 136,* 887–894.

Neugarten, B. L., Moore, J. W., & Lowe, J. C. (1968). Age norms, age constraints, and adult socialization. *American Journal of Sociology, 70,* 710–717.

New York Times, Feb. 1, 1981, p. 22EY.

Newcomb, T. M. (1943). *Personality and social change.* New York: Dryden.

Newell, A., & Simon, H. A. (1961). Computer simulation of human thinking. *Science, 34,* 2011–2016.

Nicholls, J. G., Licht, B. G., & Pearl, R. A. (1982). Some dangers of using personality questionnaires to study personality. *Psychological Bulletin, 92,* 572–580.

Nielsen, S. L., & Sarason, I. G. (1981). Emotion, personality, and selective attention. *Journal of Personality and Social Psychology, 41,* 945–960.

Nisbett, R., & Ross, L. (1980). *Human interference: Strategies and shortcomings of social judgment.* Englewood Cliffs, NJ: Prentice-Hall.

Nomikos, M. S., Opton, E. M., Jr., Averill, J. R., & Lazarus, R. S. (1968). Surprise versus suspense in the production of stress reaction. *Journal of Personality and Social Psychology, 8,* 204–208.

Norton, J. G. (1982). *Introduction to medical psychology.* New York: The Free Press.

Novaco, R. W. (1976). The treatment of anger through cognitive and relaxational controls. *Journal of Consulting and Clinical Psychology, 44,* 681.

Novaco, R. W. (1977a). Stress inoculation: A cognitive therapy for anger and its application to a case of depression. *Journal of Consulting and Clinical Psychology, 45,* 600–608.

Novaco, R. W. (1977b). A stress inoculation approach to anger management in the training of law enforcement officers. *American Journal of Community Psychology, 5,* 327–346.

Novaco, R. W. (1979). The cognitive regulation of anger and stress. In P. C. Kendall & S. D. Hollon (Eds.), *Cognitive-behavioral interventions: Theory, research, and procedures.* New York: Academic Press.

Nowlis, V. (1965). Research with the Mood Adjective Checklist. In S. S. Tomkins & C. E. Izard (Eds.), *Affect, cognition and personality.* New York: Springer.

Nuckolls, K. B., Cassel, J., & Kaplan, B. H. (1972). Psychological assets, life crisis, and the prognosis of pregnancy. *American Journal of Epidemiology, 95,* 431–441.

Nygård, R. (1981). Toward an interactional psychology: Models from achievement motivation research. *Journal of Personality, 49,* 363–387.

Nygård, R. (1982). Achievement motives and individual differences in situational specificity. *Journal of Personality and Social Psychology, 43,* 319–327.

Obrist, P. A. (1981). *Cardiovascular psychophysiology: A perspective.* New York: Plenum.

Opler, M. K. (Ed.) (1959). *Culture and mental health.* New York: Macmillan.

Opton, E. M., Jr., & Lazarus, R. S. (1967). Personality determinants of psychophysiological response to stress: A theoretical analysis and an experiment. *Journal of Personality and Social Psychology, 6,* 291–303.

Orbach, C. E., & Bieber, I. (1957). Depressive and paranoid reactions. *AMA Archives of Neurological Psychiatry, 78,* 301–311.

Ortmeyer, C. F. (1974). Variations in mortality, morbidity, and health care by marital status. In C. L. Erhardt & J. E. Berlin (Eds.), *Mortality and morbidity in the United States.* Cambridge, MA: Harvard University Press.

Ortony, A., & Clore, G. L. (1981). Disentangling the affective lexicon. In *Proceedings of the Third Annual Conference of the Cognitive Science Society,* Berkeley, CA.

Osgood, C. E. (1966). Dimensionality of the semantic space for communication via facial expressions. *Scandinavian Journal of Psychology, 7,* 1–30.

Overmeier, J. B., Patterson, J., & Wielkiewicz, R. M. (1980). Environmental contingencies as sources of stress in animals. In S. Levine & H. Ursin (Eds.), *Coping and health.* NATO Conference Series III: Human Factors. New York: Plenum.

Overmeier, J. B., & Seligman, M. E. P. (1967). Effects of inescapable shock upon subsequent escape and avoidance responding. *Journal of Comparative and Physiological Psychology, 63,* 28.

Paloutzian, R. F. (1981). Purpose in life and value changes following conversion. *Journal of Personality and Social Psychology, 41,* 1153–1160.

Panksepp, J. (1982). Toward a general psychobiological theory of emotions. With commentaries. *The Behavioral and Brain Sciences, 5,* 407–467.

Parker, S. D., Brewer, M. B., & Spencer, J. R. (1980). Natural disaster, perceived control, and attributions to fate. *Personality and Social Psychology Bulletin, 6,* 454–459.

Parkes, C. M. (1972). *Bereavement.* New York: International Universities Press.

Parkes, C. M. (1973). Separation anxiety: An aspect of the search for a lost subject. In R. S. Weiss (Ed.), *Loneliness: The experience of emotional and social isolation.* Cambridge, MA: The MIT Press.

Parsons, T., & Bales, R. F. (1955). *Family, socialization, and interaction processes.* Glencoe, IL: The Free Press.

Pastore, N. (1949). *The nature-nurture controversy.* New York: King's Crown.

Paulhus, D. (1983). Sphere-specific measures of perceived control. *Journal of Personality and Social Psychology, 44,* 1253–1265.

Paulhus, D., & Christie, R. (1981). Spheres of control: An interactionist approach to assessment of perceived control. In H. M. Lefcourt (Ed.), *Research with the locus of control construct* (Vol. 1). New York: Academic Press.

Pearlin, L. I. (1975a). Sex roles and depression. In N. Datan & L. H. Ginsberg (Eds.), ·*Life-span developmental psychology: Normative life crises.* New York: Academic Press.

Pearlin, L. I. (1975b). Status inequality and stress in marriage. *American Sociological Review, 40,* 344–357.

Pearlin, L. I. (1980a). The life cycle and life strains. In H. M. Blalock (Ed.), *Sociological theory and research: A critical approach.* New York: The Free Press.

Pearlin, L. I. (1980b). Life strains and psychological distress among adults. In N. J. Smelser & E. H. Erikson (Eds.), *Themes of work and love in adulthood.* Cambridge, MA: Harvard University Press.

Pearlin, L. I., & Johnson, J. S. (1977). Marital status, life-strains and depression. *American Sociological Review, 42,* 704–715.

Pearlin, L. I., & Kohn, M. L. (1966). Social class, occupation, and parental values: A cross-national study. *American Sociological Review, 31,* 466–479.

Pearlin, L. I., & Lieberman, M. A. (1979). Social sources of emotional distress. In J. Simmons (Ed.), *Research in community and mental health.* Greenwich, CT: JAI Press.

Pearlin, L. I., Menaghan, E. G., Lieberman, M. A., & Mullan, J. T. (1981). The stress process. *Journal of Health and Social Behavior, 22,* 337–356.

Pearlin, L. I., & Schooler, C. (1978). The structure of coping. *Journal of Health and Social Behavior, 19,* 2–21.

Pechacek, T. F., & Danaher, B. G. (1979). How and why people quit smoking: A cognitive-behavioral analysis. In P. C. Kendall & S. D. Hollon (Eds.), *Cognitive-behavioral interventions: Theory, research and procedures.* New York: Academic Press.

Peele, S. (1981). Reductionism in the psychology of the eighties. *American Psychologist, 36,* 807–818.

Peele, S. (1983). *The science of experience: A direction for psychology.* Lexington, MA: Heath.

Pennebaker, J. W., & Lightner, J. M. (1980). Competition of internal and external information in an exercise setting. *Journal of Personality and Social Psychology, 39,* 165–174.

Perkins, C. C., Jr. (1968). An analysis of the concept of reinforcement. *Psychological Review, 76*(155).

Perri, M. G., & Richards, C. S. (1977). An investigation of naturally occurring episodes of self-controlled behaviors. *Journal of Counseling Psychology, 24,* 178–183.

Pervin, L. A., & Lewis, M. (Eds.). (1978). *Perspectives in interactional psychology.* New York: Plenum.

Peterson, C., Schwartz, S. M., & Seligman, M. E. P. (1981). Self-blame and depressive symptoms. *Journal of Personality and Social Psychology, 41,* 253–259.

Pfeiffer, E. (1977). Psychopathology and social pathology. In J. E. Birren & K. W. Schaie (Eds.), *Handbook of the psychology of aging.* New York: Van Nostrand Reinhold.

Phillips, D. C., & Orton, R. (1983). The new causal principle of cognitive learning theory: Perspectives on Bandura's "reciprocal determinism." *Psychological Review, 90,* 158–165.

Phillips, L. (1968). *Human adaptation and its failures.* New York: Academic Press.

Piaget, J. (1952). *The origins of intelligence in children.* New York: Interactional Universities Press.

Pittner, M. S., & Houston, B. K. (1980). Response to stress, cognitive coping strategies and the Type A behavior pattern. *Journal of Personality and Social Psychology, 39,* 145–157.

Pittner, M. S., Houston, B. K., & Spiridigliozzi, G. (1983). Control over stress, Type A behavior pattern, and response to stress. *Journal of Personality and Social Psychology, 44,* 627–637.

Platt, S. (1981). Social adjustment as a criterion of treatment success: Just what are we measuring? *Psychiatry, 44,* 95–112.

Platt, S., Weyman, A., Hirsch, S., & Hewett, S. (1980). The social behavior assessment schedule (SBAS): Rationale, contents, scoring and reliability of a new interview schedule. *Social Psychiatry, 15,* 43–55.

Plaut, S. M., & Friedman, S. B. (1981). Psychosocial factors in infectious disease. In R. Ader (Ed.), *Psychoneuroimmunology.* New York: Academic Press.

Plutchik, R. (1980). *Emotion: A psychoevolutionary synthesis.* New York: Harper & Row.

Plutchik, R., & Ax, A. F. (1967). A critique of determinants of emotional state by Schachter and Singer (1962). *Psychophysiology, 4,* 79–82.

Polanyi, M. (1966). *The tacit dimension*. Garden City, NY: Anchor.

Pollard, I., Basset, J. R., & Cairnscross, K. D. (1976). Plasma glucocorticoid elevation and ultrastructural changes in the adenohypnosis of the male rat following prolonged exposure to stress. *Neuroendocrinology, 21*, 312–330.

Post, H. (1976, May 31). The making of a moon man. *Harper's Weekly*, pp. 1ff.

Proshansky, H. M., Ittleson, W. H., & Rivlin, L. G. (1970). *Environmental psychology: Man and his physical setting*. New York: Holt, Rinehart & Winston.

Prochaska, J. O., & DiClemente, C. C. (1983). Stages and processes of self-change of smoking: Toward an integrative model of change. *Journal of Consulting and Clinical Psychology, 51*, 390–395.

Rabkin, J. G., & Struening, E. L. (1976). Life events, stress, and illness. *Science, 194*, 1013–1020.

Radloff, F., & Helmreich, R. (1968). *Groups under stress: Psychological research in SEALAB II*. New York: Appleton-Century-Crofts.

Rakover, S. S., & Levita, Z. (1973). Heart rate acceleration as a function of anticipation time for task performance and reward. *Journal of Personality and Social Psychology, 28*, 39–43.

Rank, O. (1952). *The trauma of birth*. New York: Bruner.

Redfield, J., & Stone, A. (1979). Individual viewpoints of stressful life events. *Journal of Consulting Psychology, 47*, 147–154.

Reich, C. A. (1970). *The greening of America*. New York: Random House.

Reisman, D. (1950). *The lonely crowd*. New York: Doubleday.

Remington, M., & Tyrer, P. (1979). The social functioning schedule: A brief semi-structured interview. *Social Psychiatry, 14*, 151–157.

Renne, K. S. (1974). Measurement of social health in a general population survey. *Social Science Research, 3*, 25–44.

Review Panel on Coronary-prone Behavior and Coronary Heart Disease. (1981). *Coronary-prone behavior and coronary heart disease: critical review.* Circulation 63, No. 6. Stephen M. Weiss, M. D., Chief, Behavioral Medicine Branch, Federal Bldg., Rm. 604, National Institute of Heart, Lung, and Blood Institute, National Institutes of Health, Bethesda, MD 20205.

Rhodewalt, F., & Davison, J., Jr. (1983). Reactance and the coronary-prone behavior pattern: The role of self-attribution in responses to reduced behavioral freedom. *Journal of Personality and Social Psychology, 44*, 220–228.

Rice, B. (1976, January). Honor thy father. *Psychology Today*, pp, 36–47.

Riley, M. W. (in press). Age strata in social systems. In R. H. Binstock & E. Shanas (Eds.), *Handbook on aging and the social sciences*. New York: Van Nostrand Reinhold.

Rissler, A. (1977). Stress reactions at work and after work during a period of quantitative overload. *Ergonomics, 20*(13).

Robertson, J., & Bowlby, J. (1952). Responses of young children to separation from their mothers. *Courrier du Centre International de l'Enfance, 2,* 132–142.

Rochlin, G. (1965). *Griefs and discontents: The forces of change.* Boston: Little, Brown.

Rodin, J., & Langer, E. J. (1977). Long-term effects of a control-relevant intervention with the institutionalized aged. *Journal of Personality and Social Psychology, 35,* 897–902.

Rogers, J. (1977). *You can stop: A smokEnder approach to quitting smoking and sticking to it.* New York: Simon & Schuster.

Rokeach, M. (1968). *Beliefs, attitudes, and values.* San Francisco: Jossey-Bass.

Rose, R. M. (1980). Endocrine responses to stressful psychological events. *Psychiatric Clinics of North America, 3,* 1–15.

Rose, R. M., Jenkins, C. D., & Hurst, M. W. (1978). *Air traffic controller health change study.* Report prepared for Federal Avaiation Administration.

Rosenbaum, M. (1980a). Individual differences in self-control behaviors and tolerance of painful stimulation. *Journal of Abnormal Psychology, 89,* 581–590.

Rosenbaum, M. (1980b). A schedule for assessing self-control behaviors: Preliminary findings. *Behavior Therapy, 11,* 109–112.

Rosenbaum, M. (in press). Learned resourcefulness as a behavioral repertoire for the self-regulation of internal events: Issues and speculations. In M. Rosenbaum, C. M. Franks, & Y. Jaffe (Eds.), *Perspectives on behavior therapy in the eighties.* New York: Springer.

Rosenbaum, M., & Merbaum, M. (in press). Self-control of anxiety and depression: An evaluative review of treatments. *Clinical Behavior Therapy Review.*

Rosenberg, M. J. (1969). The conditions and consequences of evaluating apprehension. In R. Rosenthal & R. W. Rosnow (Eds.), *Artifacts in behavioral research.* New York: Academic Press.

Rosenhan, D. L., Underwood, B., & Moore, B. (1974). Affect moderates self-gratification and altruism. *Journal of Personality and Social Psychology, 30,* 546–552.

Rosenzweig, S. (1944). An outline of frustration theory. In J. McV. Hunt (Ed.), *Personality and the behavior disorders.* New York: Ronald Press.

Rosenstiel, A., & Roth, S. (1981). Relationship between cognitive activity and adjustment in four spinal-cord-injured individuals: A longitudinal investigation. *Journal of Human Stress,* March, 35–43.

Roskies, E. (1972). *Abnormality and normality: The mothering of thalidomide children.* Ithaca: Cornell University Press.

Roskies, E. (1983). Stress management: Averting the evil eye. *Contemporary Psychology, 28,* 542–544.

Rosow, I. (1963). Adjustment of the normal aged: Concept and measurement. In R. Williams, C. Tibbitts, & W. Donahue (Eds.), *Processes of Aging* (Vol. 2). New York: Atherton.

Rosow, I. (1967). *Social integration of the aged.* New York: The Free Press.

Rosow, I., & Breslau, N. (1966). A Guttman Health Scale for the aged. *Journal of Gerontology, 21,* 556–559.

Ross, C. E., & Mirowsky, J., II (1979). A comparison of life-event-weighting schemes: Change, undesirability, and effect-proportional indices. *Journal of Health and Social Behavior, 20,* 166–177.

Rothbaum, F., Weisz, J. R., & Snyder, S. S. (1982). Changing the world and changing the self: A two-process model of perceived control. *Journal of Personality and Social Psychology, 42,* 5–37.

Rothbaum, F., Wolfer, J., & Visintainer, M. (1979). Coping behavior and locus of control in children. *Journal of Personality, 47,* 118–135.

Rotter, J. B. (1954). *Social learning and clinical psychology.* Englewood Cliffs, NJ: Prentice-Hall.

Rotter, J. B. (1966). Generalized expectancies for internal versus external control of reinforcement. *Psychological Monographs: General and Applied, 80* (Whole No. 609).

Rotter, J. B. (1975). Some problems and misconceptions related to the construct of internal versus external control of reinforcement. *Journal of Consulting and Clinical Psychology, 43,* 56–67.

Rubenstein, R. L. (1966). *After Auschwitz.* Indianapolis: Bobbs-Merrill.

Rundall, T. G., & Evashwick, C. (1982). Social networks and health-seeking among the elderly. *Research on Aging, 4,* 205–226.

Rundall, T. G., & Wheeler, J. R. C. (1979). The effect of income on use of preventive care: An evaluation of alternative explanations. *Journal of Health and Social Behavior, 20,* 397–406.

Russell, B. (1968). *The conquest of happiness.* New York: Grosset & Dunlap.

Russell, D. (1982). The causal dimension scale: A measure of how individuals perceived causes. *Journal of Personality and Social Psychology, 42,* 1137–1145.

Russell, J. A. (1980). A circumplex model of affect. *Journal of Personality and Social Psychology, 39,* 1161–1178.

Russell, J. A., & Mehrabian, A. (1977). Evidence for a three-factor theory of emotions. *Journal of Research in Personality, 11,* 273–294.

Sackheim, H. A. (in press). Self-deception, self-esteem, and depression: The adaptive value of lying to oneself. In J. Masling (ed.), *Empirical studies of psychoanalytic theory.* Hillsdale, NJ: Erlbaum.

San Francisco Chronicle, Dec. 12, 1979, p. 16.

Sapira, J. D., Scheib, E. T., Moriarty, R., & Shapiro, A. P. (1971). Differences in perception between hypertensive and normotensive populations. *Psychosomatic Medicine, 33,* 239–250.

Sarason, I. G. (1960). Empirical findings and theoretical problems in the use of anxiety scales. *Psychological Bulletin, 57,* 403–415.

Sarason, I. G. (1972). Experimental approaches to test anxiety: Attention and the uses of information. In C. D. Spielberger (Ed.), *Anxiety: Current trends in theory and research* (Vol. 2). New York: Academic Press.

Sarason, I. G. (1975). Test anxiety, attention, and the general problem of anxiety. In C. D. Spielberger & I. G. Sarason (Eds.), *Stress and anxiety* (Vol. 1). Washington, DC: Hemisphere.

Sarason, I. G., Johnson, J. H., & Siegel, J. M. (1978). Assessing the impact of life changes: Development of the Life Experiences Survey. *Journal of Consulting and Clinical Psychology, 46*, 932–946.

Sarason, I. G., Levine, H. M., Basham, R. B., & Sarason, B. R. (1983). Assessing social support: The social support questionnaire. *Journal of Personality and Social Psychology, 44*, 127–139.

Sarason, I. G., & Spielberger, C. D.; and Spielberger, C. D., & Sarason, I. G. (Eds.) (1975). *Stress and anxiety* (Vols. 1–). New York: Wiley. (ongoing series)

Sarason, S. B. (1977). *Work, aging, and social change.* New York: The Free Press.

Sarason, S. B., Mandler, G., & Craighill, P. C. (1952). The effect of differential instructions on anxiety and learning. *Journal of Abnormal and Social Psychology, 47*, 561—565.

Sarbin, T. R. (1981). On self-deception. *Annals of the New York Academy of Science, 364*, 220–235.

Sarbin, T. R. (1982). Contextualism: A world view for modern psychology. In V. L. Allen & K. E. Scheibe (Eds.), *The social context of conduct: Psychological writings of Theodore Sarbin.* New York: Praeger.

Schachter, S. (1951). Deviation, rejection, and communication. *Journal of Abnormal and Social Psychology, 46*, 190–207.

Schachter, S. (1966). The interaction of cognitive and physiological determinants of emotional state. In C. D. Spielberger (Ed.), *Anxiety and behavior.* New York: Academic Press.

Schachter, S. (1970). The assumption of identity and peripheralist-centralist controversies in motivation and emotion. In M. B. Arnold (Ed.), *Feelings and emotion.* New York: Academic Press.

Schacter, S., & Singer, J. E. (1962). Cognitive, social and physiological determinants of emotional state. *Psychological Review, 69*, 379–399.

Schaefer, C., Coyne, J. C., & Lazarus, R. S. (1982). The health-related functions of social support. *Journal of Behavioral Medicine, 4*, 381–406.

Schank, R., & Abelson, R. (1977). *Scripts, plans, goals and understanding.* New York: Wiley.

Scheidt, R. J. (1976, April). *Situational factors in the assessment of adult competence.* Paper presented at Western Psychological Association meetings, Los Angeles.

Schein, E. H. (1980). *Organizational psychology* (3rd ed.). Englewood Cliffs, NJ: Prentice-Hall.

Scherer, K. R. (1982). Emotion as a process: Function, origin and regulation. *Social Science Information, 21*, 555–570.

Scherer, K. R. (in press). On the nature and function of emotion: A component process approach. In K. R. Scherer & P. Ekman (Eds.), *Approaches to emotion.* Hillsdale, NJ: Erlbaum.

Scherwitz, L., McKelvain, R., Laman, C., Patterson, J., Duttons, L., Yusim,

S., Lester, J., Kraft, I., Rochelle D., & Leachmen, R. (1983). Type A behavior, self-involvement, and coronary atherosclerosis. *Psychosomatic Medicine, 45,* 47–57.

Schlegel, R. P., Wellwood, J. K., Copps, B. E., Gruchow, W. H., & Sharratt, M. T. (1980). The relationship between perceived challenge and daily symptom reporting in Type A vs. Type B postinfarct subjects. *Journal of Behavioral Medicine, 3,* 191–204.

Schlenker, B. R., & Leary, M. R. (1982). Social anxiety and self-presentation: A conceptualization and model. *Psychological Bulletin, 92,* 641–669.

Schlosberg, H. (1954). Three dimensions of emotion. *Psychological Review, 61,* 81–88.

Schmale, A. H., Jr. (1972). Giving up as a final common pathway to changes in health. *Advances in Psychosomatic Medicine, 8,* 20–40.

Schmale, A. H., Jr. & Iker, H. P. (1966). The affect of hopelessness and the development of cancer. *Psychosomatic Medicine, 28,* 714–721.

Schmidt, D. E., & Keating, J. P. (1979). Human crowding and personal control: An integration of the research. *Psychological Bulletin, 86,* 680–700.

Schoenberg, B., Carr, A. C., Kutscher, A. H., Peretz, D., & Goldberg, I. (Eds.). (1974). *Anticipatory grief.* New York: Columbia University Press.

Schoenberg, B., Carr, A. C., Peretz, D., & Kutscher, A. H. (Eds.). (1970). *Loss and grief: Psychological management in medical practice.* New York: Columbia University Press.

Schoenberg, B., Gerger, I., Wiener, A., Kutscher, A. H., Peretz, D., & Carr, A. C. (Eds.). (1975). *Bereavement: Its psychosocial aspects.* New York: Columbia University Press.

Schönpflug, W. (1983). Coping efficiency and situational demands. In G. R. J. Hockey (Ed.), *Stress and fatigue in human performance.* New York: Wiley.

Schönpflug, W. (in press). Goal directed behavior as a source of stress: Psychological origins and consequences of inefficiency. In M. Frese & J. Sabini (Eds.), *Goal directed behavior: The concept of action.* Hillsdale, NJ: Erlbaum.

Schutz, W. C. (1967). *The FIRO Scales manual.* Palo Alto, CA: Consulting Psychologists Press.

Schwartz, G. E. (1973). Biofeedback as therapy: Some theoretical and practical issues. *American Psychologist, 30,* 553–561.

Schwartz, G. E. (1982). Testing the biophysical model: The ultimate challenge facing behavioral medicine? *Journal of Consulting and Clinical Psychology, 50,* 1040–1053.

Schwartz, R. S. (1975). Medical intelligence. Current concepts: Another look at immunologic surveillance. *New England Journal of Medicine, 293,* 181–184.

Schwartz, S. (1970). Moral decision making and behavior. In J. Macauley & L. Berkowitz (Eds.), *Altruism and helping behavior.* New York: Academic Press.

Seeman, M. (1959). On the meaning of alienation. *American Sociological Review, 24,* 783–791.

Seeman, M. (1971). The urban alienations: Some dubious theses from Marx to Marcuse. *Journal of Personality and Social Psychology, 19,* 135–143.

Seidenberg, R. (1973). *Corporate wives: Corporate casualties?* New York: AMA-COM.

Seligman, M. E. P. (1968). Chronic fear produced by unpredictable electric shock. *Journal of Comparative and Physiological Psychology, 66*(402).

Seligman, M. E. P. (1974). Depression and learned helplessness. In R. J. Friedman & M. M. Katz (Eds.), *The psychology of depression: Contemporary theory and research.* Washington: Winston-Wiley.

Seligman, M. E. P. (1975). *Helplessness.* San Francisco: W. H. Freeman.

Seligman, M. E. P., & Maier, S. F. (1967). Failure to escape traumatic shock. *Journal of Experimental Psychology, 74,* 1–9.

Seligman, M. E. P., Maier, S. F., & Solomon, R. L. (1971). Unpredictable and uncontrollable aversive events. In F. R. Brush (Ed.), *Aversive conditioning and learning.* New York: Academic Press.

Selye, H. (1950). *The physiology and pathology of exposure to stress.* Montreal: Acta.

Selye, H. (1951–1956). *Annual report of stress.* Montreal: Acta.

Selye, H. (1956). *The stress of life.* New York: McGraw-Hill.

Selye, H. (1974). *Stress without distress.* Philadelphia: Lippincott.

Selye, H. (1976). *The stress of life* (rev. ed.). New York: McGraw-Hill.

Selye, H. (1979a). Forward. In B. Gorman, *Attitude therapy for stress disorders.* Calgary: Detselig Enterprises.

Selye, H. (1979b). *The stress of life* (rev. ed.). New York: Van Nostrand Reinhold.

Selye, H. (Ed.). (1980). *Selye's guide to stress research* (Vol. 1). New York: Van Nostrand Reinhold.

Shaffer, G. W., & Lazarus, R. S. (1952). *Fundamental concepts in clinical psychology.* New York: McGraw-Hill.

Shannon, C. E., & Weaver, W. (Eds.). (1962). *The mathematical theory of communication.* Urbana: University of Illinois Press.

Shannon, I. L., & Isbell, G. M. (1963). *Stress in denial patients: Effect of local anesthetic procedures.* Technical Report No. SAM-TDR-63-29, USAF School of Aerospace Medicine, Brooks Air Force Base, Texas.

Shapiro, D. (1965). *Neurotic styles.* New York: Basic Books.

Shapiro, D., Tursky, B., & Schwartz, G. E. (1970). Differentiation of heart rate and blood pressure in man by operant conditioning. *Psychosomatic Medicine, 32,* 417–423.

Shatan, C. F. (1974). Through the membrane of reality: "Impacted grief" and perceptual dissonance in Vietnam combat veterans. *Psychiatric Opinion, 11*(6), 6–15.

Sheehy, G. (1976). *Passages: Predictable crises of adult life.* New York: Dutton.

Shekelle, R. B., Gale, M., Ostfeld, A. M., & Ogelsby, P. (1983). Hostility, risk of coronary heart disease, and mortality. *Psychsomatic Medicine, 45,* 109–114.

Sher, K. L., & Levenson, R. W. (1982). Risk of alcoholism and individual differences in the stress-reponse-dampening effect of alcohol. *Journal of Abnormal Psychology, 91,* 350–367.

Sherif, M. (1935). A study of some social factors in perception. *Archives of Psychology, 27,* (Whole No. 187).

Shervin, H., & Dickman, S. (1980). The psychological unconscious: A necessary assumption for all psychological theory? *American Psychologist, 35,* 421–434.

Shinn, M., Rosario, M. Mørch, H., Chestnut, D. E. Coping with job stress and burnout in the human services. *Journal of Personality and Social Psychology, 1984, 46,* 864–876.

Shipley, R. H., Butt, J. H., & Horwitz, E. A. (1979). Preparation to reexperience a stressful medical examination: Effect of repetitious videotape exposure and coping style. *Journal of Consulting and Clinical Psychology, 47,* 485–492.

Shipley, R. H., Butt, J. H., Horwitz, B., & Farbry, J. E. (1978). Preparation for a stressful medical procedure: Effect of amount of stimulus preexposure and coping style. *Journal of Consulting and Clinical Psychology, 46,* 499–507.

Shontz, F. C. (1975). *The psychological aspects of physical illness and disability.* New York: Macmillan.

Shontz, F. C. (1976). Single-organism designs. In P. M. Bentler, D. J. Lettieri, & G. A. Austin, *Research issues 13: Data analysis strategies and designs for substance abuse research.* U.S. Dept. of Health, Education and Welfare, Public Health Service, Alcohol, Drug Abuse and Mental Health Administration, National Institute on Drug Abuse.

Shrauger, J. S., & Osberg, T. M. (1981). The relative accuracy of self-predictions and judgments by others in psychological assessment. *Psychological Bulletin, 90,* 322–351.

Sidle, A., Moos, R. H., Adams, J., & Cady, P. (1969). Development of a coping scale. *Archives of General Psychiatry, 20,* 225–232.

Silver, R. L., & Wortman, C. B. (1980a). Coping with undesirable life events. In J. Garber & M. E. P. Seligman (Eds.), *Human helplessness: Theory and applications.* New York: Academic Press.

Silver, R. L., & Wortman, C. B. (1980b, September). *Expectations of control and coping with permanent paralysis.* Paper presented at Symposium on Issues of Control in Health, American Psychological Association meetings, Montreal.

Singer, J. L. (1974). *Imagery and daydream methods in psychotherapy and behavior modification.* New York: Academic Press.

Singer, J. L., & Opler, M. K. (1956). Contrasting patterns of fantasy and motility in Irish and Italian schizophrenics. *Journal of Abnormal Psychology, 53,* 42–47.

Sinyor, D., Schwartz, S. G., Perronet, F., Brisson, G., & Seraganian, P. (1983). Aerobic fitness level and reactivity to psychosocial stress: Physiological, biochemical, and subjective measures. *Psychosomatic Medicine, 45,* 205–217.

Skinner, B. F. (1938). *The behavior of organisms.* New York: Appleton.

Skinner, B. F. (1953). *Science and human behavior.* New York: Macmillan.

Skinner, H. A., & Lei, H. (1980). Differential weights in life change research: Useful or irrelevant? *Psychomatic Medicine, 42,* 367–370.

Slife, B. D., & Rychlak, J. F. (1982). Role of affective assessment in modeling aggressive behavior. *Journal of Personality and Social Psychology, 43,* 861–868.

Smelser, N. J. (1963). *Theory of collective behavior.* New York: The Free Press.

Smith, R. E., & Ascough, J. C. (in press). Induced affect in stress management training. In S. Burchfield (Ed.), *Stress, psychological and physiological interactions.* Washington, DC: Hemisphere.

Sokolov, E. N. (1963). *Perception and the conditioned reflex.* Oxford: Pergamon.

Sollod, R. N., & Wachtel, P. L. (1980). A structural and transactional approach to cognition in clinical problems. In M. J. Mahoney (Ed.), *Psychotherapy process: Current issues and future directions.* New York: Plenum.

Snyder, M. L. (1982). A helpful theory. (Review of Garber and Seligman, 1980). *Contemporary Psychology, 27,* 11–12.

Speisman, J. C., Lazarus, R. S., Mordkoff, A. M., & Davison, L. A. (1964). Experimental analysis of a film used as a threatening stimulus. *Journal of Consulting Psychology, 28,* 23–33.

Spence, J. T., & Spence, K. W. (1966). The motivational components of manifest anxiety: Drive and drive stimuli. In C. D. Spielberger (Ed.), *Anxiety and behavior.* New York: Academic Press, 1966.

Spence, K. W. (1956). *Behavior theory and conditioning.* New Haven: Yale University Press.

Sperry, R. (1982). Some effects of disconnecting the cerebral hemispheres. *Science, 217,* 1223–1226.

Speilberger, C. D. (Ed.). (1966). *Anxiety and behavior.* New York: Academic Press.

Spielberger, C. D. (Ed.) (1972). *Anxiety: Current trends in theory and research* (Vols. 1 and 2). New York: Academic Press.

Spinetta, J. J., & Maloney, L. J. (1978). The child with cancer: Pattern of communication and denial. *Journal of Consulting and Clinical Psychology, 46,* 1540–1541.

Stahl, S. M., Grim, C. E., Donald, S., & Neikirk, H. J. (1975). A model for the social sciences and medicine: The case for hypertension. *Social Science and Medicine, 9,* 31–38.

Stampfl, T. (1970). "Implosive therapy." In D. Lewis (Ed.), *Learning approaches to therapeutic behavior change.* Chicago: Aldine

Staudenmeyer, H., Kinsman, R. A., Dirks, J. F., Spector, S. L., & Wangaard, C. (1979). Medical outcome in asthmatic patients: Effects of airways hyperactivity and symptom-focused anxiety. *Psychosomatic Medicine, 41,* 109–118.

Steffy, R. A., Meichenbaum, D., & Best, J. A. (1970). Aversive and cognitive factors in the modification of smoking behavior. *Behaviour Research and Therapy, 8,* 115–125.

Stendler, C. G. (1950). Sixty years of child training practices. *Journal of Pediatrics, 36,* 122–134.

Stern, M. J., Pascale, L., & McLoone, J. B. (1976). Psychosocial adaptation following an acute myocardial infarction. *Journal of Chronic Diseases, 29,* 513–526.

Stewart, A. J. (1982). The course of individual adaptation to life changes. *Journal of Personality and Social Psychology, 42,* 1100–1113.

Stewart, A. J., Sokol, M., Healy, J. M., Jr., Chester, N. L., & Weinstock-Savoy, D. (1982). Adaptation to life changes in children and adults: Cross-sectional studies. *Journal of Personality and Social Psychology, 43,* 1270–1281.

Stokols, D. (Ed.). (1977). *Perspectives on environment and behavior: Theory, research and applications.* New York: Plenum.

Stone, G. C., Cohen, F., & Adler, N. E. (Eds.). (1979). *Health psychology: A handbook.* San Francisco: Jossey-Bass.

Stone, A. A., & Neale, J. M. (1984). New Measure of daily coping: Development and preliminary results. *Journal of Personality and Social Psychology, 1984, 46,* 892–906.

Strack, S., & Coyne, J. C. (1983). Social conformation of dysphoria: Shared and private reactions to depression. *Journal of Personality and Social Psychology, 44,* 798–806.

Straits, B., & Sechrest, L. (1963). Further support of some findings about the characteristics of smokers and nonsmokers. *Journal of Consulting Psychology, 27,* 282.

Strickland, B. R. (1978). Internal-external expectancies and health-related behaviors. *Journal of Consulting and Clinical Psychology, 46,* 1192–1211.

Suls, J. (Ed.). (1983). *Psychological perspectives on the self* (Vol. 1). Hillsdale, NJ: Erlbaum.

Suls, J. (1982). Social support, interpersonal relations, and health: Benefits and liabilities. In G. Sanders & J. Suls (Eds.), *Social psychology of health and illness.* Hillsdale, NJ: Erlbaum.

Surwit, R. S., Feinglos, M. N., & Scovern, A. W. (1983). Diabetes and behavior. *American Psychologist, 38,* 255–262.

Sweeney, P. D., Shaeffer, D., & Golin, S. (1982). Attributions about self and others in depression. *Journal of Personality and Social Psychology Bulletin, 8,* 37–42.

Syme, S. L. (in press). Sociocultural factors and disease etiology. In W. D. Gentry (Ed.), *Handbook of behavioral medicine.* New York: Guilford.

Syme, S. L., & Berkman, L. F. (1976). Social class, susceptibility, and sickness. *American Journal of Epidemiology, 104,* 1–8.

Tausig, M. (1982). Measuring life events. *Journal of Health and Social Behavior,* 23, 52–64.

Taylor, J. A. (1953). A personality scale of manifest anxiety. *Journal of Abnormal and Social Psychology,* 48, 285–290.

Taylor, S. E. (1983). Adjustment to threatening events: A theory of cognitive adaptation. *American Psychologist,* 38, 1161–1173.

Thayer, R. E. (1978). Toward a psychological theory of multidimensional activation (arousal). *Motivation and Emotion,* 2, 1–34.

Thoits, P. A. (1982). Conceptual, methodological, and theoretical problems in studying social support as a buffer against life stress. *Journal of Health and Social Behavior,* 23, 145–159.

Thoits, P. A. (1983). Dimensions of life events as influences upon the genesis of psychological distress and associated conditions: An evaluation and synthesis of the literature. In H. B. Kaplan (Ed.), *Psychosocial stress: Trends in theory and research.* New York: Academic Press.

Thomae, H. (1976). Patterns of aging: Findings from the Bonn Longitudinal Study of Aging. In K. F. Riegel & H. Thomae (Eds.), *Contributions to human development* (Vol. 3). Basel, Switzerland: Karger.

Thomas, L. (1983). *The youngest science: Notes of a medicine-watcher.* New York: Viking.

Thompson, S. C. (1981). Will it hurt less if I can control it? A complex answer to a simple question. *Psychological Bulletin,* 90, 89–101.

Timnick, L. (1982, August). Now you can learn to be likeable, confident, socially successful for only the cost of your present education. *Psychology Today.*

Tinbergen, N. (1951). *The study of instincts.* London: Oxford University Press.

Tobin, S., & Lieberman, M. (1976). *Last home for the aged.* San Francisco: Jossey-Bass.

Toffler, A. (1970). *Future shock.* New York: Random House.

Tomkins, S. S. (1962). *Affect, imagery, consciousness. Vol. 1: The positive affects.* New York: Springer.

Tomkins, S. S. (1963). Simulation of personality: The interrelationships between affect, memory, thinking, perception and action. In S. S. Tomkins and S. Messick (Eds.), *Computer simulation of personality. New York:* Wiley.

Tomkins, S. S. (1981). The quest for primary motives: Biography and autobiography of an idea. *Journal of Personality and Social Psychology,* 41, 306–329.

Tomkins, S. S. (1982). Affect theory. In P. Ekman (Ed.), *Emotion in the human face* (2nd ed.). Cambridge, England: Cambridge University Press.

Tuchman, B. W. (1978). *A distant mirror: The calamitous 14th century.* New York: Knopf.

Turk, D. C., Sobel, H. J., Follick, M. J., & Youkilis, H. D. (1980). A sequential criterion analysis for assessing coping with chronic illness. *Journal of Human Stress,* June 35–40.

Turner, B. F., Tobin, S., & Lieberman, M. A. (1972). Personality traits as predictors of institutional adaptation among the aged. *Journal of Gerontology, 27,* 61–68.

Turner, R. J. (1981). Social support as a contingency in psychological well-being. *Journal of Health and Social Behavior, 22,* 357–367.

Tursky, B., & Sternbach, R. A. (1967). Further psychological correlates of ethnic differences in responses to shock. *Psychophysiology, 4,* 67–74.

Tversky, A., & Kahneman, D. (1971). Belief in the law of small numbers. *Psychological Bulletin, 76,* 105–110.

Tversky, A., & Kahneman, D. (1973). Availability: A heuristic for judging frequency and probability. *Cognitive Psychology, 5,* 207–232.

Tversky, A., & Kahneman, D. (1974). Judgment under uncertainty: Heuristics and biases. *Science, 185,* 1124–1131.

Tversky, A., & Kahneman, D. (1981). The framing of decisions and the psychology of choice. *Science, 211,* 453–458.

Tyler, F. B., & Pargamet, K. I. (unpublished ms.). The behavioral attributes of psychosocial competence.

Ursin, H. (1980). Personality, activation and somatic health. In S. Levine & H. Ursin (Eds.), *Coping and health* (NATO Conference Series III: Human factors). New York: Plenum.

Vaillant, G. E. (1977). *Adaptation to life.* Boston: Little, Brown.

Van Egeren, L. F., Fabrega, H., Jr., & Thornton, D. W. (1983). Electrocardiographic effects of social stress on coronary-prone (Type A) individuals. *Psychosomatic Medicine, 45,* 195–203.

Van Harrison, R. (1978). Person–environment fit and job stress. In C. L. Cooper & R. Payne (Eds.), *Stress at work.* New York: Wiley.

Vernon, M. D. (1962). *The psychology of perception.* Middlesex, England: Penguin.

Veroff, J. B. (1981). The dynamics of help-seeking in men and women: A national survey study. *Psychiatry, 44*(3), 189–200.

Vickers, R. R., & Hervig, L. K. (1981). Comparison of three psychological defense mechanism questionnaires. *Journal of Personality Assessment, 45,* 630–638.

Vickers, R. R., Hervig, L. K., Rahe, R. H., & Rosenman, R. H. (1981). Type A behavior pattern and coping and defense. *Psychosomatic Medicine, 43,* 381–396.

Vinokur, A., & Selzer, M. (1975). Desirable versus undesirable events: Their relationships to stress and mental distress. *Journal of Personality and Social Psychology, 32,* 329–337.

Visotsky, H. M., Hamburg, D. A., Goss, M. E., & Lebovits, B. Z. (1961). Coping behavior under extreme stress. *Archives of General Psychiatry, 5,* 423–448.

Vogel, W., Raymond, S., & Lazarus, R. S. (1959). Intrinsic motivation and psychological stress. *Journal of Abnormal and Social Psychology, 58,* 225–233.

von Greyerz, W. (1962). *Psychology of survival.* Amsterdam: Elsevier.

Vroom, V. H. (1964). *Work and motivation.* New York: Wiley.

Wachtel, P. (1977). *Psychoanalysis and behavior therapy: Toward an integration.* New York: Basic Books.

Wachtel, P. L. (1980). Investigation and its discontents: Some constraints on progress in psychological research. *American Psychologist, 35,* 399–408.

Wallace, A. F. C. (1956). *Human behavior in extreme situations: A survey of the literature and suggestions for further reseach.* Washington, DC: National Academy of Sciences (National Research Council, Disaster Study No. 1).

Wallerstein, J. S. (1977). Responses of the preschool child to divorce: Those who cope. In M. F. McMillan & S. Henao (Eds.), *Child psychiatry: Treatment and research.* New York: Brunner/Mazel.

Wallerstein, J. S., & Kelly, J. B. (1980). *Surviving the breakup: How children and parents cope with divorce.* New York: Basic Books.

Wallston, K. A., Maides, S., & Wallston, B. S. (1976). Health-related information seeking as a function of health related locus of control and health value. *Journal of Research in Personality, 10,* 215–222.

Wallston, B. S., Wallston, K. A., Kaplan, G. D., & Maides, S. A. (1976). Development and validation of the health locus of control (HLC) scale. *Journal of Consulting and Clinical Psychology, 44,* 580–585.

Ware, J. E., Jr., Brook, R. H., & Davies-Avery, A., (1980). *Conceptualization and measurement of health for adults in the health insurance study. Vol. 1: Analysis of relationships among health status measures.* Santa Monica, CA: The Rand Corporation.

Watson, D., Clark, L. A., & Tellegen, A. (in press). Cross-cultural convergence in the structure of mood: A Japanese replication and a comparison with U.S. findings. *Journal of Personality and Social Psychology.*

Watzlawick, P. (1976). *How real is real?* New York: Random House.

Watzlawick, P., & Coyne, J. C. (1980). Depression following stroke: Brief, problem-focused family treatment. *Family Process, 19,* 13–18.

Weakland, J. H., Fisch, R., Watzlawick, P., & Bodin, A. M. (1974). Brief therapy: Focused problem resolution. *Family Process, 19,* 13–18.

Weimer, W. B. (1980). Psychotherapy and philosophy of science. In M. J. Mahoney (Ed.), *Psychotherapy process: Current issues and future directions.* New York: Plenum.

Weinberg, J., & Levine, S. (1980). Psychobiology of coping in animals: The effects of predictability. In S. Levine & H. Ursin (Eds.), *Coping and health* (NATO Conference Series III: Human factors). New York: Plenum.

Weinberger, D. A., Schwartz, G. E., & Davidson, R. J. (1979). Low-anxious, high-anxious, and repressive coping styles: Psychometric patterns and behavioral and physiological responses to stress. *Journal of Abnormal Psychology, 88,* 369–380.

Weiner, B. (Ed.). (1974). *Cognitive views of human emotion.* New York: Academic Press.

Weiner, B. (1980). A cognitive (attribution)-emotion-action model of motivated behavior: An analysis of judgments of help-giving. *Journal of Personality and Social Psychology, 39,* 186–200.

Weiner, B. (1981). The emotional consequences of causal ascriptions. In M. S. Clark & S. T. Fiske (Eds.), *17th Annual Carnegie Mellon Symposium.* Hillsdale, NJ: Erlbaum.

Weiner, B., & Graham, S. (in press). An attributional approach to emotional development. In C. Izard, J. Kagan, & R. Zajonc (Eds.), *Emotion, cognition and behavior.* Cambridge, MA: Harvard University Press.

Weiner, B., Graham, S., & Chandler, C. (1982). Pity, anger, and guilt: An attributional analysis. *Personality and Social Psychology Bulletin, 8,* 226–232.

Weiner, B., Russell, D., & Lerman, D. (1978). Affective consequences of causal ascriptions. In J. H. Harvey, W. Ickes, & R. F. Kidd (Eds.), *New directions in attribution research* (Vol. 2). Hillsdale, NJ: Erlbaum.

Weiner, B., Russell, D., & Lerman, D. (1979). The cognition-emotion process in achievement-related contexts. *Journal of Personality and Social Psychology, 37,* 1211–1220.

Weiner, H. (1977). *Psychobiology and human disease.* New York: Elsevier.

Weiner, H., Singer, M. T., & Reiser, M. F. (1962). Cardiovascular responses and their psychological correlates: I. A study in healthy young adults and patients with peptic ulcer and hypertension. *Psychosomatic Medicine, 24,* 477–498.

Weiner, N. (1960). The brain and the machine. In S. Hook (Ed.), *Dimensions of mind: A symposium.* New York: New York University Press.

Weisman, A. D. (1956). A study of the psychodynamics of duodenal ulcer exacerbations with special reference to treatment and the problem of specificity. *Psychosomatic Medicine, 18,* 2–42.

Weisman, A. D. (1972). *On dying and denying: A psychiatric study of terminality.* New York: Behavioral Publications.

Weisman, A. D. (1976). Early diagnosis of the vulnerability in cancer patients. *The American Journal of the Medical Sciences, 271,* 187–196.

Weisman, A. D., & Worden, J. W. (1975). Psychosocial analysis of cancer deaths. *Omega: Journal of Death and Dying, 6,* 61–75.

Weisman, A. D., & Worden, J. W. (1976–1977). The existential plight in cancer: Significance of the first 100 days. *International Journal of Psychiatry in Medicine, 7,* 1–15.

Weiss, D. S., Wilner, N., & Horowitz, M. J. (in press). The stress response rating scale: A clinicians' measure. *British Journal of Psychology.*

Weiss, J. H. (1977). The current state of the concept of a psychosomatic disorder. In Z. J. Lipowski, D. R. Lipsitt, & P. C. Whybrow (Eds.), *Psychosomatic medicine: Current trends and clinical applications.* New York: Oxford University Press.

Weiss, J. M. (1971). Effects of coping behavior with and without a feedback signal on stress pathology on rats. *Journal of Comparative and Physiological Psychology, 77*(22).

Weiss, J. M. (1971). Effects of coping behavior with and without a feedback signal on stress pathology on rats. *Journal of Comparative and Physiological Psychology, 77*(22).

Weiss, J. M., Glazer, H. I., & Pohorecky, L. A. (1976). Coping behavior and neurochemical changes in rats: An alternative explanation for the original "learned helplessness" experiments. In G. Serban & A. King (Eds.), *Animal models in human psychobiology*. New York: Plenum.

Weiss, R. S. (1974). The provisions of social relationships. In Z. Rubin (Ed.), *Doing unto others*. Englewood Cliffs, NJ: Prentice-Hall.

Weiss, S. M., Herd, J. A., & Fox, B. H. (1981). *Perspectives on behavioral medicine*. New York: Academic Press.

Weissman, M. S., & Paykel, E. S. (1974). *The depressed human: A study of social relationships*. Chicago: University of Chicago Press.

Wellard, J. (1965). *The great Sahara*. New York: Dutton.

Welsh, G. S. (1956). Factor dimensions A and R. In G. S. Welsh & W. G. Dahlstrom (Eds.), *Basic reading on the MMPI in psychology and medicine*. Minneapolis: University of Minnesota Press.

Wessler, R. L. (1982a, November). *Alternative concepts of rational-emotive therapy and their integration with the cognitive-behavior therapies*. Paper presented at 13th Annual Conference of the Psychological Society of Ireland, Sligo.

Wessler, R. L. (1982b). Varieties of cognitions in the cognitively oriented psychotherapies. *Rational Living, 17*, 3–10.

Wheaton, J. L. (1959). Fact and fancy in sensory deprivation studies. *School of Aviation Medicine Reports*, Brooks Air Force Base, Texas, No. 5-59, 60.

White, R. W. (1959). Motivation reconsidered: The concept of competence. *Psychological Review, 66*, 297–333.

White, R. W. (1960). Competence and the psychosexual stages of development. In M. R. Jones (Ed.), *Nebraska Symposium on Motivation*. Lincoln: University of Nebraska Press.

White, R. W. (1974). Strategies of adaptation: An attempt at systematic description. In G. V. Coelho, D. A. Hamburg, & J. E. Adams (Eds.), *Coping and adaptation*. New York: Basic Books.

Whiting, J. W. M, & Child, I. L. (1953). *Child training and personality*. New Haven: Yale University Press.

Whyte, W. H., Jr. (1956). *The organization man*. New York: Doubleday.

Willems, E. P. (1969). Planning a rationale for naturalistic research. In E. P. Willems & H. L. Raush (Eds.), *Naturalistic viewpoints in psychological research*. New York: Holt, Rinehart & Winston.

Williams, A. F. (1972). Personality characteristics associated with preventive dental health practices. *Journal of American College of Dentists, 39*, 225–234.

Williams, B. W., Jr., Haney, T. L., Lee, K. L., Yi-Hong Kong, Y., Blumenthal, J. A., & Whalen, R. E. (1980). Type A behavior, hostility, and coronary atherosclerosis. *Psychosomatic Medicine, 42*, 539–549.

Williams, R. G. A. (1981a). Logical analysis as a qualitative method. I: Themes in old age and chronic illness. *Sociology of Health and Illness, 3,* 141–164.

Williams, R. G. A. (1981b). Logical analysis as a qualitative method. II: Conflict of ideas and the topic of illness. *Sociology of Health and Illness, 3,* 165–187.

Wilson, W. (1967). Correlates of avowed happiness. *Psychological Bulletin, 67,* 294–306.

Wine, J. (1971). Test anxiety and direction of attention. *Psychological Bulletin, 76,* 92–104.

Wingard, D. L. (1980). *The sex differential in mortality rates: Biological and social factors.* Unpublished doctoral dissertation, University of California, Berkeley.

Withey, S. B. (1962). Reactions to uncertain threat. In G. W. Baker & D. W. Chapman (Eds.), *Man and society in disaster.* New York: Basic Books.

Witkin, H. A., Dyk, R. B., Faterson, H. F., Goodenough, D. R., & Karp, S. A. (1962). *Psychological differentiation.* New York: Wiley.

Witkin, H. A., Goodenough, D. R., & Oltman, P. K. (1979). Psychological differentiation: Current status. *Journal of Personality and Social Psychology, 37,* 1127–1145.

Wolff, H. G. (1953). *Stress and disease.* Springfield, IL: Thomas.

Wolff, C. T., Friedman, S. B., Hofer, M. A., & Mason, J. W. (1964). Relationship between psychological defenses and mean urinary 17-hydroxycorticosteroid excretion rates, Parts I and II. *Psychosomatic Medicine, 26,* 576–609.

Wolpe, J. (1958). *Psychotherapy by reciprocal inhibition.* Stanford, CA: Stanford University Press.

Wolpe, J. (1978). Cognition and causation in human behavior and its therapy. *American Psychologist, 33,* 437–446.

Wolpe, J. (1979). The experimental model and treatment of neurotic depression. *Behavior Research and Therapy, 17,* 555–565.

Wolpe, J., & Lazarus, A. A. (1966). *Behavior therapy techniques.* Oxford: Pergamon.

Wong, T. P., & Reker, G. T. (1982, November). *Coping strategies and well-being in Caucasian and Chinese elderly.* Paper presented at 11th Annual Meeting of the Canadian Association on Gerontology, Winnipeg, Manitoba.

Wortman, C. B. (1976). Causal attributions and personal control. In J. H. Harvey, W. J. Ickes, & R. F. Kidd (Eds.), *New directions in attribution research: I.* Hillsdale, NJ: Erlbaum.

Wortman, C. B., Abbey, A., Holland, A. E., Silver, R. L., & Janoff-Bulman, R. (1980). Transitions from the laboratory to the field: Problems and progress. In L. Brickman (Ed.), *Applied social psychology. I.* Beverly Hills, CA: Sage.

Wortman, C. B., & Brehm, J. W. (1975). Responses to uncontrollable outcomes: An integration of reactance theory and the learned helplessness model. In L. Berkowitz (Ed.), *Advances in experimental social psychology* (Vol. 8). New York: Academic Press.

Wortman, C. B., & Dintzer, L. (1978). Is an attributional analysis of the learned helplessness phenomenon viable? A critique of the Abramson-Seligman-Teasdale reformulation. *Journal of Abnormal Psychology, 87,* 75–90.

Wortman, C. B., & Dunkel-Schetter, C. (1979). Interpersonal relationships and cancer: A theoretical analysis. *Journal of Social Issues, 35,* 120–155.

Wright, J., & Mischel, W. (1982). Influence of affect on cognitive social learning person variables. *Journal of Personality and Social Psychology, 43,* 901–914.

Wright, R. K., Wright, B. A., & Dembo, T. (1948). Studies of adjustment to visible injuries: Evaluation of curiosity by the injured. *Journal of Abnormal and Social Psychology, 43,* 13–28.

Wrubel, J., Benner, P., & Lazarus, R. S. (1981). Social competence from the perspective of stress and coping. In J. Wine & M. Syme (Eds.), *Social competence.* New York: Guilford.

Wundt, W. (1907). *Outlines of psychology.* Leipzig: Wilhelm Englemann.

Yanagida, E. H., Streltzer, J., & Siemsen, A. (1981). Denial in dialysis patients: Relationship to compliance and other variables. *Psychosomatic Medicine, 43,* 271–280.

Yankelovich, D. (1981, April), Searching for self-fulfillment in a world turned upside down. *Psychology Today, 15,* 151–175.

Yarnold, P. R., & Grim, L. G. (1982). Time urgency among coronary-prone individuals. *Journal of Abnormal Psychology, 91,* 175–177.

Yates, M. (1976). *Coping: A survival manual for women alone.* Englewood Cliffs, NJ: Prentice-Hall.

Yerkes, R. M., & Dodson, J. D. (1908). The relation of strength of stimulus to rapidity of habit-formation. *Journal of Comparative Neurology and Psychology, 18,* 459–482.

Young, A. (1980). The discourse on stress and the reproduction of conventional knowledge. *Social Sciences and Medicine, 148,* 133–146.

Zajonc, R. B. (1980). Feeling and thinking: Preferences need no inferences. *American Psychologist, 35,* 151–175.

Zajonc, R. B. (1984). On the primacy of emotion. *American Psychologist, 39,* 117–123.

Zautra, A., & Goodhart, D. (1979). Quality of life indicators: A review of the literature. *Community Mental Health Review, 4,* 1–10.

Zborowsky, M. (1969). *People in pain.* San Francisco: Jossey-Bass.

Zeaman, D., & Smith, R. W. (1965). Human Cardiac conditioning. In W. F. Prokasy (Ed.), *Classical conditioning: A symposium.* New York: Appleton-Century-Crofts.

Zedeck, S. (1971). Problems with the use of "moderator" variables. *Psychological Bulletin, 76,* 295–310.

Zigler, E., & Trickett, P. K. (1978). IQ, social competence, and evaluation of early childhood intervention programs. *American Psychologist, 33,* 789–798.

Zilberg, N. J., Weiss, D. S., & Horowitz, M. J. (1982). Impact of event scale: A cross-validation study and some empirical evidence supporting a conceptual model of stress response syndromes. *Journal of Consulting and Clinical Psychology, 50,* 407–414.

Zimney, G. H., & Keinstra, R. A. (1967). Orienting and defensive responses to electric shock. *Psychophysiology, 3,* 351–362.

Zubin, J., & Spring, B. (1977). Vulnerability: A new view of schizophrenia. *Journal of Abnormal Psychology, 86,* 103–126.

Zuckerman, M. (1979). Sensation seeking and risk taking. In C. Izard (Ed.), *Emotions in personality and psychopathology.* New York: Plenum.

Zuroff, D. C. (1980). Learned helplessness in humans: An analysis of learning processes and the roles of individual and situational differences. *Journal of Personality and Social Psychology, 39,* 130–146.

Zuroff, D. C. (1981). Depression and attribution: Some new data and a review of old data. *Cognitive Therapy and Research, 5,* 273–281.

Index

ERRATUM

The following reference was inadvertently omitted from earlier printings:

Pancheri, P., De Martino, V., Spiombi, G., Biondi, M., & Mosticone, S. (1979). Life stress events and state-trait anxiety in psychiatric and psychosomatic patients. In C. D. Spielberger & I. G. Sarason (Eds.), *Stress and anxiety* (Vol. 6). Washington, DC: Hemisphere.